Politics and the Environment

From theory to practice

Second edition

James Connelly and
Graham Smith

London and New York

First published 1999 by Routledge
11 New Fetter Lane, London EC4P 4EE

Simultaneously published in the USA and
Canada
by Routledge
29 West 35th Street, New York, NY 10001

Second edition 2003

*Routledge is an imprint of the Taylor & Francis
Group*

© 1999, 2003 James Connelly and Graham
Smith

Typeset in Century Old Style by Keystroke,
Jacaranda Lodge, Wolverhampton
Printed and bound in Great Britain by
TJ International Ltd, Padstow, Cornwall

British Library Cataloguing in Publication Data
A catalogue record for this book is available
from the British Library

*Library of Congress Cataloging in Publication
Data*
A catalog record for this book has been
requested

ISBN 0–415–25145–1 (hbk)
ISBN 0–415–25146–X (pbk)

Contents

CONTENTS

CONTENTS

Acknowledgements

A variety of people have helped to shape the structure, content and tone of both editions of this book and we are grateful to them all. The process of writing can be long and tortuous and we have got through four editors between the commissioning of the first edition and the production of the second. Our thanks to Caroline Wintersgill, Patrick Proctor, Mark Kavanagh and Craig Fowlie who showed great patience and offered useful suggestions. We would like to express our appreciation to the readers, who included Stephen Young, Tim Gray and Mike Kenny, for their perceptive comments on the structure of the initial proposal and the content of the first edition. A number of people provided information and feedback while we were preparing the second edition: thanks to Mattias Ask, Karin Bäckstrand, John Barry, David Benson and Stephen Lake. We have gained a great deal from the large number of students at Southampton Institute, University of Southampton and University of Strathclyde who have taken the courses on which much of this material is based. We would also like to thank various friends and colleagues from a variety of backgrounds – academics, policy officers, environmental activists – who have inspired us with their ideas and friendship. Blackwell Publishers were kind enough to give their permission to use examples drawn from Iain McLean's *Public Choice* in Chapter 4.

James would like to thank his family, young and old, for their support and diversion, Sara for keeping him on the planet, and his friends who always understood.

Graham would like to thank his family for their constant love and support and, most of all, Susan for laughter and inspiration.

This book is dedicated to Liam O'Sullivan who died last summer. Liam was a great friend and teacher, and is sorely missed by all who loved him.

Southampton
August 2002

Abbreviations

ALF	Animal Liberation Front
AONB	Area of Outstanding Natural Beauty
BAT	best available technology
BATNEEC	best available technology not entailing excessive cost
BPEO	best practicable environmental option
BPM	best practicable method
CAP	Common Agricultural Policy
CBA	cost–benefit analysis
CBI	Confederation of British Industry
CCT	Compulsory Competitive Tendering
CFC	chlorofluorocarbon
CIWF	Compassion in World Farming
CJA	Criminal Justice and Public Order Act
CND	Campaign for Nuclear Disarmament
COP	Conference of the Parties
CPRE	Council for the Protection of Rural England
CSD	Commission on Sustainable Development
CVM	contingent valuation method
DEFRA	Department of the Environment, Food and Rural Affairs
DETR	Department of the Environment, Transport and the Regions
DOE	Department of the Environment
DOT	Department of Transport
DTLR	Department of Transport, Local Government and the Regions
EAC	Environmental Audit Committee
EAP	Environmental Action Programme
EC	European Community
EEA	European Environment Agency
EF!	Earth First!

EIA	environmental impact assessment
EMAS	Eco-Management and Audit Scheme
EMS	environmental management system
EU	European Union
FOE	Friends of the Earth
GDP	gross domestic product
GEF	Global Environment Facility
GMO	genetically modified organism
GNP	gross national product
IMF	International Monetary Fund
IO	International Organisation
IPC	integrated pollution control
IPCC	Intergovernmental Panel on Climate Change
IPPC	integrated pollution prevention and control
LA21	Local Agenda 21
LETS	local exchange trading system
LGMB	Local Government Management Board
MAFF	Ministry of Agriculture, Fisheries and Food
MEP	Member of the European Parliament
NEF	New Economics Foundation
NEPP	National Environmental Policy Plan (Dutch)
NGO	non-governmental organisation
NVDA	non-violent direct action
OECD	Organisation for Economic Cooperation and Development
PPG	Planning Policy Guidance
PPP	polluter pays principle
quango	quasi-autonomous non-governmental organisation
RSNC	Royal Society for Nature Conservation
RSPB	Royal Society for the Protection of Birds
SACTRA	Standing Advisory Committee on Trunk Road Assessment
SAP	Structural Adjustment Programme
SDU	Sustainable Development Unit
SEA	strategic environmental assessment
SSSI	Site of Special Scientific Interest
TDA	Twyford Down Association
TEU	Treaty on European Union
TNC	transnational corporation
UNCED	United Nations Conference on Environment and Development
UNDP	United Nations Development Programme
UNEP	United Nations Environment Programme
UNFCCC	United Nations Framework Convention on Climate Change
WCED	World Commission on Environment and Development
WTA	willingness to accept
WTO	World Trade Organisation
WTP	willingness to pay
WWF	World Wide Fund for Nature

Introduction

Why environmental politics?

Can anyone claim that they are unaware of environmental issues anymore? Surely we all know something about the hole in the ozone layer, oil tanker spills, deforestation of tropical rainforests, the building of roads and dams in environmentally-sensitive areas, public anxiety about the safety of mass-produced foods, or growing concern about the impact of climate change. Again, we are familiar with images of environmental protest: Greenpeace anti-whaling actions on the high seas, anti-roads activists bulldozer-diving, digging tunnels and building tree villages, protesters uprooting GMO trial crops, or standoffs between police and activists outside meetings of the World Trade Organisation and other global institutions. And finally, we are familiar with governments attempting to respond to these issues. An example of success is the securing of global agreements to ban CFCs to halt the destruction of the ozone layer; an example of failure is the well-publicised refusal of the United States to agree to binding reductions in carbon dioxide levels as a response to the processes of climate change.

Environmental issues and concerns are, then, simply a part of our everyday life and cannot be ignored. An obvious question that follows from this is why is it so difficult to secure effective environmental policy? There are a number of answers to this question and these will be explored in further depth as the book progresses. However, one reason is the nature of environmental problems themselves. Environmental problems are often highly complex and interconnected: a high degree of uncertainty frequently exists in attempting to ascribe cause and effect and in generating effective solutions. Added to this, environmental damage can be irreversible and many environmental problems involve high levels of risk to human and environmental health and well-being. This is a difficult combination of characteristics and it is important to ask whether governments and other institutions and groups have the capacity to respond effectively. A large part of this book is dedicated to answering this question.

However, these characteristics of environmental problems do not in themselves make environmental politics distinctive; they simply indicate that the environment is nothing more than another, albeit highly complicated, policy area. However, our contention in this book is that green politics is not simply a substitution of one policy focus with another, and that to think of it in that way is to misconstrue the significance of what is at stake. Why should this be so?

Green politics is not, then, politics as usual through a green lens. But what is it that is distinctive and challenging about environmental politics? It is our contention that green politics rests on two fundamental insights which provide the impetus for a searching re-examination of existing political, social and economic practices. These are, first, a recognition of the finite nature of the planet's physical resources – 'limits to growth', and, second, an attention to the ethical dimension of humanity's relations with the non-human world. We will briefly examine each in turn.

The significance of the limits to growth thesis can be grasped by reflecting on two short parables. The first is known as 'the tragedy of the commons' (Hardin, 1998: originally published in 1968). We are asked to imagine a pasture used for grazing cattle, open to all, and to accept that each herdsman will try to keep as many cattle as possible on this common pasture. Everything is fine while the number of animals that graze stays below the carrying capacity of the land. However, as Garrett Hardin writes:

> [T]he rational herdsman concludes that the only sensible course for him to pursue is to add another animal to his herd. And another; and another. . . . But this is the conclusion reached by each and every rational herdsman sharing a commons. Therein is the tragedy. Each man is locked into a system that compels him to increase his herd without limit – in a world that is limited. Ruin is the destination toward which all men rush, each pursuing his own best interest in a society that believes in the freedom of the commons. Freedom in a commons brings ruin to all.
>
> (Hardin, 1998, p. 26)

Substitute fish for cattle and the open seas for pasture and we have the problem of over-fishing; substitute cars for cattle and the atmosphere for the pasture and we have the problem of climate change. There are ecological limits to the use of the environment: overuse of resources by self-interested actors can lead to environmental destruction and irreversible damage.[1]

The second parable develops this line of thinking by reflecting on the manner in which resource consumption, pollution and population levels tend to grow exponentially. A French riddle illustrates the suddenness with which exponential growth approaches a fixed limit:

> Suppose you own a pond on which a water lily is growing. The lily plant doubles in size each day. If the lily plant were allowed to grow unchecked, it would completely cover the pond in 30 days, choking off the other forms of life in the water. For a long time the lily plant seems small, and so you decide not to worry about cutting it back until it covers half the pond. On what day will that be? On the twenty-ninth day, of course. You have one day to save your pond.
>
> (Meadows *et al.*, 1972, p. 29)

This riddle is quoted in the 1972 report *The Limits to Growth* and is used to reinforce the view that humanity has limited time in which to change its ecologically-insensitive patterns of growth. As the report concludes:

> If the present growth trends in world population, industrialization, food production, and resource depletion continue unchanged, the limits to growth on this planet will be reached sometime within the next hundred years. The most probable result will be a rather sudden and uncontrollable decline in both population and industrial capacity.
>
> (ibid., p. 23)

In retrospect the methodology and findings of *The Limits to Growth* have been shown to be overly simplistic and pessimistic. There is also much controversy about the meaning of 'limits': are they fixed or can human ingenuity and inventiveness extend these limits? However, the report did succeed in focusing attention on growing global tensions surrounding resource depletion and environmental damage, and its central theme – that infinite growth in a finite system is impossible – has become a 'foundation stone of Green political thinking' (Dobson, 1991, p. 13).[2]

The insights generated by considering the tragedy of the commons and limits to growth are complemented by the second fundamental insight of environmental thought: the ethical dimension of humanity's relations with the non-human world. If we start by simply considering environmental goods merely as resources for human use, important moral and ethical issues arise. Questions of social and international justice come to the fore: for example, how are we to respond to the present uneven distribution of environmental resources and quality? Are there grounds for redistributing 'ecological wealth'? And these questions of social justice are complemented by questions of intergenerational justice, namely the obligations we may have to future generations. In other words, not only do we need to think about the distribution of environmental goods and bads across the present generation, but also with regard to future peoples. In many ways these questions of distribution are familiar to much contemporary political theory. However, environmental politics adds a couple of 'twists'. First, reflection on the finite nature of physical resources – the limits to growth – means that we have to consider questions of intra- and intergenerational justice with regard to the carrying capacity of ecological systems. Overuse and over-exploitation may lead to irreversible damage. So, green politics recognises that there will be tensions between our obligations to the current and future generations; but also that these often competing demands of justice must be resolved in the context of limited physical resources.

As if this was not enough, environmental ethics then adds a second twist. Greens do not want to conceptualise nature simply as a resource for human use and (re)distribution. A fundamental element of much green thinking is that non-human nature has ethical standing in its own right. The strongest of green moral positions holds that nature has independent, intrinsic value – value in itself – and that this must be respected in our ethical and political lives. Deep ecologists, for example, believe that 'the equal right to live and blossom is an intuitively clear and obvious value axiom' (Naess, 1973, p. 95). Such a principle, if adopted, would have an extraordinary impact on the way in which we structure our relations with the non-human world. Thus the obligation to present and future generations is complemented by a third obligation: to non-human nature.

But the idea of the ethical standing of non-human nature is far from uncontroversial. For example, which aspects of the non-human world have ethical standing and on what grounds? Should we be concerned with intelligent beings, sentient beings, all life forms, or with all entities, including the inanimate? And where is our focus to be? Is it with individuals, species or whole ecosystems? Is the value of such entities merely instrumental or is it intrinsic? Is the natural world of value only in so far as it serves human purposes or does it possess value independently of those purposes? And finally, questions are raised about the relative importance of any obligations to the environment compared to our obligations to present and future generations.[3]

So, in our opinion, environmental politics does add something new to the study of politics. Fundamental to environmental thinking (and differentiating it to a certain degree from other strands of ethical and political thought) is the significance placed on the limits to growth and the ethical standing of non-human nature. Debates about the importance of these insights is common currency within environmental thinking and even where beliefs on these matters are not explicitly stated, they nonetheless have implications for green political thought and action.

Sustainable development

The growing prevalence and influence of green ideas are illustrated by the frequent use of the term 'sustainable development' on the part of a wide range of actors both inside and outside the environmental movement. We might consider the impact of the idea of sustainable development as a victory for green thinking. After all it must surely raise questions about the legitimacy of current ecologically-insensitive patterns of economic growth that threaten irreversible environmental damage and lead to discussions about our broader relations with non-human nature. As such it would appear to be a hospitable discourse for the more radical ecological vision of small-scale, decentralised, low-impact societies. Sustainable development opens up the possibility of a restructuring of contemporary economic, social and environmental relations.

But in practice the case is more complex and compromised by political expediency. The well-known and oft-quoted definition from the Brundtland Report, *Our Common Future* – 'development that meets the needs of the present without compromising the ability of future generations to meet their own needs' (WCED, 1987, p. 8) – is now as familiar a part of the rhetoric of multinational corporations as it is of environmentalists. The radical cutting edge that constitutes a challenge to orthodox political and economic arrangements has been blunted. The point is not that there is anything wrong with the broad Brundtland definition, rather that everything hinges on its interpretation. Interpreted loosely it can be used to justify almost any activity in the present so long as we leave broadly equivalent means and resources to those in the future. Interpreted more rigorously it implies that virtually all of our activities in the present should be subject to the closest possible scrutiny to ascertain their full environmental effects, and that many of them might fail the simple test of long-term sustainability. Recently, debates around sustainable development have come to be dominated by a particular interpretation – ecological modernisation – which is garnering widespread support and interest among a range of actors including business, governments, international organisations and more mainstream environmental groups. The key idea here is that economic development and environmental protection are not mutually exclusive. Economic growth can be environmentally efficient, thus generating an apparent 'win–win' situation in which the benefits of contemporary industrial society are retained while its burdens on the environment are progressively dispelled. This view allows modern technological societies to dig themselves out of the ecological trouble they dug their way into in the first place. This solution has the additional benefit of not asking us to give up on the type of lifestyle to which we in the high-consumption societies have become accustomed. The nature and impact of ecological modernisation will be a theme that re-emerges throughout the book.

Even though the concept of sustainable development has been subjected to considerable strain, constantly threatening to pull it out of shape, we believe that it remains an important concept, perhaps the most fundamental concept, in green thinking. Sustainable development can be used to generate criteria against which the success of green transformations can be judged. The very fact that it is already part of common political currency and hence subject to the market place of political bargaining and counter-definition may (paradoxically) be an advantage. All sides wish to appropriate sustainable development to justify their own activities. Greens are thus in a position to insist that its professed adherents publicly explain their interpretation and demonstrate convincingly how their policies respect the principle. In this debate, greens can point to the core ideas that it embodies, challenge alternative interpretations, and thereby reclaim its radical thrust. Different actors will at least be contesting the issue using the same vocabulary, and will be faced with the challenge of justifying their favoured interpretation if they wish to continue to appropriate the term in political debate and discourse. The core ideas embodied within the concept of sustainable development are thus central to the arguments developed within this book.

Core ideas within sustainable development

1 **Environment–economy integration**: integrating economic development and environmental protection in planning and implementation.
2 **Futurity**: explicit concern with the impact of current activity on future generations.
3 **Environmental protection**: reducing pollution and environmental degradation and protection of the non-human world.
4 **Equity**: commitment to meeting the basic needs of the poor of the present generations and to equity between generations.
5 **Quality of life**: recognition that human well-being is constituted by more than economic growth and prosperity alone.
6 **Participation**: recognition that sustainable development requires institutions to be restructured to allow all voices in society to be heard in decision making.

(adapted from Jacobs, 1999a, pp. 26–7)

Sustainable development is an umbrella concept: on analysis we find that it unites a number of related concepts which are central to green political thought, but which themselves are equally contested. The manner in which these different concepts are understood and then balanced against one another leads to different conceptions or interpretations of sustainable development.

The six core ideas and concepts implicit within sustainable development can be interpreted in a number of different ways. First, the recognition that social and economic practices are inseparable from the natural environment requires integration of economic development and environmental protection: but what relative weight should be attached to economy and environment? Can we 'trade off' environmental loss against economic gain? Are man-made and natural capital substitutable or is there a critical level of natural capital that should be sustained? Second, what is the nature of obligations to future generations and what do they entail practically? What sacrifices do the current generation need to make? Third, what is the meaning of 'environmental protection'? Is it merely a conservation ethic that aims for efficient use of resources purely to serve human welfare; or a commitment to live within limits or the carrying capacity of bioregions; or a recognition of the independent, intrinsic value and status of non-human nature? Fourth, is a commitment to social justice based on desert, merit or needs? To what extent does social justice clash with intergenerational obligations? Fifth, what does quality of life entail? Is economic welfare an accurate indicator of well-being? If not, how is it to be measured? Finally, what sort of political institutions can support participation? Should participation simply involve consultation between elites in government, business and civil society or does it require new forms of citizen empowerment? Does it necessitate decentralisation? Is the market the most effective form of individual sovereignty and direct democracy or is it a mechanism of political disenfranchisement?

As can be seen from the variety of questions that can be raised from an analysis of the ideas embodied within sustainable development, it is not surprising that it is a contested concept. Almost all the themes of environmental ethics and political thought are played out within this conceptual space. Different conceptions or interpretations of sustainable development offer competing interpretations of the constituent ideas and then prioritise them in different ways. Thus, for example, ecological modernisation places great emphasis on the importance of environment–economy integration, but holds that such integration can take place within a (green) capitalist framework; participation is interpreted as including major 'stakeholders' – government, industry and mainstream environmental organisations – within the policy process. In complete contrast, radical greens reject the interpretation of sustainable development as ecological modernisation, challenging the idea that advanced industrial, high-consumption lifestyles can be made environmentally sensitive. Here successful integration of environmental considerations within economic, social and political decision making requires the establishment of small-scale, self-reliant communities which recognise the intrinsic value of nature. Sustainable development cannot be achieved without fundamental reassessment and restructuring of values, practices and institutions. These two extremes of environmental thought offer contrasting visions of the green society;[4] it is with such competing interpretations of sustainable development and their implications for the theory and practice of environmental politics that this book engages.

The structure of the book

The book is divided into three parts. At the end of each chapter is a case study which draws out a particular theme raised in the previous discussions. Part I addresses issues central to environmental thought and political action. It begins, in Chapter 1, with a philosophical and ethical examination of the way in which we reason about and value the environment and it considers our moral obligations not only to the natural world but also to existing and future generations. In Chapter 2, the focus shifts to the conflicting ideological positions held by greens. The tensions between the political beliefs and assumptions found within environmental politics are explored and particular emphasis is placed on the analysis of ecological modernisation. Chapter 3 concludes the first part of the book by looking at the diverse nature of the environmental movement: green parties, environmental pressure groups and other forms of environmental organisation. The diverse elements of the environmental movement draw their inspiration from different ideas within environmental ethics and political thought.

Part II is concerned with analysing some of the background issues which must be faced in the development of environmental policy. Chapter 4 considers why it is so difficult for governments to formulate and implement effective environmental policy. Four complementary factors are introduced: collective action problems, the issue–attention cycle, bounded rationality and the exercise of power. In many ways this is a depressing onslaught of barriers within the policy process. However, the end of the chapter offers some ideas as to how the policy process can be greened; some of these themes are then further developed in the next two chapters. Chapter 5 compares and contrasts three different types of policy instrument available to governments to respond to environmental problems: command-and-control through mandatory regulation; economic instruments that alter incentives within markets; and voluntary approaches which aim to alter attitudes and values. Chapter 6 returns to the question of how we value the environment; this time with specific reference to judging the environmental impact of projects, programmes and policies as well as overall progress towards sustainability. Environmental economists argue that in order for environmental impacts to be effectively internalised within decision making, they need to be valued in monetary terms and thus incorporated within cost–benefit analysis and national income accounting. Many greens are suspicious of such monetary valuation and argue for alternative methods such as environmental impact assessment and the use of quality of life indicators.

In Part III, the focus shifts to an examination of the extent to which effective environmental governance has been established at international, European, national and local levels. Of particular interest is the manner in which environmental problems and the challenge of sustainable development have been interpreted and understood by policy makers and the extent to which these considerations have been integrated into policy making and implementation. Chapter 7 addresses the international dimension, focusing on the nature of international politics and the global economy and examining the challenges facing the development of meaningful global environmental agreements. The role of the Rio Earth Summit in 1992 is analysed and returned to in the chapters that follow. Chapter 8 looks at the emergence of the European Union as an environmental actor. The European Union often acts in its own right on the international stage as well as playing a supra-national role in the development of environmental policy in its member states. In Chapter 9, our attention shifts to the extent to which nation states have embraced the environmental and sustainable development agenda, with particular reference to the development of pollution-control policy and sustainability strategies. The final chapter, Chapter 10, analyses the manner in which local government has responded to the emerging agendas, in particular engagement with Local Agenda 21, a product of the Rio Earth Summit.

Finally, in our conclusion, we draw together the different elements of the book, stressing that it is imperative that we respond to both the practical and theoretical challenges thrown up by the emergence of environmental politics.

Suggestions for further reading

There are a number of introductory books to the different aspects of environmental politics. Many of them tend to focus on one particular issue, whether environmental thought, the green movement, or the policy process. These will be highlighted at the end of the relevant chapters. There are a small number of books that offer an introduction to more than one area of environmental politics. Neil Carter *The Politics of the Environment: Ideas, Activism, Policy* covers much of the same ground as this book, but with a different emphasis. Robert Garner has recently produced a second edition of his *Environmental Politics: Britain, Europe and the Global Environment* which offers a complementary analysis of recent developments in the field. Luke Martell in *Ecology and Society* provides an introduction to environmental thought and the green movement, but does not engage with the policy process. Stephen Young *The Politics of the Environment* remains an extremely short, accessible and cheap introduction. *The International Encyclopedia of Environmental Politics* edited by John Barry and E. Gene Frankland contains concise entries for key environmental concepts, individuals and organisations. Finally, Stephen Croall and William Rankin *Introducing Environmental Politics* is an entertaining introduction for those who like pictures.

Notes

1   The collective action problem implicit within the tragedy of the commons is discussed in more depth in Chapter 4.
2   The Club of Rome's report, *The Limits to Growth*, is analysed in more detail in Chapter 2.
3   Environmental philosophy and ethics is the focus of Chapter 1.
4   Competing political visions within green political thought are discussed in Chapter 2.

Part I

ENVIRONMENTAL THOUGHT AND POLITICAL ACTION

ENVIRONMENTAL
ECONOMY AND
POLITICAL ACTION

Environmental philosophy

> Underlying environmental arguments are beliefs, not always explicitly formulated, about the relative priorities of human, animal and plant life, and the whole ecology of the planet.
>
> (Peacocke and Hodgson, 1989, p. 87)

Responsible environmental action requires serious reasoning about environmental issues. We need a clear grasp of the terms we use, the values we espouse, and our beliefs about what we consider it morally proper to do. Do we have responsibilities towards the environment? What might these responsibilities be? From what sources are they derived? The chapter begins with a brief examination of some of the basic terms and concepts, such as 'environment' and 'nature', followed by a discussion of the relationship between human beings and the natural world. Next, the relationship between environmental ethics and conventional approaches in ethics is analysed in order to situate the demand for a new, environmentally-sensitive ethic. What possibilities and resources are offered by different philosophical approaches and traditions? The discussion then turns to a consideration of the values we associate with the non-human world; values which inform the way we act towards the environment, be it direct-action protests or environmental policy making. However, our considerations need to go beyond purely environmental values and the chapter concludes with an analysis of global distributive justice and justice to future generations. Reasoning about environmental issues requires us to attend to our duties towards present generations, future generations and the non-human world. The case study at the end of the chapter engages with the ethical (and other) issues raised by genetically-modified organisms (GMOs)

Reasoning about nature and the environment

Terms and concepts

The terms 'nature' and 'environment' are, of course, central to any discussion. What is 'natural' is usually defined as that which takes place independently of human agency; it is contrasted with the artificial, with the results of human skill or artifice. The natural, in total, constitutes a single world or system of nature (Collingwood, 1946, p. 30). In this sense the term is broader than the term 'natural' in 'natural history'; it refers not merely to natural objects as they appear to us, but to the underlying principles governing their being and organisation. However, as John Stuart Mill recognised, there is also a sense in which everything is natural:

> It thus appears that we must recognize at least two principal meanings in the word nature. In one sense, it means all the powers existing in either the outer or the inner world and everything which takes place by means of those powers. In another sense, it means, not everything which happens, but only what takes place without the agency, or without the voluntary and intentional agency, of man.
>
> (Mill, 1874, p. 8)

John Passmore discusses a related issue in distinguishing the terms 'nature' and 'environment':

> I shall, of necessity, be using [nature] in that sense in which it includes everything except man and what obviously bears the mark of man's handiwork. For what is in question is man's moral relationships to a nature thus defined. In another fundamental sense of the word – 'whatever is subject to natural law' – both man and man's artifacts belong to nature; nature can then be contrasted, if at all, only with the supernatural. And sometimes it will be necessary to use the word in that broader sense. The word 'environment' is often substituted for the collective 'nature'. But other people, their actions, their customs, their beliefs are the most important ingredient in our environment.
>
> (Passmore, 1980, p. 5)

Passmore here introduces the further point that 'nature' is not synonymous with the 'environment'; we can, for example, contrast the 'natural environment' with the 'built environment'. The term 'environment' in this narrow sense implies an environment for some creature or collection of creatures, whether plant or animal. Here, an 'environment' is an 'environment' for something. But we also frequently use the term 'environment' more broadly to refer to the whole of the natural world – from ecosystem to biosphere – within which human beings and all other parts of the plant and animal world have their being. 'Environment', then, is not coterminous with 'nature', and 'nature' itself has several meanings, not all of direct relevance to environmentalism.

Again, although they are often used interchangeably, we frequently need to distinguish terms such as 'preservation' and 'conservation'. Preserving something implies keeping it exactly as it is without human interference; conserving something, on the other hand, might imply managing its existence through human intervention. Thus saving of natural resources for later consumption can be conveniently referred to as 'conservation', while saving from the adverse effects of human action might be better referred to as 'preservation'. Passmore points out, however, that preservationists and conservationists will not necessarily see eye to eye:

> On a particular issue, conservationists and preservationists can no doubt join hands, as they did to prevent the destruction of forests on the West Coast of the United States. But their motives are quite different: the conserver of forests has his eye on the fact that posterity, too, will need timber, the preserver hopes to keep large areas of forest forever untouched by human hands. They soon part company, therefore, and often with that special degree of hostility reserved for former allies. So it is as well that they should be clearly distinguished from the outset.
>
> (ibid., p. 73)

Typically, conservation requires human intervention whereas preservation requires its complete absence: hence, when environmentalists talk of 'wilderness' they are referring to the idea of a region from which human activity and its effects are absent.

For preservationists, the natural world is typically assigned a value in itself, an intrinsic value; for conservationists the concern is with its value for human purposes.

Human beings and the natural world

Human duties to the natural world arise both from our ability to consider our place in relation to nature and also from the fact that we can exercise enormous power (for good or ill) over it. We consume resources; we pollute the environment with waste products; and we create landscapes or reclaim land from the sea. And not least it might be said that man 'has certainly won the contest between animal species in that it is only on his sufferance that any other species exist at all, amongst species large enough to be seen at any rate' (Quinton, 1982, p. 217). Second, human beings not only cause environmental destruction, they are also able to develop and implement solutions to that destruction. Although we are 'natural' in origin we cannot hide behind the 'natural' and deny responsibility for our actions and their consequences. Our capacity for reasoning does not lift us clean out of the natural world, but enables us to do what those without this capacity cannot: to reason about the natural world and our place within it. The ability to manipulate the natural world in accordance with our own ends goes together with the ability to reason about our exercise of that power; but as it would appear that our ability to reason about our responsibilities still lags behind our ability to manipulate nature, we are currently faced with the challenge of generating an ethics suitable for our predicament. Of course, the recognition of human responsibility does not necessarily result in our doing the right thing: before we act we need to be clear about what we are trying to do.

Does this mean that we need a new environmental ethic comprehensive enough to provide a justification for all our environmental duties? The call for a comprehensive new ethic should be examined carefully. There are two reasons to be sceptical of such a demand. The first is that it may be the case that our existing moral values and traditions already provide (or could be reasonably adjusted to provide) what those who call for a new ethic are asking for. The second is to query whether a new ethic is possible even in principle. From where could a 'new ethic' emerge and how could people possibly be persuaded to adopt it? In what sense, that is, could a 'new ethic' be new? Surely if we mean something entirely other than, and independent of, our current moral traditions then this is either inconceivable; or if conceivable, it is impossible to imagine anyone being given good reasons for adopting it. On the other hand, we could perhaps translate the call for a new ethic into a demand for a fundamental shift in the focus and priorities of our existing moral concerns. As such, a new ethic would emerge from what we already have, drawing on resources implicit within our moral traditions. This move, if successful, has the merit that the moral radical would be appealing to beliefs and values we already implicitly possess. Understood as a plea for a significant shift in the focus of our moral concerns, the demand for a new environmental ethic expresses a justifiable doubt in the ability of our traditional systems of thought and belief (as they currently stand) to provide us with a satisfactory framework within which we can situate our environmental concerns. By gathering our newly emerging intuitions concerning the environment into a coherent and systematic whole, moral theory may provide us with a comprehensive environmental ethic which is both rooted in our moral traditions and sensitive to concerns they are incapable of addressing in their unrevised form. We need, then, to examine our moral traditions to see how well they are suited to (or can be adapted to) our new moral concerns.

Three moral traditions and the environment

Which, if any, of the theories and traditions characteristic of the Western world can support an environmentally-sensitive ethic? Which is best able to provide intellectual support to our sense of having a duty to preserve nature, to conserve resources for future generations and to act justly towards those in the South affected by our economic and environmental policies? Clearly a lot is being asked for here, because the feature common to most hitherto existing types of moral theory is their exclusive focus on human concerns. It is reasonable to expect, therefore, that they will be better equipped to deal with questions of (say) distributive justice than the intrinsic value of nature. A complete environmental ethic, by contrast, has to reach beyond those concerns and extend its range to cover the sentient, the living and the non-living. It will modify our entire scale of values: human beings and their interests will still be important, but their interests will no longer be the only interests worthy of consideration. Environmental ethics, then, presents a challenge to traditional ethics: it raises questions about duties not only to animals, but also towards plants and inanimate objects and natural phenomena. In the Western world we are the inheritors of a wide variety of forms of moral thinking. It would not be possible to discuss all of these strands of thought and so we shall briefly examine three moral traditions which have currency in contemporary debates: stewardship, utilitarianism and respect for life. Later in the chapter we will discuss the contractarian tradition, a more explicitly anthropocentric (human-centred) form of thinking, in relation to questions of distributive and intergenerational justice.

Stewardship

In the West our moral values are still largely shaped by a broadly Christian tradition. This is true irrespective of our individual religious affiliations, or lack of them: the Christian ethic permeates the fabric of our moral life and history. The Christian attitude towards nature in general splits into two strands: one in which the natural world is regarded as being there essentially for man's sole instrumental use; and another in which we have duties of stewardship to the natural world. The former view, in which nature is regarded as something to be exploited for its materials, as a source of knowledge leading to power and control over it, is typical of the modern scientific attitude. In paganism the natural world is understood as populated by spirits or gods and hence to be approached in a spirit of reverence and awe. By contrast the Christian view regards nature as created (but not 'inhabited') by God. This provides the ideal conditions for natural science and its associated technology to emerge and to dominate nature (White, 1994; Foster, 1992). This is the legacy of the 'scientific revolution' typified by the work of sixteenth- and seventeenth-century figures such as Francis Bacon, who largely took the view that human beings stood over and above nature. Nature was there solely for man's use. Human needs and wants were paramount and nature, in one way or another, existed to satisfy them. This is a classic formulation of what is frequently termed 'strong anthropocentrism'.

The alternative view, based on the principle of stewardship, has coexisted with the first and is rooted in a different reading of the book of Genesis. However, the issue here is not which is the correct biblical reading, but which attitude has been dominant. Lynn White (1994) argues forcefully that Christianity in practice has been committed to an exploitative attitude, sowing the seeds of the contemporary environmental crisis. But the alternative interpretation has never been entirely absent and its insights have much to offer contemporary thinking. Robin Attfield argues that the Christian tradition should be viewed as one in which the injunction to be master of the natural world implies not a rapacious attitude towards it, but the contrary. It implies that we should have dominion in the sense of being a steward appointed by God to look after and cherish both the garden he has given us to cultivate and the creatures who live in it (Attfield, 1991, pp. 20–33). We do not unconditionally own parts of the planet, but hold them on trust. Such a view leads naturally to an ethic of environmental concern. It is certainly likely to be environmentally superior to a view in which property rights are held to be absolute, in which all parts of the natural world are held to be merely means to human ends, and where we have a right to do exactly what we want with our property even at the expense of those who come after us. The principle of stewardship is an example of 'weak' or 'enlightened' anthropocentrism.

The key biblical passage here is the book of Genesis in which man was created to have 'dominion over the earth and over every creeping thing that creepeth upon the earth', to 'be fruitful and multiply and replenish the earth and subdue it' (Genesis 1:26; 1:28; 2:15). It is clear from these passages that human beings are permitted to use nature. However, it is far from clear that they have been granted an unlimited right of exploitation, such that they have no duties towards the natural world. A word like dominion needs to be considered carefully: 'man's dominion' should perhaps be interpreted as the granting of trust to humans, giving them stewardship to look after nature on behalf of God. It should not be thought of as justifying despotism or tyranny, but as the responsible exercise of a trust. The tradition of stewardship derives from this interpretation. Human beings, although they have a privileged place in nature, are exhorted to act responsibly and with consideration towards the natural world.

> In the first place, creation is God's and humans are simply a part of it. Nature is seen as a whole, interdependent in its basic diversity and variety. Human beings, like other creatures, are created 'out of the earth'.
> (Watson and Sharpe, 1993, pp. 222–3)

Human beings were created in God's image, but what does this imply? The World Council of Churches commented that this meant that humans should be seen as 'reflecting God's creating and sustaining love' and that 'any claim to the possession and mastery of the world is idolatrous' (ibid., p. 223). In the light of this, 'dominion refers specifically to the task of upholding God's purposes in creation rather than imposing humanity's self-serving ends' (ibid.). Thus the symbolism of the garden is important: humanity's role is to tend and keep the garden which God has granted it dominion over; the injunction to replenish implies that it should be kept fertile and not overworked.[1] The concept of stewardship has thus moved to the centre of modern Christian thinking. As Michael Watson and David Sharpe argue:

> [S]tewardship is today the generally accepted understanding within Christianity . . . of the role given to humanity in creation, in its relations with the rest of nature. This can be interpreted as co-worker with God in creation, but in no sense as co-equal. For it signifies that humanity's position is that it is tenant and not owner, that it holds the earth in trust, for God and for the rest of creation, present and to come.
>
> (Watson and Sharpe, 1993, pp. 223–4)

Principles of stewardship include responsibility for the whole earth; solidarity of all people; the need to take a long-term view. As such they offer a critique of existing capitalist relations and are congruent with broad principles of sustainable development.

Of course, this tradition is anthropocentric, and it has rarely been used to justify radical environmental thought and action (although much protest concerning cruelty to animals could be traced to its influence). But it should not be overlooked as a source of environmental concern. At the very least it resonates with the sense that certain things should not be done, despite their undeniable human benefits, and that wanton acts of despoliation or cruelty or over-exploitation of natural resources should be avoided as exceeding the legitimate role which mankind has been granted in relation to the natural order.

Utilitarianism

For utilitarianism, actions should be judged by their consequences, not their intrinsic rightness. Desirable consequences typically include pleasure (or the avoidance of pain), happiness, well-being, or simply the satisfaction of preferences. The moral goal is held to be the maximisation of welfare in a society through calculation of which actions[2] will bring about the greatest aggregate benefit, or, as Jeremy Bentham phrased it, 'the greatest happiness of the greatest number'.

Clearly much of our practical reasoning is intuitively utilitarian, and it is important both to recognise this and to appreciate the scope and limits of utilitarianism, especially as it applies to debates in matters of public policy.[3] For the moment, however, we shall look at one interesting application of utilitarianism – the justification of vegetarianism. Although utilitarianism has traditionally been applied to solely human concerns, there is nothing in principle preventing its extension to the non-human world. Given its focus on maximising welfare in a society, the question now becomes who counts as *belonging* to that society. Peter Singer, in his influential book *Animal Liberation* (originally published in 1975), argues that the relevant moral community comprises all those able to feel pain or pleasure. He picks up on one aspect of utilitarianism – the promotion of pleasure and the avoidance of suffering – and combines it with Bentham's dictum 'each to count for one and none for more than one'. From this starting point he constructs an account of our obligations to animals by recognising our kinship with other sentient beings. Animals, like humans, can feel pain and suffer and this simple fact means that we can include them in our calculations of aggregate welfare. The reason for this inclusion is not their intellectual abilities or powers of reason. Just as having a higher degree of intelligence does not entitle one human to use another for their own ends so it does not entitle humans to exploit non-humans. The right question to ask, insisted Bentham, was not 'Can they reason? Can they talk? but, Can they suffer?' (Bentham, 1960, p. 412). It is the capacity for suffering and/or the enjoyment of happiness which generates the right to moral consideration. This capacity is a prerequisite for having interests, and for Singer animals have interests which we should consider:

> If a being is not capable of suffering, or of experiencing enjoyment or happiness, there is nothing to be taken into account. This is why the limit of sentience (. . . a convenient . . . shorthand for the capacity to suffer or experience enjoyment or happiness) is the only defensible boundary of concern for the interests of others.
>
> (Singer, 1983, p. 9)

This line of reasoning might appear to lead to the conclusion that we should regard all animals as deserving equal consideration to each other and to ourselves. But this does not follow: Singer is arguing for treatment as an *equal*, not for equal *treatment*. Pains and pleasures have equal significance; but this leaves open the question of identifying relative levels of pain or pleasure. The key point here is that his argument implies that we should not treat other sentient beings merely as means to our ends: they are sentient beings with interests which we should take into account. In so far, for example, as our dietary practices cause avoidable suffering to animals, and in so far as this suffering is not a necessary precondition for our own survival, any utilitarian calculus leads to the conclusion that we should cease those practices. He is not arguing that animals should be treated equally to human beings, but that their interests should be taken into account in a way in which they currently are not.

Singer's utilitarianism thus enables him to generate a powerful argument against the exploitation of animals for human purposes. At the minimum this provides grounds for the cessation of intensive, factory farming; at its strongest, an argument for vegetarianism. However, Singer has to allow that this cannot be an absolute prohibition, because utilitarianism aims at maximising aggregate net welfare, and his utilitarianism thus does not provide a principle which would absolutely prohibit any particular act. Even the dictum 'each to count for one and none for more than one' needs to be carefully understood. On the one hand it has the effect of addressing attention to the interests of creatures which otherwise we might ignore in moral calculation; on the other it is not so much a call to equality of treatment as an insistence that the suffering of each creature counts as one unit in the overall calculation of aggregate welfare. Hence it serves as no protection of the interests of any individual creature, including humans. It is merely an insistence that their capacity for pain and pleasure be taken into account in the calculation of welfare as a whole. Singer's inclusion of animals and their capacity for pleasure and pain within our moral framework is important because it quite rightly directs attention to that suffering and away from the view that human beings are quite separate from, and do not need to concern themselves with their impact on, the animal kingdom. But, by the same token, Singer's argument cannot give us any absolute respect for animal life as such. Neither can it provide us with the other elements which we would regard as necessary for a comprehensive environmental ethic. In its emphasis on individual sentience, it can provide no clear guidance for our concern with protecting species, non-sentient life forms or natural objects. Singer's argument thus works well, but only within its self-imposed constraints. It can offer nothing outside the framework of sentience and suffering. But this is not to diminish its importance. It has had an enormous practical effect in generating debate about animal–human relationships, converting many people to vegetarianism and leading them to further consideration of other environmental issues.

Animal rights?

What would it mean to grant rights to animals? Many have argued that rights can only be possessed by beings able to understand what it means to possess a right, and that therefore animals cannot possess rights. One reason for this conclusion is that it is argued that rights are necessarily linked with duties and responsibilities in such a way that possessing a right implies that some person or body has a corresponding duty to uphold that right. If this is so, rights can only be granted to beings who are able to fulfil their duties as full and responsible members of their society. Where does this leave animals? If, as many argue, 'the capacity for moral autonomy . . . is basic to the possibility of possessing a right' (Carruthers, 1992, p. 144), this would seem to rule animal rights out completely.

Supposing for the moment that we accepted that animals do not have rights: would this mean that we would be free to treat them in any way we like? The short answer is no, because morality (what we should and shouldn't do) is a much broader thing than rights. Morally we would still care for animals and legally it is possible to extend protection to animals without accepting that they have rights as such. John Rawls argues that although animals are not entitled to strict justice, it is nonetheless wrong to be cruel to them and to destroy species: we have duties of compassion and humanity towards animals, but they fall outside the scope of rights as understood within contract theory (1972, p. 512).

These duties towards animals and other non-humans would not be *direct* duties. Joel Feinberg suggests that 'we ought to be kind to animals, but that is quite another thing from holding that animals can claim kind treatment from us as their due. . . . We may very well have duties *regarding* animals that are not duties *to* animals, just as we may have duties *regarding* rocks, or buildings, or lawns, that are not duties *to* the rocks, buildings or lawns' (1991, p. 372).

We can have duties towards animals without saying that they have corresponding rights; would we be happy, then, to say the same about human beings who were unable to recognise, understand or claim rights for themselves? It would seem that we might be led to the conclusion that infant human beings do not possess rights because they cannot understand the concept, claim their rights, nor assume any corresponding duties. Many would be extremely unhappy with such a conclusion and would argue that all human beings have rights, whether they are full moral

continued

3 |5/5064

agents or not. However, if we allow that infants (who are unable to claim their rights or understand the idea of a right) might possess rights, should we not by the same token take seriously the possibility of granting rights to animals? Is it possible, after all, to argue that animals possess moral rights? And, if they do, should some or all of them become legal rights, that is, rights enforceable in law? And, if they have rights, how extensive are they? Would they be fully comparable in all respects with the rights of human beings, or would they be rights of a lesser order?

Most animal rights theorists stop short of arguing that the rights of animals are identical with the rights of humans and argue that, in effect, animal rights would be lesser rights. If that is so, it might be asked what is the point of granting rights at all? A related question is whether, if some animals are granted rights, *all* animals should be granted rights, or only those closest to human beings genetically, or in appearance or intelligence. There is a growing movement of opinion that the great apes – gorillas, orangutans and chimpanzees – should be protected from extinction by being granted rights. If this were to be done then killing these apes who so very closely resemble human beings would be tantamount to murder.

Utilitarian arguments are in general open to a further range of criticisms, perhaps the most important being that they can lead to the justification of conclusions which we would find morally repugnant. As Samuel Scheffler puts it in a discussion of classical utilitarian doctrine: 'because it is concerned to maximise total aggregate satisfaction or utility, classical utilitarianism demands that we channel resources to the relatively well-off whenever that will lead to the required maximisation' (Scheffler, 1994, p. 10). The point is that a concern with the aggregate level of satisfaction can end up justifying ill treatment of individuals precisely because individuals as such are not important within the theory. Only the aggregate level of satisfaction is important. Considerations of this sort lead philosophers such as Bernard Williams (1973, 1985) to a wholesale rejection of utilitarianism in both this and other more modern and subtle forms. It is easy to think of examples in which we could increase overall well-being by treating a particular person as a means to our ends, by redistributing their goods or even parts of their body so as to improve the welfare of others. In so far as such a redistribution increases the net level of welfare, utilitarianism, it is argued, should embrace it. By contrast, in everyday life we would object because we are inclined to insist that there are limits which are based on the intrinsic worth or value of people.

Again, we can see that it would be difficult to extend utilitarianism in such a way as to generate a full environmental ethic. While it has a place in our moral reasoning, utilitarianism is not usually assumed to be a fully satisfactory answer to our environmental concerns. In so far as it attaches absolute value to one end – welfare – utilitarianism is incapable of dealing with other considerations satisfactorily. For example, it is hard pressed to account for the value we might wish to place on the existence or well-being of things independently of our own individual welfare. Again, it cannot easily adapt itself to our moral intuitions concerning the value of life, the value of ecological systems, the existence of species, as well as the more anthropocentric concerns of justice.

Respect for life

Another possibility might be to ground an ethic on the notion of respect for life, irrespective of sentience. The notion of 'reverence for life' is indelibly associated with the life and work of Albert Schweitzer. However, there are problems with such an approach. On what grounds do we have this respect? Where does it come from? Is it a feeling natural to all thinking beings able to reflect on the complex subtleties of living organisms? It certainly cannot come from any sympathy, any sharing of suffering or feeling if the organism is not itself sentient. A related problem is what the idea implies for us: it can hardly be an injunction not to consume or use living organisms, because we need to eat to live. Perhaps it is an injunction to recognise the value of what sustains us; a reminder that we should not be wasteful, wanton or destructive without good cause. In other words, it is an insistence on the moral considerability of living things; not an absolute prohibition on use or consumption. Such an interpretation has value: like Singer's argument, it draws our attention to what we otherwise might overlook and extends the bounds of moral consideration. Hence it would appear to have a role to play in any environmental ethic. But there are still two problems. First, it fails to establish priorities: what, for example, is the relative worth of animals and plants? What are the occasions on which we can consume either or both of these things? Second, it fails to extend our obligations to the non-living world.

Thus 'reverence for life' cannot provide the ethic we need. It leaves too many unanswered questions. For example, life may have intrinsic value, but this claim cannot account for the value we assign to other natural features such as mountains, rivers and lakes, and it ignores the problem of what 'life' is. But it is important to value life even though we cannot perfectly preserve it: to live a life is necessarily to take other life. It is important to recognise that we should take account of living things in considering the effects of our actions. Granted its limitations, can this approach be developed and used as part of a wider environmental ethic?

One way is to argue that all objects, whatever their outward appearance, are really in some sense alive or conscious. Such a view would get around the problem of the attribution of value to non-living objects by insisting that there are no non-living objects. Whatever the metaphysical merits of this point of view, even its proponents doubt that it can help in our moral reckonings as we must necessarily be ignorant of its character (Sprigge, 1997, p. 130). It seems far better simply to accept that we have duties and not to try to base them on life or sentience alone. There is, however, one ingenious way of resurrecting the 'life' argument so that it applies to everything: by granting honorary life to inanimate objects as part of a whole organism. If, for example, we were to accept the Gaia hypothesis propounded by James Lovelock (1979) to the effect that the world as a whole is a living self-regulating biosystem, comparable with other biological organisms, then we can of course apply a life-ethic to all of the earth and to every part of it, including those parts of it usually regarded as not living. Such an approach challenges the tendency to regard things in isolation, neglecting their interrelatedness. Rocks and rivers, considered in isolation, are non-living things, but considered as part of a wider organism they should be granted the respect we grant to life as such. However, this position stands or falls with the tenability of the Gaia hypothesis itself.

Independently of the truth of the Gaia hypothesis, however, it might be possible to establish an intermediate position. By considering the matter at the level of eco-systems and recognising interdependence we can achieve essentially the same results as if we adopted the Gaia hypothesis, without a commitment to the view that the whole earth is a living organism. Thus we could argue that rivers, rocks, forests and species should be assigned value because, through their interactions, they form and support ecosystems which are as fundamental to our considerations as any individual animal or plant. Any entity within an ecosystem can be seen to be morally considerable in virtue of its position as part of a wider 'living' whole. Each item has honorific life status where it is not already a living being. Living beings themselves derive some of their importance from the role they play within the ecosystem. The interrelatedness of living and non-living entities becomes central to our considera-tions. Aldo Leopold's 'Land Ethic' can be seen to have a place here. He declares that: 'A thing is right when it tends to preserve the integrity, stability and beauty of the biotic community. It is wrong when it does otherwise' (Leopold, in Dobson, 1991, pp. 240–1). This is a broader conception than mere reverence for life, as it includes reference to the whole biotic community and thereby escapes some of the strictures already noted. However, it perhaps tends too far in the opposite direction (as does the idea of Gaia in its own way) by assigning too little value to the individual and too much to the whole.

This more holistic understanding of value in nature has important consequences for the relation between the self and the environment (Mathews, 1991). Arne Naess, the inspiration behind deep ecology, exhorts us to adopt an intuitive sense of 'life' which would encompass the biological/geological whole in which we are embedded. The deep ecological conception of self rejects 'the man in the environment image in favour of the relational, total-field image'; it tends towards the principle of 'biospherical egalitarianism'; it emphasises ecological concepts of 'diversity and symbiosis' (Naess, 1973, pp. 95–100).[4] Bringing Naess and Leopold together, we arrive at the view termed 'autopoietic intrinsic value theory' in which intrinsic value is attributed to all entities that are 'primarily and continuously concerned with the regeneration of their own organization activity and structure' (Eckersley, 1992, pp. 60–1). Such entitites are ends in themselves and hence have intrinsic value. Combining the recognition of intrinsic value with an expanded notion of the self brings together the biocentric (life-regarding), ecocentric (ecosystem-regarding) and anthropocentric views through a reconsideration of the way we understand and experience the world.

The Eight-Point Platform of Deep Ecology

1 The well-being and flourishing of non-human life has intrinsic value, independent of human usefulness.
2 The richness and diversity of life contribute to the realization of these values and are values in themselves.
3 Humans have no right to reduce this diversity except to satisfy vital needs.

---

4   The flourishing of human life and culture is compatible with a substantial decrease in the human population, while the flourishing of non-human life requires this decrease.
5   Present human interference in the world is excessive, and the situation is worsening.
6   Policies affecting basic economic, technological and ideological structures must change.
7   The ideological change is mainly that of appreciating life quality (dwelling in situations of inherent value) rather than adhering to an increasingly higher standard of living.
8   Those who subscribe to the above have an obligation to implement the necessary changes.

(Devall and Sessions, 1985, p. 70)

The interrelatedness of all living and non-living entities could be seen as the basis of an inbuilt human sense of oneness with the environment in which we are embedded. Transpersonal ecology, as expounded by Warwick Fox (1990), seeks to comprehend this sense by looking at the question of the self. We tend to think of the self as isolated, opposed to other selves and separate from the rest of the world. But this atomistic understanding is in many ways false, as anyone who feels strongly for another knows when faced with their pain, fear or struggles. The fact that we can empathise with other humans is important, and lies at the heart of moral motivation. But we can also empathise with other animals in their suffering and joy. Transpersonal ecology seeks to show that we have and should develop a wider sense of self. If we can cultivate this wider sense of self by identifying with other human beings, Fox argues that we can extend the boundaries of our selves outwards to embrace the larger ecological whole. This is not the imposition of our 'selfish', strong anthropocentric self on the rest of the world. On the contrary, a wider self transcends our particular desires and wishes by emphasising empathy with the selfhood of other beings with which we share the world (Eckersley, 1992, pp. 61–2).

Although deep and transpersonal ecology emphasise the interrelatedness of all entities, it is not clear how this expanded consciousness helps us to approach ethical conflicts and the practical problems that flow from them. Human beings necessarily make interventions in the natural world in order to survive. Non-intervention is not an option. When we intervene we need to weigh the effect of alternative courses of action. It is not clear that such ecological consciousness can help with the details of such considerations. We must make choices about which entities are significant, which are to be given priority, which direction our development should take. How are we to weigh the claims of different living and non-living entitities? In these terms deep ecological thinking may be limited. However, if we are to develop a more ecologically enlightened ethics, it must be rooted in a transformed, embedded sense of self. Transpersonal and deep ecological approaches may offer certain insights of value to this project of transformation.

We have examined three different approaches to the moral questions of the environment. Each approach can be associated with different ways of valuing the world. Utilitarianism lays the emphasis on sentience, on the ability to suffer or feel pleasure, and hence on how we treat animals displaying these features. Animals are seen as being equal with humans in respect of their sentience, but the consequence is that a gulf arises between sentient and non-sentient beings. The stewardship tradition generates a broader view in which human beings are seen as benevolent. It is precisely because humans are conceived of as standing over and above nature, and are thought of as rational beings made in God's image, that they are given the responsibility of caring for the natural world and the creatures within it. Respect for life, in its wider sense, emphasises the continuity of humans with the whole of the natural world. There is no great gulf between human and non-human nature, sentient or non-sentient being. All are part of a wider whole. Each moral tradition makes a distinctive contribution to the way in which we value the natural world, and in looking at the issue of value in more detail we may draw on each to a greater or lesser extent. We have inherited a plurality of value orientations towards the natural world and all have something to offer.[5] The theoretical task is how to combine these different aspects of our ethical heritage into a coherent theory able to underpin practice.

The nature of value and the value of nature

The centrality of value to environmental ethics becomes apparent as soon as we start asking ourselves serious questions about why we want to protect the natural environment. In considering this, it is helpful to draw a broad distinction between instrumental and intrinsic value.

We attribute instrumental value whenever we regard the non-human world as valuable in so far as it is or can be appropriated by human beings. (Strictly speaking this is *anthropocentric* instrumental value, as all living creatures appropriate their environment in various ways.) What might be termed 'strong' instrumental value interprets this as direct use of the natural world in the sense of consumption, production and exploitation. What follows from an insistence that the value of nature is or should be instrumental to the purposes of humankind? In so far as the well-being or survival of people is dependent on the survival or well-being of the natural environment, people have a strong incentive for protection and preservation. But there is an important consequence: human action in maintaining any aspect of the natural world is made contingent upon the interests people happen to have (or think they have). If they do not have (or do not think that they have) those interests there would be no purely instrumental reason for preserving or protecting certain parts of the natural world. While environmental concern based on people's interests alone might be practically effective in gaining support for certain policy outcomes, it is a perilously weak foundation for an environmental ethic. The role of enlightened self-interest in environmental politics as a spur to environmental action is of the greatest importance and its practical political value should not be underestimated; but it does not amount to an environmental ethic. While including such instrumental concerns, an environmental ethic needs to go beyond contingent human interests and the direct relation between the environment and human welfare.

What might be termed 'weak' instrumental value,[6] by contrast, covers non-exploitative attitudes to nature, that is, attitudes which lead to appreciation but not consumption of the natural world. For example, it is clearly possible to appreciate features of the natural world aesthetically. A person might say that the sight of a flock of geese flying overhead is of value in that they appreciate it spiritually and aesthetically and value it accordingly. Interference with the spectacle would spoil it: we wish only to appreciate it as a spectator. Value of this kind is 'the value which an object has through its ability to contribute to human life by its presence . . . the kind of value which attaches to things whether alive or not which are interesting to watch or study, or beautiful to contemplate, or which heal us when we are with them' (Attfield, 1991, pp. 151–2). Thus, to think of the geese aesthetically is to ascribe them weak instrumental value in that their value lies in their relationship with our human desires and purposes; to think of the geese merely as a food resource, by contrast, would be to ascribe them strong instrumental value. Again, we frequently experience a sense of wonder in contemplating the natural world and this enters into our desire for scientific knowledge in which we can contemplate the wonderful and the beautiful with a sense of awe and humility (O'Neill, 1993).

Contrasting sharply with instrumental forms of value, we find an approach in which we consider that even if certain things possessed no instrumental value for human beings, whether as providing material for consumption or for aesthetic contemplation or enjoyment, they should nonetheless still be protected and preserved for their own sake. This would be to assign intrinsic, non-anthropocentric value to the aspect of the environment concerned, be it an individual animal or an ecosystem. The term 'intrinsic value' has a number of senses.[7] In everyday life we are likely to use the term in either of two different ways. First, to mean that values are objective, that is to say, found in the object and not simply imputed by an observer. To say that beauty lies in the object is to say that beauty is a property of the object and that the observer, in ascribing beauty, is recognising it as located in the object, not simply in the eye of the beholder. Second, the term might be used to indicate that the value something possesses is not only objective but is independent of its instrumental value to something else. It has freestanding, self-sufficient value in its own right simply for being what it is in itself. Thus we often say that human life is intrinsically valuable and therefore should be protected, preserved and enhanced; human beings should be treated with respect in virtue of their humanity alone and not treated simply as means to the ends of other people.

In environmental debate the term intrinsic value is typically used in ways which combine the above characteristics and it is also used rhetorically to extend the range of moral attention beyond human concerns. It is not denied that human beings have intrinsic value, but they are not held to be the only things which possess such value. Typically, in discussions concerning the moral status of animals, for example, sentient creatures are granted intrinsic value. However, as we have shown in our earlier discussion, it can also be argued that living, non-sentient beings and non-living natural objects, such as rivers, forests, and wilderness, possess intrinsic value. If so, they deserve to be granted moral considerability and their interests or well-being should be taken into account and might very well divert, prevent or modify our actions, whether they be building a road through a particular landscape or building a dam and destroying the habitat of a small fish.

The inescapability of anthropocentrism: who values?

To think clearly about the values we associate with the environment we need to distinguish clearly *who* values from *what* is valued. The value of something depends on human consciousness in the sense that, beyond the purely instrumental response that we associate with animals satisfying their basic needs, only human beings can ascribe and determine value. Without human beings there would be (in the relevant sense) no value. However, this does not mean that objects cease to have value when they cease to be thought about. Some things have not yet been valued, but this does not mean that they suddenly change from being valueless to being valuable at the very instant that they are valued by a conscious entity (Attfield, 1994, p. 204). Human beings ascribe value, and to this extent value is rooted in human consciousness, but when they make valuations they are recognising value rather than arbitrarily creating it. To show that values are not arbitrary one can simply ask how one would respond if asked to attribute a greater value to a pebble than to a bird or to a piece of grass than to a tree. There is a scale of value, the precise details of which can be debated and revised, but in which the broad outlines are firm. We neither value everything equally nor do we assign things no value at all.

Anthropocentrism is often taken to be the view that only human beings have moral standing or that it is only the interests of human beings that in the end matter. However, there is also a weaker sense in which it is recognised that the interests of other beings should be taken into account. To make this clear we need to make a further distinction between the claim that it is human beings who *assign* value, and the separate claim that it is only humans and their interests that are *of* value. The first is necessarily true; the second is the real ecological point at issue. Environmental ethicists, responding to what they take to be strong anthropocentricism, often make the claim that there is value in nature itself separate from the process of valuation. Such a belief in the existence of objective intrinsic value is termed non-anthropocentrism. Such a position appears incoherent as it seems to fail to recognise the necessity of human consciousness in recognising value (Hayward, 1995, pp. 62–72; Thompson, 1990, pp. 147–60). The important distinction, then, is between different forms of anthropocentrism: strong and weak.

The fact that value is assigned or recognised by human beings does not in itself imply that values are anthropocentric in the sense of privileging human beings over the rest of nature. There is nothing inconsistent, that is, in human beings valuing the interests of other natural objects or beings above the interests of human beings. In other words it is important to distinguish who is *asking* the questions from who *benefits* from the answer given (Williams, 1995, p. 234). Only human beings ask these sorts of questions and values are to that extent human-based or anthropocentric in a weak sense. In this context a better term than anthropocentric is *anthropogenic*. Anthropogenic value originates from, but is not necessarily beneficial to, human beings. In this sense even the intrinsic value attributed by deep ecologists to the natural world is anthropogenic or weakly anthropocentric. As Andrew Dobson recognises:

If there were no human beings there would be no such conceptualized thing as intrinsic value, and it is an open question whether there would be any such thing as intrinsic value at all. In this sense, any human understanding will be (weakly) anthropocentric, including the green movement itself.

(Dobson, 2000, p. 55)

What is valued?

Holmes Rolston suggests that there are at least ten different areas of value associated with nature. They are worth consideration as they extend our tripartite classification into a spectrum of value allowing for a subtle appreciation of a wide range of human and non-human activities.

Aspects of environmental value

Economic: provider of resources for humans.
Life support: sustains and enhances life.
Recreational: recreation, contemplation and activity.
Scientific: the development of scientific inquiry.
Aesthetic: enjoyment of beauty; awe, wonder and humility in the face of the sublime.
Life: variety of living entities.
Diversity and unity: complexity and simplicity; relation of the parts to the whole.
Stability and spontaneity: continuity and change.
Dialectical: the interrelatedness of the social and the natural.
Sacramental: religious awe.

(Rolston, 1981, pp. 113–28)

Rolston is drawing attention here to the enormous variety of ways in which nature can be valued: our categories of instrumental (both strong and weak) and intrinsic value provide the primary colours on the spectrum; these further categories, the intervening shades. This variety serves to encourage us to seek out the different values that we associate with nature. It is a mistake to suppose that there is only one form of environmental value; we need to be open to a plurality of possible sources.

In what we have said with respect to our inherited traditions of thought and the variety of values that can be associated with the natural world, we have shown that all aspects of the natural world should be seen as morally considerable. This is not to say that everything is of equal value, nor that the significance of different aspects is obvious. What we have tried to show is that the onus of justification has shifted. Good reasons now need to be given by those who wish to exploit the environment. They will have to show that the significance of the developments they propose outweighs the significance of the natural entities that their activities would affect.

Duties to the human world

Thus far we have focused on moral responsibilities to the natural world; we now turn to responsibilities to humanity. The above discussion of the relation between humanity and nature simplified the issue by speaking of humanity's relationship with the natural world. But 'humanity' is not a single entity: it is divided by nation, state, class, gender, race and other forms of social cleavage. Hence issues of justice between nations and across social cleavages have a bearing on the question of the way we treat nature. Some radical environmentalists appear to take the view that only our obligations to the natural world have significance, or that, given the size and urgency of the environmental crisis, they should take priority over human affairs: but this is not our view. The challenge faced by environmental ethics is to balance the competing claims of the natural and the human worlds, not to ignore one set of claims entirely. To do so would be to make a comparable mistake to that made by those who insist only on the importance of human well-being in the world. Both extremes are morally flawed.[8] We now turn to a consideration of our duties to present and future humanity.

Global distributive justice

There are great disparities in wealth and income between the world's nations, and this informs our deliberations about aid, trade, and development and our concern with famine, poverty and suffering. But what, if anything, does this have to do with environmental issues? What links the morality and politics of global inequality to specifically environmental concerns? A general answer is that human settlements exploit their environment in various ways, and some patterns of resource use are environmentally damaging whereas others (relatively) are not. Some patterns of living are sustainable in that there is no reason in principle why they cannot be continued indefinitely; others are not sustainable given scarce resources and modes of consumption which over-exploit the resources available and destroy the environment with their detritus. Some environmental destruction is the consequence of affluence, for example, carbon dioxide emissions as a result of car use; other forms of destruction are the consequence of poverty, for example, destruction of forests for fuel or shelter where clearance leads to erosion. Distributive and environmental concerns are therefore intrinsically interconnected at this level.

Certain forms of environmental degradation can neither be contained nor solved purely at a local level. Climate change and ozone depletion, for example, affect the planet as a whole and their solution requires global cooperation. Isolated local action is simply insufficient. Environmental policy is thus faced with the dilemma that while the environmental problems caused by prosperity, such as global warming, ozone depletion and acid rain, are well recognised, the North is unwilling to jettison or modify the lifestyle which creates the problems. At the same time the South actively wishes to adopt some of the environmentally damaging aspects of that lifestyle as it develops. It is this, with its implied steep increase in consumption of fossil fuels and use of non-renewable resources, which will magnify the very problems we are trying to solve. If solutions have to be global, and if this requires a change in the way people live and develop, we need to generate international environmental regimes which will solve the problem of collective action by securing worldwide agreement on key issues. Agreement will not be secured unless the settlement is seen and felt to be fair by those affected, and this brings in the issue of global distributive justice. Thus the relationship between environmental policy, environmental ethics and questions of global distributive justice becomes clear. An unjust world will not succeed in solving global environmental problems.[9]

From the South's perspective it frequently appears that the North is demanding a degree of restraint and sacrifice which it is not prepared to submit to itself. The demand to forswear the benefits of industrialisation so long enjoyed can easily be construed as hypocrisy, and there is a view that the problem is very much of the North's own creation and that therefore the onus should be on the more industrialised nations to take responsibility. This leads to Southern nations making conditions for their having to accept stringent universal environmental standards and to a demand for material compensation for forgone benefits and technological assistance in finding and providing environmentally-sensitive alternatives. If, for example, burning coal pollutes the atmosphere, creates acid rain and leads to climate change, then the onus is on the North to provide alternative, environmentally-sensitive technologies. Again, if it is not thought desirable to use refrigerators which contain CFCs, contributions will have to be made towards developing new forms of technology which will overcome the problem. The South cannot be denied its right to develop in whatever direction it sees fit. The view that the North should not simply make demands but should provide compensation and alternative forms of technology was expressed very sharply by the Indian Environment Minister in 1990, over demands for the less industrialised nations to refrain from using ozone-depleting technology. Her view was that India should not sign the Montreal Protocol unless she was promised both financial assistance and the technology to make alternative chemicals.

Thus humanitarian moral concern with global distributive justice is frequently allied to a pragmatic political imperative: no justice, no cooperation; no cooperation, no solution. The South may be economically weak, but it can have, on occasion, the power of veto in global environmental policy affecting patterns of production and consumption. This forces a proper consideration of global distributive justice. However, in practical terms, the South may not have the bargaining or veto power to force the issue. Here we can only appeal to moral considerations. What is required, perhaps, is an impartial set of principles which can be subscribed to by all, including the weakest of the world's nations. In so far as environmental concern is rooted in the adverse effects of environmental degradation on human health and well-being, such principles must apply equally to all human beings irrespective of their location. We cannot be morally justified in solving environmental problems by exporting them. There is no moral reason to deny others the welfare we would wish to enjoy ourselves; it cannot be morally right to inflict the adverse consequences on to other people merely because they are in no position to object. To test our good faith we should perhaps be prepared to consider the extent to which we would be willing to accept the principles governing international policy if we were situated elsewhere.

Take the issue of natural resources. The distribution of natural resources around the globe is uneven. Some countries are sitting on large oilfields and others are sitting on an empty desert; some countries have good supplies of fertile land and water and others do not. What follows from this uneven and unequal distribution of resources? Does it follow that each country has an absolute right to the resources situated within its territory? Or does it follow, on the other hand, that they should be shared? There is a broad agreement that certain uninhabited parts of the world – the poles and the oceans – belong to the world as a whole and their exploitation is regulated or prevented through international agreement. Clearly this approach does not currently prevail in respect of inhabited countries: but nonetheless the issue of ownership, responsibility and control is a live debate. This will be picked up in Chapter 7. Does Brazil have the right to do just what it likes with its rainforests, or can international intervention be justified to protect them? Does the lucky accident of proximity to fuel or food stocks allow a country to enjoy a monopoly of that resource? How far are we justified in applying certain basic principles of justice to these cases?

The dominant ethical approach to these issues is drawn from the contractarian tradition in moral and political theory. This analyses rights and duties as the outcome of a hypothetical contract in which we try to understand what our rights and duties would be if we were able to stand back and look carefully at the matter without the intrusion of personal interests and selfish desires. Such a theory attempts to justify moral principles by showing that they would be agreed upon by rational agents in certain ideal circumstances. Its purpose is to exhibit the rationality of moral rules (Carruthers, 1992, p. 36).

In his *A Theory of Justice* (1972), John Rawls challenges us to think through the principles of justice we would choose if we did not know what our situation in life was, what we were going to be, and what benefits or burdens we have in life. He assumes that people's moral judgements are more likely to be unprejudiced if the peculiarities of their own situation and interests are unknown at the point of discussing general principles of justice; if we do not know who or what we are, we cannot bias the conclusion in our own favour. He refers to this condition of choice, and the associated lack of knowledge about ourselves and our circumstances as, respectively, the 'original position' and the 'veil of ignorance'. They are designed simply to clarify our thinking on these issues by forcing us to be impartial, by positing a situation in which, although we want the best for ourselves, we cannot directly choose a way of ensuring that we will emerge better off than anyone else. Rawls assumes that we are prepared to commit ourselves to whatever principles emerge out of our deliberations and he maintains that rational actors would choose principles of justice which would act as yardsticks for assessing the basic structure of a society.

The general conception of justice that Rawls claims we would accept is that 'all social primary goods – liberty and opportunity, income and wealth, and the bases of self-respect – are to be distributed equally unless an unequal distribution of any or all of these goods is to the advantage of the least favoured' (Rawls, 1972, p. 303). More specifically, he argues that this could be further subdivided into two basic principles. The first is that each person is to have an equal right to the most extensive total system of equal basic liberties compatible with a similar system of liberty for all; the second that social and economic inequalities should be arranged so that they are both (a) to the greatest benefit of the least advantaged, and (b) attached to offices and positions open to all under conditions of fair equality of opportunity. For present purposes the most important of these principles is the idea that social and economic inequalities should be to the greatest benefit of the least advantaged. This he terms the 'difference principle' and the basic point is that it assumes equality and holds that inequalities can only be justified if they are to the benefit of the least well-off in society.

These principles of justice can be used in our evaluations of the distribution of wealth and income. Rawls remarks that 'the natural distribution is neither just nor unjust; nor is it unjust that men are born into society at some particular position. These are simply natural facts. What is just and unjust is the way that institutions deal with these facts' (ibid., p. 102). The issue, then, is how we respond to the natural distribution, and we can do this in a Rawlsian fashion by asking what principles would be agreed to by countries who were denied knowledge of certain particular facts about themselves. Or, to put it more concretely, what principles would be chosen by representatives of the world's nations if they did not know whether they were from the USA, Somalia, Sweden or Bangladesh? It is not hard to imagine that globally-acceptable principles of distributive justice might look something like Rawls's principles and that they would justify and endorse some forms of global redistribution through aid and trade, perhaps the writing-off of various forms of international debt, and perhaps a more widespread sharing of the world's resources. In return, various forms of intervention into the hitherto sovereign affairs of nations would be justified and accepted: the over-exploitation of a country's natural resources (forests or flora or fauna, for example) would no longer be tolerated and the countries affected would accept this consequence as the outcome of a fair international regime from which they in turn benefit. Elements of such an interpretation of justice can at times be found in the discussion and output of some international agreements, although it is still far from being a central consideration of all parties. There would of course be enormous implications for international relations and specifically for thorny issues such as sovereignty. Aid, for example, is typically given directly to governments, but this is to ignore the internal distribution of power, wealth, income and opportunities within each state. However, if we try to give aid directly to individuals or groups within a state and ignore governments, we create all sorts of ethical and political problems. Whichever way these arguments go, it is at least obvious that any globally-successful environmental policy must issue in a re-thinking of our attitudes towards sovereignty and ownership and point in the direction of the recognition of the world as a resource common to all its inhabitants.

Justice and future generations

The actions of those living in the present will affect those living in the future. In the past we were probably confident that the effects of our actions would be (on the whole) benign and that those coming after us would be the privileged and grateful beneficiaries of our research, technology and investment. This assumption is no longer so prevalent. People worry about the world in which their children or grandchildren will grow up. They worry that their future is bleak. Neither can we simply reverse our patterns of behaviour, thereby removing this fear and restoring our lost optimism: what future generations will inherit is in large part already determined by what has already been done. We cannot take away the carbon dioxide or the chlorofluorocarbons from the atmosphere, although, given political will and wisdom, we can reduce future levels of emissions. In some instances we have already imposed a requirement on future generations to find alternatives for the energy sources that we are exhausting and we have also bequeathed to posterity the task of clearing up the consequences of our inadequate knowledge of toxic-waste disposal. We are currently storing nuclear waste which will remain highly toxic for a million years; we are doing this despite the fact that we do not yet know for certain how best to store it safely. Our obligations to future generations depending on the safe storage of nuclear waste extend to at least 30,000 generations.

Intergenerational justice is only one aspect of environmental ethics, but it stands at the junction of numerous environmental policy issues. This is obvious when we reflect on the requirements of sustainable development which requires, in the words of *Our Common Future*, that we meet 'the needs of the present without compromising the ability of future generations to meet their own needs' (WCED, 1987, p. 43).[10]

Intergenerational justice concerns what we ought to leave to the generations who will succeed us in respect of resources, pollution and environmental damage, flora and fauna, biodiversity, wildernesses, and so on. But what sort of obligations are these? It is generally accepted that there is a strong obligation to avoid harm to others, but it is sometimes held that we also on occasion have obligations to go beyond this and to improve the welfare of others. This raises the question of whether we are obliged to make our successors better-off than we are or to ensure that they are no worse-off. Should we, for example, ensure that pollution and environmental degradation gets no worse, or try to restore environments (so far as possible) to their 'original' state? Related questions include what constitutes harm; what constitutes benefit; and what substitutions future generations will find acceptable where we cannot pass on to them exactly the same mixture of environmental resources as we ourselves inherited. Whatever the precise nature of the answers, surely it is possible to agree that we have some obligations to future generations? An affirmative answer immediately raises the question of how far into the future we should think of our obligations stretching. How far into the future should we set our sights? Should we focus only on generations immediately following ours, or should we set our sights on 30,000 generations? The answer depends on, first, the source of our obligations, and second, on whether our priority is to avoid harm or promote positive good. If the priority is to avoid harm, it is plausible to argue that this must be a relatively open-ended commitment, especially in the case of irreversible, non-remediable damage, such as the extinction of species or the poisoning of the planet through nuclear radiation. Here, because the actions or their effects are non-reversible, what affects one generation will affect all those succeeding it. The present generation can help or harm future generations, but future generations cannot help or harm us, at least not in the same sense.[11] We have power over them in that we can promote our own interests at the expense of theirs, if we so choose. Future generations are, it might be said, both powerless and vulnerable.

Why do we have obligations to future generations?

The boundaries of our moral concern extend outwards as we include our contemporaries, other species, and perhaps other aspects of the natural world, within the bounds of a relevant moral community. We are now being asked whether or not to include currently non-existent members of future generations within the relevant moral community. Some argue that we can have no obligations to non-existent entities; others argue that our priority ought to be the needs and interests of the generation to which we belong and that justice begins in our own time. This is not necessarily a selfish response as it could include the acceptance of important and costly obligations to other members of our current generation. Lying behind these issues are further questions: are obligations to people remote from us in time or space weaker than those to people closer to us? Is there a significant moral difference between remoteness in time and in space? Most people would agree that we do, in fact, have obligations to those remote from us in space; and we do also behave as if we have obligations to those remote from us in time as well. However, it might be argued that the obligations are of different degrees of strength or intensity: even so, to allow that we have any obligation at all to future generations makes a difference to what we ought to do in the present.

Whatever we do we cannot duck the question because increased knowledge of the likely consequences of our actions inevitably brings in its train the sort of imaginative sympathy which generates a sense of moral responsibility. For example, we possess a great deal of knowledge about the plight of peoples in the South and we accept obligations to help in various ways. We know about famine and suffering and this generates moral sentiments. It does not necessarily follow that we do what we think we ought to do, but the recognition that there is a problem leads us to search for the causes and to consider possible remedies. In this respect we are in a vastly different position to people 200 years ago who can hardly be blamed for not helping people in other parts of the world when they were ignorant of the fact that they were suffering. We are familiar with media representations of people suffering in other countries: to turn away from the pictures unmoved is an act of a different nature from simply not knowing that the suffering existed at all. However, there are no media representations of future generations and we are in that sense in the position of those 200 years ago ignorant of suffering elsewhere in the world; but we do know that people will suffer, even if we shall not live to see that suffering for ourselves. Are we not morally responsible for the foreseeable consequences of our actions, irrespective of whether we live to witness them for ourselves? Surely simple recognition of this responsibility generates obligations to future generations?

There are some things about which one cannot know today that one will have an obligation to tomorrow. For example, tomorrow an elderly infirm person might need to be helped across the road, or a child to be saved from drowning. We do not know that this will be the case but we can agree that if it were the case then there would be an obligation to do something about it. By parity of reasoning, if we did not know that future generations were going to exist then we could not know that we had an obligation to them. However, we do know that future generations are going to exist; we do know, that is, that the generational equivalent of the old person or the drowning child will exist; and we know this now. We know it before they exist, and this means that we have to act on this now. If I knew the child was going to place itself in danger of drowning tomorrow then I would have an obligation to do what I could today to prevent that happening. Future generations are, in this respect, like the child who is in danger of drowning tomorrow. And it does not matter that we do not know who the future generations are; after all, it makes no difference who the drowning child is either. A sceptic might argue that future generations might not exist: true; but so what? It is irresponsible and stupid to act as if they will not. Furthermore it is only at the moment that they cease to exist that our obligations to them will in turn cease.

This is a general argument which establishes, if successful, a broad conclusion. Another argument might be to again draw on the work of Rawls by using the contractarian model. One obvious way of doing this is to imagine that the positions were reversed and that our generation swopped places with a future generation: 'If we were living 500 years hence, do we think we would wish that in respect of a particular problem we had been living now instead of then? If we do then our present way of acting is a selfish one' (Cameron, 1989, p. 72).

In this way, Rawls's theory could be applied to the consideration of obligations to future generations: all we would have to imagine is that the participants in the original position do not know to which generation they belong and that they might belong to *any* generation. This approach, however, goes beyond what Rawls himself argued for in *A Theory of Justice*. There he postulated that the participants in the original position were contemporaries, although they did not know to which generation they actually belonged. This prevented him from generating obligations to future generations out of the central premise of his theory. Brian Barry (1991) suggests that Rawls should simply have followed through the internal logic of his own argument and scrapped that part specifying that all people in the original position are contemporary and know that they are.[12] The veil of ignorance could then be employed to conceal from participants to which generation each of them belonged, and out of this procedure principles of intergenerational justice would be chosen. These principles would inevitably apply to and between generations many generations removed from each other: it would be much more far-reaching than Rawls's theory of justice would allow.

Despite the attractions of the extended Rawlsian approach it has often been argued by some that we should be concerned only with immediate posterity. Rawls himself actually holds that responsibilities to posterity are based on ties of affection to the next generation (Rawls, 1972, pp. 128–9).[13] Broadly, it is argued that moral obligations arise from within life in a community within which one becomes entangled in a network of mutual dependencies and comes to accept the corresponding rights and duties. Obligations arise out of actual relations with people, and thus there can be no obligations to those who will live long after we are dead. An extension of this view is to argue that obligations rest on a sense of moral community. Obligations can be extended outwards to include members of communities recognisably similar to our own. Whether or not we have obligations to future generations depends, on this view, on whether we expect them to live in ways that would lead us to regard them as part of our moral community. If we think they will develop in ways we disapprove of then we have no obligations to them. Thus Golding (1972) argues that we have obligations to those in a community with its reciprocal relationships; and that there may be possible obligations to future people, but only where they have a conception of the good life with enough in common with ours. He then goes on to argue that as we do not know what the interests and desires of people in the far future will be, it is therefore pointless worrying about them. We want to protect the natural world to provide our descendants with resources for them to enjoy, or because we think they will share our values concerning the value of the natural world. But what grounds do we have for assuming that people in the far future will adhere to the same values and desires and have the same needs? It is a fair assumption to make for those living in the immediate future – but is it not dangerous to be too sure about what those coming after that will want? And is it not possible that they might choose to live in ways which we could never regard as being acceptable in terms of our own moral community? Given these possibilities, why then should we impose obligations on ourselves to conserve, preserve, protect, maintain or enhance things which people in the future might simply not want or deserve?

But, to take issue with Golding's argument, the point about intergenerational justice is not reducible to whether we share other people's conception of the good life; we can agree that conceptions of what constitutes the good life can and will differ from our own. Nor is it about their interests in the sense in which this is related to their conception of the good life. It is something more fundamental: it is about the possession of life itself, not so much concerned with the conception of the good people choose, as with the very possibility of them being able to choose a conception of the good at all. This point is forcefully made by Barry when he argues that future generations will be alike in certain key respects.

> It is true that we do not know what the precise tastes of our remote descendants will be, but they are unlikely to include a desire for skin cancer, soil erosion, or the inundation of all low-lying areas as a result of the melting of the ice caps. And, other things being equal, the interests of future generations cannot be harmed by our leaving them more choices rather than fewer.
>
> (Barry, 1991, p. 248)

This point can be generalised: if, for ourselves, we would prefer that earlier generations had left us a greater amount of choice and variety in the natural world, environment and resources, is it not the case that generations following us would appreciate being left the same variety? True, we do not know exactly what they will want and value; but precisely for that reason it is better to widen their choice rather than to narrow it, to give them more opportunities rather than fewer.

Justice to nature

The concept of justice is normally assumed to be applicable only to human beings, and more controversially (as we have seen) to animals. For theorists such as Rawls, the notion of justice is (strictly speaking) only applicable to humans and their communities. However, there are protagonists for the view that we can treat nature itself justly or unjustly. The question is whether, in Brian Baxter's phrase, 'we should expand the idea of the community of justice to include at

---

continued

least some elements of non-human nature' (2000, p. 50). If we take the view that there is no sharp cut-off between the human world and the natural world, and if we allow that the needs and interests of non-human nature should have weight in our deliberations, we might easily find ourselves becoming reluctant to accept that the concept of justice should be reserved to the human world alone. Hence Nicholas Low and Brendan Gleeson distinguish between environmental justice, 'the justice of the distributions of environments among peoples', and ecological justice, 'the justice of the relations between humans and the rest of the natural world'. Nonetheless they regard environmental justice and ecological justice as two aspects of the same relationship (1998, p. 2). Many of the ideas here parallel the arguments for and against animal rights; clearly all forms of environmentalism lead to or presuppose some extension of our moral concerns, but the issue here is whether we need to use the language of rights and justice in articulating those concerns. There are many who would argue, echoing what we said about animal rights, that what we have here is a good idea couched in the wrong language.

Practical questions

In general it is rare to find anyone arguing against the existence of obligations to future generations, although some argue that our obligations extend only to the generations immediately succeeding ours. In the latter case the expectation is that, as and where it is appropriate and possible, the torch of intergenerational justice will be passed down the generations, thereby ensuring continuity over many generations. In this sense the difference between those advocating a limited and those advocating an extended conception of intergenerational justice is easy to overstate. However, what constitutes passing the torch depends on the issue. If our obligations are relatively open-ended this may generate a sharp clash between justice for those living in the present against justice for those living in the future. Given that resources are finite, any consumption will have an effect on choices available for those in the future. This raises a tangled web of problems going far beyond what can be dealt with here, although some, in particular the question of the substitution of natural and man-made resources, will be dealt with in later discussions of sustainable development (see case study in Chapter 6). It is worth commenting that the answer to the question partly depends on the distinctions made earlier between avoiding harm and promoting welfare (as did Barry's riposte to Golding), between reversible and irreversible damage, between certain and probable harm. As has already been argued, an obligation to avoid certain types of actual harm is open-ended; an obligation to promote the welfare of others presupposes that we in fact know what constitutes their welfare. Here Golding's argument is a telling one. But the point about natural resources, for example oil or coal, is not so much whether later generations inherit stocks so much as that they inherit sufficient energy means, irrespective of what form this energy takes. If we take seriously the view that each generation has obligations only to its immediate successors, each generation would have the duty of ensuring that it passed on to its successor the equivalent in energy terms to that it itself inherited. This could be a heavy duty and one better shared over several generations – a possibility which presupposes a much greater continuity of environmental concern over time and hence a concern not only with immediate posterity, but with distant posterity. As Cameron argues: 'Our obligation to the generations after this immediately succeeding one can be thought of as mediated through our obligation to enable that next generation to discharge its obligation to all its successors' (Cameron, 1989, p. 72). Of course any action we take now may be in vain. Future generations may simply not care, may believe that different issues are more significant, or develop technologies which make our actions redundant. But we cannot know any of this and hence we should act on the limited knowledge that we have.

Conclusion

We can affect other generations, but is there not a prior obligation to the needs and interests of this generation? Is there a legitimate concern that there may be a clash between intragenerational and intergenerational justice? Trying to be fair to people in the future might preclude being fair to people living now. What sorts of sacrifices are we justified in asking people to make in the present for the good of future generations? Is it possible to share the burden of these sacrifices fairly? A short answer might be that, as argued above, global environmental policy will not succeed unless questions of global distributive justice are settled first: in this sense *inter*generational justice presupposes *intra*generational justice. We will never secure justice for future generations unless we can also act justly towards all members of our own generation. Further, this is made still more difficult when we consider the claims associated with the non-human world, which at times may clash with both present and future human well-being.

Some argue that we should discriminate on the basis of time, and discriminate in favour of the present generation. The present generation is the last one which can help those alive in the present; all previous generations to our own have already done their work for good or bad. On the other hand, people in the distant future can be helped by a number of succeeding generations as well as by the present one – responsibility can be shared. Therefore the obligation of the present generation should primarily be to itself. One obvious answer to this is that there are many actions which we can take now which will engender risks or harms to future generations whatever anyone does in the future; and in these cases it makes no difference what our successors do or do not do. If we pollute the world with nuclear waste then it cannot be undone by any action taken in the future. There are always some who will argue that science will find the answer to this (and to every other problem) at some point. This is a terrible burden to leave: it amounts to not only leaving the original problem, but also the problem of finding a solution which we have admitted we cannot find ourselves.

We have to be careful, especially when considering questions of resource depletion, to distinguish needs from wants.[14] Our priority has to be to meet the needs of the present; this must take precedence over considerations for the future and non-human obligations. However, despite this, there are different ways in which we can fulfil our basic needs, some being more sensitive to future-regarding and environment-regarding duties. It should be stressed that this edict applies to present needs, not wants or superfluous desires. It must be recognised that in many cases meeting the needs of future generations or giving due consideration to environmental obligations will result in a reduced ability to fulfil wants. With the Brundtland definition of sustainable development in mind, we must try to satisfy our needs in the present in ways which neither compromise the ability of future generations to satisfy their needs, nor adversely impact on the integrity of the natural environment.

Here it can be seen how the concept of sustainable development, which we argue to be central to the environmental agenda, emerges as a complex web of theoretical, practical and ethical issues. A simple definition such as Brundtland's presupposes the answer to a range of questions: questions which arise at the intersection of the natural world, human well-being, intragenerational and inter-generational considerations. Questions of value, obligations and principles all come into play in any deliberation, and this shows that despite the seemingly abstract nature of the preceding discussion, it is central to any serious attempt to generate solutions and agree on policies on issues as diverse as climate change, the ozone layer, the development of Antarctica, global development patterns, population, resource use or toxic-waste disposal.

Case study: modifying nature[15]

Do we need genetically-modified organisms (GMOs) to save the world or do we need to save the world from GMOs? The subject of biotechnology is currently being urgently considered from a number of diverse but overlapping standpoints: ethical, philosophical, biological, political, commercial and economic. In considering the topic we find ourselves in a complicated web of argument and counter-argument, claim and counter-claim. Let us begin exploring by considering a typical set of objections to genetically-engineered herbicide resistant crops (GEHRs) as summarised by Gary Comstock:

> Those who think that we should stop research on GEHR crops do so for at least four different reasons. First, they argue, the research will lead to an increased use of chemical pesticides, and more farmworkers and consumers will be injured or killed as herbicide use escalates. Second, mutant organisms may develop in GEHR crop fields and devastate vast areas of vital crops. This would put the food supply of the entire world at risk. Third, a small handful of companies may exploit farmers and consumers by exercising monopolistic control over the seed and chemical industries. Fourth, some are convinced that GEHR research is intrinsically immoral because it crosses species boundaries placed in nature by God.
>
> (Comstock, 2000, p. 63)

Extending the implications, we can break this down into the following set of overlapping issues and concerns:

• Justice to farmers whose practices and livelihoods are threatened by increased costs of seed and fertilisers, the necessity annually to repurchase seed and their associated agro-chemicals, and subjection to the agricultural biotechnology multinationals.

- Justice to nature which is subject to unprecedented interference and technological experimentation, leading to potential loss of natural integrity and biodiversity.
- The risks posed to human and animal well-being, not only physical but political and economic. A massive experiment with both nature and the public as its subjects is currently under way: an experiment in ethics, in public perceptions of science and experts and in economic and political control. This experiment may (through its uncertain and perhaps unintended effects) lead to irretrievable and irreversible harm to nature and thereby to human well-being in all its aspects.
- Issues of inter- and intragenerational justice: are we attempting to improve our capacity to meet our needs in the present by jeopardising the well-being of future generations? If we choose not to go down the road of GM are we thereby jeopardising our ability to meet the needs of people alive in the present?
- Power and control over agriculture, ways of life and economies increasingly being vested in the hands of the multinational corporations who are able to patent life forms, seeds and crops previously 'owned' by indigenous peoples, who dominate research and production, and who exercise massive bargaining power over governments and international organisations.

This list is no doubt incomplete, but it serves to indicate the extent to which biotechnology (for good or ill) threatens to turn our world upside down. To take a seemingly homely example: Comstock remarks that 'genetically-engineered herbicide resistant crops reverse the order of weeding. Where our great great grandparents started with seeds and then hunted for chemicals, scientists now hunt for a chemical and then look for seeds' (ibid., p. 36).

How do we begin to address these concerns? There are those for whom the answer is simple: we should simply abjure biotechnology and all its works. Complete rejectionism or 'green romanticism' (Dryzek, 1997, pp. 155–71) is an attitude in which 'biotechnology is not evaluated in terms of its potential consequences, but rejected *in toto* as the ultimate anthropocentric assault upon a sacred natural order. Scientific rationality and technical manipulation (with its atomistic conceptions and separation of human kind from its ecological context) have, in this view, been the core problems since the days of Francis Bacon' (Vogler and McGraw, 2000, pp. 124–5). And others, in particular eco-feminists, suggest that the Promethean urge to control and technologise the world proceeds from a masculine view of science which in turn leads to ever-increasing control and power over the disadvantaged, most typically women (Bretherton and Steven, 2000). Most of the world's farmers, as Vandana Shiva (2000) reminds us, are women in developing countries, and control is in danger of being wrested from their hands.

This view of science tends to be bound up with a fear of the unknown, of monsters that might be unleashed, of genetic pollution with unknown consequences, if, for example, increased use of GM leads to the creation of superweeds. As Francis Manning mildly observes: 'it has to be noted that . . . science has been relatively weak at predicting potential outcomes when a foreign species is introduced into a new environment' (2000, p. 23). It would seem rational, therefore, to argue that 'what is important is that we adopt a critical approach, a "healthy" fear, the kind that helps one imagine the worst in order to prevent it from happening' (Louett, quoted in de la Perriere and Seuret, 2000, p. 51).

One aspect of this fear is the thought that we might be on the verge of unleashing a situation in which we are permanently condemned to chase after the unforeseen consequences of our very attempt to control nature; it is the thought that science has outstripped human wisdom and that

continued

as a result of trying to 'control' nature, nature will elude our control in dangerous and worrying ways. Caution, it is urged, not hubris, is what we need, and we should recognise that our ability to control nature has run ahead of our ability to create human institutions in which power over nature can be safely and wisely exercised. A suspicion of this sort was powerfully voiced by R.G. Collingwood at the start of the Second World War:

> Bacon had promised that knowledge would be power, and power it was: power to destroy the bodies and souls of men more rapidly than had ever been done by human agency before. . . . It seemed almost as if man's power to control 'Nature' had been increasing *pari passu* with a decrease in his power to control human affairs. . . . [I]t was a plain fact that the gigantic increase since about 1600 in his power to control Nature had not been accompanied by a corresponding increase . . . in his power to control human situations. And . . . that the ill effects of any failure to control a human situation were more serious now than they had ever been before, in direct proportion to the magnitude of the new powers put by natural science . . . into the hands of the evil and the good, the fool and the wise man. Not only would any failure to control human affairs result in more and more widespread destruction as natural science added triumph to triumph, but the consequences would tend more and more to the destruction of whatever was good and reasonable in the civilized world; for the evil would always begin using the engines of destruction before the good, the fool always before the wise man.
>
> (Collingwood, 1939, pp. 90–1)

This is a powerful indictment and a valuable reminder that humans should be wary of technological short cuts to perfection. Further, control over nature goes hand in glove with control over humans; and the terrible irony that some fear is that the ideal of control over nature may lead to nature out of control at the same time as humans are placed more and more firmly in the grip of those powerful bodies who seek to control it. But where in all this is wisdom to be found? Many argue that it can be found in traditional practices and indigenous agricultural knowledge and that it is more prudent (on every level) to work with and develop these practices than to mortgage our world to the promise of the techno-future sold to us by technocrats and multinational corporations. As Robert de la Perriere and Franck Seuret ominously remark: 'We are only at the beginning of a gigantic privatisation process that is taking place at world level' (2000, p. 9).[16]

Bearing these fears in mind, how are we to proceed? What forms of reasoning should we employ? One of the difficulties is that biotechnology is not one thing but many, comprising different approaches, products and possible outcomes. That is why the issue is so difficult to capture politically and administratively. Currently, politically speaking, each example of bio-technology tends to be dealt with case by case, because (outright rejection aside) each example raises different issues and concerns. If we were to reject the whole enterprise – an approach attractive to many – are we rejecting all interference with nature? But if so, does it follow that we should cease the interference in which we have already been engaged for millennia? Where, if anywhere, are we to draw the boundaries between justifiable interference and non-justifiable interference? Bringing together the scientific and the political, Shiva is clear on this point:

> There is a difference between ecological boundaries and socially constructed boundaries. The difference between herbivores and carnivores is an ecological boundary. It needs to

be respected for the sake of both cows and humans. The difference between the value of human life in the North and South is a politically constructed boundary. It needs to be broken for the sake of human dignity.

(2000, p. 65)

In her adoption of an attitude of respect towards both nature and human beings, Shiva neatly encapsulates both the ethical and the political dimensions of this issue: both the need to take care of the natural world and the need to ensure justice in economic and resource allocation and to counter the power of governments and multinational corporations. But are the natural distinctions Shiva refers to really so clear cut? After all, it could be argued that genetic engineering is nothing new: merely old forms of interference and modification speeded up. Comstock points out that:

Defenders of GEHR are not unaware of criticisms. To the worry that gene-splicing represents a new and strange historical epoch, they might reply that herbicide resistant crops are nothing new. Varieties have long been selected for their resistance to herbicide and insecticides; even before genetic engineering came along we have been identifying and marketing seed that could grow in the presence of chemicals used to kill competitors. Genetic engineering only speeds up the process by cutting down on the length of time needed to come up with new varieties; what moral questions does it raise that could not be raised about traditional plant breeding techniques?

(2000, pp. 56–7)

On this view the difference between the old and the new is a difference in degree, not kind. An obvious riposte is that this underplays the nature of the difference, because direct operation on the genetic constitution of organisms is qualitatively distinct from older forms of selective breeding. We now combine genetic material across species boundaries in ways which it is hard to imagine ever occurring either through natural processes alone or through any possible form of selective breeding: for example, using fish genes to protect strawberries from frost. Two broad sorts of objections to these new practices arise: the first are intrinsic objections based on the idea that genetic modification is unnatural; the second are extrinsic objections based on the unforeseen adverse consequences of genetic manipulation.

Intrinsic objections to GMOs centre on the claim that it is unnatural to genetically engineer plants, animals and foods. What counts as being unnatural can be distinguished along the following lines:

- it is unnatural to transfer genes from one species to another;
- to engage in biotechnology is to play God;
- biotechnology is world-changing technology, an activity that should be reserved to God alone;
- it arrogates historically unprecedented power to ourselves; use of biotechnology exhibits arrogance, hubris, and disaffection;
- it is unnatural because it is to transfer the essence of one living being into another; it is unnatural because it changes the telos, or end, of an individual biological entity;
- it illegitimately crosses species boundaries;
- it is unnatural because it causes harm to sentient beings;

continued

- to engage in biotechnology is to commodify life; it disrespects life by patenting it;
- it is unnatural because it disrupts the integrity, beauty, and balance of creation.

(Comstock, 2000, pp. 183–4)

The items on this list, it should be remarked, comprise a vast range of objections and each item is not necessarily dependent on its neighbours. Some objections might appear compelling, others less so: either way, the claim that biotechnology is 'unnatural' requires a lot of conceptual unpacking if it is to escape the fate of being merely a handy slogan.

Extrinsic objections focus on the allegedly harmful consequences of GMOs, and conclude that biotechnology should not be pursued because of its anticipated adverse effects on animals, ecosystems, and humans. The objections can be reduced to a list of items not necessarily mutually dependent:

- by introducing genetically-engineered foods there is a substantial risk that agricultural biotechnology will do more harm than good to human health;
- there is a risk that it will perpetuate social inequities in developed economies where it will lead to advantages for larger agribusiness farmers that will be unjustly denied to smaller family farmers;
- there is a risk that it will harm subsistence farmers by perpetuating social and economic inequities between the more developed economies with their well-capitalized farmers, and developing economies, with their under-capitalized farmers;
- there is a risk that it will harm future generations by foreclosing possibilities for them to feed themselves;
- there is a risk that it will harm ecosystems by leading to environmental catastrophe through release into the wild of virulent genetically-modified organisms, plants, and fish;
- there is a risk that it will do more harm than good by narrowing plant germplasm diversity, and reduce the quality of air, soils, and ground and surface waters;
- there is a risk that it will harm research animals, livestock and wildlife, by causing them to suffer or die, or prevent them from continuing as a species.

(Comstock, 2000, pp. 225–6)

Conclusion

The obvious point to make is that if we adopt an approach based on practical assessment of consequences, we need to know what those consequences are or might be. However, as Alan Russell and John Vogler point out, 'GM technology tends to confound established "risk assessment" procedures which require that both probabilities and outcomes be relatively well defined. Instead this new technology is characterised not so much by uncertainty but typically by ignorance' (2000, p. 7). In other words, any approach to genetic engineering which is not inherently cautious and respectful of ethical, political, and economic sensibilities is wrong. We might accept GM, but if we do it should only be, at most, on the basis of qualified and careful endorsement of particular technologies in particular contexts; Promethean endorsement should be rejected.

Suggestions for further reading

Two useful edited collections of essays are Robert Elliot *Environmental Ethics* and Robin Attfield and Andrew Belsey *Philosophy and the Natural Environment.* Elliot's collection includes a number of 'classic' articles which have shaped the development of environmental ethics. Attfield and Belsey's book is more contemporary and broader in scope. Two of the most thorough and engaging contributions to environmental ethics and philosophy are Robin Attfield *The Ethics of Environmental Concern* and Kate Soper *What is Nature?.* A more recent survey of the field can be found in Christopher Belshaw *Environmental Philosophy.* John Benson *Environmental Ethics* is an excellent introduction to the sub-discipline and includes brief extracts from classic texts. Mark Smith *Thinking Through the Environment* is a collection of extracts from essays on environmental ethics and intergenerational justice. There are a number of interesting books on the issue of justice. Andrew Dobson *Justice and the Environment* is a good summary of debates within environmental philosophy and is complemented by his edited collection *Fairness and Futurity.* Avner de-Shalit *Why Posterity Matters* is also valuable. The journal *Environmental Ethics* includes both mainstream and more radical contributions; *Environmental Values* is a well-regarded journal in the field of environmental philosophy.

Notes

1   In addition, Genesis 1: 29 seems to indicate that our diet should be a vegetarian one: 'And God said, Behold, I have given you every herb bearing seed, which is upon the face of all the earth, and every tree, in the which is the fruit of a tree yielding seed; to you it shall be for meat.'

2   *Which* actions in the case of act utilitarianism; which *type* of actions performed as a rule in the case of rule utilitarianism. For our present purpose the distinction will be ignored. For an introductory discussion of the various forms of utilitarianism see Plant (1991, Chapter 3).

3   Utilitarian reasoning can be seen to be the basis of welfare economic decision-making procedures such as cost–benefit analysis (CBA). The extension of such procedures to incorporate environmental values is a central concern in Chapter 6.

4   The political implications of deep ecology are explored in Chapter 2.

5   For a discussion of moral pluralism and environmental ethics see Stone (1987); Brennan (1988, 1992). For a contrary view see Callicott (1990).

6   Some, such as Frankena (1979), refer to this as inherent value but, given that the term 'inherent' is so frequently used as a synonym for 'intrinsic', it seems better to adopt a different formulation.

7   Different interpretations of intrinsic value are discussed by O'Neill (1993, pp. 8–25).

8   Further, attempting to ignore human claims is also politically flawed in its contradictory hope for a mobilisation of human support and action while at the same time ignoring the legitimacy of human claims. Public policy requires public support and needs to be seen as justifiable by those affected by its implementation. Unjust policies, or policies with unjust outcomes, should be opposed not only because they are unjust, but also because injustice generates opposition which renders policies unworkable and hinders the achievement of environmental goals and aspirations.

9   The nature of collective action problems is explored in Chapter 4; the politics of international environment and development issues is discussed in Chapter 7.

10   *Our Common Future* was published by the World Commission on Environment and Development (WCED) in 1987 and and is usually referred to as the Brundtland Report after its chair, Gro Harlem Brundtland. For more on this report see Chapter 7.

11   This point is contested by O'Neill (1993, pp. 26–43). While his is a valuable discussion it does not substantially affect what is argued for here, although his remarks concerning damage to the reputation of the present generation is a strong one.

12   The reason Rawls did not do this is because of the strong tendency in his work to see justice as a relation of mutual advantage based on reciprocity, and there can of course be no reciprocity if one of the contracting parties does not yet exist.

13   Passmore holds a similar position (1980, pp. 91ff).

14   Distinguishing needs from wants is not as simple a matter as the Brundtland definition appears to suggest. See Plant (1991, pp. 184–220).

15   A different version of this case study first appeared as a review article in *Environmental Politics* (Connelly, 2002).

16   A polemical account of the extent to which this is already happening, together with some of its consequences, can be found in Monbiot (2000).

Green ideology

> Ecocentrism preaches the virtues of reverence, humility, responsibility, and care; it argues for low impact technology (but it is not anti-technological); it decries bigness and impersonality in all forms (but especially in the city); and demands a code of behaviour that seeks permanence and stability based upon ecological principles of diversity and homeostasis. . . . The technocentric ideology, by way of contrast, is almost arrogant in its assumption that man is supremely able to understand and control events to suit his purposes.
>
> (O'Riordan, 1981, p. 1)

This chapter turns to more political questions within contemporary environmental thinking. For example, what might a future sustainable society look like? Can we derive a specifically green set of institutional arrangements? Who are the agents of green political change? Is there a coherent green political ideology?[1] Within green political thought, it is common to find such questions answered with reference to two considerations: first, our ethical relationship with the natural world; and second, the limits placed on development by the finite nature of physical resources and the ability of ecosystems to withstand damage from pollution. However, neither reflection on our relations with the natural world nor scientific arguments concerning the carrying capacity of ecosystems will in themselves generate a *comprehensive* green political position. To understand the emerging form of contemporary green political thought, it is also necessary to reflect on more traditional values, such as justice, democracy and equality; to engage in a critical dialogue with other political traditions. By analysing the evolving relationship between green politics and the more established traditions of Western political thought, it can be seen that some form of environmental consideration has played a part in the development of most political traditions and that such considerations have at times been utilised to justify green political arrangements ranging from fascist to anarchist.

There remain tensions within green political thinking concerning such issues as the structure of political institutions and strategies for change. These tensions will be highlighted with reference to the themes implicit within the concept of sustainable development. Although there appears to be an emerging consensus centred on this concept, there are nonetheless widely divergent *interpretations* of what sustainable development actually requires. For many greens sustainable development challenges the logic of continued economic growth; for others, economic growth is a prerequisite of environmental protection. It is this latter conception of sustainable development, most recently understood as 'ecological modernisation', that is dominating current debates. The fact that actors as far apart as environmental direct-action groups and business associations appeal to the concept of sustainable development in support of their activities should serve as a warning that usage does not always imply precise agreement on meaning.

Politics, ethics and *The Limits to Growth*

From ethics to politics

In the previous chapter, arguments were developed to show how our relationship with the natural world might be understood philosophically and ethically. What becomes clear is that it is extremely difficult to accurately describe the ethical relationships involved and the duties and obligations that these generate. That such ethical considerations are central to the commitment of many green activists is not in doubt; the point now at issue is whether political strategies and institutional arrangements can be derived directly from such reflections and commitments. Could the belief in, for instance, the intrinsic value of all natural entities tell us anything about the ideal form of institutions? Is it possible to 'read off' political arrangements from reflections on natural processes? For example, is it plausible for political ecologists to claim that diversity in nature equates to toleration; stability to democracy; interdependence to equality; and longevity to tradition? (Dobson, 2000, p. 22). Are these claims that features of the natural world equate to social and political forms and principles coherent?

There are a number of sceptical points that need to be made here which are crucial to the development of green politics. The first is as true for green politics as it is for environmental ethics: it is simply not possible to 'read off' ethical and political principles direct from scientific concepts such as diversity, symbiosis or complexity. Normative concepts cannot be drawn directly from descriptive ecological concepts. To argue that we can 'because they are natural' is to argue in a circle. As John Barry comments, 'non-human nature gives us no determinate prescriptions about how we ought to live' (Barry, 1994, p. 383).[2] However, there may be compelling practical political reasons to argue that nature does provide a guide to action. It is important to realise that reading off from nature may be 'meaningless in political-theoretical terms, but useful from an ideological point of view where persuasion is so important . . . the symbolic potency acquired by doing so may make the price of vagueness worth paying' (Dobson, 2000, p. 22).

Again, it is far from obvious that ethical commitments to the non-human world, such as a belief in the moral worth of sentience or the intrinsic value of aspects of the non-human world, can tell us anything about whether we should commend democratic or authoritarian solutions to political questions. The link between ethical and political commitments is rarely clear-cut. In fact it is a fair criticism of environmental philosophy that it provides little in the way of *practical* guidance in the area of political change. This is not to say that ethical reasoning and ecological insights are a waste of time and play no part in political considerations. All that is being stressed is that there is no *necessary* one-to-one connection between ethical and political commitments. What such ethical reasoning can provide us with, however, is a critical standpoint from which to assess political arrangements and decision-making processes. Such reflections can help us to make judgements about the environmental sensitivity of institutional designs; for instance, in contributing towards criticism of purely economic decision-making processes such as cost–benefit analysis (CBA) which cannot adequately represent such ethical commitments. For more on this see Chapter 6.

In the previous chapter our everyday moral considerations were widened to take into account duties to present and future human generations. Considering these issues may help to articulate the point that is being made here. Such considerations do not simply stem from a particular view of values in nature, from, for example, the assertion of intrinsic value; but from a commitment to justice – a typically anthropocentric concern. Studying ecological relations will not lead us to a precise definition of what our duties and obligations to present and future generations entail; that requires adherence to beliefs beyond such reflections. However, environmental considerations and values help us to deepen our understanding of humanity's relations with the non-human world and of our political and social institutions, but *without* offering us the basis for a complete blueprint for a future sustainable society.

The Limits to Growth *debate*

If an ethical commitment to non-human nature provides a basic building-block of green political thought, the debate over the ecological limits of social and economic arrangements has provided another. In 1972, the Club of Rome, a group of prominent scientists, educators, economists, humanists, industrialists and national and international civil servants, published its report *The Limits to Growth*.[3] The report was based on an investigation of the interconnected nature of five trends that the Club of Rome believed to be of global concern: 'accelerating industrialisation, rapid population growth, widespread malnutrition, depletion of nonrenewable resources, and a deteriorating environment' (Meadows *et al.*, 1972, p. 21). Using a computer-generated world model, a series of scenarios was developed by inputting different rates of change for each factor. Central to the report (and to much green analysis that followed) is the emphasis on the interrelatedness of different trends and the exponential, as opposed to linear, pattern of growth associated with these trends. A particular characteristic of such exponential growth is the suddenness with which it approaches fixed limits (see Introduction). It is this characteristic that led to the pessimistic conclusion of the Club of Rome that the post-war rate of economic expansion and population growth could not be sustained without widespread poverty and famine, exhaustion of global natural resources and irreparable environmental damage. There is a decidedly neo-Malthusian feel to *The Limits to Growth* in line with the concerns for population growth expressed in books such as *The Population Bomb* by Paul Ehrlich, published in the same year.[4]

Conclusions of *The Limits to Growth*

1 If the present growth trends in world population, industrialisation, food production, and resource depletion continue unchanged, the limits to growth on this planet will be reached sometime within the next hundred years. The most probable result will be a rather sudden and uncontrollable decline in both population and industrial capacity.

> 2 It is possible to alter these growth trends and to establish a condition of ecological and economic stability that is sustainable far into the future. The state of global equilibrium could be designed so that the basic needs of each person on earth are satisfied and each person has an equal opportunity to realise his individual potential.
> 3 If the world's people decide to strive for the second outcome rather than the first, the sooner they begin working to attain it, the greater will be their chances of success.
>
> (Meadows *et al.*, 1972, pp. 23–4)

Since its publication, the report has been widely criticised and a number of its predictions have failed to materialise. In retrospect, some of its conclusions and modelling proved overly simplistic and pessimistic. Julian Simon and Herman Kahn took the view in *The Resourceful Earth* (1984) that the proponents of the limits to growth thesis (whether the Club of Rome or later advocates such as the *Global 2000 Report* prepared for President Carter in 1980) were guilty of gross exaggeration at best and scare-mongering at worst. Later authors such as the economist Wilfred Beckerman, in his ironically titled *Small is Stupid* (1995a), are equally scathing about such resource-depletion scare stories, pointing out that *The Limits to Growth* failed to allow for the various feedback mechanisms operative within an economy – if a good or resource becomes scarce its price rises which signals a search for new sources of that good or for suitable substitutes (see also Lomborg, 2001).[5] Beckerman's critique in many ways exposes the overly pessimistic outlook of the Club of Rome's report, although it clearly requires there to be suitable substitutes: a claim that may not always be true of certain environmental goods critical to human survival.[6] Regardless of debates concerning specific resources, ultimately economic activity depends on the health of the environment; failure to recognise this could lead to devastating consequences (Arrow *et al.*, 1998). While we must recognise its rather overstated conclusions and simplistic computer modelling, the Club of Rome report nonetheless managed to focus attention on growing global tensions surrounding resource depletion. Its central theme – that infinite growth in a finite system is impossible – has become a 'foundation stone of Green political thinking' (Dobson, 1991, p. 13).

In the same year, the editorial board of *The Ecologist* magazine co-wrote *A Blueprint for Survival* (Goldsmith *et al.*, 1972) and this was followed in 1973 by E.F. Schumacher's *Small is Beautiful*. These two seminal texts share with the Club of Rome a deep concern with the impact of human activity on the global environment. However, the solutions they suggest are significantly different. The Club of Rome argues for a concerted global response led by the major institutions of industrial societies; in contrast Schumacher and *The Ecologist* both emphasise the need to restructure society and economy on a 'human scale'. In their vision, a concerted move towards decentralisation is fundamental if society is to become more congenial and develop within ecological limits. These different visions lead to different trajectories within green politics, a fact commented on by Maarten Hajer:

> *Limits* argued for a further integration and hierarchisation in order to contain the problem (global problems required global solutions) while *Blueprint* argued for decentralisation, self-sufficiency, and self government; *Limits* accentuated the historical responsibility of social elites of business, science, and government, *Blueprint* came out in favour of self-government . . . whereas *Limits to Growth* typified very much the response to the increased importance of environmental matters from the world of business and government elites, *Blueprint* became a key reference for the radical environmental public of its time.
>
> (Hajer, 1995, p. 85)

Whichever trajectory we follow, the limits to growth thesis remains central to the green standpoint. Indeed the thesis is taken further by greens who wish to emphasise the *moral* limits to growth, and mount a socio-economic critique of the inequalities and environmental insensitivity of liberal capitalist political economy (Barry, 1994, pp. 372ff). It is also important to note that there is no necessary connection between the two core principles of green political thought: the ethical basis of our obligations to the non-human world and acceptance of limits to growth. As we shall see later in this chapter, this very issue leads to tensions between some ecosocialists who have accepted that there must be ecological restrictions to the forces of production and greens who believe that they must also widen their ethical commitments beyond purely human well-being.

Bearing in mind the distinctions drawn above, we can begin to understand why there are tensions within green political thought between ecocentric and techno-centric attitudes and between decentralised and highly coordinated institutional responses to environmental problems. It is to such differences and tensions that we now turn.

Western political traditions and the emergence of a green political ideology

Any survey of green political texts from the last two or three decades will reveal that there is a wide variety of political institutions and strategies for change endorsed as the way forward to a sustainable future. From democratic to authoritarian regimes, centralised states to decentralised communities, planned to free-market economies, party politics to grassroots activism – all have found support at some time or another.[7] Such endorsements have often been a response to particular contexts and situations: Robyn Eckersley, for instance, highlights three interconnected 'preoccupations' within green political thought which can be seen as a response to particular circumstances (Eckersley, 1992, pp. 8–20). The first preoccupation, the crisis of participation, evolved primarily during the 1960s in the civil rights movement. Its central concern is with participation in decision-making processes and issues of resource distribution, leading to a recognition of democracy and social justice as important themes within the green movement. The second preoccupation, the crisis of survival, was originally inspired by the publication of *The Limits to Growth* and *A Blueprint for Survival* and 'marked the emergence of the *global* dimensions of environmental degradation and the *common fate* of humanity' (Eckersley, 1992, p. 12). The apparent urgency of the survivalist message led many writers to call for authoritarian solutions to the environmental crisis, thereby contradicting the democratic thrust of earlier commentators. The third and final preoccupation is the belief that environmental concerns are as much a crisis of culture and human character as a crisis of nature or the use of natural resources. If this is so, a broader ecological understanding of human needs, technology, and self-image becomes essential with a recognition that it is in our interests, understood in a comprehensive manner, to become less dependent on technological responses to environmental and social problems.

These preoccupations need to be recognised and each given due weight: but it is important to realise that they may be in tension with each other. For example, green concerns often stress the need for a holistic or organicistic approach to the solution of environmental problems, but these may in turn be markedly at odds with the concern for egalitarianism and the associated demands for social change which also form part of the agenda. If these tensions can be successfully addressed, green politics might then be linked with other emancipatory political projects that call for cultural renewal and the revitalisation of civil society. As Eckersley has argued:

> This new theoretical project is concerned to find ways of overcoming the destructive logic of capital accumulation, the acquisitive values of consumer society, and, more generally, all systems of domination (including class domination, patriarchy, imperialism, totalitarianism, and the domination of nature).
>
> (Eckersley, 1992, pp. 20–1)

This is an extremely ambitious and radical remit for any political project and it would be an oversimplification to think that the values and attitudes it embodies have been developed purely from an analysis of our ethical relationship with the natural world or from the need to live within ecological limits. Equally, to view these developments as having occurred only within the last three decades would ignore a long history of attitudes to nature which have played a part in various streams of political thinking. As Andrew Vincent points out, the attitudes associated with ecology

> did not spring upon us in the 1970s with pure radical credentials. Rather, they relate to a subtle and immensely potent conjunction of attitudes to nature which have been present in European thought since the late nineteenth century. Despite their widespread promotion by different and politically diverse groups throughout the twentieth century, it is the accidental conjunction of circumstances, individuals and events in the 1970s which has provided a dynamic refocus for the ecological vocabulary.
>
> (Vincent, 1992, pp. 214–15)

We need briefly to survey some of the traditions within Western political thought in order to understand how they have helped shape green political thinking. All the traditions have something to say about human–non-human relations and, in some cases, critical reassessment has occurred in the light of green critiques. One of the central issues we need to consider is whether green political thought has developed an entirely autonomous response to our circumstances or whether it still depends on the insights of other political streams. We shall sketch historical associations between traditions and ecological thinking and highlight tensions to be found with current environmental concerns, specifically the ethical considerations of the non-human world and questions arising from the limits to growth debate. We shall also consider whether the central values of these traditions are compatible with green thinking. Ecological politics has developed from a critical relationship with many other streams of thought, and because of this it incorporates a number of diverse and contradictory tendencies.

Authoritarianism and fascism

> If scarcity is not dead, if it is in fact with us in a seemingly much more intense form than ever before in human history, how can we avoid reaching the conclusion that Leviathan is inevitable? Given current levels of population and technology, I do not believe that we can. Hobbes shows why a spaceship earth must have a captain. Otherwise, the collective selfishness and irresponsibility produced by the tragedy of the commons will destroy the spaceship, and any sacrifice of freedom by the crew members is clearly the lesser of two evils.
>
> (Ophuls, 1973, p. 224)

As this quotation shows, it is very easy to move from a perception of the seriousness of environmental problems towards a view in which, as William Ophuls argues, the choice is between 'Leviathan and oblivion'. In responding to the problems identified by *The Limits to Growth* and similar reports, writers such as Ophuls and Robert Heilbroner, while at a personal level committed to liberal and democratic values, envisaged an environmentally-benevolent Leviathan as the only political arrangement that could stop human societies from developing beyond environmental-carrying capacities. Restrictions on levels of production, consumption and population growth could not be achieved quickly enough through democratic processes, and individuals' rights and freedoms would have to be overridden in the short term in order to achieve long-term survival and lessen ecological damage. Perhaps the most consistent and influential advocate of this position has been Garrett Hardin whose 'Tragedy of the Commons' thesis (Hardin, 1998; originally published in 1968) espouses strong, centralised leadership if self-interested individuals are not to despoil environmental resources. Along with his later, more controversial 'Lifeboat Ethics' (Hardin, 1977) – which seems to many to suggest that if the developed, Western nations are to survive then they should cut off aid links with the Third World and leave them in poverty – such authoritarian ideas have often found their way into green proposals concerning population control, resource distribution and immigration. It is essential for greens to realise that many of their concepts and much of their rhetoric can have authoritarian and imperialistic overtones.

Green theorists frequently appeal to concepts of the natural, using organic metaphors, elevating the spiritual over the rational, and justifying a holistic politics which elevates the community and the state over the individual. Such ecological doctrines have often been appealed to by authoritarian and fascistic movements: for instance, pantheistic ecological considerations were fundamental to the ideology of the Nazis. Although few greens would now espouse such political arrangements, they would do well to recognise that authoritarian solutions are often lurking in the background.

Conservatism

Many of the concerns of environmentalists appear to have their roots in central conceptions within traditional conservatism. Congruence can be found with ideas of tradition, continuity, stability, organic change, prudence, rejection of totalitarianism and appeals to community. Traditional conservative and ecological theorists often share an anti-capitalist stance and romantic visions of non-human nature. In a recent defence of the deep affinity between ecological theory and conservative philosophy, John Gray adopts a common criticism of neo-liberal market philosophy, stressing the similarities of the two streams of thought (Gray, 1993, pp. 124–77). Both share a multi-generation perspective, give primacy to the common life, see danger in novelty and give a central place to the virtue of prudence. There is considerable scepticism about the possibility, inevitability or desirability of 'progress' and an emphasis on continuity and change as occurring within a developing tradition rather than in the light of a rational blueprint for society. The ideals of harmony and stability are central conceptions to both traditional conservatism and green political thought. As Michael Freeden remarks, 'conservative arguments cannot be completely disentangled or excluded from all green positions' (Freeden, 1995, p. 15).

Although there are indeed many areas of congruence, Gray's analysis can easily be construed as focusing selectively on particular areas of green thought and conservatism. Clearly the conservation and preservation streams of the environmental movement owe much to conservative and romantic visions of nature. As we shall see in the next chapter, it is often the case that in specific local environmental campaigns traditional conservatives are found in alliance with more radical, emancipatory greens. However, contemporary green analysis of social relations appears to part company with much conservative thought on various issues, although even here the case is not clear cut. Where conservative thinking tends to emphasise order, tradition and community over what it sees as abstract criteria such as social justice and egalitarianism, contemporary green political analysis typically takes these later ideas as central and is critical of apparent conservative apologies for hierarchical social arrangement. Here we find a potential paradox in green thinking, with calls for universal standards of justice and democracy coexisting with a desire to defend indigenous communities and their practices. But what if those practices, which may be environmentally sustainable, are themselves based on the dominance of a particular social group? It is with such questions that green political thought must come to terms and perhaps it would be more accurate to see conservatism and romanticism as modes of thought out of which a more comprehensive green critique is developing.

Liberalism

Environmental thought again shares a mixed relationship with the liberal tradition. Although influenced in many ways by early liberal thought, particularly ideas of rights, freedom and democracy, the most recent turn in liberal thought, namely neo-liberalism and laissez-faire free-market economics, appears incompatible with the central tenets of green thinking. In the previous chapter on ethics the influence of two early liberals, Jeremy Bentham and John Stuart Mill, has already been noted. Bentham's utilitarian views on public policy have found favour among animal rights theorists where sentience and the ability to suffer pain are central to considerations of the proper treatment of animals. Many of Mill's ideas are similarly resurfacing in green texts. Herman Daly (1992), for instance, has championed the steady-state economy (see the case study at the end of Chapter 6) which was first adumbrated in Mill's *Principles of Political Economy*. Recent work has attempted to demonstrate that liberalism and environmentalism are far from incompatible (Wissenburg, 1998) and liberal approaches to environmental problems have been used to argue for the extension of rights to both future generations and to other living things (Eckersley, 1995b, 1996). Appeals to nineteenth-century liberal ideals such as public space and deliberation, civic virtue and civil society, show that certain streams of liberal thought are central to green visions of future sustainable societies (Sagoff, 1988, pp. 146–70).

However, it would be fair to say that where many connections can be made to these classic liberal values, the rise of neo-liberal or New Right thought in recent times has been viewed with horror by the majority of environmentalists.

> Individualism, the pursuit of private gain, limited government and market freedom are contradicted by radical ecology commitments to the resolution of environmental problems as a collective good and to the intervention and restrictions on economic and personal freedoms to deal with them. Liberal economy is seen to underpin the commitment to economic expansion and accumulation and to the identification of wealth and material advancement with progress and improvement.
>
> (Martell, 1994, p. 141)

Such material accumulation is seen by many green writers as spelling ruin and destruction for human and ecological communities, putting increasing pressure on social and environmental relations (Dryzek, 1992, pp. 18–26). Further, the neo-liberal conception of well-being as a correlative of material acquisition is viewed as a complete misrepresentation of what is important to a human life. There would appear to be serious contradictions between neo-liberal market logic and environmental imperatives. Recently, though, there has been a response to such criticisms by advocates of 'free-market environmentalism'. For such neo-liberals, ecological problems such as Hardin's 'Tragedy of the Commons' are the result of a lack of well-defined property rights and price mechanisms; rather than reducing the impact of the market we need to extend its role (Anderson and Leal, 1991, 1998). This is very much a counter move by the New Right in order to deflect greens' anti-free market claims and to rework environmental problems in neo-liberal rhetoric. It is important, however, to note that the rejection of a free market approach to environmental problems does not necessarily mean that greens must be totally anti-market: the market and price incentives and disincentives can be used as part of environmental policy without being seen as the *whole* of policy (see Chapter 5 for a fuller discussion of this issue).

In more general terms, the individualism which lies at the heart of liberalism, whether in its political expression (the insistence on rights and liberties) or in its economic expression (the insistence on markets), creates a problem for environmentalists who are attempting to develop new forms of community and political participation relevant to a sustainable society. Much green thinking has a greater affinity with various forms of communitarianism, both in its insistence on the essential relationship of an individual to a society (as opposed to the liberal conception of society as being nothing more than the creation of pre-existing bearers of rights) and in its insistence on responsibilities rather than merely on the assertion of rights.

Marxism and socialism

It is very common to find the criticisms levelled at capitalism and liberal free-market ideology mirrored in discussions on socialism and communism. As Jonathan Porritt argues: 'Both [capitalism and socialism] are dedicated to industrial growth, to the expansion of the means of production, to the materialistic ethic as the best means of meeting people's needs, and to unimpeded technological development' (Porritt, 1984, p. 44). For writers such as Porritt, both are forms of the 'super-ideology' of industrialism, with the former communist states displaying a record of environmental protection as bad as (if not worse than) Western nations. Although socialists share green concerns for poverty relief and egalitarian redistribution of resources, increased wealth generation is often seen as essential in order to finance such policies. Greens argue that socialist thought does not take into account the physical limits to wealth production, seemingly believing in the ability of science and technology to overcome scarcity. Further, it is argued that the environment is only considered in terms of its direct impact on the well-being of humans. Socialists have responded by accusing greens of having an idealised vision of the non-human world and providing 'in essence a defence of middle-class privilege and exploitative class and neo-colonialist relationships' (Hay, 1988, p. 26). However, between these rather polarised positions the continuing debate between greens and socialists has in the last few years resulted in the re-examination of their shared attitudes in light of the apparent hegemony of neo-liberal thinking. It is both simplistic and narrow either to take the former communist bloc as the basis of criticism of all Marxist and socialist ideas, or to view greens as only interested in the ecological effect of production.

There are at least four areas where fruitful connections have been made and where the green analysis has been deepened by socialist reflections – and vice versa. First, in the area of political economy, socialist thought exposes in some depth the destructive power of capitalist societies. Such an analysis has helped deepen and refocus the ecological critique of industrialism. Socialists have often adopted the sceptical view that greens have seemed willing to ameliorate the ecological impact of capitalism rather than call for a full-scale transformation of economic structures.

As André Gorz argues:

> It is . . . time to end the pretence that ecology is, by itself, sufficient: *the ecological movement is not an end in itself, but a stage in the larger struggle.* It can throw up obstacles to capitalist development and force a number of changes. But when, after exhausting every means of coercion and deceit, capitalism begins to work its way out of the ecological impasse, it will assimilate ecological necessities as technical constraints, and adapt the conditions of exploitation to them.
>
> (Gorz, 1980, p. 3)

The centrality of growth, the injustice of the existing distribution of wealth, and the short-term interest in profit maximisation of free-market ideology might be seen as common elements within socialist and green thought. However, for more mainstream socialists the generation of material wealth is not in itself a problem, rather the method of its production and distribution. Here we do find a tension between those socialists who are willing to accept the ideas of natural limits to economic expansion and an ecological dimension in political economy (Hayward, 1995, pp. 115–27) and those who seem overly optimistic and share the Promethean belief that the problems of poverty, injustice and inequality can be solved through the abolition of scarcity by technical means.

Marx largely viewed nature as something to be dominated and used for human purposes. Where he identified and denounced exploitation it was the exploitation of class by class through their different places within the relations of production (the pattern of ownership, property, law and control over the forces of production); the forces of production and their domination over nature he much admired. The task, as he saw it, was to harness the technological possibilities of exploiting nature in the service of a fundamental change in the social relations of production in which the surplus labour value of the worker no longer accrued solely to the benefit of the capitalist class. For Marx, the question of the desirability of exploiting nature, or the limits to such exploitation, were not a matter of concern, and nature as such was not ascribed value independently of its instrumental value to human beings in allowing them to develop and progress. The ecological dimension cannot, therefore, be straightforwardly grafted onto orthodox Marxism, requiring as it does a reorientation of human relations with the natural world.

The second area of interest is the question of agents of change. Although often providing clear prescriptions for a future sustainable society, green political thought has often been rightly criticised for inadequately theorising strategies for change. On the other hand, orthodox Marxism has a ready-made explanation of both the causes of change and the agents of change. With its emphasis on the forces of production and its analysis of the social relations of production, it could confidently state that the main agent of change would inevitably be the working class. But the Left is now in a position of turmoil on this issue, with the traditional Marxist emphasis on the working class as the vanguard of political revolution becoming increasingly unconvincing. Both green and socialist writers have turned their attention to political strategies that incorporate, for instance, new social movements, the unemployed, communes, and more traditional parliamentary routes. We shall return to this issue in Chapter 3.

The third area of critical debate centres on the role of institutions, particularly the state, both in processes of change and in any future society. Many ecosocialists tend to view the green commitment to a decentralised society as a romantic, utopian ideal that is doomed to failure, would result in further inequalities, and be unable to tackle large-scale environmental problems because of a lack of coordination. An enlightened state is often seen to be essential if a sustainable future is to be achieved.

> If one is honest, however, about the objectives which an ecologically enlightened state would set itself, it is difficult to avoid concluding that the state, as the agent of the collective will, would have to take an active law-making and enforcing role in imposing a range of environmental and resource constraints.
> (Ryle, 1988, p. 60)

It is worth noting however that there are streams of socialist thought based on decentralist values which do not put so much stress on statism. Writers such as William Morris, Erich Fromm and Ivan Illich, whose work has often been ignored within left-wing thought dominated by reformist and revolutionary statist political thinking, are now being reinterpreted and given their due in the light of the ecological imperative to restructure societies.

Finally, much has been written about the Marxist attitude to the non-human world. The early writings of Marx can be interpreted as showing an awareness of the interconnectedness and dialectical relationship of humanity with the rest of nature and the alienation of both under systems of capitalism. However, even with such a positive interpretation and the concept of nature as 'man's inorganic body', it is clear that Marx's dialectics are orientated specifically at the self-realisation of humanity through the domination and transformation of nature (Benton, 1993, pp. 23–57). Socialists are often charged with being interested in environmental concerns only in so far as there is a direct effect on human well-being. In response, greens are often vilified for a tendency towards mysticism and romanticism. But do differences in orientation of this sort necessarily issue in differing policy implications? For the most part it might not seem so. However, it is easy to see how on specific issues, for example species extinction, there might be no relation between human well-being and the threatened species. Socialists could then apparently offer no reason for protection. But this may not be the final position: socialist beliefs do not necessarily rule out consideration of non-human entities, even if in practice they have focused their attention primarily on human welfare. There are certainly a number of post-Marxists, such as Herbert Marcuse, who recognise the link between the domination of man by man and nature by man and look forward to the re-enchantment of the non-human world. More recently, writers such as André Gorz, David Pepper, Ted Benton, Tim Hayward, Michael Jacobs and James O'Connor have done much to reconcile the apparent differences between socialist and green political thought. The ecological dimension to political economy has been generally accepted as a paramount concern and 'red–green' dialogue on political, social and economic arrangements is an area of extremely fruitful work.

Anarchism and decentralised communitarianism

The political arrangement supported by many radical greens is along anarchist lines, where the ideals of egalitarianism, non-hierarchy, local empowerment and democracy, self-reliance and diversity are often central concerns. This arises out of a deep mistrust of traditional forms and bearers of political authority, and a desire to challenge them and to re-assert that power and authority lies with people and their communities. The writings of late nineteenth- and early twentieth-century anarchists, such as Peter Kropotkin, can be seen as precursors to the more recent *A Blueprint for Survival* (Goldsmith *et al.*, 1972). Anarchist arguments for decentralisation of social and political institutions are taken to be absolutely necessary if a sustainable society is to emerge. This vision can be contrasted with some of the more authoritarian responses to *The Limits to Growth* report discussed earlier.

As with other traditions of thought, the ecoanarchist stream is not unified and can be subdivided into social ecology and ecocommunalism (Eckersley, 1992, pp. 145–69). The most influential social ecologist is undoubtedly Murray Bookchin whose analysis of environmental problems is based on a perceived connection between the exploitation of nature and the exploitation of human beings.[8] Contemporary society is seen as socially, economically and politically irrational and anti-ecological in that the competitive capitalist system is based on hierarchical relations of command and obedience within which nature is commodified. It is only when the domination of human over human is overcome that the domination of nature can be transcended. This will only occur in decentralised, autonomous and radically democratic communities.

Such an analysis is very different from that of the ecocommunalists who draw extensively on deep ecology (Naess, 1973, 1989; Devall and Sessions, 1985). Here the humanity–nature relation is central, sometimes to the exclusion of relations between humans. Under the influence of deep ecological insights, bioregionalists, such as Kirkpatrick Sale (1985), hold that communities must learn to live within the carrying capacity of their specific bioregion. In many ways there is a resonance within bioregionalism of certain 1970s survivalist views that self-sufficient, small-scale communities are the only feasible response to an imminent environmental catastrophe.

The deep ecological position is frequently criticised for simply 'reading off' ethical and political principles from ecological concepts such as diversity, symbiosis and complexity: on what grounds can we derive ethical or political principles direct from such scientific concepts? Arne Naess's conception of deep ecology, and particularly his commitment to 'biospherical egalitarianism', has been vociferously challenged by Bookchin who argues, at times polemically, that the de-centring of humans in such a political position has a tendency towards anti-humanism and misanthropy. For Bookchin, too much emphasis is placed on the mystical qualities of the human–non-human relationship, on the development of an ecological self or consciousness, while the social, political and economic roots and realities of the environmental crisis are ignored.[9] It is true that both social and deep ecology wish to confer the 'maximum political and economic autonomy on decentralised local communities', that their 'anarchism is grounded in, or otherwise draws its inspiration from, ecology' and that both positions provide a strong defence of 'the grass roots and extra-parliamentary activities of the Green movement' (Eckersley, 1992, p. 145), but the important differences between deep and social ecology must also be recognised.

The anarchist belief that the state must be either bypassed or abolished leads to much heated debate within green political thought. The state is viewed as the prime example of an oppressive agent and a defender of hierarchical social, economic and political power relations. Also it is seen to be too far removed and centralised to deal with local environmental and social problems. However, for many critics, and particularly ecosocialists, the removal of the state and subsequent emergence of autonomous communities is viewed as overly idealistic and utopian and fails to take account of fundamentally important state functions.

First, there is some concern over how the internal political structure of decentralised communities would be controlled. For social ecologists, radical participatory democracy is fundamental. But, for bioregionalists it is living within the ecological-carrying capacity of a bioregion that is of prime importance rather than the political arrangements of a society. This is clearly implied by Sale:

> Bioregional diversity means exactly that. It does not mean that every region of the north-east, or North America, or the globe, will construct itself upon the values of democracy, equality, liberty, freedom, justice, and other such like *desiderata*. It means rather that truly autonomous bioregions will likely go their own separate ways and end up with some quite disparate political systems – some democracies, no doubt, some direct, some representative, some federative, but undoubtedly all kinds of aristocracies, theocracies, principalities, margravates, duchies and palatinates as well. And some with values, beliefs, standards and customs quite antithetical to those that the people in this room, for example, hold dearest.
>
> (Sale, in Dobson, 1991, pp. 80–1)[10]

Thus the stress placed on the value of diversity can be interpreted to mean a radical diversity of institutional forms. Hence, some of the more politically-sensitive questions concerning authoritarian solutions to population, immigration, punishment and the like return to the fore. There is a further issue surrounding the value of diversity which is so central to the rhetoric of anarchists – could a small-scale society support physical and cultural diversity and difference internally? Do not small, self-contained communities often lead to conformity and ostracise difference? In this respect the state may be viewed as the guarantor of democracy and the defender of political freedoms and difference.

Second, there is a question of distribution of resources: is it just that some communities or bioregions would be environmentally more abundant than others? This reflects issues of intragenerational justice between the North and the South raised in Chapter 1. Is there not some obligation for those who live in resource-rich locations to redistribute to those less fortunate? A similar issue is raised in terms of transboundary and large-scale environmental impacts. A small-scale community is likely to respond to local environmental problems more sensitively than a more centralised authority, but without some form of over-arching authority, how are cumulative, supra-community problems such as acid rain or climate change to be faced? How are claims between communities over the impact of transboundary pollution to be settled?

Finally, the question of strategy is underdeveloped. How are we to get to this utopia of decentralised communities from the present state structure and the increasing globalisation of capital and culture? Many radical greens are fundamentally at odds with the idea of achieving this outcome through parliamentary means. Such processes necessitate concessions and leave too much power with too few individuals. If the means must be consistent with the ends then it is no surprise that potentially corrupting processes are vilified and in general lifestyle changes and the development of alternative communities and practices are endorsed. Although the wider political significance of such extra-parliamentary activities may at times be limited, the influence of anarchist thought, with its belief in local political action and its challenging of existing institutions and the interests they represent, is evident in much green political thinking.

Feminism

'Ecological feminism' is an umbrella term which captures a variety of multi-cultural perspectives on the nature of the connections *within* social systems of domination between those humans in subordinate positions, particularly women, and the domination of non-human nature. . . . Ecofeminist analyses of the twin dominations of women and nature include considerations of the domination of people of color, children, and the underclass.

(Warren, 1994, p. 1)

Ecofeminist analysis shares the broad concern of the feminist movement as regards the elimination of gender bias – or more widely, all forms of bias towards subordinated groups – and the development of non-gendered or non-interest dominated political, social and economic practices and institutions. Values and characteristics usually conceived of as feminine, such as humility, care and nurture, are seen to be seriously undervalued in patriarchal societies with a detrimental effect on how we conceive of our relationships with non-human nature. In addition, ecofeminists argue that there are connections between the domination and oppression of women and of nature. This leads not only to a variety of ecofeminist positions that have strong political connections to existing political traditions, for example liberal, Marxist and socialist feminisms (Warren, 1987), but also variations based on the interpretation of the link between the domination of women and nature (Plumwood, 1986, p. 121).

The various accounts of the source of the links between the subordination of women and the domination of the natural world seem to fit into two main categories. First, there is an argument that dominant philosophies have traditionally operated on the basis of various dualisms in which women and nature are both allocated an inferior position with respect to men and their projects. It is argued that this differentiation has had real historical consequences across all forms of human knowledge and practice, be it in art, science, education, ethics or politics. These consequences have led to attitudes justifying the exploitation of women and the natural world and can be seen as an expression of what is often termed strong anthropocentrism. Second, there is an account of domination which stresses the physiological and psychological *difference* between men and women. Here women are taken to be biologically closer to the natural order by virtue, for example, of their capacity for childbirth and nurture.

It is these conceptual connections that in many cases cause tensions and disagreements both within ecofeminist analysis and within the wider feminist movement. The second stream of ecofeminism highlighted often promotes the idea of a biologically- and psychologically-determined connection between women and nature. Women must be in the vanguard of environmental change simply because they are closer to and understand the natural world in a way that men can never achieve. Such biological and psychological determinism, however, emphasises a fundamental difference between the sexes which for many critics could be used as the basis for further domination and servitude. Clearly there are controversies within ecofeminist thought with other commentators simply wishing to argue that a more environmentally-sensitive society needs to articulate those principles, values and characteristics traditionally associated with the feminine, but potentially accessible to all humanity. This latter position is invaluable in highlighting the power relations that lead to the marginalisation and exclusion of women, indigenous peoples and others, and the possibilities for radical institutional change called for by many within the green movement.

A new ideology?

Should green political thought be understood as an ideology in its own right? It is common to find writers claiming that green thinking represents an overcoming of Right–Left distinctions and, on occasions, that it represents a complete break from traditional political thought; for others it is a new ideology that can take its place alongside the more established ideologies such as conservatism, socialism, liberalism or anarchism. It would seem however that the answer to our question is problematised by the fact that there is wide disagreement as to the meaning of the term 'ideology': it is an essentially contested concept within political theory.[11]

Michael Freeden (1995) analyses ideologies in terms of the core, adjacent and peripheral concepts of which they are composed. Given such an understanding, one should expect an overlap between different ideologies in that they may hold many concepts in common. However, the place assigned to these concepts within the whole, and hence their relative significance and meaning, will vary from ideology to ideology. In analysing green ideology, then, one should not expect that all its values and principles will be completely different from other ideologies; rather, one should expect to find some features in common, but contained within a whole whose overall thrust is substantially different. In this chapter, we have argued that at the core of green political thinking is the belief that our ethical relations with non-human nature and the finite character of resources need to be central in political reflections; beyond these two core ideas, green political thought must rely on insights from other traditions. So, are these core themes enough sufficiently to demarcate green political thinking from other ideologies and doctrines?

Of the green political theorists who have argued that it is possible to demarcate a green ideological position, one of the most significant and influential is Andrew Dobson. He argues that 'ecologism' represents a new ideology in its own right.

Ecologism provides a critique of contemporary political, economic and social arrangements and offers a prescription of how the world ought to be organised that differs fundamentally from the insights of other modern political ideologies. Dobson's position rests on an important distinction between 'ecologism' and 'environmentalism':

> *environmentalism* argues for a managerial approach to environmental problems, secure in the belief that they can be solved without fundamental changes in present values or patterns of production and consumption

> and

> *ecologism* holds that a sustainable and fulfilling existence presupposes radical changes in our relationship with the natural world, and in our mode of social and political life.
>
> (2000, p. 2)[12]

The central claim in his book *Green Political Thought* is that environmentalism can be easily assimilated into more traditional ideologies (as we have witnessed above). This is simply not the case with ecologism. Briefly, ecologism argues for radically different political, economic and social arrangements based on a reorientation on the part of individuals and society towards non-human nature. The ecological society is post-industrial and small-scale. Politically it favours local face-to-face participatory democracy. The economic vision is one of self-reliance and labour-intensive processes based on low-impact technology. Although there are other conceptions of post-industrial utopias (Frankel, 1987), the vision of ecologism is significantly different:

> Ecologism envisages a post-industrial future that is quite distinct from that with which we are most generally acquainted. While most post-industrial futures revolve around high-growth, high-technology, expanding services, greater leisure, and satisfaction conceived in material terms, ecologism's post-industrial society questions growth and technology, and suggests that the Good Life will involve more work and fewer material objects.
>
> (Dobson, 2000, p. 199)

It is environmentalism (using Dobson's terms) that is having the greatest impact on present policies, practices and ideas. The vision of ecologism may simply be utopian. Nevertheless, Dobson argues that it

> provides the indispensable fundamentalist well of inspiration from which green activists, even the most reformist and respectable, need continually to draw. Green reformers need a radically different picture of post-industrial society, they need deep-ecological visionaries, they need the phantom studies of the sustainable society, and they need, paradoxically, occasionally to be brought down to earth and to be reminded about limits to growth. Dark-green politics remind reformists of where they want to go even if they don't really think they can get there.
>
> (2000, p. 202)

The ideology of ecologism is the conscience of green politics.

Dobson makes an important point here about the role of utopian visions in political movements. The question remains whether he has isolated the single green ideological vision. Alternatively he may be over-emphasising a particular stream *within* a wide range of possible coherent green political positions that can be understood as a reaction against the domination of a strong anthropocentric or technocentric attitude, where nature is simply seen as something to be mastered and controlled. Might it not be better to understand green political thought as a critical perspective which has forced existing political traditions to undergo an internal analysis and re-think of their fundamental premises and concerns, as well as providing a critical space for convergence and debate between traditions? Or is this simply 'environmentalism'; a watering-down of radical green insights? Rather than attempting to define the definitive ideological form for green politics, we may be wise to be cautious and to reflect on Martin Ryle's warning that 'the mere invocation of "ecology", crucial as it is, does not in itself determine in a positive sense the future development of social and political reality' (Ryle, 1988, p. 7).

Tensions and mutual distrust, both theoretical and practical, abound within green political thought, for instance over the role of the state and the limits of decentralisation, or the identification of agents and processes of change. Political commitments such as justice, democracy and liberty cannot be developed from purely ecological considerations, although ecological ideas can have implications for their preferred form. It is perhaps easier in many ways to draw out what contemporary green political thinking rejects, such as authoritarian solutions and free-market capitalism, than provide an unambiguous account of a unitary green ideological position. Contemporary green ideas can perhaps best be understood as developing from a fluid, critical reflection on traditional areas of political thought, particularly areas of socialist, anarchist and feminist thinking, with ecological concerns as a necessary, but not complete, part of that reflection.

Sustainable development, ecological modernisation and beyond

Whether or not we are able to discern a definitive form of green political ideology, its privileged position within the writings of green theorists is certainly not mirrored in more mainstream discussions of environmental politics. It is the ideas and practices of sustainable development that dominate proceedings. It is indisputable that the concept of sustainable development grew out of green political thought. However, to what extent does green political ideology remain 'the indispensable fundamentalist well of inspiration' (Dobson, 2000, p. 202) in current debates and practices?

As we saw in the Introduction, much rests on how the concept of sustainable development is to be interpreted and employed by those interested in environmental problems. Agreement on the importance of the concept of sustainable development can be found across the ideological spectrum. Groups as diverse as neo-liberal free-marketeers and radical bioregionalists agree that it is significant, but disagree about its implications. Consensus on the importance of a concept such as sustainable development can disguise the extent of the divergence in the ways in which it is understood by different people and interests. Different groups share the concept, but have different conceptions of sustainable development: sometimes it would seem that all there is in common between them is the very phrase 'sustainable development' itself. It is an essentially contested concept and institutional arrangements, policies and strategies for change do not simply follow from its invocation.

But although the concept of sustainable development is contested, contemporary debates are nonetheless dominated by a particular interpretation: ecological modernisation. Environmental politics raises the question of the compatibility of economic growth and environmental protection; sustainable development is the conceptual framework within which these questions are typically explored. Ecological modernisation adopts a distinctive stance on the question of economy–environment integration, challenging 'the fundamental assumption of conventional wisdom, namely that there [is] a zero-sum trade-off between economic prosperity and environmental concern' (Weale, 1992, p. 31). Ecological modernisation, it is claimed, offers a 'win–win' scenario whereby economic growth and environmental protection can be reconciled. As Hajer states:

> [E]cological modernisation can be defined as the discourse that recognises the structural character of the environmental problematique but none the less assumes that existing political, economic, and social institutions can internalise the care for the environment.
>
> (Hajer, 1995, p. 25)

The Brundtland Report (WCED, 1987) is a seminal text in the development of ecological modernisation in that it emphasises the mutual reinforcing of economic growth, social development and environmental protection (see Chapter 7). As with *The Limits to Growth* report, environmental degradation is linked with patterns of economic development. However, Brundtland concluded that continued economic growth is essential for environmental protection. This interpretation of sustainable development has been widely endorsed at all levels. It is easy to understand why such a definition of sustainable development could be supported by many different parties (including governments, businesses, reform-minded environmentalists and scientists) in that it apparently offers the panacea of combining economic growth and environmental protection. A theoretical and practical consensus is emerging around the discourse of ecological modernisation; this challenges the more radical green idea that fundamental reorganisation of the major institutions of modern society is a necessary precondition of long-term sustainable development. Ecological modernisation leaves essentially unchallenged the system of industrial production, the capitalist economy and the centralised state (Mol and Spaargaren, 2000, p. 19). The widespread political support for the conception of sustainable development as ecological modernisation is forcing many radical greens to disown the concept they originally coined. They do not want to be drawn into what they see as a false or misleading consensus which might serve to legitimise the existing institutional order and thereby blunt the edge of radical critique (Sachs, 1993; Goldsmith, 1992).

A number of commentators have attempted to characterise the core ideas within ecological modernisation theory.[13] What emerges is that it is optimistic about the ability of policy makers, scientific experts and businesses to integrate ecological concerns into everyday practices. In the policy-making realm, the adoption of techniques and principles such as integrated pollution control (IPC), the precaution- ary principle and economic instruments are seen as ways of refocusing current economic development.[14] The environment is no longer seen as a free good; markets are made sensitive to the cost of environmental destruction and pollution; and anticipation and prevention is preferred to simply reacting to environmental problems as they arise.

Features of ecological modernisation

1 **New policy-making principles**, e.g. from react and cure to anticipate and prevent; integrated pollution abatement; integrating environmental concerns into all ministries; techniques allowing firms to integrate environment into cost–risk calculations, such as polluter pays, cost–benefit analysis, risk analysis, precautionary principle, tradeable pollution rights, pollution charges and taxes.
2 **A new role for science** in policy making, especially ecological systems science. Experts take central control.
3 **Environmental protection seen as a source of growth** since low- and non-wasteful anticipatory technologies generate profit.
4 **Nature reconceptualised** as a public rather than a 'free' good, so efficiency involves internalising environmental costs.
5 **Burden of proof reassigned** to the suspected polluter, not to the damaged party.
6 **Policy-making process opened up** to include new participation and partnerships, e.g. between business and NGOs. Voluntary agreements rather than command- and-control regulation are encouraged.

(from Pepper, 1999, p. 3)

Ecological modernisation is an attempt to increase the environmental efficiency of the economy both at the macro-economic level (by signalling a shift away from energy- and resource-intensive industries) and at the micro level (by moving from 'end-of-pipe' to clean technologies).

> Advocates of ecological modernisation argue that . . . changes, at both macro-economic and micro-economic levels, have the potential to make significant improvements in the environmental performance of industrial economies. Ecological modernisation is thus presented as a means by which capitalism can accommodate the environmental challenge. Rather than environmental protection being a threat to capitalism, it is seen as a spur to a new phase of capitalist development.
>
> (Gouldson and Murphy, 1997, p. 75)

It becomes clear why ecological modernisation has been so widely embraced (Dryzek, 1997; Hajer, 1995). For governments it offers an alternative, integrative policy approach which compares favourably with earlier ad hoc, remedial attempts to deal with environmental problems and it allows them to 'square the circle' between previously antagonistic environmental and business interests. Environmental problems are no longer seen as in fundamental opposition to capitalism, and this clearly also allows the business world to embrace the idea: from being villains of the piece, businesses have a new and virtuous role as important actors in the development of an ecologically-modern society. Ecological modernisation offers businesses the possibility of cost savings in production, clean technology and new market opportunities in pollution-control equipment and other 'green' products. And for reform-minded environmental organisations there is the promise of improved environmental conditions, the environment is taken seriously by decision makers in the public and private sectors, and increased opportunities for access to the corridors of power emerge.

Ecological modernisation is more than an idea or theoretical construct. Its advocates argue that a number of advanced capitalist nations are already developing along these lines and that we are witnessing a 'decoupling' of economic growth from ecological damage.

> Over the past decade, Germany, the Netherlands, Japan and the Scandinavian block appear to have achieved above OECD average improvements across a range of industry-related national environmental indicators, including water quality and air pollution emissions. In these countries there is now evidence of a decoupling of GNP growth from the growth of environmentally harmful effects, including increased economic output with decreased energy and materials consumption per unit of GNP.
>
> (Christoff, 1996a, p. 479)

This adds up to a challenge to the fundamental green critique of large-scale industrialised economies. The claim is that we can move beyond opposition and confrontation towards cooperation and mutual coexistence between the interests of capital and the interests of the environment. Ecological modernisation aims to 'green' capitalism. But, on closer inspection, does it fulfil its promise?

Challenging/reconstructing ecological modernisation

It will not come as a surprise that the concept of ecological modernisation (and the practical claims made on its behalf) have been the object of much analysis and debate within green politics. Its faith in environmental solutions rooted in continued (although re-focused) capitalist, industrialised, scientific and technological development immediately raises the suspicions of those sympathetic to a more fundamental green outlook. A number of distinct criticisms have emerged that question the truth of ecological modernisation's decoupling thesis, challenge its perceived neglect of issues of social justice, dispute its conceptualisation of nature, doubt its faith in technological and scientific progress and take issue with the role played by the green movement itself.

The decoupling thesis has been challenged, first, because many apparent examples of decoupling have only been achieved through a displacement of high energy-consuming and polluting industries to less-industrialised countries: quite simply, environmental damage has been exported. Furthermore, increased efficiency of resource use makes no practical difference if consumption of goods increases and the economy continues to grow. Even in the few countries where industrial sectors have achieved absolute decoupling, the improvements have been small and environmental impact remains at unsustainable levels. It is also worth noting that decoupling (where it has happened) has not occurred in the systematic manner that ecological modernisation theory might suggest. It has largely been an unexpected and unanticipated consequence of contemporary changes in the global economy. The question thus still remains: can positive government intervention achieve similar outcomes over the long term (Gouldson and Murphy, 1997, pp. 76–8)?

Second, the theory of ecological modernisation is charged with a failure to address pressing issues of social justice, because environmental preservation is no longer regarded as fundamentally contradicting capitalist development. On this view, ecological modernisation ignores social contradictions. It ignores questions of justice on two fronts: both within industrialised nations and between highly industrialised and Third World nations (Hajer, 1995, p. 32). It is argued that ecological modernisation theory is silent on questions of the distribution of environmental goods and bads, focusing primarily on the overall domestic environmental impact of national economies in the industrialised part of the world. Environmental justice campaigners within industrialised nations highlight the unequal distribution of environmental risks; for example, the siting of toxic waste-disposal facilities close to lower socio-economic neighbourhoods (Schlosberg, 1999; also see Chapter 3). On a more global level, we have already seen that the ecological modernisation of national economies may only be achievable through the export of polluting industries and the degradation of environmental resources in less-industrialised nations. For writers such as Martin Khor, we must not lose sight of the role that capitalism plays in the continuation of poverty and environmental degradation:

> This is the ultimate environmental and social tragedy of our age: the scientific knowledge that could be properly used to provide for every human being's physical needs is being applied instead through industrial technology to take away resources from the Third World largely for the production of superfluous goods. Meanwhile, the majority of Third World peoples sink deeper into the margins of survival.
>
> (Khor, 1992, p. 38)

Advocates of sustainable development have been criticised for promoting development patterns that are culturally and ecologically insensitive to the needs and values of less-industrialised nations (Shiva, 1992). However, at least the concept of sustainable development has 'global reach' – its pretensions towards global responsibilities and interconnectedness offer opportunities for alternative non-technocratic and non-patriarchal conceptions of development to emerge. Even the much maligned (by radical greens) Brundtland Report *Our Common Future* stresses the fulfilment of needs in its much-quoted definition of sustainable development: 'development that meets the needs of the present without compromising the ability of future generations to meet their own needs' (WCED, 1987, p. 43). The very next sentence in the report emphasises that it is 'the concept of "needs", in particular the essential needs of the world's poor, to which overriding priority should be given' (ibid.). But within the discourse of ecological modernisation questions of Third World development appear to be neglected: ecological modernisation is a discourse of (and for) highly industrialised nations.

Third, ecological modernisation fails to engage with the moral critique offered by greens. Admittedly nature is integrated in decision-making processes, particularly economic policy, and is no longer viewed as a free good. However, there remains a highly instrumental view of nature because the discourse is that of ecoefficiency in which a reorientation towards the natural world is promoted for reasons of efficiency and not ethics. This is manifest in the promotion of policy techniques such as extended cost–benefit analysis. Environmental impacts are internalised, but only in economic terms. Although there may be pragmatic arguments for this internalisation, greens typically argue that it misrepresents the different types of value that we associate with the non-human world. The nature of aesthetic and ethical values is misrepresented in economic terms (see Chapter 6). Further, such valuation appears to reinforce a technocentric worldview.

Fourth, the trajectory and characterisation of modernisation as being (or as leading to) ecological modernisation is questioned within sociological theory. Ulrich Beck's formulation of the *Risk Society* (1992) contends that with the emergence of potentially devastating technological advances, such as nuclear power and bio-technology, the attention of government has shifted from the distribution of wealth to the distribution of risks. The unintended and unexpected side effects of indus-trialisation, such as nuclear contamination, climate change and the impacts of genetic modification, potentially affect all – no one can escape. In the risk society everyone is a potential victim of ecological devastation. And it is the institutions of industrial society that are implicated in environmental damage: there is a loss of legitimacy and trust in politicians, scientists, businesses, etc., and widespread anxiety and dis-enchantment with scientific and technological progress. The very actors that are seen as fundamental to the establishment of ecological modernisation no longer enjoy public support.

Finally, there is a widespread suspicion among more radical greens that ecological modernisation is simply a strategy of political accommodation: 'a rhetorical ploy that tries to reconcile the irreconcilable (environment and development) only to take the wind out of the sails of "real" environmentalists' (Hajer, 1995, p. 33). Reform-minded environmentalists are enthusiastic in the greening of capitalism, but capitalism it remains. The danger is that the radical critique of the environmental movement is blunted (if not neutralised) and the very structures and institutions responsible for continuing ecological decline are legitimised by apparent green approval.

An alternative trajectory: ecological democratisation

In some senses we are back to the environmentalism–ecologism debate discussed above (Dobson, 2000). Ecological modernisation is one possible conception of environmentalism. It is a managerial approach that does not fundamentally challenge social, economic and political practices. Admittedly production and consumption are to be made more ecologically sensitive; but overall, the debate is technical rather than ethical, promoting technical responses to environmental problems. But if, as we have suggested, 'ecologism' is a merely utopian vision, are ecological modernisation and the darker risk society the only two conceivable and practicable possibilities?

An alternative trajectory appears to be emerging within contemporary green political theory, one that might be termed 'ecological democratisation'. Although ecologism may provide succour for the imagination, its rejectionist stance towards 'modernisation' is typically found to be unappealing. However, the technocratic character of ecological modernisation is also deeply problematic, especially with the spectre of risk society looming large. And it is this weakness in ecological modernisation – the loss of legitimacy of the dominant institutions of industrial society in the eyes of the public – that offers a glimpse of an alternative to ecological modernisation. It is only through the democratisation of technological, economic and political decision making that the legitimacy of (and trust in) institutions will be rebuilt. A theory of ecological democratisation begins to emerge.

If we are to move towards a more sustainable and equitable future, social, political and economic institutions will need to adapt to new ways of doing things. However, contemporary institutions at all levels (global to local) lack legitimacy in that they are implicated in the growing disparity of wealth within and between societies, increased environmental degradation and the inability to act within the confines of the global capitalist system (Dryzek, 1987, 1992). Their practices and interpretations of sustainable development are seen to favour the interests of particular politically-influential groups within society and are relatively unconcerned with the experiences and needs of the disenfranchised. Unsurprisingly the motives of the state and other institutions are distrusted, leading to feelings of political alienation, cynicism, and general apathy towards political institutions (Offe and Preuss, 1991, pp. 164–5). It would seem, then, that the crisis to which contemporary green politics must respond can best be understood as a crisis of representation, or more accurately, a crisis of misrepresentation. Knowledge of, and ethical commitments to, non-human nature are frequently misrepresented in technical, economic and political decision-making processes by 'experts' and by our political representatives. How then, in such circumstances, can institutions be trusted to develop sustainable policies and practices? One answer is that meeting the demands of sustainable development requires radical political restructuring to reflect the experiences and needs of all sectors of society. Opportunities need to be available to challenge the environmental and social implications of current practices. Decision-making processes need to be designed to ensure that the voices of the disenfranchised are heard and different interpretations of sustainable development and our relations with the natural world explored. Is it possible to design institutions to guard against the manipulation of the political agenda by powerful elites?

Certain key themes begin to emerge from our reflections on the nature of green politics and the connection between sustainable development and democracy. Contemporary capitalism primarily requires governments to protect private capital and to ensure continued economic growth. Under such conditions, environmental considerations (where they conflict with capital accumulation) are unlikely to be given priority. The demands of sustainable development appear to be at odds with the logic of capitalism. This may be a further reason for greens to adopt a more critical stance towards ecological modernisation as currently understood. Sustainable development points towards the priority of democracy over capital accumulation. It requires the democratic control of development patterns. Greens may have good reason to be democrats.

However, theorists such as Robert Goodin are more sceptical about the necessity of democracy within green political thought and practice. In his view, greens should be concerned primarily with achieving sustainable ends rather than with the justice of the means: 'To advocate democracy is to advocate procedures, to advocate environment is to advocate substantive outcomes: what guarantee can we have that the former procedures will yield the latter sort of outcomes?' (Goodin, 1992, p. 168). But he has overlooked precisely what we have stressed in this chapter, which is that environmental concern can lead to the advocacy of a number of substantive outcomes. Greens subscribe to a range of values and practices and do not universally agree on a single blueprint for a sustainable society. If this is the case, the manner in which we debate which ends to pursue clearly becomes extremely important. Political spaces need to be opened up within which alternative conceptions of the future can be suggested and challenged. Thus questions concerning ends are (it turns out) inseparable from questions of means. Sustainable development is as much about democracy as it is about limits to growth and our ethical relationship with the non-human world.

The extension of different forms of democratic participation offers a strong alternative to ecological modernisation, an alternative which connects ecological thinking with other streams of emancipatory thought, such as critical theory and feminism. Making these connections is without doubt politically and theoretically important. As a result of the interchanges between greens and contemporary democratic theorists, alternative conceptions of democracy have emerged that are likely to be more sensitive to environmental issues. Of particular interest is deliberative or discursive democratic theory which directly responds to the problems of representation and authority raised earlier.[15] The core idea behind deliberative theories is that decisions should only be regarded as legitimate if they derive from a process of argument and deliberation in which all citizens have an equal right to be heard, in which arguments are won and decisions made only through the force of the better argument, and in which other forms of power and political influence derived from wealth or patronage have no place. Joshua Cohen provides a useful characterisation of deliberative politics:

> The notion of a deliberative democracy is rooted in the intuitive ideal of a democratic association in which the justification of the terms and conditions of association proceeds through public argument and reasoning among equal citizens. Citizens in such an order share a commitment to the resolution of problems of collective choice through public reasoning, and regard their basic institutions as legitimate in so far as they establish the framework for free public deliberation.
>
> (Cohen, 1989, p. 21)

Hence deliberative institutional designs are participatory in that the values and needs of all groups in society form the basis of political deliberation and the legitimacy of actions and institutions is rooted in reasoned agreement. Only when citizens are able to see that their political and ethical commitments to environmental issues are genuinely taken into account will they begin to regain trust and interest in political debate and action.

Greens committed to such a form of ecological democratisation emphasise a number of features of democratic deliberation (Smith, 2001). First, deliberative institutions are likely to be more 'ecologically rational' in that they have the ability to respond to the high levels of complexity, uncertainty and collective action problems associated with many contemporary environmental problems (Dryzek, 1987). Deliberative institutions are seen as promoting improved information flows by actively engaging numerous voices, including those individuals and groups with direct experience of the effects of environmental change who are too often marginalised from political decision-making processes. When faced with high levels of uncertainty and risk, deliberative institutions promise an ingenious mechanism through which the application of scientific and technological knowledge and expertise might be democratically regulated – an institutional setting within which the barriers between 'expert' and 'lay' knowledge can be challenged and reformulated (Beck, 1992; Barry, J., 1999).

Second, democratic deliberation promotes the articulation of preferences and judgements that are 'public-spirited' in nature (Miller, 1992). In public discussion it is difficult to defend the typically narrow self-interested preferences of those who wish to despoil and degrade the environment. Democratic deliberation offers conditions within which conflict between different values, such as environmental protection and social justice, can be understood and explored (Torgerson, 1999a; Smith, 2000) and under which more environmentally-sensitive attitudes, practices and development paths can be promoted.

Third, democratic deliberation rests on an active notion of citizenship that might be the basis for political and cultural change and the development of a practice of ecological stewardship. Democratic deliberation offers conditions under which citizens will encounter and reflect upon ecological knowledge and values and are more likely to internalise these in their judgements and practices (Goodin, 1996; Barry, J., 1999). Such internalisation and social learning can profoundly reshape the boundaries of existing political citizenship beyond the nation state, generating 'additional and occasionally alternative transnational allegiances ranging from the bio-regional through to the global, as well as to other species and the survival of ecosystems' (Christoff, 1996b, p. 159). Deliberative processes provide a conducive arena in which to expose citizens to alternative ways of conceptualising relations between human and non-human worlds.[16]

Deliberative democracy does not necessarily require complete decentralisation, although more locally-based decision-making procedures would clearly allow a greater degree of participation. Deliberative democracy is not the same as direct democracy. The former does not necessarily require total participation of all citizens, but rather a reasoned decision-making process to which all voices have access. As has already been noted, larger-scale institutions are also necessary to tackle transboundary and global environmental problems. The contemporary world is characterised by the dispersed nature of information and knowledge and the plurality of values and commitments. Deliberative institutions would be designed to respond to this.

Deliberative democracy can also be seen as 'ecological' in so far as it is characterised by the notion of appropriate scale. The idea of deliberation cuts across existing political and economic boundaries, because, as Dryzek argues, 'the size and scope of institutions should match the size and scope of problems' (Dryzek, 1995a, p. 26).

Conclusion

Green politics responds to the lack of attention given on the one hand to the ethical standing of non-human nature and on the other to the limits to growth implicit in the finite nature of the planet. As we have seen, recognition of these concerns is insufficient in itself to generate a *comprehensive* political doctrine in its own right. Greens necessarily need to engage in debates about the nature of democracy, justice, equality, etc. The outcome of these debates cannot be pre-determined by analysing the two core insights alone. Whether we believe that a distinct green ideological position has emerged or not, green politics provides powerful critical ground from which to challenge existing and potential ideas and practices.

Nowhere is this critical engagement more necessary than with the analysis of the concept of ecological modernisation. Although greens are concerned about the way nature is conceptualised, much of their critique rests on commitments to social justice and effective democratic institutions. However, the green analysis of ecological modernisation remains somewhat ambiguous. Ecological modernisation could be seen as an idea and practice that undermines more demanding visions of the green society and overwhelms the more fundamental green critque. Alternatively, as Hajer has asked, 'one may also wonder whether ecological modernisation does not in fact have a much more profound meaning and could be seen as the first step on a bridge that leads towards a new sort of sustainable modern society' (Hajer, 1995, p. 4).

Case study: principles and policies of the green political programme

Much of the discussion in the above chapter has focused on the principles and concepts of green political theory. The aim of this case study is to analyse the nature of the green political programme. What sort of policies do greens promote? On what principles are these policies based? The policy platform of the Green Party of England and Wales is used as the basis of this analysis.[17]

Statement of Core Principles

Life on Earth is under immense pressure. The environment around us is threatened with massive destruction. Conventional politics has failed us because its values are fundamentally flawed. The Green Party isn't just another political party. Green politics is a new and radical kind of politics guided by these core principles:

1 Humankind depends on the diversity of the natural world for its existence. We do not believe that other species are expendable.
2 The Earth's physical resources are finite. We threaten our future if we try to live beyond those means, so we must build a sustainable society that guarantees our long-term future.
3 Every person should be entitled to basic material security as of right.
4 Our actions should take account of the well-being of other nations and future generations. We should not pursue our well-being to the detriment of theirs.
5 A healthy society is based on voluntary co-operation between empowered individuals in a democratic society, free from discrimination whether based on race, colour, sex, religion, national origin, social origin or any other prejudice.
6 We emphasise democratic participation and accountability by ensuring that decisions are taken at the closest practical level to those affected by them.
7 We look for non-violent solutions to conflict situations, which take into account the interests of minorities and future generations in order to achieve lasting settlements.
8 The success of a society cannot be measured by narrow economic indicators, but should take account of factors affecting the quality of life for all people: personal freedom, social equity, health, happiness and human fulfilment.
9 Electoral politics is not the only way to achieve change in society, and we will use a variety of methods to help to affect change, providing those methods do not conflict with our other core principles.
10 The Green Party puts changes in both values and lifestyles at the heart of the radical green agenda.

The first two core principles of the Green Party in the Statement above will be familiar by now: the recognition of (1) the values associated with the non-human world; and (2) the physical limits to growth. The relentless pursuit of material affluence and economic growth is seen as the root of both the unsustainable use of environmental resources and the failure to recognise the interdependence between humans and their environment. Changes in patterns of *consumption* and our understanding of well-being lie at the heart of the green political programme. Traditional political platforms are concerned with disagreements over the *distribution* of resources. Distributional justice is key to the green programme, but policies also call into question what is being produced, how and why. Our current lifestyles and attitudes and the structure of our political, social and economic institutions are implicated in the environmentally- and socially-destructive aspects of modern capitalist economies.

Many aspects of the green programme are directly related to the first two core principles and primarily promote the conservation of resources. Capitalist economies tend to be linear in the sense that resources are depleted, products produced and consumed and finally disposed of into the environment as waste, frequently causing pollution. Greens argue that this linear process, which as economies grow becomes more intense, needs to become circular and reduced in size. Products should be more durable and when their initial use is over, they should not be disposed of, but rather repaired or recycled – utilised as resources for other production processes. There is a hierarchy for resource consumption and waste management which would be central to a green economy.

continued

The waste-management hierarchy

1 Reduction of overall consumption
2 Selective consumption – maximum use of secondary materials, durable, reparable and recyclable products
3 Waste minimisation
4 Re-use
5 Recycling (including composting)
6 Disposal to landfill only as last resort (long-term policy to phase out completely)

It is interesting that recycling, which is perhaps one of the most popularised (shallow) 'green' proposals, is not the primary focus of waste management. Recycling can often be seen as an attempted technological fix to make capitalist economies less environmentally damaging. A green economy considers recycling only as an option after reduction of consumption, re-use and the like.

The rise in 'green consumerism' is regarded in a similar way to recycling – at best only a partial improvement on present consumption patterns and at worst an attempt to make capitalism appear more ecologically friendly. Where publications such as *The Green Consumer Guide* (Elkington and Hailes, 1988) exhort consumers to wield their consumer power to force manufacturers to develop more ecologically-sensitive production processes, the bottom line is that consumption patterns need to be reduced rather than simply refocused.

Energy policy would again follow a similar hierarchy to resource and waste management. Conservation of energy becomes just as important as the consistently ignored and underfunded low-impact, renewable 'soft' energy options such as wind, sun and wave. Although these energy paths may not themselves generate enough to fulfil current demand, a reduction in consumption and conservation of energy would reduce this demand substantially. Measures such as energy and carbon taxes would be introduced to facilitate this change to a conservation society and the move from non-renewable fossil fuels to renewable sources. This use of fiscal instruments to reduce the throughput of energy and raw materials is a key aspect of the green programme. The tax base itself would be altered in a move away from taxes on work and labour (for instance, income tax on the poor and national insurance), to be replaced by taxes on environmentally-damaging practices such as intensive energy usage, polluting industrial processes and the use of scarce raw materials. In this sense the tax system would focus on activities that ought to be discouraged from the standpoint of attaining a sustainable future. The polluter pays principle (PPP) becomes central. For a more detailed discussion of 'green taxes', see Chapter 5.

The importance placed on the development of new renewable energy and pollution-control technologies challenges the frequent portrayal of greens as 'anti-technologists' or 'neo-Luddites'. There certainly are greens who espouse reactionary attitudes towards any form of technological development, but they tend to remain peripheral figures within the environmental movement. There is however a widespread recognition that technology tends to shape contemporary society, creating new wants and desires; its social and ethical impact often leading to a sharp separation of humanity from the natural world. Strong anthropocentric, Promethean attitudes of control and domination abound. For greens this attitude and relation to technology must be reversed.

Technology should be used appropriately in a manner which both aids the development of humanity in its widest, enlightened sense and has as little impact on the non-human world as possible. Nowhere is this more obvious than in the attitude of greens towards nuclear power, a focus of consistent campaigning by almost all sectors of the green movement. A potentially highly destructive energy source has been developed while low-impact alternatives have consistently been ignored. The potential impact of nuclear technology is not simply a concern of the present generation – we are leaving future generations the legacy of dealing with the highly radioactive waste products of our energy generation (see Chapter 1). This is perhaps the most obvious example of both the present generation's over-optimistic belief in the promise of science to provide technological solutions to environmental problems and their failure to consider fully their obligations to the future. Inseparable to these considerations is the recognition that the nuclear energy and arms industries are inextricably linked. The idea of weapons of mass destruction that could obliterate all forms of life on the planet is simply anathema to green thinking.

Again, policies on agriculture have been developed in opposition to current unsustainable industrialised, intensive farming methods. The two core principles of green political thought combine to offer a strong critique of current practices. The mechanisation of farming and indiscriminate use of chemical fertilisers, pesticides and herbicides put high levels of stress on the land and pollute the soil, air and water courses. Wildlife and biodiversity is threatened through the loss of habitat and pollution and the introduction of monocultures, often promoted by the biotechnology industry. Intensive practices undermine humane animal husbandry. Although greens do not necessarily believe eating meat is wrong per se, they abhor contemporary factory-farming methods. Food safety, particularly in the light of BSE, use of animal hormones and GM foods, has become a crucial issue and organic farming, particularly at a community level, is held up as the way forward for agriculture.

Needs, justice and self-reliance

The policies discussed above are directly related to the two core insights of green political thought. The recognition of limits to growth provides the rationale for conservation of resources and the search for low-impact technology and energy sources. The desire for a humane and organic agricultural policy promotes a more sensitive relationship with non-human nature. The strong anthropocentric attitude underlying many industrial practices is questioned, particularly the potentially ecologically-devastating nuclear industry.

But it would be a disservice to the green platform if we imagined that green policies reflect a concern with only limits to growth and our ethical relations with non-human nature. Quite clearly the 'Statement of Core Principles' at the beginning of this case study is far broader. Justice and equality are key principles within a green economic, social and political framework grounded in the 'satisfaction of needs' rather than wants, a 'reconceptualisation of the nature of work' and a 'commitment to economic self-reliance' (Ekins, 1986, p. 97). As the 'Philosophical Basis' of the Green Party's *Manifesto for a Sustainable Society* states:

> As human beings, we all have the potential to live co-operatively and harmoniously with each other, and with reverence and respect for the complex web of life of which we are a part. Yet is has become increasingly obvious that the potential cannot be realised while basic human needs remain largely unmet.
>
> (PB106)

continued

> By basic needs we mean not only the physiological needs of food, water, air, shelter and sleep, but also psychological needs. These include the need for love, respect, autonomy, security, and meaningful activity within our communities.
>
> (PB107)

The green programme is committed to a strong account of social justice and equity, based on the universal provision of needs and ecological security.[18] Later in the Philosophical Basis, it is argued that 'a sense of insecurity will prevent individuals from acting in accordance with ecological constraints. A guarantee of security will not secure voluntary ecological behaviour, but it is a necessary precondition' (PB307).

This account of basic needs or security is tied in with a reconceptualisation of work and the economy. The green platform aims for a move away from the connection of meaningful work with paid employment. Outside the 'formal' wage-economy people engage in activities whose worth is undervalued in contemporary society – parenting, caring, community volunteering, etc. These activities of the informal economy are fundamental to both the economic and social spheres of life. Primarily to fulfil the conditions for social justice, greens argue that there should be a universal basic income scheme. This would provide all citizens with a level of income sufficient to cover basic needs, replacing the current means-tested benefits system that often acts as a barrier to those who wish to take part-time employment or work on informal community-based activities. Critics question whether the incentive to work would remain (particularly given that the green vision is labour intensive) or whether the tax base can deliver such a scheme. This later issue is particularly problematic if economies are to be reduced in scale – there may simply not be enough money to re-distribute. However, this is a long-term problem, and in the long term greens would expect our conception of money, work and community relations to have changed significantly. They point to local money and trading schemes, such as LETS (local exchange trading system), which have particular application in deprived areas, as offering the potential for more congenial community-based, not-for-profit forms of trading and organisation (see Chapter 3).

The green platform is firmly internationalist in its desire to ensure universal basic needs fulfilment and global justice. The reduction of conflict through aid, diplomacy and provision of appropriate technology and the end to the arms race and arms trade are fundamental policies. Greens are not however complete pacifists and there is a recognition that the armed forces and military intervention in a peacekeeping role may be necessary. Although the green programme has global pretensions, local self-reliance remains a fundamental principle. The removal of debt and the restructuring of global economic institutions such as the World Bank, International Monetary Fund and the World Trade Organisation would aim to promote self-reliance. The transfer of aid and appropriate technology would promote the provision of basic needs through health care, education, family planning and self-sufficiency in food and energy. The idea of developing self-reliance is at the heart of the green position on global trade which would become the exception rather than the rule. Shipping goods across the world is both polluting and inefficient. It also means that transnational corporations tend to have a high degree of influence on world markets, often leaving localities relatively powerless, particularly in the South. This does not mean that more economically-developed countries do not have a duty to help such nations develop, but that this development should lead to nations and localities being able to provide for the basic needs of their population. Such an emphasis on self-reliance places greens in obvious opposition to the current trend towards global market liberalisation. Their position is often understood as a form of protectionism. However, it is protectionism of a particular kind – the development of local economies to provide for local needs (Goldsmith and Mander, 2001).

This principle of localism means that politically the green programme calls for decentralisation and local democracy. Decisions should be made at the lowest appropriate level. Thus we find that greens are deeply concerned with the centralising tendency within the European Union and with the development of a single European currency.[19] The EU is seen to be too remote from its citizens and dominated by economic interests. A democratic deficit exists. This does not mean that there is support for withdrawal from the EU; after all, it is seen as the appropriate political level for certain activities such as setting minimum ecological standards, safeguarding human and animal rights, redistributing resources within Europe and resolving disputes. However, decentralisation of political power wherever possible takes priority.

Finally, not only is prevention the order of the day when it comes to pollution and ecological destruction, but it is also the key principle of social policy. Currently, the majority of health services are focused on treating the symptoms of illness, with relatively few resources devoted to tackling the causes. Not only would more emphasis be placed on public health care, but preventative measures such as reducing pollution and traffic accidents, and ensuring food safety, are just as much aspects of health policy. The interconnectedness of different policy areas is obvious; ecologically-sensitive policy integration is at the heart of the green programme. Controversially, the green programme also advocates politically contentious policies towards crime and drugs. These policies have both libertarian and communitarian roots. For example, the decriminalisation of drug use is a libertarian policy; whereas criminal justice has a more communitarian focus, with an emphasis on rehabilitation, community service and restorative justice.

Conclusion

The green platform is far from single-issue and is developed from a broad range of principles. These principles are not purely 'ecological' and go beyond a concern about limits to growth and the value of non-human nature. Social justice based on the provision of basic needs, social policy that draws on liberal and communitarian principles, and economic and political decentralisation and democratisation are at the heart of a distinctive programme that sets the green programme apart from the policies of traditional political parties.

Suggestions for further reading

The first and most reliable survey of green political ideology (now in its third edition) is *Green Political Thought* by Andrew Dobson. Another recent overview is John Dryzek *The Politics of the Earth*. The literature on green political thought is growing in sophistication. Three particularly influential works are John Barry *Rethinking Green Politics*, Tim Hayward *Ecological Thought* and Robyn Eckersley *Environmentalism and Political Theory*. There are a number of good readers available.

The best on green political thought is probably John Dryzek and David Schlosberg *Debating the Earth: The Environmental Politics Reader* which is a collection of 40 classic articles and chapters. Both Andrew Dobson *The Green Reader* and Mark Smith *Thinking Through the Environment* contain shorter selections from key texts. The literature on ecological modernisation is relatively recent. For a defence and analysis, see Arthur Mol and David Sonnenfield's edited collection *Ecological Modernisation Around the World: Perspectives and Critical Debates* (originally a special issue of *Environmental Politics*). The journals *Environmental Politics* and *Capitalism, Nature, Socialism* frequently publish articles on green political theory.

Notes

1   At this point we can simply take 'ideology' to be a coherent set of principles explaining the world and intended to guide political action. We shall return to its essentially contested nature later in the chapter.

2   As we shall see later, this criticism can be levelled particularly at deep ecology – the ethical and political status of the ecological concepts of diversity, symbiosis and complexity are central to Arne Naess's seminal article on the deep ecology movement (Naess, 1973).

3   Even before the publication of *The Limits to Growth*, a number of authors, notably Rachel Carson in *Silent Spring* (1962), had been instrumental in raising the level of environmental awareness. However, it was the Club of Rome's report which provided the first comprehensive attempt to analyse the connections between economy, society and environment which now forms the basis of much environmental thought.

4   Malthus (writing in 1798) argued that the exponential growth of population would outstrip food supply. Hence he was a forerunner of present-day concerns with the limits to growth.

5   So successful is this feedback mechanism that Beckerman claims that we are better off in respect of all of the resources covered by the Club of Rome. Beckerman amusingly entitled the box in which he gave the reserve figures 'How we used up all the resources that we had and still finished up with more than we started with' (Beckerman, 1995a, p. 53). His point is that although resources are finite, we do not know what their *absolute* quantity is: it is easy to assume that we have reached an absolute limit when we have reached only a *relative* limit; a limit relative to present prices, technological ability, desire for the resources and so on. Once feedback mechanisms come into play, he argues, we might find that the resource is in effect rationed, that we develop suitable alternatives, or that it is now worth developing techniques for gaining access to hitherto inaccessible resources.

6   We shall return to this point in our case study of weak and strong sustainability at the end of Chapter 6.

7   Chapter 3 will highlight the 'broad church' of organisations and approaches which constitute the environmental movement. This diversity derives from the wide variety of political and ethical commitments that greens can and do endorse.

8   Bookchin has been developing the principles and practice of social ecology for around three decades. Two of his more important works are *Toward an Ecological Society* (1980) and *The Ecology of Freedom* (1991).

9   For an example of Bookchin's vitriolic outpourings against deep ecology, see 'Social Ecology versus "Deep Ecology"' (1987).

10   Sale is perhaps better described as a decentralist communitarian than as an anarchist.

11   Essentially contested concepts are ones where their use 'inevitably involves endless disputes about their proper uses on the part of their users' (Gallie, 1964, p. 158).

Dobson discusses the contested nature of the concept of ideology in the Introduction of *Green Political Theory* (Dobson, 2000, pp. 1–12).

12   Other influential writers who offer a well-defined green ideological position include Arne Naess, whose distinction between 'deep' and 'shallow' ecology motivates much green writing and action (Naess, 1973), and Tim O'Riordan, whose differentiation between 'ecocentrism' and 'technocentrism' is illustrated in the quote at the beginning of this chapter (O'Riordan, 1981, p. 1). For further distinctions and classifications, see Eckersley (1992, pp. 60–71), Young (1992) and Vincent (1993). Such classifications can be useful, but they do seem to caricature and fix what often prove to be rather fluid and in some cases inconsistent positions (Barry, 1994).

13   See, for example, Dryzek (1987), Pepper (1999), Hajer (1995), Christoff (1996a), Mol and Spaargaren (2000) and Gouldson and Murphy (1997).

14   See later chapters for more detailed discussions of these policy principles and instruments.

15   See, for example, Barry, J. (1999), Dryzek (1987, 2000), Eckersley (1999), Goodin (1996), Hayward (1995) and some of the essays in Doherty and de Geus (1996).

16   Gunderson offers some evidence that deliberation on ecological issues has a transformative effect on citizens' worldviews (Gunderson, 1995).

17   *The Manifesto for a Sustainable Society* is perhaps the most systematic green political platform of any green party. The Green Party of England and Wales may have been able to focus on its core values, principles and philosophy in detail because it has been relatively undisturbed by electoral successes! (see Chapter 3). The Green Party policies can be accessed on www.greenparty.org.uk/. For an analysis based primarily on the *Programme of the German Green Party*, see Goodin (1992, pp. 181–203). For further discussions of the green programme, see Dobson (2000, pp. 62–111), Irvine and Ponton (1988), Real World Coalition (1996), Porritt (1984), Robertson (1989) and Ekins (1986).

18   The classification of basic human needs is problematic. For a general discussion see Plant (1991, pp. 184–220).

19   Green Parties across Europe differ in the extent to which they are hostile to further European political and economic integration.

The environmental movement

> The ecology movement, when viewed as a whole, draws its force from a range of arguments whose ethical underpinnings are really quite divergent and difficult to reconcile.
>
> (Soper, 1995, p. 254)

Environmental protest in one form or another has scarcely been out of the news over the past few years. The public has become familiar with images of anti-road direct actions and Reclaim the Streets parties in the UK; protests against the shipping of nuclear waste in Germany; Greenpeace campaigns against the dumping of the Brent Spar, whaling, and the nuclear testing at Mururoa Atoll; and more recently street protests and violent conflict at international political and economic conferences. But this is just the tip of the iceberg. These forms of protest may grab the headlines, but the activities of the environmental movement go well beyond direct action. There are many different groups with a range of aims and strategies. The environmental movement encompasses a wide variety of people, interests and groups, which differ in the goals they seek and in the means they employ. It comprises green political parties, a vast array of pressure groups and direct-action organisations, activists in the mainstream political parties, green businesses and consumers, and those seeking alternative lifestyles. What are these people and groups trying to achieve and how are they trying to achieve it? In Chapters 1 and 2 we examined the core ideals of environmental politics. This chapter focuses on the nature of the environmental movement, how different sections of the movement aim to achieve their goals and how they see themselves in relation to each other. As it progresses, the focus will move away from the examination of attempts by greens to work directly within party structures or to influence policy through pressure-group activity, to those who eschew the parliamentary road and look towards the transformation of communities and local practices. The case study investigates the emergence of the anti-roads movement in the UK in the 1990s.

An environmental movement?

Is there an identifiable environmental movement? Is there a single unified movement working together harmoniously, with agreement on means and ends? Clearly there is a movement in a loose sense in that there is a range of groups and organisations committed to environmental protection and change. But, as Kate Soper indicates, within this movement there is a wide variety of activities and justifications 'whose ethical underpinnings are really quite divergent and difficult to reconcile' (Soper, 1995, p. 254). Considering the practices of organisations as divergent as the National Trust (NT) and Earth First! (EF!) makes this point: both of these groups can claim to be part of the environmental movement. These divergences can and do result in tensions and clashes. For example, recent attempts to site wind turbines have met with opposition not only on aesthetic grounds, but also because they might affect bird sanctuaries and other habitats. There is a clash here between the advocates of alternative energy and the advocates of wildlife and habitat conservation. There is not necessarily any way of reconciling their differences, yet both sides claim the mantle of environmentalism. It would seem that it is a mistake to think of the environmental movement as a single actor (Yearley, 1994, p. 156).

From the early 1960s there has been a renewed concern about the environment. Groups established before this time, such as the Royal Society for the Protection of Birds (RSPB) in the UK and the Sierra Club in the USA, have increased their membership substantially and many new organisations, frequently more radical in their approaches and demands, have been formed in the last three decades or so. Although it is hard to ascertain precisely the levels of support that they enjoy, the membership of environmental groups in the UK has roughly doubled each decade from 1960 until 1990: about 4.5 million people currently belong to an environmental organisation.[1] The table below gives an indication of the membership trends over the past twenty years. As can be seen, there has been a steady growth in membership overall, but the aggregate figure masks clear differences between organisations such as the National Trust on the one hand, whose membership has grown steadily over the past twenty years, and the more radical groups such as Friends of the Earth and Greenpeace whose membership tends to fluctuate. Membership of Greenpeace has declined rapidly from its peak in the early to mid 1990s, while membership of FOE peaked in 1997 at 114,000. These fluctuations perhaps indicate a difference between groups whose primary focus is campaigning and those which provide amenities and additional benefits to its membership.

Table 3.1 Membership of UK environmental groups[2]

	1980	1985	1990	1995	1999
Greenpeace	10,000	50,000	380,000	380,000	176,000
FOE	12,000	27,000	110,000	110,000	112,000
WWF	51,000	91,000	247,000	220,000	255,000
Ramblers	36,000	50,000	81,000	109,000	129,000
National Trust	950,000	1,323,000	2,032,000	2,293,000	2,643,000
CPRE	27,000	26,500	44,000	45,000	49,000
RSNC	140,000	165,000	250,000	250,000	280,000
RSPB	321,000	390,000	844,000	890,000	1,004,000
Total	1,547,000	2,122,500	3,988,000	4,297,000	4,648,000

Green parties

In September 1988, Mrs Thatcher famously surprised the political world by delivering a speech on the environment to the Royal Society. As an astute politician, she recognised that environmental concerns had caught the public imagination. In many ways the speech appeared to be a radical conversion, a recognition that the environment should be at the forefront of any political party's programme. As it turned out, this new-found environmentalism was more rhetoric than substance; nonetheless it propelled green considerations into the political mainstream in the UK and thereby created space for debate. Traditional parties are now required to respond to the challenges posed by the popularity of green issues, scientific evidence on the depletion of the ozone layer and climate change, and the claims that radical changes in living patterns are necessary. So, with the recognition by mainstream parties of the environment as an important policy issue, is there any need for green parties?

The old-established parties are frequently referred to by greens as the 'grey' parties and often reviled as part of the problem, not part of the solution. Although most parties within liberal democracies have begun to take notice of environmental imperatives, it is frequently charged that they are merely pandering to transient shifts in public opinion, attempting to deflect the challenge of the newly formed green parties and to attract the votes of a more environmentally-conscious younger generation.[3] They are accused of 'greenwashing' their policies rather than seriously re-thinking and reformulating their political doctrines. Given that the established parties are typified by a commitment to some form of industrialism and economic growth, greening their policies amounts to little more than amelioration, with no serious challenge to the existing patterns of consumption, production and lifestyle. This can be understood as a form of ecological modernisation with its strong conviction that economic growth and environmental protection can be reconciled. A weak form of environmentalism predominates. As an example, responses to climate change and acid rain have been slow where the problems result from existing industrial practices. When solutions have finally been proposed and accepted, they have typically been technocentric: technical solutions tend to be sought. Radical social and economic change is not seen as a plausible political option.[4]

The first green party was established in 1972 in New Zealand, followed a year later by 'People' in the UK which was to become the Green Party in 1985. Perhaps the most well-known and successful party, die Grünen, emerged in West Germany in 1980.[5] Green parties have been established in almost all liberal democracies, typically seeing themselves as offering a radical alternative to the policies and politics of the 'grey' parties. As die Grünen's Petra Kelly famously contended:

> As Greens, it is not part of our understanding of politics to find a place in the sun alongside the established parties, nor to help maintain power and privilege in concert with them. Nor will we accept any alliances and coalitions. This is wishful thinking on the part of the traditional parties, who seek to exploit the Greens to keep themselves in power. . . . We are, and I hope we will remain, half party and half local action group – we shall go on being an anti-party party.
>
> (Kelly, in Dobson, 1991, pp. 193–4)

But in 1998, less than two decades after its formation, die Grünen became a junior partner in the federal government in Germany. Should this be viewed as a success? In comparison, the Green Party of England and Wales has no representation in the UK parliament.[6] The short history of green parties is at times traumatic with a series of conflicts around ideology, organisation and strategy. A comparison of the key events in the history of die Grünen and the Green Party of England and Wales allows us to consider the future of green parties and the extent to which they can be understood as 'anti-party parties'.

Explaining the differential electoral impact of green parties

Given the short history of green parties (less than three decades) they have been relatively successful in electoral terms, establishing a presence in parliaments and more recently in executives.

The electoral impact of the Greens

Europe-wide

1999 green parties represented in the parliaments of the majority of west European nations and in at least five governing coalitions: Belgium, Finland, France, Germany and Italy.

Die Grünen

1983 won seats in both Länder (regional) and federal (national) elections.
1985 first involved in Länder governing coalitions with the SPD.
1993 formation of Alliance '90/die Grünen (unification with East German citizens' movements).
1998 entered the German government in a coalition with the SPD.

Green parties in the UK

1989 15 per cent of the overall vote in the European elections (but no green MEP elected).
1999 one Member of the Scottish Parliament and two MEPs elected in English constituencies.
2000 three members of the Greater London Assembly elected.
       greens hold a number of local council seats in the UK, concentrated particularly in areas such as Oxford and Stroud.

European Union

1999 increased representation from 27 to 38 MEPs (from 11 member states).

Crudely, the measure of success or failure, if taken to be the level of party representation in legislative assemblies, is a function of the electoral system. Although the highest-ever vote received by a green party was that achieved in the UK in the 1989 European elections, the party only achieved representation at European level in 1999 with the election of two MEPs. There is still no national level representation.[7] By comparison, die Grünen has consistently achieved electoral success. Quite simply this difference is related to the electoral systems operative in each country.

The failure to translate votes into parliamentary seats in the UK arises from the nature of the plurality or 'first past the post' system which militates against small parties with diffuse support. This is a system in which each of the 651 constituencies elects one representative; the candidate with the highest vote wins the seat. Because voting is constituency based, the Green Party has simply not had enough concentrated support to achieve a breakthrough at national level. Even when it achieved its vote of 15 per cent in 1989, a vote that in many ways can be seen as a backlash against the lack of environmental concern in the traditional parties,[8] it did not do well enough in any single constituency to win a European seat. In British politics second place has no electoral impact. Within the European Union the UK's electoral system was unique; if the election had been conducted according to one of the systems of proportional representation in operation in the rest of Europe, the Green Party could have won up to twelve seats. When the European electoral system was changed to a more proportional system for the 1999 European elections two Green MEPs were elected. Similarly the electoral system introduced for the Scottish Parliament and the Greater London Assembly was crucial to the election of one Green MSP and three MLAs.

The system used in these latter two elections resembles the German system in which 'first past the post' is supplemented by a party list resulting in a more proportional outcome. There are particular features of the German system that have been attractive for die Grünen. First, a vote above 5 per cent automatically secures a level of legislative representation. However, this also acts as a 'barring clause': parties must overcome the 5 per cent threshold to achieve *any* representation. This has had the effect of preventing fragmentation and acts as an incentive to construct alliances across green, left and feminist boundaries; alliances that may well not hold where this incentive is absent.[9] Second, electoral costs are refunded in Germany if a party receives at least 0.5 per cent of the national vote. Finally the federal system in Germany provides meaningful opportunities to gain both political experience and public exposure. Apart from the 1990 're-unification' election (see later), die Grünen has had continuous representation in the Bundestag and the European Parliament since 1983. Thus, moves towards electoral reform and regional assemblies offer UK green parties opportunities to begin to follow in the steps of their more successful German cousins. But does this electoral success come at a price?

Fundi-realo controversies

The short history of green parties has been one of electoral success, but also a history of internal conflicts over ideology, organisation and parliamentary strategy, typically referred to as fundi-realo conflicts. As the name suggests these are conflicts between fundamentalist and realist factions within the party. However, the nature of the factions is complicated because their composition alters according to the issue in question. Thus one could be, for example, an organisational realist, committed to the need for centralised leadership, and a parliamentary fundamentalist who believes entering into coalitions inevitably leads to compromise.

The three axes of the fundi-realo conflict

- **Ideology**: ecological or green-left.
- **Organisation**: grassroots democracy or increased centralisation/strong leadership.
- **Parliamentary strategy**: oppositional or coalitional.

The fundi-realo conflict over the principles of organisation has been the site of the most determined political battles within green parties. Certainly this is the case in the UK and Germany. For many activists, commitment to grassroots democracy is central, not only to their vision for society, but also to their vision of how green parties themselves ought to be organised. This commitment raises important questions concerning party organisation and the nature of leadership. Their radical democratic commitment is at odds with the hierarchical structures of traditional parties and the 'cult of leadership' that this generates. However, pragmatic greens argue that success in electoral politics requires an identifiable leadership: figures that the public trust and recognise. Radicals believe, on the other hand, that structures should be open and non-hierarchical, that leadership and responsibility should be collective.

Green parties were typically established on the principles of grassroots democracy with party members guiding and even mandating elected officials in the party. In Germany, die Grünen was very much viewed as the mouthpiece of extra-parliamentary social movements (Poguntke, 1993; Wiesenthal, 1998). Green parties embraced a series of institutional mechanisms in an attempt to promote grassroots democracy and prevent a concentration of power. The principles of rotation and incompatibility were particularly important. Official posts were to be rotated with limited terms of service (usually one or two years) and no re-election. Additionally the incompatibility rule prohibited the simultaneous holding of official positions, the most obvious implication being that parliamentary representatives could not hold any official position within the party. This sense of collective leadership is most publicly visible in the form of official party spokespersons (one male, one female) who change regularly and are never parliamentary representatives. The concentration of power and the cult of leadership are to be avoided at all costs. However, these and other mechanisms have been the subject of much contention.

In the light of its performance in the 1989 European elections, the issue of leadership became central to debates about how the Green Party of England and Wales should develop. A group of well-known public figures within the party launched Green 2000, a structural reform programme to streamline party organisation. High profile members such as Jonathan Porritt and Sara Parkin believed that if the party was to capitalise on its success then it needed to adopt a more professional and realistic attitude to leadership, presentation and decision making. There were recognisable and popular figures within the organisation and they should be charged with enhancing its image with the public. But for a sizeable number of party members, specifically many of the party activists, this violated deeply held beliefs and would also have resulted in a loss of grassroots influence, leaving power in the hands of a small executive. A very public rearguard action was fought that not only led to the resignation of some of the most prominent figures, but also to a decline in membership. This acrimonious infighting contributed to the abysmal showing at the 1992 general election and although structural changes have taken place, the party is still recovering from the fall-out a decade later.[10]

For die Grünen, questions of leadership and organisation have been even more pressing given their representation in the Bundestag. The conflict became particularly acute during the 1990 election which exposed the party's inability to respond rapidly to a changing political environment, in this case the unification of West and

East Germany, which die Grünen opposed.[11] Given the widespread popularity of unification it was electoral suicide to stand in opposition to the process. Critics argued that organisational deficiencies meant that the party was unable to respond effectively to these circumstances and led to die Grünen only attracting 4.8 per cent of the vote in West Germany, thus failing to gain any representation in the Bundestag for the first time since 1983. This episode may be illustrative of the difficulties facing a party lacking strong centralised leadership when circumstances demand a swift response to unforeseen changes in the political landscape. As Brian Doherty argues: 'Factionalism in the greens may be no stronger than in other parties, but the power held by the grassroots means that it is more important to the parties' effectiveness' (Doherty, 1992, p. 115). Some of the organisational principles of green parties appear to be incompatible with effective and efficient electoral performance (Poguntke, 1993). The pragmatic realist argument for structural reform was eloquently expressed by Herbert Wiesenthal:

> The most serious effects were those brought by rotation and the incompatibility rule. They prevented the accumulation of experience and the building-up of stable informational and communication links with other actors inside and outside the party. *The tight chronological and functional restriction on the mandates ran counter to the interdependent nature of the problems with which green politics is concerned.* Because party functionaries and members of Parliament were not allowed to stand for office again, they lost an important incentive to communicate with the grass-roots, they 'became detached' and concerned themselves only with that which they personally considered to be important. Accountability and willingness to assume responsibility dwindled. Because there was a strict ban on plurality even of party offices . . . an important channel of communication between the different levels of the organisation was lost.
>
> (Wiesenthal, 1998, pp. 175–6)

Die Grünen had already made some changes to the rotation rule at the parliamentary level after their initial electoral successes in 1983. Party policy had been to rotate representatives to ensure and maintain the collective and non-hierarchical nature of their approach to politics. But a number of the elected greens, including Petra Kelly, argued that it was necessary for them to continue in their positions if they were to work efficiently within the bureaucratic structures of the Bundestag. It took time to acclimatise to the day-to-day demands of, and to work effectively within, the assembly. For others, however, Kelly and her associates had succumbed to the very cult of leadership against which she had previously preached and the radical edge of green politics was being blunted. Many radical activists became disillusioned with this accommodation to the political status quo. Rudolf Bahro, a leading 'fundi', was so incensed by what he took to be the inevitable subversion of the ideals of die Grünen that he resigned. He believed that it was simply impossible for a party of whatever sort, and however self-critical, to escape the common fate of all parties: 'At last I have understood that a party is a counterproductive tool, that the given political space is a trap into which life energy disappears, indeed, where it is re-dedicated to the spiral of death' (Bahro, 1986, p. 211).

With the electoral failure in 1990, organisational pragmatists were able to successfully highlight the fragmentation that was taking place in the party. As Thomas Poguntke argues: 'The shock of the unexpected electoral defeat in the 1990 Bundestag election was skilfully exploited by Green reformists to initiate substantial structural reform aimed at drawing lessons from a decade of alternative politics and making the party politically more efficient' (Poguntke, 1993, p. 391). Communication was breaking down between members of the legislative assemblies (national and regional) who were ineligible to stand on policy-making bodies within the party and party officials who had no legislature experience, but were able to mandate legislative members. The party could be seen as fragmented 'into a multiplicity of different spheres of action, in which actors operated in parallel or against each other, instead of cooperating' (Wiesenthal, 1998, p. 176). In the wake of the unification election, die Grünen partially abolished the incompatibility rule and the main policy-making forum now includes Bundestag and Land representatives.

The impact of organisational realists should not be overstated. Even after internal reforms green parties are still characterised by their commitment to grassroots democracy, particularly by comparison with the traditional 'grey' parties. However, the experience of green parties does raise the question of whether it is possible, within contemporary electoral politics, to fully embrace participative forms of organisation and collective leadership. Certainly much of the success of die Grünen appears to be related to the popularity of individuals such as Joschka Fischer, whereas in the UK there is at present no equivalent political personality.

The future of green party politics?

In 1998 die Grünen became part of the national governing coalition with the SPD with ministers in high profile posts. For example, the popular Joschka Fischer became Foreign Minister.[12] This apparent success has raised a number of tensions. Most obvious is that coalition government has required compromise on core policies such as the environment, nuclear energy and citizenship rights (Lightfoot and Luckin, 2000). Green ministers were instrumental in the highly controversial decisions to allow German military involvement in Kosovo and to transport nuclear waste back from France. Both policies were vehemently attacked by large sections of die Grünen and the wider green movement. But at the same time the recent scandal over BSE and broader concerns about food safety has provided the political opportunity and legitimacy for a Green minister for Consumer Protection, Food and Agriculture to attempt to reform the unsustainable agricultural industry.

Two questions remain about the compromise required in government. First, what effect will this have on the electoral support for the greens? It will now be hard for them to stand as the radical alternative to the traditional governing parties. Second, compromise may paradoxically subvert green principles and goals. As John Dryzek remarks: 'it would be ironic indeed if the major impact of the German Greens were to render German capitalism, and German economic growth, more ecologically sustainable – and less in need of a green critique' (Dryzek, 1995a, p. 299). Certainly the current situation of die Grünen is a long way from Petra Kelly's original vision of the anti-party party.

While die Grünen must wrestle with the implications of coalition and com-promise, it can still claim a role as the focus and voice for environmental politics within the legislature and it is still considered to be an influential element of a wider national movement extending from the grassroots to the Bundestag and on into the European Parliament. But what of its UK counterparts? The relative lack of electoral success means that the British environmental movement is unable to capitalise on access to a comparable parliamentary platform. Short of election-time publicity, there seems little that the Green Party can offer, since it has no unique access to Whitehall decision making which is not already open to pressure groups. As Christopher Rootes argues:

> In other European countries, where Green parties are represented in parliament, the ecological and environmental cause benefits from enhanced visibility and access and, sometimes, from financial support as well. There, ecologists may use Green parliamentary representatives as a conduit for influence through the formal political process or, as in Germany, they may employ a dual strategy of party and movement, in which the party serves to channel into the formal political process issues which have been raised by the extra-parliamentary movement. In Britain, neither strategy is available; the poor prospects for a Green party under present electoral arrangements compel ecologists and environmentalists to adopt other tactics.
>
> (Rootes, 1995, p. 79)

Environmental pressure groups

As pointed out in the introduction, environmental pressure groups tend to be the most visible element of the environmental movement. But what is a pressure group? How are we to characterise the diversity of organisations which are identified by the use of this term? Apart from a loose affinity, what do the RSPB and Reclaim the Streets have in common? Wyn Grant defines a pressure group as

> an organisation which seeks as one of its functions to influence the formulation and implementation of public policy, public policy representing a set of authoritative decisions taken by the executive, the legislature, and by local government and the European community.
>
> (Grant, 1989, p. 9)

This is a useful working definition, although, as will be shown, not all environmental organisations would claim to be seeking to directly influence policy. For certain anarchical groups such as Earth First! (EF!), public policy, and even the state itself, are objects of suspicion, the very cause of the current environmental crisis.

An important distinction is frequently made between different types of group in terms of who or what they represent. First, cause or promotion groups represent a belief or principle; they act to further that cause. Membership is not restricted: anyone who accepts the belief or principle can join. Most of the well-known environmental organisations fit into this category. Friends of the Earth (FOE), the

World Wide Fund for Nature (WWF) and the Council for the Protection of Rural England (CPRE) are all committed to particular ideals and as such are best described as cause or promotion groups. Second, by contrast, interest or sectional groups represent a particular section of the community, defending their common private interests. Membership tends to be restricted to that sectional interest. The Country Landowners' Association (CLA), the Society of Motor Manufacturers and Traders (SMMT) and the Confederation of British Industry (CBI) are all well-known interest groups whose political activities are based purely on enhancing the interests of their members.

A further distinction can be made between 'insider' and 'outsider' groups. Insider groups have gained a degree of legitimacy and may be consulted by government departments and agencies on matters of policy. For example, the RSPB is frequently consulted as a matter of routine by the environment ministry and members of the road lobby such as the Automobile Association (AA) and the Road Haulage Association (RHA) by the transport ministry.[13] However, in itself insider status says nothing about the level of influence that these groups enjoy, rather it simply means that they can be considered part of the department's policy community. Outsider groups do not have this access. For some, this is a problem as they wish to engage in a constructive relationship with officials but have been unable to gain recognition. The New Economics Foundation (NEF), for instance, has little or no influence in departments such as the Treasury; Compassion in World Farming (CIWF) has had little consistent impact on agricultural policy. Other outsiders (such as EF!) are ideologically opposed to any positive relationship with government. However, the distinction is not always clear-cut for two interconnected reasons. First, some groups stand at the threshold of official recognition; their status is unclear and they stand in an ambiguous relationship with Whitehall. Second, it is frequently the case that a group has insider status with one department or agency but not with others. WWF and CPRE are examples in that they clearly have close working relationships with environment ministers and civil servants but have no meaning-ful status within the Treasury. This differential access will no doubt continue, given that the state is becoming more fragmented: many departmental responsibilities have been devolved to arm's-length executive agencies and quasi-autonomous non-governmental organisations (quangos). For environmental pressure groups with limited resources, this situation creates difficulties in that they campaign across a whole range of issues. This is further exacerbated by the fact that well-resourced sectional interest groups, opposed to the environmental agenda, have insider status, even to the point of having their representatives appointed to quangos.

In response to the power of vested 'anti-environmental' interests, green groups have often mobilised themselves into networks and coalitions. The paradigm case of an horizontally-organised network is the environmental justice movement in the United States. The movement differs from traditional 'white middle-class' environmental organisations in that it focuses on the environmental risks, such as the location of toxic dumps and polluting industries, that have a disproportionate impact on the poor and ethnic minorities. The environmental justice movement does not rely on a national leadership or central bureaucracy, but rather is organised as a network of local groups fighting environmental threats to their neighbourhoods (Schlosberg, 1999). Coalitions of more traditional pressure groups have emerged when they have been able to overcome their competitiveness and recognise that it is a waste of limited resources to campaign independently on the same issue. When this is particularly successful, an 'umbrella' group emerges. In transport politics, Transport 2000, formed in 1973, is an obvious example comprising (among others) FOE, CPRE, rail unions and public-transport user groups. More recently, in 1996, the Real World Coalition was established to promote the full range of issues implicit within sustainable development: environmental protection, global poverty and security, inequality, and democratic renewal. A number of the UK's leading pressure groups, including FOE, WWF, Christian Aid, Charter 88, Oxfam and Save the Children Fund, issued a wide-ranging manifesto, *The Politics of the Real World* (Real World Coalition, 1996), followed a few years later by *From Here to Sustainability* (2001). In the run-up to the 1997 election the Coalition issued a direct challenge to the major political parties to implement twelve key reforms.

The Real World Coalition's 'Action Programme for Government'

- increased public investment in local, community and voluntary enterprises;
- ecological restructuring of the tax system;
- enactment of a Bill of Rights;
- increased international development aid;
- strategy for affordable housing;
- integrated transport programme;
- substantial reduction of the UK's carbon dioxide emissions;
- enforceable code of conduct on international arms transfers;
- strategy to increase consumption of fresh and nutritious food;
- reform of international trade to safeguard social and environmental standards;
- binding legal protection for Sites of Special Scientific Interest;
- alternative social and economic indicators.

The formation of coalitions, at whatever level, whether policy or grassroots, is a positive step forward in two respects. First, combining resources, knowledge and expertise enables groups to boost their impact and effectiveness. Second, and this is especially true where such coalitions cut across hitherto discrete campaigning areas, it gives the groups involved an opportunity to explore issues of mutual concern; it is a learning process for those participating.

Forms of action

While recognising that the categories used to define pressure-group politics are not watertight, knowing where a group stands in relation to the insider/outsider and cause/sectional distinctions is helpful to understanding the tactics and forms of action it chooses or is forced to employ. As the table below demonstrates, pressure-group action can range from informal or formal lobbying or petitioning through to large-scale marches and direct action.

Forms of action

Informal contact and influence through discrete lobbying behind the scenes, often with transfer of personnel. For example, ex-ministers and civil servants from the former Department of Transport (DOT) often move to positions in the British Roads Federation (BRF).

Formal lobbying through governmental institutions and bodies. For example, FOE makes submissions to standing committees (such as the Standing Advisory Committee on Trunk Road Assessment) as well as having a seat on the UK Sustainable Development Commission.

Letters and petitions to MPs and ministers from group members and the general public organised in a concerted manner. For example, in their successful campaign against sow stalls, CIWF inundated MAFF with letters and petitions.

Scientific research and reports to establish the credibility of green concerns. For example, FOE has been responsible for breakthrough reports on the impact of acid rain, the global timber trade and nuclear power.

Consumer boycotts designed to highlight industrial malpractice. For example, a number of development groups have called for a boycott of Nestlé products. The company has been accused of swamping Southern nations with baby milk powder which people are unable to use safely because water supplies are contaminated.

Court action where it is believed that official procedures have not been adhered to. For example, protesters against the M3 extension through Twyford Down challenged the DOT for their failure to abide by the EC directive on environmental impact assessment.

Demonstrations and marches which provide obvious visible evidence of public support. For example, the massive numbers that turned out for a series of anti-nuclear demonstrations organised by the Campaign for Nuclear Disarmament (CND) in the 1980s.

Media stunts to gain widespread public exposure. For example, Greenpeace has become famous for its skill in attracting media attention to issues such as whaling and nuclear testing.

Non-violent direct action where activists engage in acts of civil disobedience and eco-sabotage. For example, EF! has been involved in monkeywrenching, mass trespass and 'bulldozer diving' on road-construction sites.

Violent direct action where the aim is to injure those directly involved in practices that are environmentally destructive or harmful to animals. For example, the ALF has sent letter bombs to particularly prominent vivisectionists.

While, within their overall strategies, environmental pressure groups may use one or more of these forms of action, their choice of tactics will be dependent upon their status and principles. Approaches may range from moderate or conventional to more radical, hard-edged and conflictual means. The former tactical style is to operate within established procedures, working through dialogue and consultation in a cooperative manner. Typically demands are not absolutist, and groups are prepared to negotiate, frequently willing to compromise to reach agreed solutions. The latter approach is characterised by more confrontational and uncompromising tactics; demands often being absolutist, allowing little or no space for compromise. Clearly, different forms of action can be used in different ways: for instance, the production of a scientific report could be the basis for conventional dialogue and negotiation or, more radically, as the basis of confrontation with, and challenge to, government or industrial experts. Further, these tactics are not necessarily mutually exclusive; environmental pressure groups will frequently adopt an array of approaches in their campaigning. These points can be illustrated by looking at how two of the most well-known organisations, Greenpeace and Friends of the Earth (FOE), have approached campaigning and the problems that their apparent success has brought.

Greenpeace and FOE: the institutionalisation of environmental pressure groups?

Both Greenpeace and FOE have their origins in a repudiation of the moderate, conventional lobbying tactics of more traditional pressure groups. With the rise of environmental concern in the late 1960s and early 1970s, many people saw the need for a new, more direct form of campaigning. The apparent urgency of the environmental crisis was the spur to the creation of these groups, ushering in a new style of environmental protest and a new breed of protester. Activists were committed to confrontational forms of direct action, a style of campaigning that they quickly discovered to be of great interest to the media. This media exposure led to high levels of public support. From radical beginnings both organisations have grown, achieving international standing with an active presence in all parts of the world.

FOE was founded in the USA in 1969 by David Brower who had become disillusioned with the staid traditionalism of the Sierra Club. Two years later FOE was established in the UK. Although rightly famous for its high publicity campaigns, exemplified by the early, innovative dumping of non-returnable Schweppes bottles outside the company's London headquarters in 1971, FOE has never limited itself to a single form of protest. In the early 1970s it published a number of path-breaking reports including Paul Ehrlich's *The Population Bomb*. Success came early with Rio Tinto Zinc abandoning its plans to mine areas of Snowdonia National Park and the British government banning imports of leopard, cheetah and tiger skins. Equally, its campaigns against the nuclear industry and the use of CFCs have been models of imaginative and well-researched action. It has not simply lobbied government, but has taken direct action against industry, for instance its leading role in the successful boycott of the DIY stores which imported hardwoods from unsustainable rainforest sources.

Over the past three decades the level of commitment and technical expertise of FOE has gained the respect not only of the general public but, perhaps, more importantly, certain sections of the political establishment. In the UK, for instance, it is impossible now to regard them purely as an outsider group. While FOE activists continue to engage in confrontational activities, and although it provides resources and support for other groups such as the Third Battle of Newbury,[14] it has assumed a more conventional and, at times, insider role in relation to specific departments and agencies. After the publication of *Sustainable Development: The UK Strategy* in 1994, FOE accepted the invitation to sit on the UK Round Table on Sustainable Development, now subsumed within the UK Sustainable Development Commission.[15]

Internationally, FOE has taken advantage of the new-found status of non-governmental organisations (NGOs) in United Nations forums; for example, presenting detailed submissions to the Commission on Sustainable Development (CSD). At the opposite end of the organisational structure, its semi-autonomous local groups have begun to take an active role in local government initiatives such as Local Agenda 21. As an organisation, FOE has recognised that participation in local to global political forums offers a valuable opportunity for change.[16] In many ways this is a far cry from its radical beginnings and it has not always escaped criticism for a perceived softening of approach. However, the organisation appears to be doing its best to negotiate a difficult and largely unexplored terrain where governments are recognising some of the implications implicit within a commitment to sustainable development. How should a group such as FOE respond to requests from government and industry for help in developing programmes of action? FOE appears to be attempting to have the best of both worlds, juggling high-profile actions alongside participation in governmental bodies. At present it appears adept at performing this balancing act, although its more radical edge has been sacrificed in order to grasp the opportunity to participate in policy communities where it perceives a changing climate which promises new possibilities for an environmental voice.

Greenpeace was also launched in the United States by renegades from the Sierra Club in 1971, with protests against nuclear testing in the Aleutian Islands to the west of Alaska. In 1977 Greenpeace was established in the UK. Greenpeace took direct action to the limits, frequently shocking the public by the heroic audacity of its activities. Images of activists riding the waves in small inflatable dinghies, placing themselves between whaling ship and whale, underneath toxic drums suspended from dumping ships and their dumping zone, or riding headlong into nuclear test zones, were soon relayed worldwide. Never before had the reality of environmental issues been so graphically presented. A perhaps naive attempt by young idealistic activists to save the world by their own actions quickly led to the recognition that their activities generated huge media interest which could be exploited to further their aims. The media were hungry for images such as these and the scare stories they embodied. In recognising the power of the media, Greenpeace began to tailor its actions for maximal effect, with the media being recruited as accomplices in the process. Direct actions undertaken by FOE and others often seemed amateurish by comparison. Discussing the early years of Greenpeace, Fred Pearce comments:

> The stories that Greenpeace weaves are so beguiling that, according to one insider, 'News desks will often suppress stories of campaigning cock-ups because they like the Greenpeace image too much.' . . . Greenpeace has over almost two decades maintained an image of swashbuckling success.
>
> (Pearce, 1991, p. 20)

But does this swashbuckling image hide the complexity of the environmental agenda? Critics have often charged Greenpeace with a selective approach to the environment, picking and choosing those issues which are simple and media friendly. As Pearce contends: 'To make the image work, Greenpeace needs a clear, simple message. It is good at being against things, but finds being in favour of them harder; and complex issues, such as Third World agriculture or reafforestation, tend to pass it by' (ibid.).

To a certain extent, where Greenpeace has tended to keep things as simple as possible, FOE appears less afraid of tackling and admitting the complexity of environmental problems. But Greenpeace's direct and uncompromising approach led to huge popular acclaim and rapidly increasing membership levels and financial support. In 1990, Greenpeace UK was receiving around £5 million per annum which allowed it to branch out into other activities such as research. Although it has steadfastly refused to participate directly in government policy communities, its research has influenced policy discussions both nationally and internationally. In fact, the reports by Greenpeace scientists have in some cases been the most reliable form of evidence available to many countries, particularly those from the South, during international negotiations. Again, with respect to the International Whaling Commission (IWC), Greenpeace's evidence concerning whale numbers and the infringement of international agreements has been influential, particularly when simultaneous large-scale actions are employed to attract media and public attention. For many nations Greenpeace has too much influence and its activities are seen as subversive. Nowhere was this suspicion better illustrated than by the 1985 sinking of the *Rainbow Warrior* in Auckland, New Zealand. Greenpeace activists were preparing to renew their protests against French nuclear testing in Mururoa Atoll, a frequent target for the organisation, when French secret service agents planted two limpet mines on the ship, sinking it and, more horrifically, killing a photographer in the process. The international outcry was enormous; membership and support soared.

Does this success have a price? Greenpeace has become an international multi-million-dollar organisation with a bureaucracy to match. It is no longer a small group of committed activists with no responsibilities beyond their own commitment to the non-human world. Quite clearly the growth of the organisation has had a substantial impact. Whereas in its formative years, issues could be raised and pursued immediately and with impunity, in the present climate, activists are forced to consider the financial effect of any proposed actions. Perhaps popular success and the financial rewards this brings have become a burden. Hardcore activists, central to the development of Greenpeace's distinctive approach, have increasingly become disillusioned, often resigning from, or being asked to leave, the organisation. To their mind Greenpeace has gone soft, abandoning its earlier radical and courageous cutting edge. Two issues illustrate their concerns.

First, although Greenpeace had hitherto steadfastly refused to endorse prod-ucts and industrial processes, in Germany it has recently backed the development of non-CFC- or HCFC-based refrigerators and a low-emission, low-consumption car. Supporters of these initiatives argue that they are developing a new form of direct action: 'solutions orientated campaigning'. Opponents decry such ventures, believing that they legitimise and capitulate to the very consumer- and car-based culture that they are committed to calling into question.

Second, in the early 1990s, as part of its continuing campaign against nuclear reprocessing at Thorp, Greenpeace attempted to stage a concert on the grounds of the Sellafield nuclear site. Sellafield gained an injunction, banning all protesters from entering the site. Greenpeace was concerned that if it broke the injunction its substantial assets would be sequestered. In response the media were treated to the spectacle of the internationally successful pop group U2 standing alongside Greenpeace activists just below the high-water mark by the nuclear plant. Greenpeace declared that it could go no further for fear of what the courts might do. But was this really the action of a hardcore direct-action organisation? For many it was not. Indeed, for some it symbolises the decline of the original wave of radical campaigning groups. Even though Greenpeace has recognised this predicament and more recently re-engaged in high-profile, daring actions such as the 1995 campaigns against the dumping of the Brent Spar and the latest round of French nuclear testing, in many ways it has been usurped by a new breed of environmental protester and new forms of organisation, which embody the spirit and idealism of the early Greenpeace.

Greenpeace, the media and the Brent Spar episode

Greenpeace's relationship with the media has been crucial to its success. As already noted, much of the organisation's effectiveness in bringing environmental issues to widespread public attention can be traced to the ways in which it manages or at times even manipulates the media. Greenpeace frequently presents newspapers and television stations with footage and stories which are published and broadcast without proper independent scrutiny. But it appears that Greenpeace might now be the subject of a media backlash on two fronts. First, Greenpeace faces the problem of media fatigue: their direct-action stunts are no longer considered spectacular and novel. Second, the media have become suspicious of Greenpeace after the Brent Spar episode. What seemed at first to be an almost perfectly coordinated campaign against Shell's proposal to dump the Brent Spar oil platform at sea turned into a media-relations fiasco. Greenpeace combined scientific evidence of toxic residues with the spectacle of activists boarding and occupying the platform, and national campaigns against Shell service stations. Shell backed down, agreeing to dismantle and dispose of the rig on land. The media proved to be willing accomplices in forcing this change of policy. However, Greenpeace's estimate of the level of toxic residues turned out to be seriously flawed, which the organisation was quick to admit. This left various editors rather embarrassed over their previous one-sided uncritical reliance on Greenpeace's interpretation of the situation. The vicious response in the subsequent editorials was unprecedented and it is far from clear whether Greenpeace has been able to rebuild the relationship of trust with news editors.[17]

The story of FOE and Greenpeace is one of a move away from their initial outsider status towards growing influence with both governments and businesses. Although Greenpeace does not formally engage with governments to the same extent as FOE, it would be difficult not to classify them both as insider pressure groups. However, the insider/outsider typology tells us little about the changing nature of the two organisations. In contrast, social movement theory offers us an understanding of institutionalisation and the type of choices facing environmental pressure groups.

Hein-Anton van der Heijden argues that we can understand the process of institutionalisation along three axes: (1) organisational growth; (2) internal institutionalisation; and (3) external institutionalisation (van der Heijden, 1997, pp. 31ff). Organisational growth occurs in response to an increase in the size of an organisation's constituency and financial resources. The degree of internal institutionalisation is related to the level and sophistication of the bureaucracy of organisations, the increase in professionalisation rather than relying on volunteers and a growing centralisation of power. Finally, external institutionalisation is witnessed in the changing nature of an organisation's action repertoire with a move away from unconventional actions such as demonstrations and direct action and towards more conventional and routinised activities such as lobbying, press releases and the production of scientific and technical reports.

Drawing on a range of social movement studies, Mario Diani and Paolo Donati argue that environmental organisations 'are shaped by their response to two basic functional requirements, *resource mobilisation* and *political efficacy*' (Diani and Donati, 1999, p. 15). Organisations are faced with two basic choices. The first concerns the resources they choose to mobilise: either the time of volunteer activists or the money of supporters. Organisational models are either participatory or professional. The second choice relates to action repertoire (or political efficacy): whether to engage in disruptive or conventional forms of political negotiation. Diani and Donati argue that the history of social movements in Europe is typically a move from participatory protest organisations to public interest lobbies. The ideal case is Germany where widespread direct action of the 1960s and 1970s has gradually transformed itself into a highly successful green party and a number of well-respected pressure groups (Rucht and Roose, 1999).

Does the recent history of the UK environmental movement follow the same pattern? Have we experienced gradual institutionalisation, as groups develop from participatory protest organisations into public interest lobbies? In contrast to other European nations, the UK never really witnessed mass-participatory environmental organisations in the 1970 and 1980s. In particular, the anti-nuclear movement was not as active or radical as many of its European counterparts. Although it does have local groups, FOE has always been relatively centralised and Greenpeace has consistently kept a tight control over actions bearing its name. The lack of an aggressive, disruptive participatory movement can be explained to a certain extent by the favourable political opportunity structure in the UK: environmental groups have enjoyed comparatively easy access to decision makers. Aggressive direct action has seemed unnecessary.

Greenpeace in particular has never been interested in mass mobilisation; direct action has other ends:

Spectacular, risky actions by professional campaigners do not aim at mobilising sympathisers, but rather at attracting media attention and thus commanding financial support from the general public. Unconventional disruption defines a model of 'vicarious activism' which is actually media-orientated rather than grassroots-orientated. . . . Greenpeace presents a peculiar blend of professional and confrontational traits.

(Diani and Donati, 1999, pp. 24–5)

Grant Jordan and William Maloney have gone so far as to describe both FOE and Greenpeace as 'mail-order protest businesses' (Jordan and Maloney, 1997). Members' involvement is typically through their chequebooks. This is not a disparaging comment: on the basis of individual donations, FOE and Greenpeace have been able to develop into effective national and international environmental pressure groups. It is important to remember that these groups are not, and never have been, mass-participatory organisations.

The new wave of direct action and civil disobedience in the UK

The early 1990s saw a quite remarkable rise in the level of non-violent direct action (NVDA) against environmentally-destructive practices in the UK. Inspired by the activities of Earth First! in the USA, the radical green network was established in the UK in 1991. Originally focused on rainforest actions, the network rapidly turned its attention to anti-roads protest (see Wall, 1999; Doherty, 1999; Seel *et al.*, 2000). The new mood of defiance first captured national attention in 1992 in the attempted defence of Twyford Down and then spread throughout the country (see the case study at the end of this chapter). The new direct-action network had no central organisation or membership. Tactics became more sophisticated with the development of tree houses, aerial walkways and tunnels. Pictures of activists placing themselves in immediate danger against the onslaught of construction machinery became familiar, the image of 'manufactured vulnerability' (Doherty, 2000) being somewhat reminiscent of earlier Greenpeace actions.

The response of the British state to this new wave of NVDA was repression. Under the provisions of the 1994 Criminal Justice and Public Order Act (CJA), the UK government criminalised certain forms of protest: actions that had previously been legal or subject only to the civil law were now classified as criminal. With respect to the environmental movement, the CJA most obviously criminalised forms of trespass which have direct impact on, for instance, road protests and hunt saboteuring.[18]

Provisions of the Criminal Justice and Public Order Act (1994)

The Act defines two new offences which will criminalise a variety of peaceful political activities:

---

continued

- **aggravated tresspass** – tresspass which occurs with the intention of disrupting or obstructing any lawful activity as defined by the police. It is also a criminal offence to disobey the orders of any police officer who has directed a person to leave land.

- **trespassory assemblies** – this empowers police to obtain an order banning assemblies held on land without the owner's permission which may result either in 'serious disruption to the life of the community' or 'significant damage to a site of historical, architectural or scientific importance'. Police are also empowered to stop people whom they believe to be travelling to such an assembly.

Ironically, as the then Conservative government's aim was to fragment and disperse protest and its support, the CJA itself became a focal point of resistance and led to the formation of coalitions between different communities and groups. Apart from attacking the rights of environmental protesters, the CJA criminalised the activities of, among others, travellers, squatters and ravers. All over the country new alliances and campaigns sprang up both in an attempt to halt the passage of the legislation and to develop even more imaginative forms of protest and community projects as activists exchanged skills and experience. This new grassroots activist movement is often referred to as 'DIY culture' (see later). Rather than putting a stop to protest and frightening off would-be activists, the years directly following the introduction of the CJA witnessed some of the most audacious, inventive and innovative protests. For example, the Reclaim the Streets party held on the M41 in the summer of 1996 attracted thousands of politicised people from all walks of life to dance on what is normally one of the busiest stretches of road in London. Again, eco-protesters were national news as they tunnelled under proposed road schemes in Fairmile, Devon and at the site of a new runway at Manchester Airport.

None of the direct actions actually stopped the specific developments, although many activists argue that it was the anticipated levels of protest and the public outcry it would inspire that caused the then Department of Transport to withdraw plans for a river crossing through ancient Oxleas Wood in London. By the mid-1990s the roads programme underwent a fundamental review that saw many of the controversial road schemes shelved. Without doubt much of the rethink can be related to public expenditure concerns, but the prohibitive costs of policing protest and the rise of awareness of the environmental impacts of road building were also part of the explanation of policy change.

The legitimacy of direct action

Activists typically argue that direct action is part of a long tradition of civil disobedience against illegitimate activities of the state.

An act of civil disobedience is an act of illegal, public protest, nonviolent in character. That is to say: the civilly disobedient act must be a knowing violation of the law, else it would not be disobedient; the act must be performed openly, being one of general community concern of which the agent is not ashamed; and the act must be intended as an objection to some law or administrative policy or public act.

(Cohen, 1970, p. 469)

But what counts as justifiable civil disobedience is not always clear-cut. In a liberal democracy most people are clear as to the legitimacy of most actions and forms of protest. Under most circumstances a political rally is recognised as legal; at the other extreme violent actions directed against individuals would be seen as illegal and condemned on moral grounds. But between these extremes lies a disputed area: the realm of civil disobedience. Many people recognise that, although breaking the law is generally wrong in principle, in some cases where a law seems to contravene deeply held beliefs and ideals, or stops people acting on these beliefs, actively disobeying those laws is legitimate.[19] The problem, however, is which laws and which beliefs and ideals? Although not answering this question directly, for an act of civil disobedience to be legitimate, it is generally assumed that it must be non-violent, take place in the open, with a willingness to accept the consequences, and after all the legal means of democratic persuasion have been exhausted. Interestingly, the practice of monkeywrenching, the disabling of machinery and damage to property, would not in these terms generally count as justifiable civil disobedience. But some committed activists are willing to accept the consequences of their actions and believe it is legitimate to stop environmentally-destructive developments in this manner; as EF! proclaim, there can be 'No Compromise for Mother Earth'. Within the environmental movement as a whole there tends to be general revulsion to the idea of justifying physical harm to persons (militant animal rights activists aside), although there is some sympathy and support for the monkeywrenchers.

But how are we to explain the rise in direct action? After all, the history of the environmental movement would appear to be one of gradual institutionalisation. As Doherty argues:

> In 1991 the British environmental movement was well organised and well supported but politically moderate. It was assumed that there was no prospect of a more radical environmental movement emerging and no likelihood of significant protests on environmental issues. Yet in that year new radical environmental protest groups emerged which posed a challenge to this established view of the environmental movement.
>
> (Doherty, 1999, p. 275)

Three interconnected explanations for the changing nature of environmental protest can be offered. First, there was growing dissatisfaction and disillusionment with the campaigns, ideology and structure of once-radical environmental pressure groups such as FOE and Greenpeace. FOE's decision to withdraw from the campaign against the M3 at Twyford Down over fears of sequestration of funds was seen as symptomatic of a wider malaise among the established organisations. It is argued that FOE and Greenpeace's dependence on maintaining high levels of subscription and financial support from relatively pragmatic supporters affects their action repertoire and campaign focus. The new activists were also critical of what they perceived as the 'single-issue' approach of environmental groups. Typically activists embraced a more comprehensive anti-capitalist ideology that went beyond roads and narrow environmental concerns. The broader anti-capitalist orientation of direct action became clear as activists recently moved from road protests to more globally-significant targets such as the World Trade Organisation. The more established, highly professionalised and bureaucratic environmental organisations offered few opportunities for radical activists to participate in actions. Direct participation and engagement was seen as a critical principle in the more comprehensive ethos of protesters. As one activist states: 'That's the pull of direct action: in a world where the individual feels increasingly helpless, direct action instils a sense of power and confidence. It brings people together and gives them hope' (Marman, 1996, p. 5).

Second, the founders of the EF! network were able to draw on existing and emerging counter-cultural networks. Many had been active in existing environmental organisations such as FOE and the Green Party and had access to the green networks associated with the *Green Anarchist, Green Line,* Green Student Network, the *EF! Journal* in the USA and *The Ecologist* (Wall, 1999). Contacts were built with the existing peace, anti-nuclear, animal liberation and rainforest campaigns and ideas, resources and action repertoires were exchanged. As we have already noted, the reaction of the state to green and youth counter-cultures also led to further mobilisation: the campaign against the Criminal Justice Bill (later to become the CJA) galvanised into an alliance between environmentalists, dance culture, hunt saboteurs, New Age travellers and other 'marginal' groups in opposition to the government. High youth unemployment and mass higher education fed DIY culture. And the emerging counter-culture was also able to draw on new technologies of networking and protest such as the Internet, video and mobile phones, which made mobilisation and coordination so much easier.

Finally the unprecedented road-building programme of the Conservative government offered a highly symbolic and politically-charged target for mobilisations. As Derek Wall contends: 'accelerated road-building and other forms of large-scale construction provided grievances around which different demands could be mobilised. At cherished localities such as Twyford or Claremont in East London, roads acted as a potent symbol of global environmental damage and a concrete threat to valued sites laden with cultural and natural significance' (Wall, 1999, p. 95). Additionally EF! activists were able to develop alliances with and draw support from already existing local opposition groups who had been fighting the road schemes through more conventional means (Cathles, 2000).[20]

The change in transport policy has led to a change in focus for direct action. The most obvious target of mass mobilisations is now international economic and political conferences. Since the street protests in Seattle in 1999, almost every major international conference has been the scene of mass demonstration, often with violent confrontation between a small minority of the activists and the police. Whether these broad anti-globalisation mobilisations can be sustained and how states respond are perhaps two of the key questions for the future development of the direct-action movement.

Transforming everyday life: from green consumerism to green communes

Up to this point the activities of the green movement have been investigated with direct reference to its relations with the legislature and policy process. However, this emphasis in no way exhausts the scope of environmental activity. By moving away from more conventional understandings of party and pressure-group politics and towards the way individuals and groups have sought to change their everyday practices, other important aspects of the green movement can be brought into focus. There are perhaps three distinct areas of activity that are worth consideration. The first is frequently termed 'green consumerism' and ranges from changing purchasing and consumption patterns (for example, buying ecologically-sensitive products) through to the establishment of green businesses. The second area of activity is that associated with third-force organisations (TFOs) in the social economy. These tend to be community-based, not-for-profit groups which develop local projects such as wildlife site conservation, neighbourhood recycling initiatives, and reclamation of derelict land. Finally, attention will turn to individuals and groups whose practices are a direct challenge to the existing system. This challenge has taken two principal forms: green communes and DIY culture. Green communes, while separating themselves from mainstream society, at the same time aspire to be actually existing utopias: exemplars for future political and social arrangements. DIY culture is a more recent phenomenon. Rather than separation from society, those involved aim to disrupt, and offer alternatives to, conventional practices. An example of this might be the squatting and refurbishing of a derelict building to provide a community space, a place of shelter for the local homeless. Whereas green communes typically seek rural isolation, DIY activists often operate within inner cities. Clearly all the activities mentioned, from green consumerism to DIY culture, can and do affect the formulation and implementation of public policy; however, the point is that for these areas of green action, influencing the policy process is not necessarily the prime concern. It is the alteration of lifestyles, through changing existing everyday practices and patterns of behaviour, that is central.

Green consumerism

Everyone is a consumer of one sort or another. The question that green politics poses is how and what should be consumed? The 1980s saw a rise in what has been termed green consumerism, the easiest, most accessible and culturally acceptable form of green action. The promotion of 'green' products, such as lead-free petrol, and activities such as recycling, have become commonplace.

Principles of green consumerism

The green consumer avoids products which are likely to:

- Endanger the health of the consumer or of others;

---

continued

- Cause significant damage to the environment during manufacture, use or disposal;
- Consume a disproportionate amount of energy during manufacture, use or disposal;
- Cause unnecessary waste, either because of over-packaging or because of an unduly short useful life;
- Use materials derived from threatened species or from threatened environments;
- Involve the unnecessary use of – or cruelty to – animals, whether this be for toxicity testing or for other purposes;
- Adversely affect other countries, particularly in the Third World.

(Elkington and Hailes, 1988, p. 5)

There is no doubt that green consumerism can be very powerful. Through a realisation that their purchasing power can have an impact, people have come to believe that they can make a change for the better; to a certain extent green consumerism has empowered individuals. In principle, the aggregation of individual market transactions forces industry to change its practices, for example, by encouraging it to switch from polluting and wasteful products to more environmentally-friendly alternatives. This is an extension of the logic of the consumer boycott, moving from action against a single readily-identifiable product (such as the 1988 FOE campaign against aerosols containing CFCs) to the use of consumer pressure in all markets. Alongside existing companies which have responded to green consumer demands by producing additional 'green' products, a space has opened up for green companies and businesses. These can take the form either of established companies recognising the need to change their production processes or of completely new companies formed on the basis of environmental principles. But what does a company have to do to be 'green'? Considerations would surely need to include the production and retailing process as a whole, from the impact of the extraction of raw materials and the energy efficiency of production through to the environmental and social costs of transport and packaging. The source of raw materials, the effect and destination of waste products created in production processes and the recyclability and durability of products would become key concerns.

In the late 1980s green consumerism was at its height: the book *The Green Consumer Guide* and the magazine *The Ethical Consumer* both sold well, and companies, most prominently perhaps The Body Shop and the Cooperative Bank, increased their public profile and market share. But within a few years green consumerism began to suffer a backlash from both consumers themselves and green activists. The consumer backlash can be attributed to a number of causes. First, the initial wave of enthusiasm for green issues declined as Western economies moved into recession and traditional concerns – job security and economic opportunity – reasserted themselves. Combined with this, the novelty of 'being green' wore off. Issue attention and the perennial political focus on economic considerations are problems that the green movement has yet to overcome (see Chapter 4). Second, markets have been flooded by products purporting to be environmentally friendly. This leads to suspicions that existing products are simply being re-packaged and that their green claims are spurious. Even when consumers wish to buy green there is no readily understandable standardised information or labelling to enable product comparison.

Perhaps the most fundamental criticisms have, however, emerged from the more radical elements of the environmental movement. The very idea and possibility of green consumerism itself has been challenged. While green consumerism might conceivably make markets less environmentally destructive, it fails to challenge the logic of accumulation and the patterns of consumption inherent in the capitalist system. Simply, green consumerism argues that when choosing between products, the choice should be made according to a scale of green and ethical criteria; which product is 'greenest'? But surely the environmental challenge questions the need for certain types of product in the first place? True, we can judge between the environmental impact of alternative makes and models of cars; we can choose the most environmentally friendly. But is not an 'environmentally-friendly car' a misnomer? Is not the prior decision whether to buy a car or not the more fundamental issue? As Sandy Irvine argues:

> A truly green consumer would be asking first and foremost 'do I really need all these things?' It would involve a change to thinking in terms of what is the minimum necessary to satisfy essential human needs, rather than novelty, fashion, status and all the other hooks of materialism.
>
> (Irvine, in Dobson, 1991, p. 224)

Green consumerism does not fully attend to the demands of sustainable development. It is no more than a first step and if seen as more, as a panacea, there is a real danger of complacency – all that being green would entail is shopping more wisely and recycling waste paper. This is not to disparage the efforts of dedicated green businesses, it is simply to argue that sustainability requires a reconsideration of the role of private companies and the market.

Third-force/social economy organisations

> Around the country, in many of Britain's most deprived urban neighbourhoods, in its rural areas, and even in its more affluent suburbs, tens of thousands of voluntary, community-based organisations enable local people to improve the conditions of their localities and take some control over their own lives. . . . [T]hey come in a variety of forms and meet many different kinds of needs, identified by local people. They are already creating jobs, work and incomes. But their activities are barely recognised by mainstream political debate.
>
> (Real World Coalition, 1996, pp. 96–7)

There is a variety of organisations and activities, particularly at a local level, that do not fit comfortably into the standard category of cause/interest pressure group. Neither can this community-based activity be understood purely in terms of public-sector policy and funding or private investment and entrepreneurial venture. Third-force organisations – also known as social economy organisations – have sprung up in fields as diverse as health, housing and homelessness, education, and the arts; for example, drug projects, housing cooperatives, literacy schemes and community carnivals and theatre. Specifically environmental TFOs have also emerged in many communities. These range from local wildlife conservation projects and recycling initiatives, through to local exchange trading systems (LETSs) and 'veg boxes' which link residents with local organic farms (Young, 1996, 1997).

Why have TFOs emerged? In fact, such community-based enterprise has always existed, operating in the space between the public and the private. However, in the last decade there clearly has been increased participation and activity in this sector as the potential of TFOs has been recognised. Inaction on the part of government and industry has led to community action filling the vacuum. This inaction can be traced to a number of sources: lack of will and indifference; lack of resources because of tight public expenditure or the absence of profit-making potential; or a principled belief that such initiatives should be relatively autonomous, self-organised community developments. The majority of projects and initiatives are not completely independent: funding and expertise are frequently sought from public and private institutions. The difference is that TFOs are taking responsibility and developing the activities themselves. Many conservation and environmental improvement initiatives fit this pattern, as do wider enterprises such as housing cooperatives and health projects. But, as the Real World Coalition recognises: 'Most of them suffer from a severe lack of resources. Given greater support, there is enormous scope for their expansion' (Real World Coalition, 1996, p. 97).

But some TFOs retain almost complete independence: LETS is an excellent example. LETS operates independently of the existing economy, with members bartering skills, resources, time and goods among themselves, using their own currency or credit notes. A coordinator logs the interactions, credits and deficits. No conventional money changes hands: when an individual does some work for another, this is credited to the individual's account by the LETS community. The person for whom the work was done then has a general obligation to repay the community; no individuals are ever directly in debt to each other. For this reason, LETS appears particularly attractive to economically-deprived sections of the community and has been seen as a potential solution to 'social exclusion, poverty and inability to work' (C. Williams, 1995, p. 4; see also Fitzpatrick and Caldwell, 2001). From its inception in Vancouver in the early 1980s, LETS has gained increasing popularity in many countries, including the UK, Australia, Canada, New Zealand and France. There are over 350 LETSs in the UK involving around 30,000 people (Walker and Goldsmith, 2001, p. 265). In 1995 it was estimated that UK LETSs were trading the equivalent of at least £1.5 million.

For green activists LETS offers a practical example of an alternative to the logic of capitalist markets and the individualism they engender. Work is reconceptualised in terms of community activity. A utopian ideal drives these developments and in many ways LETS can be seen as a direct challenge to existing market relations.[21]

Green communes and DIY culture

Central to the green critique is a recognition that the creation of a green society requires not only opposition to prevailing patterns of consumption and political values, but also the generation of alternatives: alternative technologies, democratic institutions, forms of community, social relations, and conceptions of work. Rather than the established actions of pressure groups or the weak environmentalism of green consumerism, a more fundamental way to counter modern capitalist society is to opt out altogether, to form new communities and counter-cultures with like-minded people. There has always been a number of environmental activists who believe that the only real way forward is to found green communes: actually existing utopias (Pepper, 1991; Sargisson, 2001). In many ways the more recent DIY culture can be seen as a further expression of this impulse (McKay, 1998; Brass and Koziell, 1997; Jordan and Lent, 1999). Environmentally-sensitive forms of social, political and economic organisation should be small-scale, self-reliant (or even self-sufficient) and autonomous. By comparison with existing societies, these communities would necessarily be frugal, although the face-to-face, direct forms of democratic self-governance that their proponents argue ought to be established would allow space for new forms of cultural creativity and expression.[22]

Many experiments in alternative communities can best be understood in terms of the survivalist views characteristic of the early 1970s, as a response to the perceived imminence of ecological collapse. These communities saw themselves as separate from the doomed conventional system. In contrast, other green communes have been established as exemplars: demonstrations and visions of alternative possibilities. Perhaps the leading visionary of this position is Rudolf Bahro. Disillusioned with conventional party politics, Bahro argued that 'a new Benedictine order' should be founded to act as a spiritual beacon, a green utopian reality for us to aspire to (Bahro, 1986, pp. 86–91). To a certain extent, a number of existing rural, self-reliant communities and cooperatives could be understood in this way; perhaps the most well known and well documented being the Centre for Alternative Technology (CAT) at Machynlleth, Wales. However, green communes have frequently failed to sustain their initial utopian ideals. Many have had serious internal problems. Living within small communities can have drawbacks, particularly for those premised on the imminence of eco-collapse. For communes established as exemplars other difficulties have emerged, most prominently the tendency to be reabsorbed within the very society in opposition to which they had previously defined themselves. This is the fate that has befallen CAT. Over the last two decades, as environmental awareness in the general population increased, the attraction of alternative technologies grew. Rather than a green commune separate from the rest of society, CAT has become a successful visitor and educational centre. This is a potential paradox for such ventures: success in attracting attention tends to diminish the very conditions vital to their own existence as a separate entity. But the idealism of many activists means that the idea of establishing green communes still appeals and their place in the wider environmental movement is assured.

DIY culture is a relatively recent phenomenon. In the UK it emerged from a coming together of like-minded groups in opposition to the Criminal Justice Bill (later the CJA), its roots including the squatting, direct action and the underground dance cultures. Organisations such as the Freedom Network, initially formed in opposition to the CJA, developed broader agendas as those involved recognised common ground. *SchNEWS*, the weekly publication of Justice? in Brighton (one of the most prominent groups in the DIY network), illustrates the wide range of issues extending beyond simple opposition to a single act of parliament.[23] As the compilers of *The Book*, a directory of DIY organisations, argue:

> This Book is symptomatic of a new awareness, a force of empathy, wit, vision and community spirit which has given a fresh sense of empowerment and freedom. The scapegoated have become united like never before. The old channels of protest and party politics are dead. DIY culture is creating homes and entertainment by the people for the people captured in the philosophy of Deeds not Words.
>
> (Anon., 1995, pp. 1–2)

For activists such as George Monbiot, the development from single-issue opposition to the active promotion of green alternatives is essential:

> The direct action movement is the most potent popular force of the 1990s, yet it has one fundamental and potentially fatal weakness. So far it has been largely responsive. The Government proposes a road or a bill and the movement opposes it: the Department of Transport and the Home Office have set the direct action agenda. Political change does not take place until the opponents of government fight for what they're for, rather than simply for what they're against.
>
> (Quoted in McKay, 1996, p. 127)

In contrast to green communes, DIY activities tend to be urban-based, dealing head-on with the adverse effects of contemporary society. Derelict land and empty properties have been squatted and made available to activists, artists and the community at large. In many cases those involved are committed to supporting people whom society has left behind or forgotten: the homeless, the elderly and the mentally ill. The seeds of new social relations are being sown within some of the most deprived urban areas. Further, through these initiatives, environmentalists have been forced to address issues extending beyond conventional environmental boundaries and to make alliances with other types of activist. This wider recognition is important as it moves green politics beyond single issues; but at present the idealism of many activists is an inadequate preparation for some of the harsh realities that they now face. This was particularly evident in the case of the 'Pure Genius' eco-village in Wandsworth. In May 1996, supporters of This Land is Ours, an organisation committed to challenging established property rights, occupied derelict land owned by Guinness. Over the preceding few years Guinness had been trying to get planning permission to build a supermarket and luxury flats on the site. Taking advantage of the local community's opposition to these plans, the campaigners aimed to build a model sustainable village, a development that would respond to community needs rather than private profit. Five months later Guinness won a court order to remove the protesters and the dwellings and reclaimed land were flattened. In many ways the establishment of this new community had been successful as it had forced the political issue of local land rights and community needs into the media and public domain. But beneath the veneer of success other tensions were becoming increasingly apparent. 'Pure Genius' was attractive not only to environmentalists, but also to many of those who had nowhere else to go.

[U]topians and protesters had no training in dealing with the mentally disturbed, beyond common sense and sympathy (of which there was a lot). 'How do you deal with people on heroin? People with guns and knives? We have no support network. Some of these people need hospital care, many need professional help,' said Sarah last month. 'We are having to spend more and more time looking after people. That's fine but you can't expect us to build a community in these circumstances.'

(Vidal, 1996, p. 3)

Pure Genius highlights the attempts of activists to go beyond the single-issue politics of groups such as Greenpeace that often neglect the complex interconnectedness of social, political, economic and environmental issues. But the fact that leading green campaigners placed the blame for the 'failure' of the occupation on the 'mentally disturbed', who like other communities of interest should 'clear off and find their own spatial and political commons', raises uncomfortable questions about the inclusiveness of green and other radical politics (Beresford, 1999, pp. 40–1).[24] Environmental concerns are not clear-cut and cannot always be simplified for media and public consumption. DIY activists are beginning to recognise that the separation of environmental from pressing social, economic and cultural concerns is a nonsense: the construction of effective coalitions across lines of difference is key to the future development of green politics.

Conclusion

This chapter has not sought to provide a compendium of environmental activity; its aim has been to show the range and forms that such activity can take. Although various terms and categories have been introduced to try to make sense of the diversity of groups, their ideals and approaches, it needs to be recognised that in practice many transcend these boundaries. However, the categories act as useful pointers enabling us to appreciate the tactics and choices open to the green movement.

What is striking is the range of tactics and forms of action deployed. This should not surprise us, given the diversity of ethical and political commitments represented within green thinking. This takes us back to the identity of the green movement as a 'movement'. Its diversity allows the possibility of action in many different forms and at many different levels – from inside the legislature to grassroots community development, all political spaces are exploited. Although networks and coalitions are increasingly being formed, action is not necessarily concerted. Many groups which are in principle campaigning against similar policies and developments would not wish to be seen to be in alliance. For example, the gaze of the National Trust and Earth First! may at times converge on similar issues, but the likelihood of, and desire for, a strong association is non-existent. In many cases the tactics and forms of action favoured by different green organisations are scorned by others in the same 'movement'. Despite this mutual suspicion the different emphases may actually be positively reinforcing. As Dave Foreman, a prominent American Earth Firster!, argues:

[T]he actions of monkeywrenchers invariably enhance the status and bargaining position of more 'reasonable' opponents. Industry considers main-line environmentalists to be radical until they get a taste of real radical activism. Suddenly the soft-sell of the Sierra Club and other white-shirt-and-tie eco-bureaucrats becomes much more attractive and worthy of serious negotiation. These moderate environmentalists must condemn monkeywrenching so as to preserve their own image, but they should take full advantage of the credence it lends to their approach.

(Foreman, in Dobson, 1991, p. 229)

To answer our original question, then, with another: does the environmental movement need to be homogeneous? Diversity, which appeared at first to be a weakness, may turn out to be the green movement's strength.

Case study: Twyford Down and the formation of an anti-roads movement

In the UK, direct action against road construction projects seems commonplace. The images of protesters physically placing their bodies between machinery and environment, being 'cherry-picked' from trees and aerial walkways and taking their protests underground are all familiar. It is perhaps surprising then to consider that such actions are a comparatively recent phenomenon, beginning in late 1992 at Twyford Down in Hampshire. The story of the Twyford Down campaign reaches back over two decades – the initial public inquiry for the extension of the M3 occurring as early as 1971. It is worth dwelling on some of the aspects of the movement as it was without doubt one of the major influences in the evolution of a national anti-roads campaign and it is an exemplary case of how environmental groups can be 'mobilised out' of the political process, a point that we shall return to in Chapter 4. The events surrounding Twyford Down have become part of campaigning 'folk lore'.

M3 public inquiries

The first public inquiry in 1971 endorsed the extension of the M3 near Winchester through the water meadows along the line of the Itchen Valley. Between then and the follow-up inquiry in 1976, local people and organisations came together under the banner of the M3 Joint Action Group. Support was received from powerful landowners such as Winchester College. With the help of John Tyme, a lecturer at Sheffield Polytechnic who had worked with local campaigners to force the abandonment of the M16 inquiry in the Aire Valley, the M3 inquiry was disrupted and the Inspector judged that a full-scale examination of the scheme was necessary. Not only John Tyme, but others including the Headmaster of Winchester College, were ejected from the proceedings at various points in what was perhaps the first direct action associated with this scheme (Tyme, 1978, pp. 31–42).[25] In 1980, the Inspector ruled against the M3 extension only for the Department of Transport (DOT) to offer a new route which would cut through Twyford Down. At the 1985 public inquiry, there was a lack of real opposition since Winchester College itself had offered to sell the Down to the DOT and both Hampshire and Winchester Councils were in broad support of the project. However, once local people realised the extent of the damage to the landscape that would be caused by the new route, the Joint Action Group was reformed. After concerted pressure, during which time Winchester District Council was persuaded to come out against the scheme, the inquiry was re-opened in 1987. But, this time the inquiry was lost, with the Inspector deciding in favour of the cutting. The proposal of a tunnel which had widespread local support was rejected. In response, members of the newly formed Twyford Down Association (TDA) challenged the DOT in the High Court for failing to implement the EC's environmental impact assessment directive and when that failed they appealed to the European Commission itself.[26] While the European appeal was under way, though, construction work began. TDA kept the question of Twyford Down in the political and media spotlight and in the 1992 general election the local MP, the then Roads Minister Christopher Chope, lost his seat. However, the Conservative government won the election with the promise of extending the roads programme and were able to affect the outcome of the EC review during the Maastricht negotiations. With construction under way, local activists were faced with the option of resigning themselves to defeat or continuing the campaign in a new form now that all the legal and political institutional processes had been exhausted. For many, the battle was far from over.

The biased nature of the public inquiry process

Before moving on to discuss the wave of direct action that followed, it is worth reflecting on some of the aspects of the public inquiry process which meant that the odds were generally stacked against the anti-road protesters. A public inquiry into a road proposal is the first official opportunity that people in the UK have to deliberate on questions of transport. Generally a decision has already been made as to the preferred route of the proposed road; the DOT has already decided that a road needs to be built.[27] As early as 1936, the Trunk Road Act gave the Ministry the sole authority for initiating and deciding upon trunk road schemes. The Highways Act 1980 continued in the same vein: 'by giving the Ministry a direct executive responsibility for this one aspect of transport only, it inevitably resulted in an organisational commitment to inter-urban road building at the expense of an overall and balanced view of transport needs' (Kay, 1992, p. 18). To further unbalance proceedings and discredit the 'participation' process, inspectors are appointed by the DOT. Thus the DOT is the sole authority for initiating and deciding on trunk road schemes – 'judge and jury of its own case' (ibid., p. 17). It is perhaps informative to note that over a five-year period, only five out of 146 public inquiries have gone against the DOT (Rowell, 1996, p. 332). Because the issues that are open to debate are so narrowly defined, public inquiries provide only a 'veneer of participation'. Objectors are not allowed to challenge either government policy or to challenge the use of particular decision-making procedures, in this case an elaborate form of cost–benefit analysis (CBA) known as COBA. Inspectors have always ruled such challenges illegitimate. 'They [objectors] have been told that it is government policy to rely on both COBA and forecasts in making decisions about new roads, and that scrutiny of government policy is the business of Parliament' (Adams, 1995, p. 1). There is much to be said about the use of CBA in decision making and it will be a central theme of Chapter 6. For now a few comments which should expose the dubious assumptions upon which decisions are based will suffice. Such assumptions cannot be challenged at any point in the public inquiry process.[28]

Calculations of time savings are the dominant benefits of any trunk road proposal and represent the foremost quantification of the DOT's policy objective 'to assist economic growth

continued

by reducing transport costs' (DOT, 1989, p. 4; 1992, p. 20). 'Typically, time savings account for 85 per cent to 90 per cent of the gross benefits of a trunk road scheme' (DOT, 1991, p. 5). Using economic valuation techniques, the DOT assigns a figure of 153.2 pence per hour per person for non-working time journeys (at 1985 prices) (DOT, 1987, p. 5). There are at least two areas of concern here. First, the time-saving valuation within COBA has no regard for those individuals who have strong environmental commitments and may have been prepared to accept a longer journey time in the knowledge that a sensitive landscape such as Twyford Down was being conserved. As Stephen Atkins writes, 'the likelihood is that many people find that their short-term travel behaviour choices are being used to justify decisions that they would not support "politically"' (Atkins, 1990, p. 8). Simply because they use a stretch of road, it is assumed that all drivers will prefer a quicker journey. Second, there is a problem of aggregating small increments of time such that benefits of £100 million are apparently achieved. It is assumed in economic analysis that an individual accords the same value to a large time period as to the equivalent aggregation of small time periods. If, for instance, an individual saves one minute every day using a proposed road scheme in non-working time, it is assumed that the aggregation of those small daily savings is valued in the same way as a single period of six hours. Outside the limited assumptions of neo-classical economic theory, it is questionable as to whether such small time savings are even noticed and even if they are, whether they are of any productive use compared to the longer time span to which they are apparently equivalent. In 1990, the House of Commons Transport Select Committee argued: 'The assumption that small increments of time have real economic value when aggregated over a large number of vehicles is unsubstantiated' (quoted in Bray, 1995, p. 9). When the aggregation of time savings is commonly in the range of £100 million and is the principal quantified benefit of a scheme, the cogency of such assumptions needs to be challenged.

One of the major costs of road construction is the price of land. However, it can be shown that the incorporation of market prices for certain types of land may result in an acute underestimate. Green belt land, Sites of Special Scientific Interest (SSSIs) and Areas of Outstanding Natural Beauty (AONBs) are protected areas, ones which have severe development restrictions attached to them. As the DOE stated in *This Common Inheritance* (at the same time as the government was promoting the roads-building programme), there is an objective 'to protect the best of urban and rural environments so that we can pass on to our children what we value most about our own heritage' (DOE, 1990, p. 80). Surely Twyford Down, part of an AONB, an SSSI and home to two scheduled ancient monuments, was such an environment? However, where a decision is made to propose a road scheme through such environments,[29] the value of the land is then incorporated. But one of the primary features of such areas is that they have planning restrictions attached to them, and so the market price is extremely low; a price that clearly misrepresents the important scientific, aesthetic or amenity value of the land in question. Not only is an area of local or national importance to be lost, but its value is taken to be *less* than ordinary agricultural land. The DOT's own standing advisory committee has recognised this paradox: 'the cost of acquired land . . . may be a serious underestimate of its social value if the land is subject to severe restrictions on development' (SACTRA, 1992, p. 96).

Finally, it is frequently argued that when COBA produces apparent benefits to the economy of millions of pounds, the environmental and social impact of schemes tends to be overlooked. As Atkins points out: 'Recent public policy has been dominated by concerns over "value for money" in public expenditure. In this context a measure that purports to show cash returns from public investment has a greater influence on decision-makers' (Atkins, 1990, p. 7). The expertise of economists is not open to challenge and as such the idea of public participation is degraded. As Ray Kemp contends, 'the professionalisation of planning with the introduction of technical terms and standards, bureaucratic and legal devices, may be seen to have led to merely token public involvement in many important planning matters' (Kemp, 1985, pp. 183–4). The public inquiries that were held on the M3 extension are prime examples of this tokenism.

Direct action on the Down

Following the exhaustion of political and legal procedures and standard forms of protest, the nature of the campaigning began to change. In order to raise public and media awareness, demonstrations took place on the site itself. Actions that stopped short of full confrontation were coordinated by TDA and FOE. The transition from one form of protest to another is described by Barbara Bryant:

> As far as the Twyford Down campaign itself is concerned, the transition from conventional campaigning tactics (consciousness-raising, legal representation at public inquiries, political lobbying, high-profile events) to non-violent direct action was not an easy one. The rationale behind such a transition was overwhelmingly clear: in February 1992, TDA activists and Friends of the Earth (who had been working together for more than a year) argued that the government was itself breaking the law in proceeding with preliminary works *before* the EC has ruled on the complaint before it concerning breaches of the Environmental Impact Assessment Directive. This unlawful behaviour entirely justified the use of responsible, non-violent direct action to slow down or even prevent the work continuing. A railway bridge due for demolition was therefore occupied on 14 February by Friends of the Earth.
>
> (Bryant, 1996, pp. 300–1)

FOE and TDA continued such actions for a couple of weeks, successfully halting construction before an injunction was served against FOE. At this point

> lawyers advised them that to break it would risk contempt of court proceedings, which would result in fines of up to a quarter of a million pounds. This would bankrupt the organisation. FOE left the site, leaving a breach that was soon filled by the direct action protesters.
>
> (Lamb, 1996, p. 6)

The changing nature of the campaign continued with local people and green activists taking more confrontational but non-violent direct action (NVDA) against the construction. It is interesting that many of the direct action activists felt that FOE had let them down by pulling out. This reflects the tension between the newly-emerging direct-action (dis)organisations and the more established and well-resourced pressure groups discussed earlier in the chapter. As well as the financial and legal problems that they could have faced, the new activists caused a problem for FOE 'who were anxious about being associated with mass illegal protests over which they had no control' (Doherty, 1997, p. 149).

continued

In late 1992, members of a newly-formed local group, Friends of Twyford Down, as well as members of Earth First! and the Dongas Tribe who had camped on the Down, began 'bulldozer-diving' and 'crane-sitting', squatting the proposed route on St Catherine's Hill. What followed was to set the scene for future confrontations around the country. One incident in particular made protesters realise the physical power that could potentially be unleashed upon them. 'Yellow Wednesday', 9 December 1992, saw private security guards (Group 4) hired for the first time to ensure that the site was cleared for the contractors. The violence meted out to the protesters, with the police looking on, shocked those present and those who viewed the footage on national television.

Undeterred, the Twyford campaign continued throughout 1993, slowing down the construction process and in the end adding some £3.5 million in security costs, including the hiring of private detectives by the DOT to gather information on the protesters.[30] The year 1993 also saw seven activists jailed for breaking court injunctions and returning to the site. Further, the DOT attempted (unsuccessfully) to recoup the £3.5 million by suing a group of 67 protesters indiscriminately picked from a particular action that involved thousands. Although the road was completed in late 1994, Twyford radicalised groups all over Britain where previously they might have given up the fight after the public inquiry had given the go-ahead. As Jonathan Porritt writes:

> The trauma of Twyford Down galvanised thousands of people into a host of actions that might otherwise never have taken place. It was so horrific, so visible, so palpable. Even now, there is no amount of cosmetic landscaping and tree planting that can conceal the sheer scale of the wound inflicted on the countryside. It screams out at you, and will go on screaming out to all with ears to hear and eyes to see. . . . Ruling politicians and their self-serving advisers consistently underestimate the power of symbolism in politics. Long after the Twyford Down campaign was lost, and the Dongas had been brutally routed, Twyford Down continues to work its magic as a symbol of opposition to undemocratic, ecologically wanton road-building, wherever it takes place.
>
> (Quoted in Bryant, 1996, p. 299)

The emergence of a national anti-roads movement

It is important to remember that before the 1990s there was no national anti-roads campaign coordinating the independent actions of local groups fighting specific schemes. Organisations such as Transport 2000 and FOE had campaigned at policy level against the road-building programme and in support of an integrated transport policy; but at the level of individual schemes there was no real movement. This began to change in the 1990s. After having successfully coordinated local opposition throughout London against the London Road Assessment Studies in the late 1980s, ALARM, the umbrella body for over 150 London-based groups, went national. *Roads for Prosperity*, published by the DOT in 1989, promised a £23 billion national roads programme. Alarm UK's response strategy was to set up a network supporting local groups fighting proposed road schemes before, during, or after a public inquiry. Alarm UK became 'a central, umbrella organisation which supplies local groups with information on transport, environmental and campaigning matters, which staged occasional nationwide stunts (including a "Stop That Road Week") and which held conferences where the groups could meet' (Alarm

UK, 1996, pp. 13–14). By 1995, about 300 local groups opposing particular road schemes were members of Alarm UK.

With their experience of direct action from Twyford Down and the realisation that road schemes were under construction all over the UK, a small group of Friends of Twyford Down members set up Road Alert!, in many ways a sister organisation to Alarm UK. As Rebecca Lush, one of the protesters who went to jail for their actions, explains: 'Many people have been inspired by the protests that have sprung up since Twyford and have wanted to defend their land too. Road Alert! exists to help these people by passing on protest skills and helping others to get involved' (Alarm UK, 1996, p. 21).

Without doubt the actions at Twyford Down acted as a spur to non-violent direct actions at, for example, Pollock, Bath, Leytonstone, Stanworth Woods near Blackburn, and most recently at the Newbury and Exeter–Honiton bypasses and the proposed new runway at Manchester Airport. The courage and commitment of activists is beyond doubt and we are witnessing a new form of flexible, non-hierarchical and spontaneous protest. Certainly the techniques and forms of organisation utilised by activists are becoming more and more sophisticated.[31] Direct action offers the possibility of new forms of political action in the face of political institutions that stifle meaningful public participation and that are unresponsive to environmental values. Even with the introduction of draconian legislation such as parts of the Criminal Justice and Public Order Act, the anti-roads movement still embodies the spirit of opposition and a creative and empowering energy. As Tim Allman, another founder of Road Alert!, contends:

There were a lot of people who didn't like what was happening around them, but who didn't see what they could do that would make much difference. Direct action changed all that. It empowers people. It makes them feel that they are individuals, can make things happen.

(Alarm UK, 1996 , p. 21)

Thus the Twyford Down campaign, while unsuccessful in its immediate goal of halting the destruction of the Down, was successful as a spur to further direct action across the country (Seel *et al.*, 2000; Doherty, 1999). And the direct action that followed has become more sophisticated and generated increasingly widespread public support. Twyford Down showed both that the public inquiry system is seriously flawed and that the standard legal and political channels of influence are weak and unresponsive. Furthermore, concern is no longer limited to particular local schemes but to the roads-building programme as such and the way in which public discussion of road schemes is limited and circumscribed by an inadequate inquiry system. As Chris Gillham, a veteran of the Twyford Down campaign and an individual far removed from the media image of the dreadlocked, unemployed youth, remarks:

I came from a background of concerned but respectable and restrained involvement. I spent years in formal committees of preservation groups, not achieving very much. Here is the justification, whenever it is needed, for non-violent direct action. The system allowed us to spend decades in argument, and huge sums of money, making an intellectually unshakeable case, only for the system to brush it all aside. When you hear the brazen words 'democratic process' and 'rule of law', reply quietly with 'Twyford Down'.

(Road Alert!, 1996, case history no.3)

Suggestions for further reading

For a cross-national comparison of green parties in the 1990s, see Dick Richardson and Christopher Rootes's edited collection *The Green Challenge. Green Parties in National Governments*, edited by Ferdinand Müller-Rommel and Thomas Poguntke (originally a special issue of *Environmental Politics*), provides an up-to-date analysis. The literature on the changing nature of environmental pressure groups and direct action is developing rapidly. Of particular interest is Christopher Rootes's edited collection *Environmental Movements: Local, National and Global* (also originally a special issue of *Environmental Politics*). Peter Rawcliffe *Environmental Pressure Groups in Transition* is a well-researched analysis of the changes within the UK environmental movement. On the rise in direct action, Ben Seel, Matthew Paterson and Brian Doherty's edited collection *Direct Action in British Environmentalism* and Derek Wall's study of Earth First! in the UK *Earth First! and the Anti-Roads Movement* are both highly accessible and informative. The journal *Environmental Politics* frequently contains articles on all aspects of the environmental movement. The magazines *The Ecologist* and *Red Pepper* provide up-to-date information on current green campaigns.

Useful websites

GreenNet: www.gn.apc.org
Greenpeace: www.greenpeace.org.uk
Friends of the Earth: www.foe.co.uk
WWF: www.wwf.org.uk
Earth First!: www.eco-action.org/efau/aulast
Reclaim the Streets: www.gn.apc.org/rts
Undercurrents: www.undercurrents.org
SchNEWS: www.schnews.org.uk
Green Party of England and Wales: www.greenparty.org.uk
The Ecologist: www.theecologist.org
New Economics Foundation: www.neweconomics.org
Sierra Club: www.sierraclub.org

Notes

1   This equates to approximately 8 per cent of the total population. However, it is important to remember that many people will belong to more than one organisation, so these figures may be an over-estimate caused by double counting. Further, more decentralised, direct-action orientated organisations such as Earth First! and Reclaim the Streets do not have 'membership' in the same sense as more orthodox groups.

2   Figures drawn from McCormick (1991), Office for National Statistics (1992–2001) and directly from the organisations concerned.

3   Within the mainstream political parties in the UK there are activists attempting to green the parties from the inside. The two most successful internal groupings have been the Socialist Environment and Resources Association (SERA) within the Labour Party and the Liberal Ecology Group.

4   Witness, for example, the length of time it took for the British government to admit that emissions in the UK were responsible for the acidification of lakes in Scandinavia; and the intransigence of the US government in climate change negotiations which would result in binding reductions in carbon dioxide emissions.

5   After unification in 1993 die Grünen merged with the East German citizens' movement and was renamed Bundis 90/die Grünen. In this chapter we will simply refer to die Grünen.

6   The Scottish Green Party is an independent organisation.

7   In fact, the Green Party could be said to have had 'half' an MP: Cynog Dafis was elected to the House of Commons in 1992 on a joint Plaid Cymru/Green Party platform.

8   The wave of public enthusiasm for environmental issues that resulted in this level of support for the Green Party was the background to Mrs Thatcher's Royal Society speech.

9   Wiesenthal argues that the electoral success of die Grünen is not only related to the political opportunity structure, but also to Germany's post-war political *culture*. There was a lack of socialist opposition that represented minority interests such as women's rights and ecological concerns (especially nuclear risks). The citizens' initiatives in the late 1970s gradually transformed into the more coordinated die Grünen (Wiesenthal, 1998, pp. 163–8).

10   For a compelling insider's account of the divisions in the Green Party since its inception, see Wall (1994).

11   Most greens were not against unification per se, rather they argued that rapid reunification would be a process of almost cultural imperialism: East Germany would be swamped by the culture of the West with little or no recognition that the West might have something to learn from their Eastern counterparts.

12   Die Grünen achieved 6.7 per cent of the vote overall. However, 7.3 per cent was achieved in the West; whereas the 4.1 per cent in the East meant that there is no political representation from the former East Germany. Die Grünen had previously been in red–green coalitions in a number of regional governments.

13   The structure of Whitehall has changed considerably over the past few years. The infamous Ministry of Agriculture, Fisheries and Food (MAFF) became part of the Department of the Environment, Food and Rural Affairs (DEFRA) after the election in 2001. The Department of Transport (DOT) was merged into the Department of the Environment, Transport and the Regions (DETR) in 1997, which then became the Department of Transport, Local Government and the Regions (DTLR) in 2001 and then was reorganised again into the Department for Transport (DfT) a year later. We will reflect on the implications of these changes in Chapter 9.

14   The Third Battle of Newbury was the group protesting against the construction of the Newbury by-pass.

15   The strategy was published as the UK's response to Agenda 21 signed at the Rio Earth Summit. See Chapter 9.

16   These trends will be addressed in more detail in Part III of this book.

17   For more on the Brent Spar episode see Dicken and McCulloch (1996), Bennie (1998) and Jordan (2001).

18   The Prevention of Terrorism Act 2000 gives the Home Secretary new and wide-ranging powers of proscription which could potentially further affect radical direct action organisations.

19   In the mid-1990s in a Gallup poll survey in the UK, 68 per cent of respondents were prepared to entertain the idea of civil disobedience in defence of a cause they believed in (Bryant, 1996, p. 302).

20   Anti-roads activism thus became an interesting combination of NIMBY (not in my backyard) and NIABY (not in anyone's backyard). Not surprisingly critics who argued that protesters did not oppose developments in principle, but merely object to their

proposed location (their backyard), now criticised the eco-activists for being outsiders who did not understand the needs of the community!

21 For an accessible guide to using and running LETS, see Peter Lang's *LETS Work* (1994). The New Economics Foundation's newspaper *News from the New Economy* has regular articles on LETS and similar community-based initiatives. A comparable scheme, Time Dollars, has emerged in the last decade in the USA (see Walker and Goldsmith, 2001).

22 As was argued in Chapter 2, however, certain advocates of green communes, particularly bioregionalists, are not at all concerned with the establishment of democratic forms of self-governance; living within ecological limits takes precedence over political arrangements. In practice, though, existing communes have largely been founded on a principle of democratic renewal.

23 Justice? has been compiling its weekly newssheets into annual publications since 1996. Recently it has published these in collaboration with *SQUALL*, the magazine for 'sorted itinerants', under the title *SchQUALL*.

24 Beresford also notes that at its launch in 1996, the broad-based Real World Coalition (discussed earlier in the chapter) included no groups representing people with disabilities or mental health service users.

25 During the 1970s, John Tyme became a well-known figure at public inquiries, both presenting the case against road building and inciting disruptions. His book *Motorways Versus Democracy* (1978) is a detailed account of his fights against road proposals and the lack of accountability of the then Department of Transport.

26 Environmental impact assessment (EIA) is discussed in Chapter 6.

27 Although the DOT was merged into the Department of the Environment, Transport and the Regions (DETR) in 1997, it is unclear whether this had any meaningful effect on decision-making processes. In 2001, environment and transport were again separated with the formation of the Department of Transport, Local Government and the Regions (DTLR). For the sake of clarity we shall continue to refer simply to the DOT. See Chapter 9 for further discussion of the changing nature of the UK administration.

28 Objectors do have the right to challenge the accuracy of the actual figures within the COBA calculation. However, they cannot challenge the use of COBA itself. Occasionally, inquiries have been won or at least abandoned on the basis of inaccurate figures.

29 English Nature estimated that the DOT's 1989 *Roads for Prosperity* road programme threatened 161 Sites of Special Scientific Interest (SSSIs), and English Heritage calculated that over 800 important archaeological sites could be affected.

30 Private security firms, such as Brays in Southampton, have become established actors in the present political climate, collecting information on direct-action activists for the DOT and the contractors.

31 See *Road Raging: Top Tips for Wrecking Roadbuilding* produced by Road Alert! for a description of the techniques and organisations involved in direct action.

Part II

THE BACKGROUND TO ENVIRONMENTAL POLICY

Chapter 4

Rationality and power in environmental policy making

It is not terribly difficult to know what needs to be done, though it is of
course immensely difficult to get the relevant actors (government and
other) to do it.

(Barry, B., 1999, p. 116)

Why is it so difficult to make rational environmental policy? Even where we know
what needs to be done from an environmental perspective, emerging environmental
policy is often too weak to fulfil its ambition. This chapter offers a series of
explanations as to why attempts to integrate environmental considerations within
policy making is often frustrated. To begin with it is important to remember that
difficulties for policy makers are created by the nature of environmental problems
themselves. As we discussed in the Introduction to this book, environmental
problems are often complex, interrelated and have effects at different scales – local
to global. When responding to environmental problems we are typically faced with
a high degree of uncertainty about both the cause of the problems and the impact
of possible policy options. Undesirable unanticipated consequences are always
a possibility. Interventions into the environment may also be irreversible: for example,
the extinction of species cannot be reversed. Finally, many environmental problems
involve a high degree of risk. When risk is combined with irreversibility and
uncertainty, we begin to understand why developing policy responses can be a rather
difficult process.

But the nature of environmental problems is only part of the reason why it is
difficult for rational environmental policy to emerge. What this chapter highlights
is the way in which the characteristics of environmental problems combine with
problems in the policy-making process itself. Our investigation will begin with an
analysis of the nature of collective action problems. This is a body of issues arising
from the fact that the solution to environmental problems is necessarily a collective
one. Hardin's theory of the tragedy of the commons, which we discussed briefly in
the Introduction, will be analysed in more depth along with the problems associated
with voting cycles. There are a number of obstacles standing in the way of achieving
collective action and it is important to understand their characteristics prior to
considering the forms that any solution might take. The case study at the end of the
chapter further develops the analysis of collective action problems, drawing on the
example of pollution control in US cities. Second, we will examine the idea of the
issue–attention cycle. Environmental problems may exist, but it does not follow that
there is any political interest in these problems nor any desire to solve them: all
political issues are subject to the fortunes of public and political fashion and interest.
Public interest in environmental issues fluctuates. Third, we will consider the idea
of bounded rationality and how it affects the policy process. We need to understand
that the manner in which we conceptualise environmental problems is constrained
both by individual and organisational knowledge and behaviour. Fourth, we will
consider how the exercise of power further compromises the rationality of the policy
process. Just because a group may have a legitimate grievance or policy proposal
does not mean that it will necessarily be able to affect decisions. Individuals, groups
and organisations differ in their access to the means of making or influencing policies
and decisions. Being right about an issue is not sufficient if there is little or no
opportunity to ensure that one's viewpoint will be heard. An analysis of the concept

of power will help explain why some issues make the political agenda, while others fail to gain a hearing.

These four barriers and constraints to policy making – collective action problems; issue–attention cycles; bounded rationality; and the exercise of power – affect the emergence of environmental policy. These problems can be overcome to a certain extent through changes to the machinery of government, including the application of green policy principles, administrative techniques and tools, structural reorganisations and policy instruments. The emergence of new forms of environmental governance may offer opportunities to 'green' the policy process.

Collective action problems

Even where we recognise that something ought to be done, there still remains the everyday political problem of agreeing on what is to be done and how best to implement the agreed solution. It may be hard or even impossible to get agreement on what course of action should be taken; and it is also very common to find that all those involved want something to happen but that nonetheless nothing happens. Why is this? Very often it is because none of us individually is prepared or able to make something happen. Either we do not want to bear the burden ourselves or we take the view that it cannot be done by just one or two people, but only by a concerted effort. We may conclude that it is not worth trying to do anything unless others are involved. Thus, recognising the existence of an environmental problem and its possible solutions constitutes only the first step towards a satisfactory resolution of the problem.

Global environmental action: the plurality of actors

The practical collective action difficulty can be clearly recognised if we consider just how many actors need to coordinate their activities to solve global environmental problems such as climate change. These include:
- the United Nations
- global economic institutions, e.g. the World Trade Organisation
- the European Union
- national governments
- sub-national governments
- government agencies, including environmental-protection agencies
- private corporations
- voluntary associations and pressure groups
- households
- individuals

A common underlying feature of the political difficulty in achieving a workable solution is the problem of collective action. In many cases, for example over-fishing in the world's oceans, we can see that, although there is a general recognition of the problem, it is still extremely difficult in practice to prevent it. It remains in the interest of individual countries to continue present practices even though they are aware that this will lead to a diminution of fish stocks. This is because they know that if they do not take the fish someone else will. Why, then, should they be the ones to lose out? The same applies to carbon dioxide emissions. Scientific evidence concerning the danger of climate change does not automatically entail that nations or individuals will reduce their own emissions. They might recognise the problem and consider that something should be done, but they are reluctant to contribute to a solution.

Thus, it often seems, paradoxically, that cooperation is least likely where those involved stand to lose most. This is particularly the case at the global level. There is open access to the atmosphere and stratosphere – they are common property, priced at zero, and are therefore likely to be overused. We all get the benefits or the disbenefits; that is, no-one can be excluded from the benefits of clean air or the disbenefits of increased ultraviolet-B radiation. However, we are reluctant to assume the individual cost of ensuring the benefits or avoiding the disbenefits. Public goods of this type can only exist through cooperative action and yet cooperation in such a case is extraordinarily hard to attain and still harder to enforce. Where there is a public good which can be secured only through the cooperation of a vast number of individual actors, there is always an incentive for individuals to 'free-ride' – to benefit from the public good without contributing towards it. It might be argued that so long as the public goods concerned *are* provided then it does not matter whether or not there is free-riding – after all, the future of the planet is at stake. But the problem lies in the fact that where free-riding is possible, the provision of the public good itself may be endangered. Our concern here is not so much the moral one of the ethics of free-riding, but the practical one of securing sufficient agreement to act where the threat of free-riding undermines the conditions for securing agreement (Pearce *et al.*, 1989, p. 12).

Collective action problems arise where an individual's contribution to a problem or its solution is at most a tiny part of a much larger whole, and where their actions one way or another seem to make little or no difference. So every car driver blames every other car driver for the traffic jam in which they sit on the way to work; and as they sit immobile in their cars reflecting on the fact that the carbon dioxide they are emitting from their exhausts contributes to climate change, each driver sees little point in reducing their car use unless everyone else does the same. Everyone is waiting for everyone else to act first, the result being that no one acts at all.

We recognise this as an everyday occurrence: the discipline known as rational choice theory extends the analysis by generalising from the assumption that individuals are self-interested, egoistic, rational, utility maximisers, to the conclusion that achieving voluntary collective action is necessarily fraught with difficulty.[1] People are assumed to be, in general, self-interested; they are assumed to be largely concerned with themselves and their immediate family; they are assumed to be rational in the sense that they can act consistently, given the preferences they happen to have; and they are assumed to be interested in maximising their own welfare rather than in operating according to abstract moral principles. Rationality, then, is defined in terms of the choice of means, not the choice of ends. To be rational is to be able to choose the most effective, most efficient and most economical means to achieving what one wants, whatever that happens to be.[2] We shall investigate two particularly relevant issues within rational choice theory: voting paradoxes and the 'tragedy of the commons'.

Voting paradoxes

Suppose a protest group is trying to decide where and how to campaign but it cannot reach consensus. Whatever decision members make will be binding on all, because they cannot afford to divide their efforts. One or other course of action must be chosen and the tactics agreed. For the sake of argument, let us suppose that everyone in the group is not purely self-interested – they all share the same broad goals and are willing to assume the burden of acting. They will not free-ride on the efforts of others. But the problem of collective action does not fall away. The group still has to make a collective decision based on the individual views or preferences of its members: individual preferences have to be aggregated into a collective choice and this raises the question of which formal procedures they use to make the decision. An obvious answer would seem to be that they make a decision by voting. This appears to be a fairly straightforward thing to do – until we reflect a little further. There are of course a number of well-recognised issues associated with choosing an electoral or voting system, some of which are to do with criteria such as fairness to parties or groups of voters. As we saw in Chapter 3, these issues are important in green politics. For example, the nature of the electoral system has been an influential factor in determining the electoral success of green parties. However, our present concern is the obstacles to securing collective action on environmental issues, and there are other, more technical, aspects of voting theory directly relevant to this issue.

Representative assemblies and committees typically vote to reach decisions, and structures of decision making have evolved which stipulate the way in which votes should be conducted. It might seem intuitively obvious that the only relevant factor determining the outcome of a sequence of votes is the number of votes each proposal attracts, but in fact this is not necessarily so. It is perfectly possible, for example, for circumstances to arise in which there is no overall winner and in which the outcome is entirely dependent on seemingly irrelevant factors such as the order in which the votes are taken. This seems a rather curious possibility which might have significant consequences, so it is worth a look. Let us suppose that in a local council there are three parties, none with overall control, and that two are needed to form a coalition on any issue for it to be adopted as policy. Each party has its own transitive set of preferences: that is, they are in a stable order of priority. Given this we can consider the way in which different outcomes might arise. The issue under consideration is whether to build council houses, private houses or a park on a plot of vacant land.[3] The parties' preferences are summarised in the table below.

Thus, party A prefers council houses to private houses to a park, and because its preferences are transitive, we can infer that it would prefer council houses to a park if given a straight choice between the two. In the table we can see that (in a straight vote between any two alternatives) two parties prefer council houses to private houses; two prefer private houses to a park; and two prefer a park to council houses. Given this, it is clear that there can be no simple question of deciding which policy

Table 4.1 The parties' preferences

Preference	Party A	Party B	Party C
1	CH	P	PH
2	PH	CH	P
3	P	PH	CH

Key: CH = council houses; PH = private houses; P = park.

there is a majority for, because (in a straight contest between two proposals in each round of voting) a majority can be found for *each* proposal. In most formal voting procedures there are rules governing how votes are to be taken, and this would normally mean that those voting should be given a choice between only two proposals at a time. Thus, once all the amendments to the substantive motion have been tabled, the amendments are usually voted on in turn, at each point there being a straight choice between two alternatives. Finally there is a run-off between the remaining two alternatives and whichever gains a majority wins. In the case under consideration the only thing which will determine the outcome is not any particular majority as such, but the order in which the votes are taken. Michael Laver explains how this works:

> If council housing had been presented first, it would have been rejected by a coalition of parties B and C, each of which preferred something else. Once council housing had been rejected, the run-off between private housing and a park would provoke parties A and C to combine and choose private housing. On the other hand, if a park had been presented as the first matter for decision, it would have been rejected by a coalition of parties A and C. This would have resulted in a run-off between council and private housing. Parties A and B would have combined to choose council housing. Again, if private housing had been presented first, it would have been rejected by parties A and B. The park would have won the run-off with council housing, since it was preferred by parties B and C.
>
> (Laver, 1983, p. 153)

In other words, *any* of the outcomes might have been chosen, and which was chosen depended solely on the *order* in which the alternatives were considered. A majority of voters preferred an alternative to each outcome. The final outcome is therefore not independent of the order in which the votes are taken, but on the contrary, entirely dependent on that order. This may seem a surprising result, but it is remarkably difficult to devise systems of voting in which the outcome is independent of the order of voting. The above example is the simplest version of a voting cycle in which each of the three alternatives can be defeated by another of the three.

The possibility of a voting cycle obviously presents a challenge to anyone who believes that voting is a straightforward matter; but there are also other possible consequences. So far we have assumed that each party will vote in accordance with their preference orderings as shown in the table. However, it might be in *someone's* interest, if they know the other parties' preferences, to vote tactically. Tactical voting is where a party or person votes against their real preference in order to secure the best outcome possible under the circumstances. If we apply the possibility of tactical voting to our example above we can see that if, for example, the first vote to be taken were private houses against council houses, and Party A votes in line with its true preference ordering by voting for council housing, council housing would win, but it would then lose in a straight run-off against the proposal for a park. But this is Party A's least preferred option. Thus if Party A is canny and has sufficient knowledge of the other parties' preference orderings, it might be wiser for it to vote for private housing (its second preference) in the first round, thus securing a run-off between private housing and a park in which private housing wins. By not voting in accordance with their true preferences in the first round of voting, and in accordance with their true preferences only in the second round of voting, Party A secures the provision of private housing which, although it was not their first preference, it undoubtedly prefers to a park which was its last preference.

These themes will be picked up again and illustrated in the case study at the end of this chapter. For the moment the general point is that greens need to be aware of the way in which voting and other decision-making processes can affect outcomes in policy making and how they might be manipulated by other actors.

Collective irrationality: the tragedy of the commons

The example we have just been considering is concerned with some of the formal problems of decision making – it is an example of that branch of rational choice theory known as social choice theory. As such, it assumes only that people are rational and utility maximising, not that they are necessarily self-interested or egoistic. However, in looking at the problem of collective action, we can add to this formal problem in aggregating preferences by making additional assumptions about people's motivation. The branch of rational choice theory known as public choice theory applies the methods and assumptions of economics to political decision making. As we saw above, in our earlier example of the traffic jam, the outcome of individuals acting rationally in their own self-interest can lead to a form of collective irrationality which is in no one's interest.

A classic and frequently cited example of this sort of problem is Garrett Hardin's 'The Tragedy of the Commons' which we briefly discussed in the Introduction. Hardin asks us to imagine a pasture open to all and to accept that each herdsman will try to keep as many cattle as possible on this common pasture. Although under certain conditions the number of people and the number of animals they graze may stay below the carrying capacity of the land, a day will arrive where this is no longer so and where 'the inherent logic of the commons remorselessly generates tragedy' (Hardin, 1998, p. 26).

> As a rational being, each herdsman seeks to maximise his gain . . . he asks, 'What is the utility to me of adding one more animal to my herd?' This utility has one negative and one positive component.

1 The positive component is a function of the increment of one animal. Since the herdsman receives all the proceeds from the sale of the additional animal, the positive utility is nearly +1.
2 The negative component is a function of the additional overgrazing created by one more animal. Since, however, the effects of overgrazing are shared by all the herdsmen, the negative utility for any particular decision-making herdsman is only a fraction of –1.

Adding together the component partial utilities, the rational herdsman concludes that the only sensible course for him to pursue is to add another animal to his herd. And another; and another. . . . But this is the conclusion reached by each and every rational herdsman sharing a commons. Therein is the tragedy. Each man is locked into a system that compels him to increase his herd without limit – in a world that is limited. Ruin is the destination toward which all men rush, each pursuing his own best interest in a society that believes in the freedom of the commons. Freedom in a commons brings ruin to all.

(ibid.)

By substituting examples we can see why seas are over-fished, air and water polluted, the ozone layer damaged and the emission of greenhouse gases hard to reduce. In each case there is a free good, whether a natural resource or an environmental 'sink' into which we pour our pollution. Because the good is free we over-consume it, and although over-consumption and its consequences are not in the interest of everyone collectively, it is in the short-term interest of each individual to continue to consume as much as they can. Thus the tragedy of the commons, the possibility of collective irrationality, lies at the heart of many environmental problems.

To avert the tragedy Hardin offers two possible solutions. First, he argues that individual property rights in what were previously the commons ought to be created so that people either own their own land or someone owns the land as a whole and charges people for grazing rights. In either case there is an incentive to ensure the long-term provision of grazing, and it is precisely this incentive which is absent in the commons.[4] Where there is such an incentive, and where a market might work in bringing about the desired environmental goal, the establishment of property rights might be the best solution. This view, generalised, becomes free-market environmentalism (see Chapter 5). However, there are limits to what markets can do and that is why Hardin argues, second, that certain issues are not amenable to the allocation of private property rights and thus require strong action on the part of governments. For example, our right to have as many children as we wish will lead, in Hardin's view, to the misery of overpopulation and bring ruin to all: we must therefore abandon 'the commons in breeding' and this will require 'mutual coercion, mutually agreed upon' (Hardin, 1998, p. 32). In many later writings (for example, Ophuls, 1973, 1977) this phrase has been interpreted as providing support for a strong authoritarian response to environmental problems.

Hardin's solutions are not the only ones available and (as we shall see later) his conception of human behaviour in terms of rational self-interest has been challenged. However, the idea of the tragedy is useful: using the idea of the self-interested individual as a heuristic device allows us to develop policy instruments for a 'worse case scenario'. Policy instruments discussed in the next chapter – such as regulation (or command-and-control) and economic instruments – are typically used on the grounds that otherwise environmental goods will be over-consumed. For now, however, it is enough to realise that collective action problems raise difficult issues for the generation of effective environmental policy.

Public opinion and the issue–attention cycle

Democratic governments cannot develop environmental policy in a vacuum. They require public support. Otherwise public opinion will discipline governments at the ballot box. Obviously the movement of influence is not simply a one-way matter of public opinion affecting government action. Rather, there is a complex relationship of cause and effect between government policy and wider public opinion. Nonetheless, policy making is strongly affected by the nature of public opinion. As far as environmental knowledge and literacy is concerned, the populations of contemporary liberal democracies are perhaps the most environmentally aware, with public opinion indicating a large degree of sympathy towards environmental issues. But we have to recognise that the relationship between the existence of this sympathy and actual policy making is not simple.

An attempt to capture the typical trajectory of environmental issues in the public and political domain was offered by Anthony Downs in his influential article 'Up and down with ecology – the "issue–attention cycle"' (1972). In this piece Downs identified five stages in the issue–attention cycle.

Downs's issue–attention cycle

1 the pre-problem stage
2 alarmed discovery and euphoric enthusiasm
3 realising the cost of significant progress
4 gradual decline of intense public interest
5 the post-problem stage

In the pre-problem stage an environmental problem exists and is recognised by a few actors, for example, pressure groups or scientists, but it has not yet captured public interest or attention. In the second stage the problem is 'discovered' both by the wider public and also by decision makers, who typically display a self-confident belief that the problem can be solved. Usually the media plays an important role during this stage in fanning the flame of public opinion with sensational headlines and reports – a point which environmental groups such as Greenpeace have learnt to exploit to their advantage (see Chapter 3). However, for many environmental problems, it is soon realised that the costs of finding a solution may be high. A good example here is climate change. Individuals are generally not willing to reduce their use of private vehicles – the practice and technology that is at least partially responsible for this environmental problem. Where a relatively inexpensive technological fix is not possible and solutions may require major behavioural change and/or social or economic restructuring, political will and public interest begin to wane. At this point there may be acceptance of a simple amelioration of effects, or symbolic action, rather than the elimination of causes. The widespread recognition of the costs involved leads to a sense of discouragement on the part of some and boredom on the part of others. The wheel of public attention turns round as other issues become increasingly prominent; as it turns media and public attention is directed elsewhere as new, more exciting topics arrest their attention. In many ways the disappearance of an issue from the media in itself creates the impression that the issue has gone away and been 'solved'. The final stage of the cycle sees the issue languishing in a limbo until there is another resurgence of interest and the cycle begins anew.

What are we to make of such cycling of public interest? On a positive note, we need to recognise that once an issue has been round the cycle, things will not be quite the same again. This is because there will have been some kind of institutional response: organisations adapt to issues as they go round the cycle (Peters and Hogwood, 1985). The creation in 1970 of the Department of the Environment in the United Kingdom and the Environmental Protection Agency in the United States are both excellent examples of the institutional implications of the issue–attention cycle. These institutions were founded in response to the wave of environmental consciousness and activity that began in the late 1960s. As interest in the environment waned they did not disappear. And, when environmental issues came round again, there was an institutional base from which to develop more effective policy. As we shall discuss later, this institutionalisation may have some unexpected drawbacks; however, it does indicate some degree of progression as issue–attention cycles revolve.

One of the more negative aspects of the issue–attention cycle is that such variations of public opinion make effective policy making more problematic and raise the likelihood of purely symbolic responses to problems, particularly on the part of policy makers who are not genuinely committed to solving the particular issue in question. Further, the issue–attention cycle for environmental problems is strongly related to the state of the economy. Drawing on public opinion data from the UK, Robert Worcester argues:

> [W]hile a rise in concern about the economy, unemployment, health care and crime are all correlated positively, there is a significant negative correlation between nomination of these issues and the mention of the environment. ... People's concern for the environment rises when they feel economically secure.
>
> (Worcester, 1997, pp. 163–4)

For many people, environmental concerns are of secondary importance in comparison with what they see as the primary issues of economic prosperity and social welfare. Although greens would obviously wish to argue that economic, social and environmental issues are interrelated and should be considered in relation to one another, this is not generally reflected in wider public opinion. It is specific environmental issues, such as nuclear power, climate change, ozone depletion and the release of genetically-modified organisms that capture public and political attention, not the broader policy implications of sustainable development.

A final issue that needs to be recognised about public opinion is that although there is a significant level of environmental awareness and concern among the public and general expressions of support for environmental policies, this tends to remain somewhat abstract. There appears to be a gap between concern and behaviour. Reflecting on evidence from western Europe, Sharon Witherspoon argues that 'support for environmental policies drops off when citizens are asked if they are willing to make personal sacrifices for the sake of the environment, and becomes a minority interest when it relates to cutting back on car usage' (Witherspoon, 1996, p. 54). Unsurprisingly, the individuals who participate in collective activities (e.g. protests, demonstrations, support and membership of environmental groups) are typically also more consistently green in their policy preferences and more scientifically knowledgeable about the environment. However, overall, 'much public opinion relevant to environmentalism in western European democracies is confused; much is expressive, with little import for behavioural change' (ibid., p. 65). This is why, in reflecting on record UK car sales for the year 2001, George Monbiot pessimistically concluded that 'environmentalism as an argument has been comprehensively won. As a practice it is all but extinct' (Monbiot, 2002). One does not need to be in complete agreement to accept that he has a point.

Complexity, uncertainty and bounded rationality

Environmental problems are often highly complex and, as such, uncertainty haunts the policy-making process. Given our lack of comprehensive knowledge about the nature of problems themselves, the goals and objectives we are trying to achieve, the consequences of different policy alternatives, and potential unanticipated outcomes of policy interventions, we are faced with a further hurdle in developing effective environmental policy.

If we take climate change as an example, we can identify different types of uncertainty. There is uncertainty about emissions: we do not know exactly which gases we will be pumping out into the atmosphere – it depends on technical change and political progress in securing stabilisations and reductions. There is also uncertainty about climate response. Meteorological models are enormously complex and because of the vast number of inter-related variables it is difficult to make accurate predictions. Further, there is uncertainty concerning the regional impact of climate change: the world as a whole may undergo global warming, but it does not follow that each part of the world will warm up to the same extent – some parts of the world are likely to cool down. Relatedly, there is uncertainty concerning the thresholds at which the effects of climate change become a problem. We might be unconcerned by, or be able to adapt to, even a large rise in sea level; but thereafter, beyond a certain threshold, the problems might be enormous. Sometimes marginal changes have far-reaching consequences. Finally, we cannot easily predict what the political and social responses to climate change will be. Societies and governments can respond in markedly different ways: how easy is it to say how far populations will simply adapt what they do to the new circumstances, and how governments will respond in their policy making to changing circumstances?

Given this level of uncertainty, one of the fundamental questions facing decision makers is simply knowing *when* to act. Are environmental problems really as serious as environmentalists claim? Perhaps we should act only when there is absolute proof? A common technocentric and optimistic response is to agree that a particular issue is serious and demands attention, but that we can rest secure in the expectation that some technical solution will be devised if only we wait patiently. Meanwhile we can continue on our current development path. Are these responses simply cynical shirking of the issues, or genuine responses to difficult questions of choosing how to allocate the scarce resources of time and money?

We generally adopt the view that future costs are less burdensome than current costs. We do this in everyday life, and it is something which economists have formalised through the concept of discounting. The general idea is that we tend to worry less about burdens that will fall on us in the future if there is some present advantage. Therefore, while recognising that the costs will have to be paid later, we view them as of little or no immediate concern simply because they lie in the future. An economist expresses this by assigning a lower monetary value to future costs and benefits as compared with costs or benefits that face us now. We shall have more to say about discounting in Chapter 6, but whatever the general virtue of this way of looking at things – and it can hardly be denied that in life we often take this view – when we are considering environmental policy we have to look at the issues a little more deeply. Given uncertainty, should we act now to prevent future harm or wait and act later when we are more certain that we know exactly how to prevent that harm? The first approach is to anticipate problems and seek to solve them before they become serious; the second is to react to serious problems when they have already arisen. Both approaches have something to be said for them; much depends on the current state of knowledge and what we think we might come to know in the future. Again, it depends on the nature and seriousness of the problem and the nature and effects of the solution. Clearly a serious problem which requires only a small adjustment in what we do now is easily dealt with. In contrast, the solution to future problems, with potentially serious consequences, may be both technologically expensive and socially disruptive. Here the temptation to opt for reactive policies is almost overwhelming, especially if we believe – whether rightly or wrongly – that some technical fix might emerge which will enable us to solve it painlessly. This strong belief that a technological fix for environmental problems will emerge given time is widely held. As we shall see later in the chapter, the precautionary principle supported by most greens stands in opposition to such technological optimism.

Bounded rationality and the administrative mind

Our lack of knowledge about the nature of environmental problems and the possible consequences of different policy options raises fundamental questions about our capacity to develop effective environmental policy. In a classic critique of the ideal of rational, comprehensive policy making, Herbert Simon argues that we need to recognise that there are practical limits to human rationality. Decision makers operate within 'bounded rationality'. For Simon, the rationality of the decision-making process is limited or bounded by both decision makers' knowledge and capacities and the organisational environment in which decisions take place.

> It is impossible for the behaviour of a single, isolated individual to reach any high degree of rationality. The number of alternatives he must explore is so great, the information he would need to evaluate them so vast that even an approximation to objective rationality is hard to conceive. Individual choice takes place in an environment of 'givens' – premises that are accepted by the subject as bases for his choice; and behaviour is adaptive only within the limits set by these 'givens'.
>
> (Simon, 1957, p. 79)

'Givens' include the incompleteness of knowledge of consequences, the difficulties of articulating goals and objectives of policy and the limited number of policy options that come to mind. One effect of this understanding of decision making is that important policy options and consequences may be ignored.

The idea of bounded rationality has a deep impact on our understanding of environmental policy making. In our discussion of the issue–attention cycle we stressed that as issues spiral through the issue–attention cycle they never start again at the beginning when they come back into the public eye. The main reason for this is that they have typically become embedded institutionally in various ways and therefore people and organisations are committed to them even while the public gaze has been directed elsewhere. In general, institutionalisation, such as the formation of an environment ministry or a pollution-control agency, has the advantage of providing a ready-made structure within which policy responses can be channelled. However, this seeming advantage can at the same time be a drawback. Problems tend to be defined in ways which admit of solutions within the prevailing political and administrative arrangements. Governments and departments have particular inherited methods and techniques (or even habits) of dealing with issues. Drawing on Simon's idea of bounded rationality, Douglas Torgerson argues that there are limits to the 'administrative mind' (Torgerson, 1999b). The nature of the administrative mind in contemporary societies means that policy makers typically pay attention only to problems which are amenable to technological and administrative solutions. Modern 'rational' administration presupposes a vision of order and progress within which certain approaches or responses are regarded as reasonable or rational and others are not. Thus environmental problems are often responded to in isolation rather than being seen as interconnected and thereby constituting a challenge to contemporary development patterns. According to Torgerson, the administrative mind cannot admit that there might be a fundamental flaw in the whole pattern of industrial development (ibid., p. 114). Environmentalism frequently challenges this directly because it asserts or implies that progress as commonly understood may be not so much a source of order as a source of disorder, 'disrupting the natural systems upon which civilization and human life depend' (ibid.). The administrative mind accordingly seeks to denigrate those who articulate a vision different from the administrative norm:

To be dealt with, the 'crisis' had to be viewed and treated not comprehensively, as the product of a basic flaw in the whole project of industrialization, but in a manner which identified *manageable* problems. Although the problems could be regarded as somehow commonly 'environmental', they had to be defined, in operational terms, as primarily separate, capable of being solved in a manner which matched the functional differentiation of the administrative apparatus.

(Torgerson, 1999b, p. 115)

The fragmentation of issues into different government departments (such as environment, agriculture and industry) each with its own logic and policy instruments means that the interconnected nature of many environmental problems is over-looked. Solutions to complex environmental problems require more creative, imaginative and coordinated responses than the current functional organisation of the state appears able or willing to promote.

Power and influence: setting the policy agenda

As we have seen from our discussion of public opinion and the issue–attention cycle, issues do not rise up or dominate the political agenda simply because of their intrinsic importance or virtue. Of course certain political challenges are bound to attract attention, but many (perhaps most) issues need to be propelled onto the political agenda through the activities of those concerned, whether this is because it directly impinges on their livelihoods or because they take a more disinterested concern. But if different individuals, groups and organisations are competing for the attention of decision makers in this way, and if their access to resources and information is unequal, we have to accept that there will be disparities in access to decision makers, in influence on decision makers. In short, there will be power inequalities, with some groups or organisations better placed to get their way than others. That is why we now turn to the question of how the political agenda is constructed and to the concept of power.

Political success depends on power and influence: without either, a group, organisation or individual will achieve nothing, irrespective of the intrinsic merits of their case. But what do we understand by the term 'power'? In his influential book *Power: A Radical View* (1974), Steven Lukes argues that power should be studied in three dimensions.[5] The first is the exercise of power which occurs in observable overt conflicts between actors over key issues; the second is the exercise of power which occurs in observable overt or covert conflicts between actors over issues or potential issues; the third is the power to shape people's preferences so that neither overt nor covert conflicts exist. The first dimension of power corresponds to Robert Dahl's definition of power in which 'A has power over B to the extent that he can get B to do something that B would not otherwise do' (Dahl, 1957, p. 203). This is the visible exercise of power; it is clear and obvious. We can see when someone is making someone else do something. It is not necessarily physical, but it is tangible. Clearly this covers many of the cases where we would want to say that power was being exercised, but in Lukes's view it is limited as it is blind to the various and less obvious ways in which the political agenda can be controlled in a political system (Lukes, 1974, p. 57).

Thus, the first dimension needs to be supplemented by a second dimension, which Lukes characterises as the exercise of power which occurs in observable overt or *covert* conflicts between actors over issues or *potential* issues. We should not only look at what is done, at the decisions people and organisations make, but also at the non-decisions which are made when contentious policy issues are avoided or sidelined rather than subjected to obvious and observable challenge and likely defeat. This goes beyond the visible and obvious exercise of power characteristic of the first dimension. It corresponds with what Peter Bachrach and Morton Baratz term the 'second face of power'. In their view power does not simply involve examining key decisions and actual behaviour:

> Of course power is exercised when A participates in the making of decisions that affect B. Power is also exercised when A devotes his energies to creating or reinforcing social and political values and institutional practices that limit the scope of the political process to public consideration of only those issues which are comparatively innocuous to A. To the extent that A succeeds in doing this, B is prevented, for all practical purposes, from bringing to the fore any issues that might in their resolution be seriously detrimental to A's set of preferences.
> (Bachrach and Baratz, 1962, p. 948)

This is the 'mobilisation of bias', the confining of decision making to safe issues. The phrase is E.E. Schattschneider's, who argues that forms of political organisation are inevitably biased in favour of capitalising on some kinds of conflict and suppressing others, because *'organisation is the mobilisation of bias.* Some issues are organised into politics while others are organised out' (Schattschneider, in Bachrach and Baratz, 1962, p. 949).

What this suggests is two faces of power: one operating at the level of overt conflicts over key issues; the other operating through a process which might be termed 'non-decision making' where conflicts are suppressed and prevented from entering the political process. A full analysis of power thus requires the examination of both decision making and non-decision making. A decision is a choice among alternative modes of action whereas a non-decision is a decision that results in the suppression or frustration of a challenge to the values or interests of the decision maker. Non-decision making is a way of ensuring that demands for political and social change are stifled before they can be articulated, or kept hidden, or eliminated before they can achieve access to the policy process. And if all these ruses fail, a policy can be rendered impotent, ridiculous or irrelevant by inept implementation.

Although Lukes regards the idea of a second dimension to power as a valuable one, he is still not satisfied that it captures all that we mean by the concept of power; some aspects of power have still escaped the net. At this point he introduces a third dimension characterised by the idea of *latent* conflict and the affecting of interests. Latent conflict exists when there *would* be a conflict of wants or preferences between those exercising and those subject to power if the latter were to become aware of their interests. The question of interests is very important here: Lukes defines the underlying concept of power, common to all three views, thus: 'A exercises power over

B when A affects B in a manner contrary to B's interests' (Lukes, 1974, p. 27). In the first and second dimension it is relatively obvious that interests have been adversely affected because people recognise this directly when their desires are thwarted; but on the third dimension things change because Lukes introduces the idea of a 'real interest'. When we are examining the third dimension it is not necessarily obvious that someone will have gained and someone lost. Power may be exercised even if those affected by it do not feel adversely affected by its exercise. In other words, the existence of a consensus does not indicate that power is not being exercised:

> [I]s it not the supreme and most insidious exercise of power to prevent people, to whatever degree, from having grievances by shaping their perceptions, cognitions and preferences in such a way that they accept their role in the existing order of things, either because they can see or imagine no alternative to it, or because they see it as natural and unchangeable, or because they value it as divinely ordained and beneficial? To assume that the absence of grievance equals genuine consensus is simply to rule out the possibility of false or manipulated consensus by definitional fiat.
>
> (ibid., p. 24)

It should by now be clear how the above theoretical account might fit actual cases. Some people, groups or organisations obviously and visibly wield power. We might think, for instance, of the state, transnational corporations, the World Trade Organisation (WTO) or even (at times) Greenpeace. This power is sometimes highly visible, for instance, where the state uses sanctions to ensure that we keep within the law, or redefines a form of direct action as a criminal offence. The WTO has considerable power, much of which is obvious, but some is less so. For example, part of its power consists in the way that it shapes the agenda of economic growth and development, insisting that certain approaches to national economic development are not acceptable. In other cases power may be much less visible. Even where a pressure group is granted access to a government minister or department, there is not the slightest guarantee that their views will be listened to seriously, much less adopted. The meetings themselves can be used to defuse opposition because it allows government to go on to make the claim that it has consulted all the relevant parties and interests; but its decision can still be just what it always wanted it to be. Examples of this can be found where an interest lobby such as the National Farmers' Union or the British Roads Federation has succeeded in capturing the mind of a department, and where its practical success lies in simply making alternatives unthinkable. For many years it has been 'obvious' that we need new roads and motorways; to think or say otherwise has been regarded as cranky and absurd. The issue could not be seriously raised in any forum. Even in public inquiries concerning the route of a motorway, discussion is limited to the route itself. It is not possible to raise the question of whether the motorway is needed in the first place. This is an example of the 'mobilisation of bias' where some issues are organised into politics while others are organised out, and it is extraordinarily difficult to fight.[6] Frequently the most successful lobbyists are the quietest, while the ones making the noise are the ones who have been 'organised out' and who can only make an impact by highly visible and public means. Again, as we discussed in Chapter 2, it is clear that there is currently an 'acceptable' interpretation of sustainable development which is dominated by the outlook of ecological modernisation. Sustainable development is interpreted in such a way as to allow for the continuation of economic growth and production and consumption patterns which are modified to reduce their adverse environmental impact, but remain otherwise unchallenged. This interpretation is built into the reasoning of government, business and economists and is virtually impossible to challenge at the points where it matters.

The influence of policy networks

Policy making in contemporary governments is typically seen as disaggregated; it is fragmented into a large number of policy subsystems that focus on particular policy issues (Richardson and Jordan, 1979). An environment ministry, for example, may be home to a number of policy sub-systems such as pollution control, wildlife conservation, climate change, etc. Each sub-system has its own policy network which might take the form of a 'policy community' which is small in number, highly exclusive and able to frustrate major changes, or an 'issue network' in which there is more competition of ideas and a wide range of interests involved. As David Marsh and Rod Rhodes argue:

> Government is fragmented, and in many cases, individual departments and a powerful interest have developed a *common* interest and policy, and the network fosters the mutual interests of its members against outsiders. The pattern of policy making is essentially elitist.
> . . . There is clear structural inequality in the access of interests to, and their influence over, government policy making.
>
> (Marsh and Rhodes, 1992, p. 264)

The strongest policy communities are typically those dominated by either producer or economic interests (e.g. agriculture) or by professionals (e.g. health). The tight-knit communities often frustrate the efforts of environmental organisations which will typically only have meaningful access to a small number of policy networks around 'green' issues. However, even the most elitist policy communities can be opened up by external shocks. A perfect example here is the changing nature of the policy network around agriculture in the UK. Recent policy disasters such as CJD and foot-and-mouth disease have forced a rethink in agricultural policy and burst open the previously tight community of officials from the Ministry of Agriculture, Fisheries and Food (MAFF) and the National Farmers' Union. What we have now is a competition of ideas and interests more akin to an issue network. Structurally, the end of the closed agriculture policy community was reinforced by the establishment in 2001 of the Department of the Environment, Food and Rural Affairs (DEFRA) (see Chapter 9).

John Gaventa has argued that if actors have consistently been excluded or failed to achieve any degree of success in political decision making, apathy or fatalism may set in and with it acceptance in the face of the demands of powerful actors (Gaventa, 1982, pp. 20ff). Along similar lines, Brian Wynne comments that 'the powerless always tend to rationalise and thus consolidate their own impotence and apathy because to do otherwise would be to expose themselves to the greater pain of *explicit* recognition of their own neglect and marginality. . . . This kind of enculturation process *normalises and consolidates* whatever dependency and lack of agency is thought to exist. It obscures the alienation and ambivalence or worse which people may feel in relation to elites and expert institutions' (Wynne, 1996, pp. 53–5). Further, Gaventa suggests that if actors do not participate in decision-making processes they may well have an under-developed or fragmented political consciousness. For environmentalists, the very structure of political institutions and the relation between decision makers and citizens is a matter of fundamental concern.

The un-politics of air pollution

As we have seen, the exercise of power consists not only in the positive ability to get things done. It can also consist in the ability to make sure that decisions are not made or are deferred indefinitely. One way of doing this is to ensure that an emergent issue never reaches the agenda, that is, it never becomes an actual issue for a decision-making body. In *The Un-Politics of Air Pollution: A Study of Non-Decisionmaking in the Cities*, Matthew Crenson provides a good example of how a powerful local interest can prevent issues reaching an agenda. The question Crenson asks is why the issue of air pollution was not raised as early or effectively in some American cities as in others. He wanted to discover why in many cities and towns in the United States air pollution failed to become a political issue. His focus was not just on what was done, but more importantly on what was *not* done: he wanted to study both political activity and political inactivity. A serious investigation required that he had to choose towns which were, so far as possible, very similar in pollution levels and in social composition, otherwise the answer as to why one town or the other had acted on pollution could have been attributed simply to (say) the fact that one was more polluted than the other. He examined two cities in Indiana: East Chicago and Gary. Both were equally polluted and had similar populations. East Chicago took action on air pollution in 1949; Gary did nothing until 1962. So what was the explanation? In brief, it lay in the fact that Gary was largely dominated by US Steel and had a strong party organisation operating in tandem with the steel company and exercising mutually advantageous control over the labour force. The company and the party were the dominant organisations in the city. East Chicago, on the other hand, was host to a number of steel companies and had no strong party organisation. In Gary, therefore, there was a reluctance and an inability to challenge these dominant organisations. Their power was exercised simply by the fear that they could use their influence: people were afraid of their anticipated reactions; they did not necessarily have to *do* anything, their reputation was sufficient to prevent the issue being properly raised.

Crenson's conclusion was that US Steel had for a long time prevented the issue of pollution control from being raised because it was able to exploit its position as the major employer and wield power as much through reputation or fear of what it might do (for example, re-locate production). When an anti-pollution ordinance was finally enacted (as a consequence of the threat of State or Federal action), it had a considerable influence on its content. It did this without entering into the political arena or intervening in policy-making forums: its reputation for power was enough to inhibit the emergence of the issue. By not taking a clearly identifiable stand one way or the other, the company frustrated the efforts of environmentalists and others to introduce an effective pollution-control ordinance. One activist remarked that:

> The company executives . . . would just nod sympathetically 'and agree that air pollution was terrible, and pat you on the head. But they never *did* anything one way or the other. If only there had been a fight, then something might have been accomplished!' What US Steel did not do was probably more important to the career of Gary's air pollution issue than what it did do.
>
> (Crenson, 1971, pp. 76–7)

Crenson extended his analysis to other cities and reached the conclusion that the issue of air pollution tends not to flourish in cities where industry enjoys a reputation for power. Further, where industry stays silent, the opportunities of raising the pollution issue are diminished. In addition, the role of political parties and politicians makes a difference. Why was the dominant party not interested in clean air? There were some politicians in both towns who tried to raise the issue of dirty air, but they faced stiff opposition from the 'machine' politicians who controlled both towns. Some politicians might be genuinely motivated by ideology; others, by contrast, are 'non-ideological entrepreneurs' in that they deliver private goods such as jobs or contracts in return for votes. But clean air, because it is a public good, does not lend itself to this approach. Thus, in Gary, it was local politicians as much as anybody who kept clean air off the agenda (McLean, 1987, p. 35). Party politicians can manipulate public support by providing goods to particular groups; but they cannot afford to alienate the financial and other support they gain from a dominant company in their locality. Strong and influential party organisations will tend to inhibit the development of issues such as these because acceding to the demand for clean air will harm the party's political and financial support. Clean air is a public good and its costs are concentrated on industry who are likely, therefore, to be strongly opposed to it. That is why the conjunction of US Steel and a dominant party organisation kept clean air off the agenda. On the other hand, support for pollution control suffers because although all benefit, it is hard to get people together to fight for it. There is a collective action problem.[7]

The task of placing issues on to the political agenda is made still more difficult because they tend to be interconnected. Those policy analysts (typically pluralists) who believe that a plurality of roughly equal voices each have a say in decision making, and who find empirical evidence for this view by looking simply at overt, discrete, separate and unrelated decisions are unable to see that power could be exercised in many and more insidious ways than through the obvious wielding of force. Thus, it is possible that success in one issue might lead to success in others because it demonstrates the practical possibility of working together with others. Conversely, at a given moment, the pursuit of a particular issue might prevent other issues from reaching the political agenda. Astute politicians realise that they can defuse a situation by acceding to pressure on some issues and ignoring others. They can use the virtue of compromise to disguise the fact that they are stifling the emergence of issues they do not like or do not wish to address. Governments are adept at this. They can pursue 'green' policies or label already existing policies as 'green' and thereby make the claim that they have addressed environmental issues. In reality, the serious issues may have been neatly sidelined by the appearance of environmental concern driving out its substance.[8] There are, Crenson concludes, 'politically imposed limitations upon the scope of decision making' (Crenson, 1971, p. 178) which are achieved by the use of non-decision making. Simply studying the overt actions of decision makers may tell us nothing about the groups and issues which may have been excluded from the political process (ibid., p. 181).

Policy making as partisan mutual adjustment

In our earlier discussion of uncertainty and complexity, we introduced Simon's idea of bounded rationality. Charles Lindblom developed the analysis of the rationality of the policy process further: policy making is not only limited by bounded rationality, but also by the exercise of power. Bargaining and negotiation are a fundamental part of any decision-making processes. Policy emerges after a process of competition, compromise and adjustment between groups.

Lindblom shares with Simon the belief that the complexity of analysing different policy options always leads to technical problems in collecting and processing information. Again, the rationality of the policy process is undermined by a lack of information and by our inability to conceptualise complex problems and process information. In practice, decision making is simplified and proceeds by limiting the number of alternatives considered to those which differ in small degrees from existing policies. Using the method of 'successive limited comparison' or 'disjointed incrementalism', policies are analysed which differ from each other only incrementally, and which differ incrementally from the existing policy. Using disjointed incrementalism, the decision maker keeps on returning to problems, and attempts to ameliorate those problems rather than to achieve some ideal state of affairs. Policies are only considered and adopted at the margin – there is only incremental movement from the status quo. Radical policies with large-scale unpredictable outcomes are eschewed. Amelioration becomes the norm: 'A policy is directed at a problem; it is tried, altered, tried in its altered form, altered again, and so forth . . . incremental policies follow one upon the other in the solution of a given problem' (Braybrooke and Lindblom, 1963, p. 73). Adherence to the incremental approach avoids the making of serious mistakes because the method proceeds a little at a time and retreats and goes in a different direction if things do not go well.

Incrementalism is reinforced by the exercise of power. The different dimensions of power affect the decision-making process. Policy making occurs through 'partisan mutual adjustment' (Lindblom, 1965, p. 33). Lindblom suggests that we explicitly recognise the need for bargaining, compromise and agreement between affected parties in our understanding of what makes a good policy. On this view the test of a good policy is not that it maximises the decision makers' values, but that it secures the agreement of the interests involved. Lindblom's initial formulation of partisan mutual adjustment was avowedly pluralist: he believed that power was dispersed throughout society and that all groups had access to resources (whether wealth, information, people, prestige, etc.) and thus could influence the policy process. Our discussion of power above, and in particular the covert effect of non-decision making and agenda setting and the possibility that the latent exercise of power shapes our very perceptions and preferences, casts doubt on this pluralist vision of the policy process. Tight policy networks can restrict access to policy sub-systems and inequalities of power are thereby reflected in the workings of the policy process.

Lindblom's conception of policy making has often been criticised for being inherently conservative as it denies the possibility of large-scale change (Lindblom, 1979; Smith and May, 1980). In response, Lindblom has argued that very large changes can come about through disjointed incrementalism, it is just that they are built up gradually through a series of small policy successes rather than through a huge leap which might end up in disaster and would probably lack public support. Incrementalism does not need to be slow moving. Although this response has some merit, it is misleading to suppose that merely because large-scale changes can be the outcome of a number of smaller changes that this is appropriate in all cases. In particular, structural features of politics within market-orientated societies means that 'grand issues' pertaining to the structure of politico-economic life (e.g. the distribution of income and wealth, distribution of political power and corporate prerogatives) are simply left off the agenda. In this sense many large-scale environmental problems and the more challenging visions of sustainable development can be understood as 'grand issues'.

Greening the policy process

Any strong environmental programme is likely to be contested on many fronts and subjected to responses ranging from downright opposition to subtle exclusion or manipulation. The problems of collective action, issue–attention cycles, bounded rationality and insidious forms of power relations will inevitably raise their heads as people and organisations lobby to secure their position and achieve their goals. Successful environmental action requires both a knowledge of environmental goals and of the obstacles standing in the way of achieving them. This chapter has shown what some of these obstacles are. What remains to be done is to discuss possible ways of overcoming them. In what ways might the policy process be made more sensitive to environmental considerations?

A number of different approaches can be taken to raising the profile of the environment in decision making, ranging from the principles that guide policy making through to the policy instruments chosen to secure desired outcomes. Different approaches typically respond to the different types of barriers considered in this chapter. In this section we will introduce four broad approaches to reorienting the 'machinery of government' to ensure that environmental considerations are weighed in policy making: green policy principles; administrative techniques and tools; structural changes to the institutions of governance; and policy instruments. Many of these approaches will be discussed in more detail as the book progresses.

Green policy principles

A number of principles have been offered by greens that would reorientate the way policy making attends to environmental and sustainability considerations. Many of these principles have been accepted within international treaties and declarations and in national legislation and sustainability strategies. For example, the principle of integrated pollution control (IPC) has become the core principle in pollution legislation in most liberal democracies (see Chapter 9 for a more detailed discussion). IPC requires decision makers to anticipate, rather than react to, pollution and to take into account the effects of pollution on all media (land, water and air). It is not enough to consider only one medium in decision making: this will often lead to the transfer of a pollution problem to another location. Here the holistic nature of environmental problems and the necessity of an integrated response are recognised.

The polluter pays principle (PPP) again attempts to reorientate policy making. Rather than the costs of pollution being borne by the wider society, the simple idea behind PPP is that those responsible for environmental damage should be forced to pay for its social costs: it is an attempt to overcome free-riding on the part of polluters. Polluters are forced to internalise pollution costs. As we shall see in more detail in Chapter 5, the logic of PPP lies at the heart of many economic instruments. Examples include energy taxes on industry and vehicle fuels.

A third principle – the precautionary principle – is perhaps the most well known and debated of all green principles. The principle attempts to institutionalise the green orientation towards uncertainty and environmental risk. Principle 15 of the Rio Declaration (1992) defines the precautionary principle in the following widely accepted way:

> In order to protect the environment, the precautionary approach shall be widely applied by States according to their capabilities. Where there are threats of serious or irreversible damage, lack of full scientific certainty should not be used as a reason for postponing cost-effective measures to prevent environmental degradation.[9]

We argued earlier that there is often a time-preference for delaying costs, a desire not to act until there is full scientific certainty and that therefore policy making is typically reactive. The precautionary principle stands in opposition to this. The principle requires that, in conditions of uncertainty, decision makers should prevent potentially serious or irreversible environmental harm. Where scientific evidence cannot be used to prove conclusively that an activity or substance will not cause harm, the activity should not progress; the substance should not be released into the environment. The burden of proof is reassigned: for example, the burden of proof would be on industries to show that their processes do not cause long-term environmental damage. In other words, we should try to prevent pollution before it happens.

> The precautionary principle places the burden of proof in decision making on establishing that ecosystems will be protected in the face of uncertainty about the impacts of pollution. In other words, scientific uncertainty should not be taken as a reason for postponing preventative actions.
>
> (Kinrade, 1995, p. 94)

Unlike 'normal' cases where we say that someone is innocent until proved guilty, the precautionary principle insists that potentially harmful substances are guilty until proved innocent. The burden of proof should be on those who wish to engage in polluting activities to prove that they are safe before they do so. If we wait for absolute proof of the impact of a pollutant, the damage will have already been done and it will probably be impossible to reverse. If the precautionary principle were to be taken seriously in policy making we can begin to see the repercussions it might have on issues such as nuclear power, climate change and the release of genetically modified organisms.

Core elements of the precautionary principle

- a willingness to take action in advance of formal justification of scientific proof;
- a proportionality of response so that uncertain outcomes are additionally weighed to justify initial costs;
- a preparedness to provide 'ecological space' for the earth to 'breathe' essentially as a willing concession to human ignorance and some recognition of the intrinsic rights of ecological processes;
- shifting the onus of proof onto those who propose to change the order of things in ways that cannot be guaranteed to be sustainable; in other words a form of ecological charter;
- a concern for future generations and for possible adverse impacts on those alive and to be born, who can neither avoid these impacts, nor have a say in determining their cause and effect;
- a need to address 'ecological debts' through which those who have breached the margins of ecological tolerance in the past have a disproportionate responsibility to curtail their ignorance-busting habits now.

(O'Riordan, 1999, p. 285)[10]

Although the precautionary principle is widely accepted, it is possible to interpret it in a number of ways. Tim O'Riordan and Andrew Jordan point out that a weak interpretation tends to be restricted to the 'most toxic and human life threatening substances and activities' (1995, p. 197) and cost-effectiveness and technical feasibility become central concerns. This is certainly true of the Rio Declaration definition given above, which refers to the capability of states and cost-effective measures. Such an interpretation appears to resonate with the discourse of ecological modernisation (see Chapter 2). Bearing in mind the arguments advanced in Chapter 1, we can see that this formulation of the principle fights shy of accepting any deep commitment to the well-being of future generations and the non-human world, except where action requires the imposition of relatively low costs on the current generation.

By contrast, a stronger interpretation of the precautionary principle emphasises the unconditionality of our obligations towards the non-human world and future generations, even where meeting these obligations can only be carried out at considerable cost to ourselves. This interpretation is likely to be more unpopular and more strongly resisted than the former precisely because it requires more of governments, business and the public who are (perhaps understandably) reluctant to accept the radical consequences. But for greens this interpretation may be the only one worth fighting for if we are truly serious about addressing the full range of environmental problems facing contemporary and future generations and the non-human world. Adoption of the precautionary principle is desirable, but there is little or no point in adopting a version which is too weak to make any appreciable difference, especially if its adoption were to displace more radical responses to environmental problems. The problem is that the principle, understood in the strong sense, requires significant sacrifice in the present. It requires strict control of polluting and depleting activities and will therefore be opposed by all who stand to lose in the short term, whether industry, business, workers or consumers.

The ambiguous status of science within green politics

The precautionary principle is not anti-science. In fact it provides a high status for scientific evidence within policy making. More broadly, within green political thought it is fair to say we find rather ambiguous and at times contradictory attitudes to science. On the one hand, greens criticise the 'technocentrism' of contemporary society, its faith in scientific progress and the domination of a scientific worldview. On the other, an enormous amount of green concern and its related rhetoric is firmly rooted in scientific evidence, observation and predictions. It is clearly senseless to talk about physical limits to growth, acid rain, climate change or ozone depletion without reference to scientific methods and evidence. Is there perhaps a paradox here, with greens turning science on itself by using scientific knowledge to expose the effects of the application of the scientific worldview (Yearley, 1991)? There are two points to make here. First, that it is not the practice of science per se that is the problem, but rather 'scientism', that is, the belief that natural science (and only natural science) has the answer to everything and that nothing falls outside its remit. Second, one of the associated problems with scientism is the assumption of the 'purity' of science, the belief that scientific practice is neutral and therefore above the political fray. Such an understanding of the role of science in contemporary society is misleading. For example, the choice of what is deemed worthy of investigation often reflects political power relations and access to knowledge: politically and economically powerful actors typically hold the purse strings, promote research and interpret the results.[11] Further, where funding for research is forthcoming, results unwelcome to the funder might never see the light of day. Greens argue that the authority of science and its sometimes illicit presumption of detached neutrality should not remain unquestioned, and that only through the democratisation of decision-making processes can the status of scientific evidence be legitimised and the (often ignored) evidence and experience of 'non-expert' citizens also be given due consideration (Fischer, 2000; Wynne, 1996; Irwin, 1995).

Administrative techniques and tools

At the heart of green policy-making principles lies a concern that the true environmental costs of developments are not sufficiently considered in decision-making processes. A number of techniques, such as cost–benefit analysis (CBA) and environmental impact assessment (EIA), have been developed in order to internalise environmental costs and benefits in policy making. CBA is the most widely-used technique for ensuring cost-effectiveness in decisions. Environmental economists have developed ingenious methods to produce the economic valuation of environmental costs and benefits so that they can be included in CBA calculations. Their argument is that unless such costings are included, they will be overlooked in decisions. The economic valuation of environmental impacts is a contentious issue, discussed in detail in Chapter 6.

An alternative to CBA is EIA. Here environmental (and social and economic) impacts are described and summarised in both qualitative and quantitative terms in order to convey information to decision makers. EIA has been mandatory on development projects across Europe since the late 1980s and a form of strategic environmental assessment (SEA) for policies and plans will become mandatory in the near future. Again, the merits of EIA are discussed in more detail in Chapter 6.

Where administrative techniques such as CBA and EIA provide environmental information on particular projects, programmes or policies, greens also promote alternative methods for judging overall well-being. Commonly used techniques such as measuring Gross National Product (GNP) may provide information about the size and changing nature of national economies, but they are poor indicators of social and environmental aspects of sustainable development. Greens have thus been at the forefront of promoting alternative indicators of 'progress'. These have typically taken two forms: either the re-evaluation of GNP to include social and environmental costs; or the use of a broad set of indicators of well-being that cover economic, social and environmental conditions. In both cases attempts are made to weigh environmental and social impacts alongside economic considerations. Again, these different techniques are discussed at length in Chapter 6.

All of these different administrative techniques attempt to provide more detailed information to decision makers than that currently available to them. The aim is to internalise environmental information within the policy process. The use of these techniques can be seen as a response to the problem of bounded rationality: they are methods for increasing the level of information available to decision makers. However, as Lindblom recognises, the complexity of environmental impacts will still lead to technical problems in collecting and processing information and existing power alignments are likely to affect the collection and interpretation of information. Any use of administrative techniques will remain, to a certain extent, incomplete, partial and partisan (Lindblom, 1979; Gregory, 1989, pp. 145–6).[12]

Structural changes to the institutions of governance

As we discussed earlier in this chapter, environment ministries were first established in the early 1970s in response to high levels of public and political concern. Even when the issue–attention cycle moved on, these ministries retained their interest in raising environmental considerations in government decision-making processes. We have already acknowledged that although this provides the environment with a 'voice' within government, there is a danger that other departments do not see green issues as their concern: there is a lack of integration across government.

One way that such marginalisation of environmental considerations can be lessened is through the use of administrative techniques, such as extended CBA and EIA, or the promotion of green policy principles such as the precautionary principle discussed above. Another way to move towards integration is to restructure ministries so that the environment is integrated with other policy areas. Prior to 1997 the Department of the Environment (DOE) in the UK had responsibility for local government and planning. Consequently it was able to promote sustainable development within planning policy guidance (see Chapter 10). After 1997 the DOE was merged into the Department of the Environment, Transport and the Regions (DETR). Environment officials were thus able to have more influence over transport and regional policy. Further reforms took place after the 2001 election with the creation of the Department of the Environment, Food and Rural Affairs (DEFRA). This has two potential effects. On the positive side the new department could lead to a more sustainable agricultural policy; on the negative side, influence over transport and planning may be lost (see Chapter 9).

Obviously environmental ministries cannot embrace all areas of policy through such reorganisation: ministries and departments cannot cover all issues. However, one way that policy integration can be promoted is through the establishment of special units at the heart of government – within the core executive.[13] An example of this is the Social Exclusion Unit in the Cabinet Office, which attempts to coordinate the different departments, agencies and networks whose work affects social exclusion. The aim is to achieve 'joined-up government', with departments collaborating on difficult and complex policy problems rather than working in isolation. Although a Sustainable Development Unit (SDU) was established within the DETR, this is not at the heart of government and thus has difficulties in drawing other departments into collaborative arrangements. The key point to recognise here is that the architecture of government matters.

Governments do not operate in isolation and successful policy formulation and implementation typically involves other levels of government, agencies and non-governmental actors, including private companies, voluntary associations and citizens. Thus we have witnessed the emergence of stakeholder institutions which draw representatives from different sectors and levels of government. Examples here include the creation of the United Nations Commission on Sustainable Development and the UK Sustainable Development Commission which involve stakeholders from beyond national government. Different stakeholders bring with them different expertise and perspectives on environmental problems and the possibility of a more coordinated and collaborative response to the challenges of sustainable development. Innovative experiments to include citizens and community organisations within the policy-making process have also begun to emerge in recent years (Fischer, 2000; Smith, 2001). Such stakeholder and participatory institutions resonate with the demands for increased participation and deliberation from green theorists discussed earlier in Chapter 2. New forms of environmental governance are beginning to emerge that draw in organisations and individuals from beyond government itself. These will be discussed in more detail in Part III of this book.

The dangers of co-option

The merits of engaging organisations from different sectors (public, private and voluntary) in the policy-making process lies at the heart of ecological modernisation (see Chapter 2). Engagement is said to lead to social learning, creative solutions to complex environmental problems and broad social support for the policies that emerge. Critics of such close association between environmental organisations, private corporations and governments argue that it is a way of co-opting once-radical environmentalists who are seduced by the promise of political influence. Engagement does not necessarily equate to meaningful influence. Critics argue that environmental organisations are in danger of gaining small concessions, but losing their moral authority (Hajer, 1995; Jacobs, 1999a; Dryzek, 1995). The dilemma for the green movement is knowing when to cooperate and when to take a confrontational stance.

Policy instruments

The first barrier to effective environmental policy raised in this chapter was the problem of collective action. If individuals, groups and organisations do not necessarily act in an environmentally-sensitive manner then governments will need to develop instruments to ensure that sustainability outcomes are achieved. Broadly, governments utilise three types of policy instruments: command-and-control, economic and voluntary instruments. Command-and-control involves the use of mandatory regulation: legislation that requires a particular form of behaviour on the part of individuals or firms. Examples here include the banning of CFCs in production processes; or the banning of private vehicles from town centres. Command-and-control leaves little or no room for choice.

Economic instruments operate according to a different logic: they provide an economic incentive for individuals or organisations to improve their environmental performance. Environmentally-damaging actions become more costly and the pursuit of self-interest drives improvements. Thus, for example, tax regimes can be used to protect the environment.

Finally, governments can promote voluntary action. This can range from education campaigns through to the development of environmental covenants with particular industries. Whereas economic instruments work on the assumption that individuals and organisations are self-interested and driven purely by the profit motive, voluntary approaches attempt to develop more environmentally-sensitive behaviour through cooperative and consensual approaches. The effectiveness and potential of these different instruments will be discussed in more depth in the next chapter.

Conclusion

In many ways this chapter is a depressing onslaught of reasons why it is difficult, if not impossible, to produce more ecologically-rational policy. The barriers are formidable. The literature on collective action stresses the difficulties in getting people to agree and to act in concert; individual self-interest undermines the collective interest in environmental protection; and Hardin's vision of tragedy, writ large, signals widespread ecological devastation. Drawing all of the various interests together, whether international organisations, states, private corporations or citizens, to collaborate and develop common solutions appears hopeless. And this problem is made worse when we investigate the fluctuating nature of public opinion. Not only does public opinion wax and wane, meaning that environmental problems slip in and out of the public and political spot-light, but analysis of actual behaviour suggests that a significant part of the population may be environmenally conscious, but this does not translate into more ecologically-sensitive practices and lifestyles. Without meaningful public support, will (or can) effective environmental policy emerge?

The rationality of the policy-making process is further undermined by the bounded nature of rationality and the exercise of power. Environmental problems are typically not addressed in their totality but, rather, compartmentalised and fragmented as departments of government attempt to respond to issues in their jurisdiction. The rationality of any response is limited and bounded by their ability to conceptualise problems, collect and analyse information and available policy instruments. Beyond questions of knowledge, the policy process is also affected by the exercise of power. Decision making takes place in a political context where some groups have access or influence on decision making and others are marginalised. Policy tends to only change incrementally as power alignments shift.

Obviously one response available to greens is to fight power with power, and cunning with cunning. At various times environmental pressure groups have been successful in breaking into or bursting open previously closed policy networks and influencing decisions. Certainly environmental policy and the influence of the environmental movement have developed markedly over the last few decades. One visible effect of environmental political pressure has been changes to the machinery of government which lead to improved integration of environmental considerations in policy making. The use of policy principles such as the polluter pays and the precautionary principle have the potential to reorientate the policy process. Administrative techniques such as CBA, EIA and alternative indicators also attempt to internalise the environment in decision making. Structural changes to the architecture of government, promoting collaboration between departments and with organisations from beyond government, have begun to emerge. And finally governments have a range of different policy instruments available to ensure improved environmental performance and behaviour. At its best a vision of effective environmental governance emerges. At its worst, critics contend that this is nothing more than the pacification of environmental unrest. The extent to which either vision is being realised is a recurrent question throughout the rest of this book.

Case study: air pollution in the United States[14]

Having introduced both the formal problems of aggregating preferences and the broader problem of collective action, it might be helpful to see how they combine in a real life example. This case study demonstrates the problem of collective action in a situation where different groups are forming and breaking de facto alliances with other groups in order to achieve their goals. It illustrates how a group can be frustrated in its purposes by trying to achieve too much and where to have aimed for less would have resulted in achieving more. The conclusion is that not only should groups be careful about which actors they form alliances with, but also that they should learn to appreciate and understand the logic of collective action.

The Legislation

New Source Pollution Standards (NSPS) were rules introduced in the USA for emission control, following lobbying and legislation, which all new plants emitting effluents (especially power stations) had to meet. For *existing* plants the rules demanded that the total ambient level of sulphur dioxide pollution in the local atmosphere must not exceed a certain threshold. *New* plants were required to achieve a *reduction* in emissions.

The legislation was designed to reduce pollution. In fact the consequence of seeking reductions of emissions from new plants was to increase their cost and keep less efficient, dirtier plants in use for longer. Sulphur dioxide was to be 'scrubbed' from exhaust gases until they were as clean as those produced by power stations burning low-sulphur coal. But the fitting of scrubbers added up to 20 per cent to the capital cost of a new plant, while old plants could be kept running for 40 years or longer. Where, then, was the incentive for a company to replace old equipment? There was none. On the contrary there was a disincentive, and the replacement of old equipment slowed down accordingly (Cairncross, 1991, p. 95). Thus the policy was both more expensive than alternatives and left air dirtier because old and dirty power stations remained in use. How did this happen? It emerged from the logic of a situation in which three broad groupings, environmentalists, coal producers and power station operators, were each seeking to achieve certain goals. The lobbying took place in two stages, based on two related but separate issues. The first issue (in 1977) was how to achieve reductions in emissions, that is, whether to employ tradeable permits, green taxes or to insist on the installation of a particular technology in power station chimneys (flue gas desulphurisers). The second issue (in 1979) was that of the level of emissions to be permitted, that is, how stringent or lenient should the legally enforced 'scrubbing' be. In the first instance a coalition of environmentalists and coal producers emerged as both were in favour of scrubbing. The environmentalists wanted strong and obvious measures to be taken to reduce pollution, and they thought that scrubbing rather than less obvious measures, such as fiscal incentives, was the answer: emission control 'scrubbers' in power station chimneys were seen as a more visible gain than changing the behaviour of utilities through the use of fiscal incentives. The coal producers wanted their coal, including that with a high-sulphur content, to continue to be burnt. For the producers of dirty coal, scrubbing enabled them to continue

continued

marketing coal which otherwise could not be sold because utilities would have purchased low-sulphur coal from elsewhere. In opposition to the coalition of coal producers and environmentalists were the power station operators who simply wanted regulations imposing the least cost on their operations. Although both groups comprising the original coalition considered the achievement of compulsory scrubbing a gain, when it came to the question of the stringency of the scrubbing, their paths diverged. At this point the environmentalists found themselves isolated as the coal producers had nothing further to gain from the alliance. A new coalition was born with the coal producers throwing in their lot with the power station operators who wanted to keep costs of production to a minimum.

At this point it is worth considering the nature of the different organisations involved in this bargaining process. Both industrial groups were internally divided. The utilities which planned new power stations (typically the larger ones) would be very much affected by NSPS; those with no such plans were not. The power station operators belonged to a weak trade association (the Edison Electrical Institute) which was made weaker by free-riding: for example, members would send inexpert delegates to its meetings. The large utilities decided to form a new organisation to lobby on the legislation: the Utility Air Regulatory Group (UARG). This was a 'privileged' group, as each member had a sufficiently large interest in the outcome of the political bargaining over NSPS to be willing to take a share of the burden of organising it, whatever the others did. Hence it was the UARG which sponsored the utilities' litigation over NSPS. The coal industry also had its own internal divisions. Coal producers whose coal was naturally low in sulphur (in the West), were not interested in scrubbers; those whose coal was high in sulphur (in the Mid-West and East) wanted scrubbers since this would allow continued consumption of their coal. Because the National Coal Association represented both high- and low-sulphur producers it was caught in the middle and could do little more than fudge the issue. The United Mine Workers' Union, on the other hand, which had most of its members in the high-sulphur coal-producing East, came out in favour of universal scrubbing; the UMWU was a strong union with political influence which could effectively and cheaply lobby for high benefits for its members. On this occasion it had a clear interest in lobbying for the introduction of scrubbing as its members' livelihoods were at stake. In addition, some of the coal producers in the East who stood to lose most if scrubbing was not enforced were sufficiently concerned to be willing to take on the costs of lobbying themselves. Thus both the utilities and the coal industry managed to solve their collective action problems and emerged as formidable lobbies in the political bargaining over the introduction of NSPS. One consequence of the bargaining over pollution control was more expensive electricity, yet no consumer lobby emerged. Once again this was because of a collective action problem: despite the collective benefits if everyone were to act in concert, the marginal utility to an individual of taking part in a consumer-group lobby is infinitesimal and therefore consumers tend to remain a 'latent' group.[15] The contrast with the utilities is quite stark.

The environmentalists[16] confused the appearance of tough action on emission controls with the reality of effective action. They took the view that forced scrubbing on new plants was preferable to no forced scrubbing, and that more stringent scrubbing was better than less, but failed to realise that the effect of introducing strenuous rules applying only to new plants would be to keep older and dirtier plants in operation for longer and that this would not reduce pollution but rather increase it. A less strenuous policy on new plants would have been less polluting overall and hence a better outcome for them, but they were unable to see this at the time. In addition, they suffered from a voting paradox (of the sort illustrated earlier in the chapter) because the lobbying over NSPS went in two stages and the order in which votes was taken partly determined the outcome.

Of course, there was no formal voting as such, but with three main actors making and unmaking alliances the effect was the same. At any given moment the most powerful lobby was the alliance with two 'votes' as compared with their opponent's one vote. In 1977 the issue was whether to legally enforce scrubbing or to adopt another policy instead. Because they saw it as being in their interests (although in each case for very different reasons), the environmentalists and the coal industry joined forces to lobby for forced scrubbing on the utilities. At this time both got what they wanted. But two years later the issue had changed. What had to be decided now was the *level* of scrubbing and the coal industry joined the utilities in a 'dirty coal/dirty air' alliance to fight off plans for stringent emission control. The utilities wanted to minimise their costs and hence preferred lenient emission levels as it kept the costs of installing new technology down. The coal producers were concerned only that their coal continued to be burnt and this was more likely if the emission controls were less rather than more stringent. Thus, the outcome of this bargaining and alliance making, as each group sought to maximise its interests, was forced scrubbing at a lenient level. If the voting order had been different, or if there had been a single straight choice between legally enforced scrubbing at a stringent level and no forced scrubbing, then the original coalition of environmentalists and coal producers would have held firm and the outcome would have been different. Environmentally speaking this would not have been the best solution, but it would have been superior to the actual outcome. The voting can be illustrated by the following table, in which the preference orderings for each lobby are represented.

Table 4.2 The lobbies' preferences

Environmentalists	Utilities	Coal producers
stringent scrubbing	no forced scrubbing	lenient scrubbing
lenient scrubbing	lenient scrubbing	stringent scrubbing
no forced scrubbing	stringent scrubbing	no forced scrubbing

The first 'vote' was a choice between forced scrubbing and no forced scrubbing. The groups for whom no forced scrubbing was their last preference (the coal industry and the environmentalists) combined to beat the utilities for whom it was their first. In the second round of voting the choice was between stringent scrubbing and lenient scrubbing. But here stringent scrubbing was bound to lose out to a new coalition formed by the coal industry and the utilities who both preferred lenient scrubbing to stringent scrubbing.

Conclusion

It is clear that although the environmentalists at first appeared to get what they wanted (in that scrubbing became compulsory), what they eventually got was far from their original aspirations. They achieved an outcome which was worse than the alternatives which they had spurned, because forced scrubbing looked tougher, with the result that they helped to convert the legislation into 'a multibillion-dollar bail-out for high-sulphur coal producers' (Ackerman and Hassler, 1981). This was hardly their intention. What lessons can be learnt from this? Clearly,

continued

environmentalists need to be tactically aware of the background conditions to their actions; they need to watch carefully to avoid falling into procedural and other traps. They also need to be aware of their real interests, and not to confuse green appearance with green reality. A policy or decision is not necessarily effective just because it looks tough and uncompromising; on the contrary, as in this case, it might be just the opposite. It is not in their interest to achieve something which merely **looks** like an environmentally radical policy; that, after all, is what they usually accuse governments and business of doing. Thus they need to make judgements both about the tactics and the suitability of policies by looking at their likely consequences in a hard-headed manner. While they might themselves not be calculating, self-interested, egotistical utility maximisers, to a certain extent they need to assume that their opponents probably are, that they are well versed and cunning in maximising their interests. That is, after all, how many environmentalists themselves portray industrial actors and governments. The message for environmentalists is therefore to watch for potential pitfalls. These may come in many shapes and sizes: some deliberate, some accidental, some procedural, some substantive, some well concealed, some obvious.

Suggestions for further reading

Matthew Crenson *The Un-Politics of Air Pollution* and John Gaventa *Power and Powerlessness* are classic studies of the politics of power in the environmental arena. Iain McLean *Public Choice* is an accessible introductory text on collective action problems, while *Global Challenges* by Todd Sandler is an extended application of these ideas to global environmental problems. Tim O'Riordan and James Cameron's edited collection *Interpreting the Precautionary Principle* highlights a number of problems facing decision makers. *Environmental Policy* edited by Wolfgang Rüdig is a two-volume set of classic articles in comparative environmental policy. Robert Paehlke and Douglas Torgerson *Managing Leviathan* is a challenging collection of essays on many of the policy problems facing liberal democracies.

Notes

1   'Rational choice' is a broad term which includes 'public choice' and 'social choice' theory. The former studies political and bureaucratic processes on the assumption that people engaged in politics and administration behave in the same way as they do when making choices in a market; the latter concentrates on the formal aspects of decision-making procedures by studying the problems of aggregating individual preferences into a rational and acceptable social choice. See Heap *et al.* (1992) and Mueller (1989) for a complete overview of the territory.

2   These assumptions can of course be challenged. It can be denied that people are really like this; or it can be argued that they are like this some, but not all, of the time; or that they only behave in this way under special circumstances; or that it is wrong to think of preferences as always fixed and immutable; and so on. It is clear that collective agreement and action is often threatened by the existence of free-riding, and that this has significance for environmental politics: this concession is enough to show that these theories may have something to offer.

3   This is not a hypothetical example: it is based on events in Liverpool in the early 1980s. The example is taken from Laver (1983, pp. 152–4).

4   Strictly speaking the problem is not one of 'the commons', but of open access to resources owned by no one. Given such ownership status, we can perhaps understand why authoritarian solutions to environmental problems have been proposed by certain elements of the green movement (see Chapter 2).

5   The detail and adequacy of Lukes's account can be challenged, as it is for example by Wrong (1979), Morriss (1987) and Hindess (1996), but commentators would agree that the aspects of power which he investigates need to be addressed. See Clegg (1989) for a good introductory overview of the debates around the concept of power.

6   For further discussion of such bias within the politics of transport see the case study at the end of Chapter 3.

7   See the case study at the end of this chapter for an extended example.

8   The 1990 UK White Paper, *This Common Inheritance*, which largely consisted of a repackaging exercise of this sort, received extensive criticism on exactly these grounds. It promised much but delivered little. Most of its more radical proposals were consigned to an appendix on the use of economic instruments in environmental policy despite the commissioning of David Pearce as an advisor. Here it is important to remember that what was considered radical was the use of economic instruments, rather than any more fundamental questioning of the UK's patterns of production and consumption. For more on *This Common Inheritance*, see Chapter 9.

9   See the appendix of Harding and Fisher (1999) for examples of contrasting statements of the precautionary principle in different international and national contexts.

10   Tim O'Riordan draws these themes from O'Riordan and Cameron (1994) and O'Riordan and Jordan (1995).

11   Michael Jacobs, for example, exposes the dangers inherent in a naive belief in the neutrality of science, arguing that many of the assumptions made in, for instance, climate change models emerge out of 'complex socio-political processes in which scientists are inevitably bound up with the commitments of the political and economic institutions responsible for funding and acting on the research' (Jacobs, 1995a, p. 1473). See the case study on climate change politics at the end of Chapter 7.

12   The case study at the end of Chapter 3 provides just one example of how political considerations can affect the use of CBA, in this case in decision making about road construction.

13   Within political science, the part of government that attempts to coordinate policy areas and networks is termed the 'core executive' (see Rhodes and Dunleavy, 1995).

14   This example is for the most part adapted from McLean (1987, pp. 62–80).

15   For a full account of 'privileged' and 'latent' groups, see Olson (1971, pp. 48–52).

16   The main environmental organisations involved were the Sierra Club and the Natural Resources Defense Council (NRDC).

Choosing the means

> There is no single ideal instrument or type of instrument, we need the full
> orchestra.
>
> (Jänicke and Weidner, 1995, p. 18)

Having identified in the previous chapter that there are a number of barriers to developing effective responses to environmental problems, it is necessary to turn to a more detailed discussion of the appropriate means for solving them. There is no single or simple answer to the question of means: it depends on the nature of the issue being addressed and on the responses of industry, consumers and pressure groups. Different problems may require different types of solution, for example, taxes, charges, targets, limits, bans, or some appropriate mixture of policy responses. As discussed in the previous chapter, collective action problems lie at the heart of many environmental issues. Thus, policy responses are often attempts to solve collective action difficulties. Industry pollutes because it is a cheap method of waste disposal; resources are depleted because it is to the advantage of each to take what they can. If environmental resources are to be used in a sustainable manner, then environmental policy has to find ways of ensuring that the actions of individuals, businesses and government are themselves sustainable.

In this chapter we will address a number of policy responses: regulation and enforcement, economic instruments and voluntary approaches. Each of these approaches responds in a different way to the collective action problem. Regulation punishes transgressors; economic instruments provide an economic incentive to improve environmental performance; voluntary approaches rely on education, persuasion and negotiation. Each policy instrument has its advantages and disadvantages. The case study at the end of the chapter investigates how policy instruments might be applied to the problem of unrestricted use of the car. Private motor-car use has led to crowded and congested roads; it is a significant contributor to climate change and user of resources and energy. As roads become more congested and travel becomes slower and more unpredictable, we consider proposals for London and the UK aimed at alleviating the problem.

Regulation and enforcement

What sort of governmental interventions are possible? The first and most easily understood is straightforward regulation and control through an appropriate regulatory body, such as the Environment Agency in the UK or the Environmental Protection Agency in the USA. Mandatory regulation or 'command-and-control' (as the standard regulatory approach is often known) typically takes the form of legislation, the issuing of orders to industry and other actors. Regulation tends to be thought of as primarily affecting industry, for example, through controls of effluents and emissions. However, regulation also directly affects the lives of private citizens, for example, banning the use of cars in a city centre. Regulations may be used to define acceptable processes, establish emissions standards or specify quality objectives. Traditionally, regulation requires the relevant agency to concern itself with the activities of an industry or plant and it can take many forms, from complete control over every aspect of a firm's activity to a more hands-off approach which assumes that firms are doing what they should unless it can be proved that they are not. Acceptable levels of emissions can be determined and companies punished where they fail to meet them. These standards may be uniform quantitative standards, identical for all firms (as is typically the case in German and EU policy), or take the form of a more flexible response, negotiating with individual companies to determine their acceptable levels of emissions.

Alternatively, standards can be set by looking at what are known as ambient levels of pollution.[1] These are 'end-of-pipe' controls: the emissions of processes are regulated. Here the local carrying capacity of a particular environment is ascertained by determining that it can assimilate pollutants up to, but not beyond, a certain level; standards would be set accordingly. Companies which exceed the standard will then be punished in some way. One problem with this is that punishment, by definition, follows the crime, and hence emerges only after the environmental damage has already been done. Further, the level of fines may be inadequate to act as a deterrent: it may be cheaper for a company to pay the fines than to change their production processes. At this point draconian measures may be needed, such as preventing the company from producing or trading either permanently or until they have changed their processes. Another problem, and one which is of central importance to the arguments for economic incentives, is that setting a standard and punishing a firm for exceeding that level creates no incentive for them to seek to *reduce* their emissions beyond the standard. They receive nothing for doing so.

Rather than end-of-pipe controls, standards are often set not at ambient levels, but based instead on the use of particular types of pollution-control technology. For example, firms may simply be required to install the best available technology (BAT). What matters here is less their actual level of emissions and its effect on the environment, but whether they are using the appropriate technology. There are problems with this approach. For example, if production increases, emissions will increase. As long as the approved technology is still being used there is little that can be done about this unless there is a separately stipulated emissions ceiling. What counts as the best available technology is also a matter of dispute; and even where it is not, it may be extremely expensive for some companies to install the best technology available. Requiring them to do so might simply put them out of business – although this may sometimes be the right thing to do. Hence, regulatory systems have evolved in which firms seeking authorisation for their manufacturing processes are required to install the best available technology *not entailing excessive cost* (BATNEEC) or the best practicable method (BPM). In addition, where discharge is to more than one environmental medium, authorisation of the industrial process concerned is often subject to the condition that it meets the requirement of the best practicable environmental option (BPEO).[2] This requires a lot of expensive, labour-intensive and time-consuming negotiation between the regulator and the regulated and there is always a danger of compromise. Inspectors and companies will inevitably find themselves in protracted discussion about what constitutes 'excessive cost' and what the 'best available technology' is at any given time. BATNEEC attempts to match the cut in pollution required of each firm to its cost structure. However, given an understandable reluctance on the part of inspectors to closing down a firm which cannot afford to install the best available technology, there is a danger that companies will continue to use inferior technology on grounds of cost and hence to continue polluting at too high a level. A stringent uniform approach, such as that typical of Germany, avoids this problem, but perhaps at the expense of a loss of flexibility in responding to individual companies' needs and to the peculiarities of a local environment.

The use of regulations is in many ways straightforward and uncomplicated; it is readily understood by governments and by the public. But, as Michael Jacobs argues, for it to work effectively certain conditions have to be met:

> To the firm or consumer, regulations offer no legal choice. Pollution or resource use above the consented level or through use of unsanctioned technology . . . is simply forbidden. The cost of non-compliance is judicial punishment: a fine or sometimes imprisonment. This means that enforcement and punishment are crucial. When enforcement is difficult, or where the level of punishment is too low, the environmental target may not be achieved.
>
> (Jacobs, 1991, p. 136)

There are some advantages to command-and-control, especially where a pollutant or a process requires an outright ban. In the case of some pollutants, for example, heavy metals, the only acceptable level of emission is zero. If a monitoring regime and appropriate deterrents are in place, simple prohibition through regulation is a sound option. Further, it is possible to act quickly: the regulator can step in and ban or reduce an emission where serious environmental damage is occurring or likely to occur. Other means of doing this may be subject to appreciable time lags. The disadvantages are, however, well documented. Command-and-control, if it is to be fully comprehensive, requires an enormous amount of knowledge on the part of the regulator of the activities concerned. It is thus time consuming and expensive. Since firms know what their productive activities entail, it may be better to set up a system in which they establish self-monitoring processes and are given incentives to reduce their polluting activities and then left to choose the best method of doing so. As we have already mentioned, command-and-control provides no incentive for firms to do better than the standard. Thus it is poor at reducing polluting activity below a fixed level, and in some cases it may allow increases as long as the appropriate technology is being employed. Further, under a regime such as in the UK, a flexible and responsive arrangement between regulator and regulated can degenerate into a cosy relationship whereby the regulator is 'captured' by those it is regulating. A regulator is said to be captured when the relationship with the industry being regulated becomes too close. This may be revealed by a circulation of personnel between the two, together with too great a willingness to listen sympathetically to the regulated industry at the expense of the public interest, consumers or the environment. Ultimately it leads to a bias in favour of the regulated industry characterised by an acceptance of its terms and agenda.

Given these problems with command-and-control regulation, might there not be other solutions which are both more flexible and more likely to achieve the desired ends? Alan Moran argues that alternative approaches are available:

> The command-and-control solution, in opting for particular means of abatement, faces an impossible task of achieving abatement efficiently. Firms

have a vast number of options in terms of their abatement equipment, its maintenance, the inputs they use and the quantity, quality and mix of their outputs. With direct controls, the regulatory authority needs to know the technological and other adjustment alternatives open to individual emitting firms in order to specify individual emission levels and technologies. Far less information is required for the implementation of taxes or marketable permits because individual emitters make their own decisions about output and emissions.

(Moran, 1995, p. 77)

It is to such taxes and permits that we now turn.

Economic instruments

Mandatory regulation clearly has its merits. But a key disadvantage is simply that it punishes transgressors for doing wrong where what is needed in environmental policy is to encourage potential polluters to do right. One way of doing this is to establish a system within which polluters have an incentive not only to avoid polluting, but to reduce their polluting activities and in so doing gain a fiscal advantage. There are two main sources of inefficiency in the command-and-control approach. First, it requires the regulator to use resources in acquiring information the polluter already possesses. Second, polluters vary in the extent to which they can abate pollution. Under command-and-control each polluter has to meet a given standard or use a particular technology. However, some polluters find it easier or cheaper than others to reduce their polluting activities. Perhaps, then, control should be concentrated on where it is cheapest to abate pollution because then the overall costs of compliance would be minimised. Economic incentives enable a polluter to choose how to adjust to the required environmental standard. Some will prefer to pay while others will prefer to install new or modified equipment. Hence there is an incentive, not found under a direct regulatory system, to reduce levels of pollution.

Just as rational choice theorists understand individual behaviour, we could conceive of firms as self-interested rational utility maximisers. Whether the motives and behaviour of individual people are best understood in this way or not, there is little doubt that the description fits profit-making companies accurately, and that at least some of the time, it is an accurate description of people's behaviour. If this is a fair assumption, would it not be possible to recognise and possibly utilise such self-interested behaviour in the formulation of environmental policy? In Chapter 4 we saw that collective action problems arise out of the aggregation of the actions of rational self-interested actors where there is an incentive to free-ride, and that it leads to an outcome which is the worst outcome for all. But must the outcome of self-interested actions necessarily be for the worst? Economists argue that the operation of the market provides a mechanism which harnesses individually self-interested actions to the good of all. In economic theory a properly working free market should produce an outcome which, although not intended by any single company or person (each of whom is assumed to behave according to their own self-interest), is nevertheless to everyone's advantage. Thus, through the operation of 'the invisible hand', self-interested individual actions lead to a collective outcome of benefit to all. It is the possibility of utilising self-interested behaviour in this way which lies behind proposals for the use of economic instruments in environmental policy. Intervention in the market is required to adjust the overall structure of incentives and disincentives and thereby modify the behaviour of producers and consumers in ways which benefit the environment.

But modifying the market in this way has a further objective. The use of economic instruments is not only concerned with providing internal incentives to polluters and resource users to reduce their emissions or to reduce their inputs. It also seeks to internalise the external costs of pollution and resource depletion. The prices of goods bought and sold in markets prior to this form of intervention tend not to include the environmental costs of production, consumption and disposal. These costs are known as 'externalities': they are external consequences of the activities of producers and consumers who do not have to pay for them or take them into account. The attempt to remedy this links these forms of economic incentive directly to the polluter pays principle (PPP). Although it is possible, in principle, to achieve PPP through direct regulatory means (if the costs to a polluter of polluting are sufficiently high, this is equivalent to forcing them to accept responsibility for the environmental damage they cause, and to pay for it), economic incentives offer a more flexible and efficient way of achieving this end:

> The lack of proper prices for, and the open access characteristic of many environmental resources means that there is a severe risk that over exploitation leading to eventual complete destruction will occur. The PPP seeks to rectify this market failure by making polluters internalize the costs of use or degradation of environmental resources.
>
> (Turner *et al.*, 1994, p. 45)

As with so many key terms in environmental politics and economics, it is possible to interpret what PPP requires in a variety of different ways. At a minimum it can be understood as merely the requirement that polluters should pay for their excess pollution. This would be seen as granting them the right to discharge their emissions up to the acceptable level free of charge. On the other hand, a stricter interpretation would require polluters to pay for *all* of their discharges to the environment, not merely those deemed to be in excess of some particular limit. This stricter interpretation, if implemented, means that polluters have an economic incentive to reduce their pollution across the board. It creates the necessary conditions for the use of economic incentives in environmental policy. Providing a continuing incentive to pollute less through internalising externalities can be a rigorous way of meeting PPP. Although direct regulation can force some internalisation of external costs, the use of economic instruments can do this while at the same time offering other advantages in pollution control. Where environmental goods are regarded as free, the cost of the production of a good is a combination of priced inputs (including labour, capital and technology) and unpriced inputs (environmental services). In such a case the market price does not reflect the true value of the resources used to produce goods and services and the market fails to allocate resources efficiently because there is a divergence between private and social cost;

that is, a divergence between the cost to the individual or company and the cost to wider society. Many environmental resources are regarded in this manner and are not currently represented in the price mechanism. As such they tend to be over-consumed and the environment degraded. Giving them a positive price signals that they are not free and that consumption entails a cost. It means that the environmental costs of production, consumption and waste disposal are reflected in the costs of economic goods and services. The costs of production are altered and the price level reflects the environmental impact of the goods produced and consumed. The new, environmentally-sensitive price indicates to consumers the full cost of producing a product. In such a system, assuming that environmental goods can be priced properly, PPP would deter over-consumption and environmental degradation.

Most economists argue that the market-based approach is more efficient and effective than command-and-control. The proper price for a good is (or should be) that which reflects the full social and environmental costs of production. In a competitive market a firm will increase production until the point where it would cost as much to produce an extra unit as would be gained from selling it. Economists then say that marginal cost equals marginal revenue and at this point production stabilises as there is no advantage to be gained by producing greater quantities. However, if production does not take proper account of the full social and environmental costs, marginal cost will be too low and, because the firm will be able to maximise profit at the higher level of production, it will produce (and consumers will consume) beyond the point at which excessive environmental and social damage is caused. Here the firm has not internalised the external cost of production. If, however, the firm is forced to include these external costs of its production process, overall costs will rise, prices will rise and demand will fall. The firm will therefore produce less and reduce its use of resources and its level of polluting emissions. Of course, matters are never quite so simple in reality. For some goods (typically necessities such as bread or fuel) consumers cannot easily find acceptable substitutes or reduce their consumption and will therefore tend to continue to buy them despite price rises. Demand will vary little with price. Economists describe goods of this type as 'price inelastic'. In these cases the firm will be able to pass on increased costs to the consumer. Thus, if we are considering imposing a tax, the impact that it will have will depend on the type of goods concerned. In principle, however, the environment should benefit either way. On the one hand, if production falls, emissions and resource use fall with it; on the other, if production remains high, the higher level of tax revenues can be used to remedy environmental damage or to engage in research on improving the environmental impact of manufacturing processes.[3]

PPP states that the polluter should pay: but who is the polluter? Is it the company or is it the consumer? We perhaps have an image of firms producing goods while remaining complacently indifferent to the pollution caused, and we think they should be punished. However, as we have already seen, companies who face increased costs may in some cases simply pass on those extra costs to the consumer. In this case the phrase 'making the polluter pay' equates to 'making the consumer pay'. Is this fair? Are the public the innocent victims of a double bind in which they suffer at the hands of the polluter and are also asked to pay for the cost of putting matters right? Before we conclude that PPP is a capitalist fraud we need to look at the issue a little closer. Who is the polluter? Who should pay? There are a number of important considerations here.

Is there a valid objection to consumers paying higher prices for environmentally-damaging products? Presumably the goods concerned are produced because there is consumer demand. But up to this point these consumers have not been paying the proper price which reflects the full environmental cost. Why should they escape their share of the extra cost? Both the producer and the consumer are 'the polluter'. Our overall pattern of consumption has a detrimental environmental effect. It would be hypocrisy to blame a firm as if they operated utterly independent of consumer demand. We are all to some extent complicit in the environmental degradation caused by the production of the goods and services we demand. However, despite these strictures, it should be remembered that existing markets do not function perfectly and that consumers have little or no knowledge or control over the processes and raw materials that firms employ. If they were fully informed about all aspects of production they might disapprove of, and object to, much that companies do. In practice, however, information is often limited, and even where it is available, consumers may be powerless if alternative products do not exist. Only in economists' models are consumers able to directly influence the mode and manner of production. In principle, the idea of consumers paying for environmental damage is fair, but in practice markets do not operate perfectly and the wishes of consumers tend not to influence the behaviour of companies to any great extent.

So far we have examined the basic principles lying behind the advocacy of economic instruments as an alternative to command-and-control and discussed their use in meeting PPP. We now need to look at possible mechanisms in a little more detail. All economic mechanisms use markets, but some modify existing markets and others create new markets. Price-based mechanisms are so called because they affect prices in existing markets through the imposition of taxes. The incentives they provide can take different forms such as the direct alteration of price or cost levels through product charges, emissions charges or input charges; indirect alteration through financial or fiscal means such as subsidies or loans for good environmental practice; or market support where government agencies stabilise prices by, for example, guaranteeing a price for recycled paper, glass or metal. Rights-based mechanisms, on the other hand, create new markets by allocating to people or firms the right to use environmental resources in the form of quotas or permits and allowing these to be traded at a price determined by the market thus created (Beder, 1996, p. 105).

Price-based mechanisms: green taxes[4]

Support for the idea of green taxes is increasing. They are seen as a flexible and efficient alternative to traditional command-and-control techniques. In principle they reduce compliance costs (the costs that polluters bear in meeting the standard) and they allow polluters to choose how best to adjust to the environmental quality standard. Polluters facing high pollution abatement costs will prefer to pay the tax; those with low costs will install equipment to avoid paying.

Taxes can be imposed in different ways and upon different things. For example, emissions charges are levied on the discharge of pollutants into the air, water or soil; user charges are related to treatment or disposal cost; product charges are levied on products that are harmful to the environment when used in production processes or when consumed. Although charges of these sort are the most commonly used economic instrument, their application has hitherto tended to be economically sub-optimal, that is, they have been set at too low a rate to achieve the environmental objectives. They have tended to be used merely as a way of raising revenue and have therefore not had a significant incentive effect (Cairncross, 1991, p. 97). However, recent proposals for green taxes require them to be more than mere revenue earners. The idea is that polluters should pay according to the estimated damage caused by their emissions and that the imposition of the tax should also change their behaviour. For example, the introduction of a landfill tax in the UK has forced local authorities to rethink their waste-disposal strategies by making other processes more economically viable. But it is important to remember that green taxes should not be seen in isolation from taxation and economic policy as a whole. They can form part of a wider strategy which seeks to change the tax dynamics of a whole economy by shifting the tax burden away from taxes on income and labour. Taxes whose rationale is merely to raise revenue are becoming increasingly unpopular. They can be replaced by green taxes which have a 'double dividend' in that they raise revenue and also have a direct positive environmental impact.[5]

Environmental taxes in the UK

- *Landfill tax* – levied on the disposal of waste to land-fill sites.
- *VAT on domestic energy consumption.*
- *Climate change levy* – a tax on business energy consumption.
- *Aggregates tax* – on the quarrying of virgin sand, gravel and crushed rock.
- *Fuel duties* – differential duties on leaded and unleaded petrol, diesel, low-sulphur diesel and liquid petroleum gas.
- *Vehicle excise duty* – vehicles with larger and less fuel-efficient engines pay higher duty.
- *Taxes on company cars.*
- *Road congestion and workplace car parking charges* (see case study).

(adapted from Commission on Taxation and Citizenship, 2000, p. 299)

From the point of view of administration, a green tax has several advantages over the traditional UK approach of quantitative emissions standards backed by low fines. The first is that they can be administered through the existing tax frame-work, and therefore there is a lower risk of evasion compared with fixed emissions standards policed through irregular on-site inspections. Second, taxes provide an incentive for further reductions in emissions, because reducing the amount of emissions reduces the amount of tax for which the firm is liable. Third, there is therefore an incentive to commit funds to research into new, less polluting forms of technology. Finally, taxes on one pollutant may have the related effect of reducing emissions of associated pollutants: for example, a tax on carbon emissions from fossil fuels may lead producers to switch to non-fossil fuels and thus simultaneously reduce the emissions of sulphur dioxide.

Green taxes are popular, in theory, because they enable government to intervene in the economy with the minimum of direct interference with the actions of firms or individuals. In principle the idea is simple: government sets a tax at a level which discourages people from buying environmentally-unsound products. If people buy products in smaller quantities the tax has done its work; if, on the other hand, they continue to buy products in significant quantities the revenue raised can be used for environmental-protection purposes. Where they work best, taxes of this sort, such as a carbon tax on fuel, succeed by significantly changing the behaviour of individuals and companies. But behaviour will only be changed if the tax is set at a sufficiently high rate. Measures such as increased taxes on road use and fuel will not measurably reduce vehicle use if the alteration is only at the margins. But even marginal changes in tax provide revenue which can be used for ameliorative purposes such as environmental enhancement projects, funding emergency services and hospitals, and research and development. However, for taxes to change behaviour as well as provide welcome extra revenue they need to be set at a rate which makes the cost of motoring so high it borders on the prohibitive.

There are, however, problems with green taxes. One is that they are often regressive in impact. For example, a carbon tax levied on domestic or motor fuel has a high impact on low-income groups, whereas the better-off can afford to pay the higher costs because fuel makes up a much smaller proportion of their total income. These regressive impacts can be offset in various ways, such as through the provision of grants or aid to those directly affected by them. The point is that their regressive nature needs to be recognised and green taxes should be thought of as part of an overall shift in taxation strategy rather than as a separate solution to a separate problem. Another technical problem with setting a tax is that it is intrinsically difficult to set it at precisely that level at which people are sufficiently discouraged from using that product to have the desired environmental effect.[6] If it is set too low the environment will suffer; if it is set too high, people and industry will protest. The problem is that one is trying to achieve a certain target in actual use and in order to do this one has to make a number of assumptions about elasticity of demand, about the relative value of goods and about the value of money. Taxes will need to be frequently re-adjusted to ensure that they maintain the same effects against a background of changing relative costs, currency fluctuations, innovations in research and development, entry into and out of an industry, and shifting patterns of consumer demand. It is possible to adjust tax rates year by year: but this is fraught with technical difficulties if the objective is to ensure consistent environmental protection, and also with political difficulties as this is highly unpopular with industry since it hinders their long-term investment plans.

And as a final cautionary note, it is important to recognise that the widespread use of green taxes requires that people and businesses understand their purpose and trust governments to use the proceeds as they claim they will. A recent EU study on green taxes shows that, on the contrary, there is general mistrust of governments and little understanding of the case for shifting taxes on to environmentally-damaging activities. The study challenges a basic principle of environmental tax reform, which is that taxes should be cut on positive items such as labour and increased on negative ones such as pollution. There is scarcely any public or business acceptance of the argument that this shift could yield both economic and environmental benefits: the 'double dividend'. Quite the opposite: they saw the approach as merely pointlessly moving money around and did not grasp the point that the relative cost of things would change. In addition, the public did not trust governmental assurances that the money raised would be used as promised (ENDS, 2002c, pp. 8–9).

Clearly a degree of caution is appropriate because no solution is a panacea, even where it has understanding and support and operates effectively; but at the same time we should be mindful of the potential advantages of green taxation, and accept that:

> Taxation is in many cases an appropriate, efficient and effective way to protect the environment. It is not the only way; it will not be suitable or acceptable in all cases, and it will almost always work best in combination with regulations and educational campaigns. But taxation to make prices reflect the full social and environmental cost of particular activities is a necessary part of a transition to a sustainable society.
>
> (Tindale and Holtham, 1996, p. 14)

Rights-based mechanisms: tradeable permits and quotas

Price-based instruments, such as taxes, rely on the workings of already existing markets and seek to achieve their objective by altering the relative prices of goods so as to influence behaviour. Rights-based responses, on the other hand, start from the view that new markets can be created or existing markets can be modified or extended. For example, markets can be created in previously free services: entrance fees to natural amenities could be charged or coastal zones could be privately owned with their owners charging for the use of waters as sewage dumps. An amenity or environmental asset which is privately owned would not be vulnerable, it is argued, to the problem of open access which we examined in Chapter 4. The owner of such an amenity has a direct financial incentive to preserve it and ensure its profitability over a period of time. This idea is central to free-market environmentalism which we discuss later in this chapter. Other approaches establish rights to pollute or rights to exploit resources and combine this with the establishment of a market in these rights. Rights-based approaches, such as tradeable quotas and permits, start with the end to be achieved, and work backwards. Industries are given the right to consume environmental resources and to trade any surplus they do not need. A market is created in the right to pollute or to consume resources: the overall level of emissions or resource use is determined in advance and the quotas or permits are left to find their own price. This avoids the need to adjust the tax rates continually and is well suited to situations in which the carrying capacity of the environment can be accurately specified and in which the optimum number of firms exists to generate a working market.

Instead of setting a pollution target in terms of price, as a tax does, this sets it in terms of quantity. . . . Under such schemes, governments set a standard in terms of, say, tons of sulphur dioxide a year. That total is then shared out among companies or power stations. Each polluter thus has a quota of gas that it can emit. If it introduces new, cleaner technology so that its emissions fall below its permitted level, it can sell its unneeded share to other polluters, or to new companies that may want to set up in the same business. Companies for whom cleaning up is relatively cheap thus have an incentive to be as clean as possible. But the dirty can also stay in business, though carrying the cost of buying more pollution credits.

(Cairncross, 1991, pp. 100–1)

Those who find it expensive and difficult to reduce their pollution costs, or who want to continue using resources, will prefer to buy permits; those with low abatement costs, or who are not tied to the use of a particular resource, will be willing and able to sell their permits. Tradeable permits have a number of advantages: they are flexible; they encourage efficiency; they encourage polluters to continually improve their environmental performance. Where a permit scheme is set up for air pollution, what matters is the total ambient level of pollution, not how much each individual polluter pollutes. For fisheries, what matters is whether the catch or yield is sustainable, not how much each individual boat catches. Tradeable permit schemes have been put into practice in various parts of the world, most successfully in the USA where a system was set up under the Clean Air Acts of the 1970s and expanded by the Clean Air Act of 1991.

Permits are seen as attractive because they avoid some of the problems associated with taxes while at the same time retaining the flexibility associated with the use of economic incentives and avoiding the perceived defects of command-and-control. With taxes there is always the problem of estimating the correct level of tax to achieve the desired effect. Permits, on the other hand, have the advantage that they can 'guarantee the achievement of particular pollution targets, because the authorities control the number of available permits. Moreover, if permits are leased rather than sold, the authorities are able to tighten the ambient targets by cutting the number of permits available' (Jacobs, 1991, p. 142).

There is thus an incentive to *benefit* the environment rather than simply (as in command-and-control systems) a punishment for harming the environment. By starting from the premise that the target is being met (although the target can be adjusted if necessary) and allowing companies to decide for themselves how to meet their share of the target, standards can be varied to reflect the conditions of the day. The authority would then act like a central bank in buying and selling securities to influence their price (Pearce and Turner, 1990, pp. 113–14).

Tradeable permit systems have the advantage that there is no need, as there is with the imposition of environmental taxes, to ascertain both the required standard and the appropriate tax rate. All that is needed is for the proper environmental standard to be identified and for permits to be distributed through a fair and acceptable procedure. The price of the permits is determined by market transactions and this removes the difficulty governments traditionally have in determining the appropriate price level. This is because a permit scheme starts from the conclusion and works backwards by setting the overall permissible levels of emissions and then allocating permits which in aggregate are equivalent to that level. Prices find their own level. Government does not therefore need to keep adjusting the tax so as to ensure that the target is being met. Permits are thus much more flexible (and in principle cheaper to administer) than command-and-control and often more appropriate than a system of taxes. There are, however, two important conditions that have to be met for a permits system to work properly. First, it has to be possible to determine the permissible overall level of emissions, and this can be difficult because it requires the ability to judge the carrying capacity of the affected environment. Second, it has to be possible to set up a market in which genuine trading can and will take place and where emissions can be monitored. This in itself is a strong reason for resisting the idea that permits schemes are some sort of environmental panacea. As with other approaches they should be used with caution and in an appropriate manner. There are problems both with too many permit holders in a market and also with too few:

> Under a tradeable permits scheme, the administrative costs could be very high if there are a great many polluters. Where there are comparatively few, the costs of administration are low, but a new problem arises in that one or two polluters may corner the market in permits and refuse to trade them. This would act like a barrier to entry for new firms and the permits could therefore contribute to non-competitive behaviour.
>
> (Turner *et al.*, 1994, p. 187)

Thus a permits scheme is unsuitable in cases both where there is a very high number of emissions sources (for example, exhaust emissions from motor cars) and also where the number of sources is so low that a few operators dominate the market. Where the appropriate conditions are not met it is better to turn to taxation, or command-and-control solutions.

There are also practical drawbacks to permits schemes which need to be borne in mind. For example, the unrestricted use of permits could easily lead to a situation in which a particular locality suffers excess pollution or resource use, simply because the focus is on the overall condition of the environment in a region, irrespective of localised 'hot spots'. Regulation in addition to a permits scheme may very well be necessary. As Jacobs argues:

> [T]radeable permits have the disadvantage that they may allow very high discharges in some places, compensated by very low emissions elsewhere. This will often be unacceptable: they therefore usually have to operate with 'backstop' regulations setting maximum discharge rates.
>
> (Jacobs, 1991, p. 142)

Although tradeable permits have to date mostly been employed in respect of air pollution, the principle can be extended to many different forms of pollution and also, as we have already seen, to the achieving of sustainable levels of resource extraction. Take, for example, over-fishing in the world's oceans. New Zealand has introduced a system of giving fishermen quotas which they can either take up or sell.

This gives them a predictable income and removes the incentive to catch as many fish as quickly as they can. It also encourages them to fish at the times when they will get the best price. This system has proved popular with fishermen themselves. By contrast, the European Union's Common Fisheries Policy is both unpopular and ineffective. Quotas are allocated each year, but tend to be set by fisheries ministers at far higher levels than official scientists recommend.

In addition to the questions relating to the effective environmental and economic workings of permits schemes, there is another practical issue which has to be addressed, and this is how the initial allocation of permits is determined. It is not enough merely to determine the aggregate level of permitted emissions: decisions have to be made as to who is to receive the permits and why. One method is to allocate permits according to past emissions levels. This can be both inequitable and also environmentally inefficient: inequitable because it is granting further pollution rights to companies in direct proportion to their previous polluting activities and inefficient unless the overall level of permits issued is for less than the current volume of emissions and the initial allocation is reduced over time. The system of allocating according to previous emissions levels is known as 'grandfathering'. The problems with this approach can be seen clearly if we look at emissions of carbon dioxide country by country. Should we give permits to those who already are, and for many years have been, emitting large quantities of carbon dioxide? This might be objected to both on the grounds that it is rewarding those who caused the problem in the first place and also that it denies to Southern nations their opportunity to achieve the higher standard of living which they see industrial nations enjoying. An alternative would be to allocate permits on the basis of population; but this is problematic in that it might be construed as an encouragement to achieve a higher birth rate. Further, it is obvious that, whatever the problems of equitable distribution of global environmental resources, we cannot afford the continued emission of carbon dioxide in anything like the levels previously achieved by the industrialised nations.[7]

How have tradeable permits worked in practice? Not surprisingly the picture is complicated: experience has varied and the details of the schemes adopted are arcane. However, from the experience in the USA, it is possible to report that most trading has been internal, that is between the plants owned by a single company. There has been some trading between firms under the offset system which requires new or expanding sources in 'non-attainment areas' (where air quality does not meet standards) to secure permits from existing firms so that the air is as clean (or cleaner) afterwards as before. This policy allows new industry to move into an area. Cost savings have been considerable, although it is difficult to give a precise figure – estimates range from $1 billion to $13 billion. Netting, which allows new, modified or expanding sources to emit within an established threshold so long as there is a transfer from elsewhere within the plant or firm, has also been used extensively. New sources are subject to stricter regulations than existing ones, and firms are therefore keen to adopt offsetting procedures when a new source starts up.[8]

Tradeable permits schemes are now being developed and implemented worldwide. For example, in the UK the Greenhouse Gas Emissions Trading Scheme started in April 2002, but it is too soon to ascertain its likely degree of success (ENDS, 2002b, pp. 6–7). Some uncertainty has also been introduced into its initial operations as the EU is developing plans for a Europe-wide trading scheme to be in place by

2005. Some aspects of the latter are at odds with the former and hence there is some reluctance on the part of businesses to commit themselves until the full EU position becomes clear (Park, 2001). Again, under the Kyoto Protocol, trading is due to begin globally in 2008. This is, however, a contentious scheme for reasons outlined in the case study on climate change at the end of Chapter 7.

Selling environmental indulgences?

The medieval practice of selling indulgences whereby sinners were assured that they would spend less time in purgatory was abolished by the church in 1563. Robert Goodin argues that green taxes or tradeable permits are a new form of selling indulgence, this time granted to polluters. Why does he believe this? Because it is:
- *Selling what is not ours to sell*: nature is not ours to sell; we are stewards not owners;
- *Selling that which cannot be sold*: stewards should protect the environment, not allow its destruction;
- *Rendering wrongs right*: with a tax or a charge (unlike a fine) it is accepted that pollution is not wrong;
- *Making wrongs 'all right'*: pollution is made undesirable but still permissible;
- *Indulging some but not all*: can the distribution of pollution rights be fair?

(adapted from Goodin, 1998)

Free-market environmentalism (FME)

FME is the rights-based approach taken to the limit. For free-market environmentalists, the existence of environmental externalities is attributed to the *absence* of markets and well-defined, enforced and transferable property rights. In their view markets should be encouraged and left to govern the allocation of resources, including environmental resources. FME not only rests on a view of how markets operate but also offers a critique of bureaucracy and the state. Both are characterised as inefficient, subject to 'regulatory capture' and corruption, influenced by special interest groups, and lacking the necessary information to effectively monitor and respond to environmental problems. From this, advocates conclude that the role of the state and associated public bureaucracies should be limited.

> At the heart of free-market environmentalism is a system of well-specified property rights to natural resources. Whether these rights are held by individuals, corporations, non-profit environmental groups, or communal groups, a discipline is imposed on resource users because the wealth of the owner of the property right is at stake if bad decisions are made. Of course, the further a decision maker is removed from this discipline as he is when there is political control – the less likely it is that good resource stewardship will result. Moreover, if well-specified property rights are transferable, owners must not only consider their own values, they must also consider what others are willing to pay.
>
> (Anderson and Leal, 1998, p. 208)

FME may appear to be an extreme response to the policy situation and in many ways it is. However, it does embody certain strengths through its attempt to systematically apply the logic of the private market and ownership. Under FME, institutions would be designed to harness self-interest through individual incentives. Within a society information is diffuse: governments and bureaucracies have great problems collecting and processing the vast amount of information necessary for centralised control. Within a market, on the other hand, prices convey and update changing information about demand for environmental goods. By comparison with governmental action FME claims to be flexible and responsive to changing environmental information and conditions. A clear (but limited) role is assigned to public bodies, typically, enforcement of a system of property rights. This reduces the costs of environmental protection: prices are used to convey information, costs are borne directly by owners and competition means that alternative suppliers of environmental goods will be available (ibid., p. 220).

Having said this, there are undoubtedly significant weaknesses in the FME approach. For example, full-scale privatisation of the commons is not feasible, especially in some of the most environmentally important and sensitive areas, such as air and the oceans. Second, FME ignores the distribution of wealth and is thus generally indifferent to questions of social justice. Finally, there is scepticism as to whether the individual actions of property holders will lead to overall sustainability. First, will all property holders really act in an environmentally-sensitive manner? Second, even if they did, would these actions necessarily lead to a coherent social outcome? Uncoordinated individual actions may simply cancel each other out.

Voluntary approaches

Most studies of policy instruments argue that either mandatory regulation or economic instruments need to be widely applied in an attempt to overcome collective action problems. Without either threat of punishment or economic incentive, it is believed that environmentally-sensitive behaviour will not emerge. There is a crucial and widely-held assumption at work here: that either the threat of punishment or an economic incentive is needed to alter the self-interested behaviour of individuals, groups and businesses.

In contrast to this rather pessimistic conception of human behaviour, policy instruments have been developed that attempt to shape the behaviour of individuals and organisations, not through threats or economic incentive, but through education, persuasion and negotiation. Whereas mandatory regulation and economic instruments are primarily focused on changing behaviour, voluntary policy instruments aim to change the underlying attitudes and values of individuals and organisations, in order to secure long-term changes in behaviour. There are (broadly) two forms of voluntary policy instruments: first, provision of information, education or voluntary standards; and second, negotiated agreements. There is a widely-held suspicion that voluntary action will not be adequate: that individuals and businesses will not take the required action. Is this suspicion warranted?

Information, education and voluntary standards

The most obvious voluntary instrument is the provision of information and education. Eco-labelling has become commonplace: the Forest Stewardship Council mark on sustainably-managed wood products has found its way into many DIY stores; energy efficiency ratings on washing machines and fridges are displayed in electrical superstores; Fair Trade teas, coffees and chocolate are widely available in super-markets. The discerning green consumer has more information and choice than ever before. One step up from the simple provision of information, civic education campaigns are familiar in liberal democracies. For example, the UK government's *Are you doing your bit?* campaign revolves around celebrities explaining simple actions (such as recycling and energy and water conservation) which anyone can do in their home. In schools, education for sustainable development has recently become a core aim for the National Curriculum in the UK. Civic and school education programmes are explicitly aimed at shaping people's values and perceptions of the environment; for example, the National Curriculum is intended to develop children's 'awareness and understanding of, and respect for, the environments in which they live, and secure their commitment to sustainable development at a personal, local, national and global level' (DETR, 2001, pp. 31–2). And not only governments and government agencies engage in such activities: the Global Action Plan (an environmental charity) promotes eco-teams – small groups of households that monitor each other's consumption of resources. The idea has proved relatively popular in the Netherlands:

> The underlying principle is that behaviour can only be changed if consumers are aware of the resources they consume. In an Ecoteam, members measure and compare their individual environmental efforts. This generates an element of social control, and gives consumers a direct sense of responsibility. The main emphasis is on measuring, on knowing the facts. Each team member calculates exactly how much electricity, water, gas, etc., is used from the outset, and progress is charted at every meeting. The team's average is also calculated at each meeting and compared to other teams and to average consumption in the Netherlands.
>
> (van Muijen, 2000, p. 161)

Beyond the legal and tax frameworks discussed earlier in this chapter, businesses have also been subjected to information and education campaigns promoting good environmental practice. Government and local authority departments and agencies frequently run conferences and workshops seeking to persuade companies of the benefits to be gained from enhanced environmental awareness and action. At a more formal level, voluntary environmental management systems (EMS) have been developed. To qualify, an organisation must satisfy a number of criteria by installing systems and procedures which allow the company to properly evaluate the effect of its activities on the environment and to ascertain how best to improve its environmental performance. Participation is voluntary, and organisations may seek certification for a variety of reasons. One important reason is likely to be environmental credibility and the possibility of being at a commercial disadvantage if they do not participate.

Environmental management systems (EMS)

Environmental management systems are being promoted both by national governments and the European Union. The international environmental management standard ISO14001 and the EU's second Eco-Management and Audit Scheme (EMAS-2) share much in common and companies can switch between them. The UK Environment Agency prefers companies to adopt EMAS in its quest to generate a lighter regulatory touch for firms that are committed to greening their operations (ENDS, 2001b, p. 6). Schemes of this sort are voluntary, but once entered into, companies have an obligation to deliver what they have agreed to: if a company chooses to register under EMAS it subjects itself to a considerable amount of external scrutiny from an independent organisation.

The objective is to promote 'continuous improvement in environmental performance' on a site-specific basis. Each individual site where a company is located must:

- adopt a company environmental policy;
- conduct an environmental review;
- introduce an environmental programme and an environmental management system;
- carry out an environmental audit; and
- prepare an environmental statement to be released to the public.

(Gouldson and Murphy, 1998, p. 60)

An accredited environmental verification agency ensures that the approach taken by the site complies with the requirements of the scheme.

There are a number of advantages of EMS and EMAS. First, such systems can provide a systematic framework for a comprehensive approach to dealing with the environment and thus create the potential for improved economic performance. Second, one of the main reasons why companies engage in what can be a time- and resource-intensive exercise is the improved image and reputation that can flow from accreditation – such a 'green' image can be important both in dealings directly with consumers, but also with other companies. Third, accreditation can lead to improved relations with regulators – we have already noted that the UK Environment Agency views commitment to EMAS as an important indicator of environmentally-enlightened business practice.

These advantages are matched by certain disadvantages. First, accreditation does not guarantee any particular level of environmental performance – a company may be producing a highly toxic product, but in a more environmentally-sensitive way! Second, for many organisations environmental management systems are costly to develop and apply. Third, there is concern that accreditation may actually lead to legislative non-compliance and engender complacency – the Environment Agency is likely to focus on those sites without EMS (Gouldson and Murphy, 1998, pp. 63–4).

Businesses generally prefer the use of voluntary means wherever possible. The Confederation of British Industry (CBI), for example, has developed an agenda for voluntary action: 'To promote voluntary efforts by business to enhance environmental performance and to ensure that the policy and regulatory framework within which business operates is consistent with the need to gain competitive advantage' (Gouldson and Murphy, 1998, p. 56). The CBI takes the view that government should set minimum standards, broad goals and priorities and otherwise leave industry to achieve these objectives in the most efficient way.

To what extent can voluntary action of this sort replace mandatory regulation or economic instruments? Business leaders typically argue that a voluntary approach is more flexible, cheaper, more effective and can be enacted more quickly. But sceptical critics argue that the real impetus to environmental improvement and innovation is the need to comply with mandatory regulations or the incentive generated by economic instruments. Without a legal requirement or economic incentive there is concern that most businesses and citizens will not be willing to change their behaviour. There is no guarantee.

Cooperation and joint environmental policy making

The belief that voluntary action will not be forthcoming, or will only be forthcoming at insufficient levels to make a real difference, rests on a particularly influential model of the problems of collective action that we discussed in some depth in Chapter 4. Without an incentive to act differently, the actions of individuals, groups and businesses are unlikely to be environmentally sustainable. Self-interest leads to environmental damage and pollution. However, empirical evidence and theoretical re-evaluation casts doubt on this pessimistic conclusion and demonstrates that there are ways in which collective action problems can and have been overcome in practice, without recourse to legal sanctions or economic incentives. Elinor Ostrom offers a number of examples where communal regimes have emerged to manage meadows, forests, irrigation and fisheries in a sustainable way (Ostrom, 1990). She has consistently argued that the assumptions supposedly central to the emergence of the tragedy of the commons are misleading and incomplete: they neglect a number of factors that may lead to the emergence of a more 'collectively rational' outcome without direct action by the state. Rather, voluntary organisations and regimes can emerge that protect environmental commons. The principal feature neglected by Garrett Hardin's model is communication between actors: he neglects the possibility that cooperation increases substantially with face-to-face communication. Ostrom demonstrates how, through communication, people use reciprocity, reputation and trust in their exchanges to develop and build their sense of and capacity for partnership. She terms these resources 'social capital': 'social capital is created and maintained by the very process of working together' (Ostrom, 1997, p. 178).[9] A free and extensive flow of communication or information enables the development of effective cooperation. This in turn allows for the development of norms and sanctions that can be validated and accepted by participants and which allow environmental resources to be managed sustainably. As Ostrom comments: 'simple, cheap talk allows individuals an opportunity to make conditional promises to one another and build trust that others will reciprocate' (Ostrom, 1998, p. 6). Participants are able to build a (voluntary) regime to protect public goods with rules, monitoring and enforcement mechanisms. Such an analysis of (local) regime formation may also help us to understand how and why international regimes on issues such as ozone and biodiversity emerge and are sustained through state interaction and dialogue.[10]

Other examples of voluntary negotiations and agreements are beginning to emerge which share many of the features of Ostrom's regimes. However, where Ostrom is particularly interested in the development of regimes independent of the activities of the state, joint environmental policy making (JEP), or negotiated agreements, focus on the development of voluntary relationships between the state and other actors, in particular businesses. JEP can thus be understood as negotiated agreements *formulated* and (importantly) *implemented* by both public authorities and private actors. JEP differs from direct regulation in that it is voluntary, and from economic incentives in that modification of behaviour occurs through negotiation and agreement. This form of policy making has evolved over the last decade or so in a limited number of European nation states and has been promoted by the EU's Fifth and Sixth Environmental Action Programmes (Mol *et al.*, 2000). To date the Netherlands has had the greatest success in the development of JEPs. Its political and institutional culture – in particular its consensus-orientated policy style – is seen as particularly supportive of the emergence and relative success of JEP arrangements. For example, packaging covenants were established in the 1989 National Environmental Policy Plan and Long Term Agreements (LTAs) on energy efficiency are a fundamental part of Dutch industrial energy policy (see the case study in Chapter 9). The more adversarial political culture of the UK has been less hospitable to the emergence of JEP, although recent examples include a more rigorous agreement with the newspaper industry to increase the recycled content of newsprint, an ambitious agreement with the semi-conductors industry to reduce energy use and the development of the climate change levy package (Shaw and Willis, 2002, p. 26).[11]

Within JEP, all the ingredients are present for supporters of both deregulation and ecological modernisation. JEP shares with mandatory regulation and economic instruments the desire for increased environmental efficiency. However, in theory, JEP has a number of advantages. First, it offers a solution to environmental problems that promotes non-hierarchical and flexible relations between industry and government. Second, and mirroring Ostrom's work, it relies on the development of consensus-orientated policy making as the basis upon which commitment, trust and reciprocity can be built. Finally, it promises inclusive negotiations involving all stakeholders and thus offers meaningful access to environmental NGOs. To what extent these conditions can be developed outside a fairly restricted number of nation states remains an open question and even in pioneer nations, there is a tendency towards the development of closed and exclusive policy networks between state and business actors with environmental NGOs and other actors left outside the agreement process. The most successful agreements appear to be backed by the implicit threat of government action (either legislation or taxation) if the negotiated agreements do not work (Mol *et al.*, 2000; Shaw and Willis, 2002).

Regulation, economic or voluntary instruments?

Studies of policy instruments often compare regulation, economic instruments and (occasionally) voluntary approaches as though one type of instrument is clearly superior to the others. This is seriously misleading. First, comparisons are not always genuine. Thus, for example, the proper comparison is not between pollution abatement secured by economic instruments and zero pollution, but between a specific economic instrument and what command-and-control achieves in practice. Second, it is important to compare command-and-control in practice with the *practice* rather than the theory of economic instruments. The tendency to compare practice in the one with theory in the other is seriously misleading. Third, given the variety of policy approaches, it is also important to distinguish between the relative merits of different types falling under the broad headings of 'mandatory regulation', 'economic instruments' and 'voluntary approaches'.

What in the end we are looking for is not the 'best' single policy instrument – as though an orchestra were reducible to a single instrument – but rather, the most appropriate mix of policy instruments to achieve the required level of environmental protection. Each policy instrument has its strengths and weaknesses, and used in an appropriate combination different instruments may well be complementary. Sensible policy in respect of the environment will therefore rely not on one mechanism to the exclusion of all others, but on a mixture depending on the conditions.

How are we to make judgements about which environmental policy instrument, or combination of instruments, to use? Jacobs suggests six criteria.

Criteria for evaluating policy instruments

- **Effectiveness**. Each method can be effective if used appropriately. However, it is worth noting that if the goal is to reduce a damaging activity quickly, it is often better to use regulations as incentives; education programmes and negotiated agreements take time to formulate, introduce and to become effective.
- **Motivation**. Taxes and permits provide a motive to constantly improve environmental performance; command-and-control does not. Voluntary approaches not only aim to alter behaviour but also the attitudes and character of polluters.
- **Administrative cost**. Command-and-control tends to have high administrative costs; taxes and permits generally reduce these costs.
- **Efficiency**. The efficiency of each type of measure is a function of effectiveness, motivation and cost: the method which maximises effectiveness while minimising costs and providing a motive to avoid environmentally-harmful acts in each particular sphere is the one which should be chosen.
- **Political acceptability**. Some solutions might be theoretically sound but hard to implement because they are, for example, seen as 'giving a licence to pollute'. Irrespective of the truth of this claim, or the claimed effectiveness of the policy, political sensitivities might lead to a reluctance to employ certain approaches.

---

continued

> • **Distributional impact**. Methods affect different groups differentially. For example, taxes tend to be regressive in that they have a greater impact on the poor. Thus they might be politically or morally sensitive and best avoided in some cases, or, where they are deemed appropriate, they may require additional measures to be taken to offset the impact on those most affected by them.
>
> (adapted from Jacobs, 1991, p. 152)

Conclusion

Collective action problems occur because individuals and organisations act in their own short-term interest. Policy instruments aim to overcome the collective action problem by offering different types of incentive. Mandatory regulation punishes those who act in an environmentally-damaging way; behaviour is altered through the threat of punishment. Command-and-control instruments are well understood and popular. However, environmental economists argue that they are not the most efficient way of changing behaviour and offer no incentive to improve performance once the legislative standard is reached. Economic instruments work on a different logic: instead of fear of punishment, individuals and organisations are given an economic incentive to improve their environmental performance. Whether economic instruments are based on altering price signals or enforcing rights to use environmental resources, it is argued that self-interest can be channelled to efficiently protect the environment. Typically debates about policy instruments revolve around which is the most effective or desirable: mandatory regulation or economic instruments.

This is to neglect a third strand of policy instrument – voluntary approaches. There is a variety of these, from information and education campaigns to negotiated agreements or joint environmental policy making between government and (typically) business. Voluntary instruments do not only aim to change behaviour, but also the attitudes that underpin the collective action problem. Thus they are a direct challenge to the model of the self-interested rational actor at the heart of the tragedy of the commons. Our interests can be understood in different ways: one interest is clearly long-term environmental sustainability.

There is a growing interest in the role that can be played by voluntary instruments and it should be recognised alongside mandatory regulation and economic instruments. We have argued that governments do not need to be dogmatic – they can pick and choose and mix and match the different policy instruments to suit the particular circumstance. Governments have a range of policy instruments to choose from: the question is whether they are willing to apply them effectively.

Case study: road congestion: the price to be paid?

Traffic congestion and pollution is clearly a major contemporary problem, especially in the small and overcrowded UK. But what form should any proposed solutions take? Should we build more roads? Provide more public transport? Ban the use of cars in cities? Charge drivers for using the roads? Charge drivers more for parking at work? Charge higher fuel and duty prices? Many policy options suggest themselves, but each has to be examined carefully and a politically-acceptable solution found: any solution is likely to incorporate different approaches into an overall package comprising different policy means. In what follows we shall briefly consider some recent proposals put forward in the UK for the reduction of traffic congestion.

Traffic congestion and pollution in cities

In the UK 89 per cent of carbon monoxide, 51 per cent of nitrogen oxides, 36 per cent of volatile organic compounds and 42 per cent of black smoke in the air we breathe is produced by road transport. It is also the fastest growing source of the greenhouse gas carbon dioxide – cars produce up to four tons of carbon dioxide each per annum and road transport contributes around 25 per cent of the UK's annual carbon dioxide emissions of 152 million tonnes. It is the only major sector which is increasing carbon dioxide emissions.

Emissions from private and commercial vehicles contribute to ill health, particularly breathing problems among children and the elderly, as well as the corrosion of buildings and vegetation. Exhaust fumes are particularly concentrated in towns and cities where the volume of motor vehicles is high and where traffic speeds are low because of congestion. Slow or non-moving vehicles release higher levels of emissions than vehicles running relatively efficiently at optimum speeds. These fumes and their products such as ozone exacerbate (and possibly help cause) asthma. Five million people have the disease, 18,000 new cases are diagnosed each week and 1,500 people die from it every year. More than one in seven children in the UK now suffers from asthma – six times as many as twenty-five years ago.

Finally, the cost of road accidents is high, both economically and personally; increased number of accidents implies higher expenditure on emergency services and hospital treatment. The increased use of cars has transformed the way people live their daily lives. Because of concerns over rising numbers of accidents, parents now increasingly drive their children to school; thus, paradoxically, increasing the likelihood of road accidents, increasing congestion and thus pollution levels. For people not driving cars, congested cities no longer feel safe and become increasingly alienating.

Since 1950 travel by car and van has increased over tenfold to 388 billion miles annually and travel by bus has halved to 28 billion miles. Over the past decade traffic growth on motorways has increased by 49 per cent. There are now 22.5 million cars on the roads in the UK: in 1970 there were 10 million. Bus fares and rail fares have both increased in real terms while the real cost of motoring has fallen. The CBI estimates that traffic congestion costs the economy £18 billion a year: a third of our urban driving time is spent travelling at less than five miles an hour.

So what can be done? Several options suggest themselves. First, we could build our way out of the problem: more roads could be constructed to accommodate the increasing volume of

continued

traffic. This demand-led approach was taken by the Conservative government in the late 1980s and directly led to the rise of the anti-road movement (see Chapter 3). Apart from the environmental damage associated with road building itself, this approach fails to recognise that new roads themselves tend to generate new journeys. Embarrassingly for the government at the time, its own Standing Advisory Committee on Trunk Road Assessment (SACTRA) pointed this out in 1994.

Second, motor cars could simply be banned from town centres with access restricted to deliveries and other specified uses. This has been done in a number of cities, although typically only for a small geographical area. On a larger scale, traffic congestion could also be reduced by stipulating that private cars are allowed access to city centres only on alternate days. A simple way of doing this is to allow access one day to cars with even-numbered licence plates and the next day to those with odd-numbered plates. In principle this encourages people to look for and demand alternative means of transport. However, where this has been tried in practice (for example in Italian cities) it has proved less effective than hoped, because many people already have two cars, and in some cases have even been known to bypass the system by purchasing another with the alternate number plate.

Third, greater use could be made of buses, trains and trams; the scope and provision of public transport could be enhanced to make it an attractive and practical alternative to car use. Even when a quarter full, a bus is more than twice as fuel efficient as a family car. It is also safer – the risk of being killed or seriously hurt while travelling on public transport is about 13 times less than in a car. Proportionately, buses and trains can efficiently convey many more people than cars; given that cars are rarely filled to capacity the disparity is even greater. Hence moves towards the greater use of buses, trams and trains could significantly reduce city centre road traffic. For example, in Paris in 2001, the mayor, Bertrand Delanoe, built seven kilometres of new bus lanes along some of the busiest roads in the city. These were divided from adjacent lanes by concrete strips preventing cars skipping into them. In Leeds 'guided busways' have been designed to do the same thing. Journey times have been halved by the use of the busway and the number of passengers increased by 75 per cent; in 2006 Leeds will also open a new tramway system which will similarly reduce the amount of road available to the private car driver; similar new tram or light-rail schemes are already running in Manchester and Croydon and one is proposed for Southampton. Elsewhere, computer-based systems giving priority to buses over other vehicles at traffic lights have been (or are being) introduced. Cardiff pioneered the scheme, and is now being followed by Aberdeen, Nottingham, Merseyside, Maidstone, Winchester, Norwich, Ipswich, Swansea and Birmingham. This is a radio system which reads signals from the buses and gives them priority when they are late and full, but makes them wait at the lights if they are early and empty. Within three years perhaps half of the UK's 40,000 buses will be fitted with this system.[12]

But we have to be careful: it would be a mistake to assume that the problem can be solved simply by shifting more and more journeys onto public transport. The fact is that since the Second World War, the number of journeys undertaken using private or commercial road vehicles has increased exponentially, not simply through displacement from public transport, but also because people now make many more journeys than they ever did before – journeys which they would never have considered making on public transport. They are reluctant to give up this freedom and flexibility. Public transport, then, while being part of the solution, cannot be the whole of it. We need to provide incentives to reduce the number of car journeys, to move people out of their cars and onto public transport; and we need to ensure that the true costs of motoring (not only personal but also social and environmental) are both recognised and paid (Maddison *et al.*, 1996).

This is a similar position to that advocated by The Royal Commission on Environmental Pollution (RCEP) in 1994. It recommended improvements in public transport, an increase in the number of bus lanes and the introduction of additional light rapid transit systems. However, it also recommended that the improvement in public transport facilities should be closely linked to policies restraining the use of private vehicles in urban areas (RCEP, 1995, pp. 248–9). It went on to argue that:

> As technology improves, local road pricing may offer environmental advantages. We recommend that the government work within the EC to develop common standards for the technology of road pricing. Decisions to introduce road pricing should be made locally after evaluating the environmental effects, including those on adjoining areas; and the revenue should be retained by the local authority introducing the scheme and used to finance public transport or infrastructure improvements which are not environmentally damaging.
>
> (ibid., p. 249)

Congestion charges in London

Under the Transport Act (2000) and the Greater London Act (1998), local authorities have the power to introduce urban congestion charges; they also have the power to introduce workplace car parking charges. In both cases revenue has to be earmarked for transport spending. The idea of road charging has recently been proposed by the London Mayor, Ken Livingstone, as a solution to the problem of road congestion.

What are the London congestion charge proposals? The plan is to introduce a congestion charge of £5 each weekday for motorists to enter a central area of the capital from 7am to 6.30pm. Cameras positioned on the zone's entry points will match car number plates against a database of vehicles that have paid the charge. Any motorist who has not paid by the end of the day will be fined. The scheme is designed to cut down on chronic traffic congestion in central London. Livingstone hopes for 10–15 per cent fewer vehicles on the road, making central London safer for cyclists and pedestrians, less polluted and easier to drive through for those who are prepared (and able) to pay. The scheme will also raise around £150 million a year for other transport policies plus an extra £30 million in fines; it is estimated to cost £600 million. Under the scheme bus travel in central London should become quicker, if not in the areas outside it. There are now more buses in London than at any time since 1965 (with 200 a year on order) and the mayor has cut fares to entice passengers on board. The London Chamber of Commerce supports the scheme. Evidence from other cities, such as Munich, suggests that the local economy benefits from a reduction in traffic in commercial and retail centres (Jeffrey, 2002).

However, objections have been raised to the scheme. The most common is that improvements to public transport need to be in place before the scheme will work. Another, voiced by those living on the fringes of the new zone, is that their businesses will be adversely affected by the plans. The concern is that there will be dead zones in London, just inside the zone boundaries, which people will avoid. Equally, there will be zones just outside the boundaries which will suffer

continued

further congestion as people travel to and park their cars at a point just before they would have to pay the charges. Despite these concerns, the scheme looks likely to go ahead in 2003 and is likely to have a serious impact. David Begg, the Chair of the Commission for Integrated Transport (CFIT), supports the scheme and suggests its extension not only to other cities but also country-wide:

> You could double the number of people travelling by public transport in Britain and it would only be equivalent to five years' growth in car traffic. And road building creates more demand. You need a charge to reduce congestion. If it is right for London and Bristol it must be right for other towns and cities.
>
> (Walters, 2002)

In Begg's view the London scheme does suffer from the two weaknesses identified – the boundary problem and the current inadequacy of public transport. That is why CFIT is proposing a national scheme of road charging which will overcome these difficulties. They propose a 'big bang' in 2010 when public-transport investment and satellite car-tracking technology are good enough to make pricing on every road in Britain technically feasible. This would complement the £180 million promised by the government to improve public transport by the end of the decade as part of its ten-year transport plan.

National road pricing

> The principle of charging motorists for the use of a scarce resource, namely road space, is absolutely sound. It is the best way in the long run to reconcile efficiency, fairness and environmental protection.
>
> (*The Independent*, 2002)

In their report, *A New Concept for Paying for Road Use* (2002), CFIT propose a scheme in which motorists would pay a congestion charge according to the level of congestion on the stretch of the road they were using. Thus rural drivers would pay no road charge while those driving in congested urban areas and on busy motorways would pay for the privilege.

A new concept for paying for road use

The Commission for Integrated Transport scheme would:

- shift some road use costs from being a tax paid to government, to paying a direct charge to use the road network – but only at congested times;
- be fiscally neutral, meaning that there would be no extra costs overall for the road user – just a different way of paying;
- charge those using congested roads at peak times of day when demand is highest;
- apply on 10 per cent (in length) of motorway network and other trunk roads, but would apply to those sections only at times affected by congestion;
- not charge where there is no congestion – 63 per cent of all travel;

- reduce the amount of traffic by 5 per cent, leading to a 44 per cent reduction in congestion nationally;
- cut pollution and make journeys by bus, car and road haulage faster, less congested and more reliable;
- bring cost savings to those who make occasional, off peak journeys or those who travel mainly on non-congested routes such as rural roads;
- not affect most rural roads which would require no charge as they do not generally have high congestion levels;
- not be implemented until the improved public transport promised in the government's ten-year transport plan is delivered and the technology (e.g. Global Positioning Technology using satellites) is more widely available.

(CFIT, 2002)

The scheme promises major cost savings to some users, cuts pollution and brings benefits to the economy, to bus passengers and to the road haulage industry. But its introduction presupposes the public transport infrastructure promised in the government's ten-year plan. The view of the CFIT is that much of the congestion on the roads is influenced by the way we currently pay to travel: 'The result is that people only think about motoring when they fill up at the pump' (CFIT, 2002, p. 2); this echoes the views of the RCEP and environmental economists who argue both that motoring is too cheap (because its real social and environmental costs are not included) and that its price structure – compared with public transport and most other goods where we pay for what we want when we want it – hides the real cost to them individually (RCEP, 1995, pp. 98–119; Maddison *et al.*, 1996). Current methods of payment contribute to the problem and not to the solution and the real cost of motoring is half what it was 30 years ago and is forecast to fall by 20 per cent over the next ten years. Therefore without radical action we will become more dependent on the car for the foreseeable future. The idea of the CFIT report is that we should pay for what we consume when we consume it: we do this with other forms of transport – why not with cars? On many forms of transport we pay according to when and how we want to travel: why should roads be different?

Conclusion

The car is almost the perfect symbol of the problems facing environmental politics. First, it is an environmentally-destructive technology: consider, for example, the resources needed for car production, the reliance on fossil fuels (a limited and highly polluting energy source), the ecological damage caused by road building. Second, it has profound cultural effects: it re-affirms the privatisation of lifestyles and reinforces economic privilege – private and flexible transport is only available for those who can afford it. And finally, it generates the archetypical collective action problem: everyone thinks there should be less traffic on the roads, but equally everyone thinks that everyone else should alter their travel habits.

We have looked at different ways of dealing with 'car trouble' (Paterson, 2000). Voluntary approaches are unlikely to produce any serious reduction as people find their cars to be useful and generally life enhancing; besides, once they have made the expense of investing in a car, the daily costs of running it are relatively low and also hidden from their day-to-day cost

continued

calculations. Attempts to control car use through limiting the number of cars people own, or by banning them in certain areas, are only likely to work in specific places and tend to be politically unpopular. Economic instruments – taxes and charges – appear to offer the way forward. People could be forced out of their cars by raising the price of motoring; the typical approach here is to dramatically increase the price of fuel or vehicle tax. However, there will be widespread cultural and political resistance to any such sweeping attempt to make private motoring more expensive.

We need to consider more precisely what the policy goal is. Perhaps it is best understood as a series of four policy steps:

1 introduce the principle of payment visibility for motoring by making motorists pay for journeys they make as and when they make them;
2 bring the cost of motoring into line with the cost of public transport;
3 discourage private motoring by making it relatively more expensive than public transport;
4 ensure that the cost of motoring reflects its full social and environmental cost.

Each step is politically daunting and any attempt to leap directly to the final step without a careful phasing in of a more efficient and reliable public transport infrastructure is likely to be both politically unworkable and economically naive. There are also other reasons for pragmatic caution. For example, we have seen that drivers are increasingly willing to protest against what they see as excessively high fuel prices: the political challenge lies in the fact that although the cost of motoring is economically and environmentally too low, most drivers regard it as too high. Another sensitive issue is that any blanket approach to the problem tends to be regressive in that the overall cost of motoring increases for everyone regardless of their ability to pay; a closely related point is that it would penalise rural drivers who rely on cars more than urban dwellers and have less access to public transport.

Road charging of the sort proposed by the CFIT appears to offer an innovative solution to a number of the problems we have identified. It certainly makes the first step identified above and progresses towards the second and third by creating some of the conditions for the provision of more reliable public transport. It promises:

• to cut congestion and pollution;
• to free up traffic flows, thereby making public transport and freight transport more predictable and reliable;
• not to penalise rural drivers;
• to charge only where there is real congestion;
• to avoid the need for massive road-building programmes or any increases in the overall level of motoring taxation.

There are, however, still drawbacks. For example, the proposals come at a time when there are potential proposals for a new substantial trunk-road building programme across England, each road designed to solve traffic problems in specific transport corridors. Here we have a stark opposition between two conflicting approaches: more roads or reduced use. Additionally, the idea is dependent on advanced forms of technology which would require a smartcard located in every vehicle. This raises concerns about civil liberties – who will have access to this information and how will it be used? The civil liberties group Liberty is concerned about these aspects of the plan as it fears that the information gathered could be misused by government and the police.

Despite the political risk of raising the costs of motoring, it is nonetheless the case that the current price of private and commercial vehicle use does not fully reflect its social and environmental costs. Innovative and creative thinking is required to respond to this pressing environmental problem. The CFIT scheme may prove to be one element within the development of an overall solution.

Suggestions for further reading

For a collection of essays on the relative merits of different policy instruments, see Robyn Eckersley's edited volume *Markets, the State and the Environment*. Stephen Tindale and Gerald Holtham develop an accessible argument in favour of re-orientating the tax system to protect the environment in *Green Tax Reform*. Andrew Gouldson and Joseph Murphy's *Regulatory Realities* offers a detailed comparative analysis of the use of mandatory and voluntary instruments in the Netherlands and the UK. Arthur Mol, Volkmar Lauber and Duncan Liefferink's edited volume *The Voluntary Approach to Environmental Policy* compares policy in Austria, Denmark and the Netherlands. Albert Weale *The New Politics of Pollution* is a classic analysis of pollution control and national approaches to sustainability. The last three texts explicitly locate their analysis within the framework of ecological modernisation. The contemporary practical application of different policy instruments is tracked by Environmental Data Services (ENDS) who produce monthly reports.

Notes

1   Debates about how standards should be set within the EU are discussed in Chapter 8.
2   For further details of the way in which such technological standards are applied in the UK in the area of industrial pollution control see Chapter 9.
3   Whether this is done in practice depends on a number of factors. In the UK, for example, hypothecation of taxes (earmarking their revenue for a particular use) has hitherto been virtually unknown; in other countries, such as Germany, the Netherlands and Sweden, it is more common.
4   Technically it would be proper to refer both to taxes and to charges and to distinguish between them. However, for the sake of simplicity we shall use the term 'tax' as a general term. See Jacobs (1991, pp. 120–4) for more on this distinction.
5   For an extended discussion of environmental tax reform see Tindale and Holtham (1996) and the Commission on Taxation and Citizenship (2000).
6   It could also be argued that there is a problem in that we are being asked to place an economic value on the environment – the problems with this will be discussed in Chapter 6. However, it could be argued that this is not the case: all that is required is that an environmental standard is set according to whatever is regarded as relevant criteria. This does not require placing an economic value on the environment, merely agreement about acceptable limits – and this applies as much to command-and-control or other solutions as it does to green taxes or tradeable permits.

7   For a discussion of the issues surrounding the economics and ethics of setting up a global carbon dioxide permit scheme see Markandya (1991). See also the case study at the end of Chapter 7.

8   For fuller details both of the terms employed and of the results of trading see Turner *et al.* (1994, pp. 182–5).

9   For a critical overview of the debates on social capital see Foley and Edwards (1999).

10   For an analysis of the similarities between Ostrom's approach to common-pool regimes and work on international environmental regimes, see Ostrom and Keohane (1994) and the other articles in that special edition of the *Journal of Theoretical Politics*. The nature of international environmental regimes will be discussed in Chapter 7.

11   Mol *et al.* (2000) provide a detailed comparative analysis of the development of JEP arrangements in three European nations: Austria, Denmark and the Netherlands.

12   Many of the details in this paragraph come from Walters and Jeffries (2001).

Valuation of the environment

> Appraisal in central government is concerned with the best use of the
> nation's resources, and the economic analysis of major decisions should
> in principle be wholly in terms of economic costs and benefits.
>
> (HM Treasury, 1991, p. 10)

If, as we have consistently argued, environmental concerns need to be placed at
the centre of our judgements (both ethically and politically) then we are faced with
a pressing *practical* problem of how to value environmental entities in decision-
making processes. The issues we raised in Chapters 1 and 2 concerning our relations
with the natural world need to be represented in decision-making procedures,
otherwise we are bound to misrepresent and distort the human condition and its
relationship with the non-human world. Two interrelated issues form the core of this
chapter.

First, how are we to assess the environmental consequences of proposed
projects, programmes or policies? Non-intervention in natural systems is clearly not
an option for contemporary societies, so we need methods by which we can weigh
the environmental, social and economic costs of proposed developments and policy
options. Initially the chapter will engage with the growing discipline of environmental
economics and the monetary valuation of ecological resources and values. Through
a discussion of cost–benefit analysis (CBA) we will investigate the limits of such
valuation techniques and the assumptions embedded within environmental economics. Potential alternatives to economic decision making such as environmental
impact assessment (EIA) will then be discussed.

The second issue that needs to be attended to concerns the measurement of
progress towards sustainable development. Traditionally, 'progress' has been defined
in relation to the growth of national economies. It will be argued that this is far
from a suitable measure of environmental sustainability in that growth usually entails
environmental and social costs, for example, increased pollution or resource
consumption. A single economic measure of progress is unlikely to be sensitive to
the different dimensions of sustainable development. An alternative approach has
seen the development of broad quality of life indicators to guide policy decisions and
other interventions into the non-human world. The case study at the end of the
chapter engages with the different ways that sustainable development is understood
within environmental economics.

Economic valuation of environmental interventions

> The need to balance the costs of an action against its benefits is intuitively
> appealing, and provides an important discipline with which to approach
> decisions.
>
> (Winpenny, 1991, p. 42)

How are we to make reasoned decisions between different policy options or
concerning whether large-scale projects such as roads and railways, industrial
complexes and the like should go ahead? How are we to judge not only the financial
implications but also social and environmental consequences? In attempting to aid

decision makers in what is necessarily a balancing of a number of positive and negative impacts, welfare economists developed a technique known as cost–benefit analysis (CBA).[1] The theory behind CBA is relatively simple and (at its core) utilitarian: the social costs and benefits of an intervention are expressed by aggregating the gains or losses to well-being (or utility) of all individuals affected. The increase or decrease in levels of individuals' utility is represented through a common measure – money. Since all these costs and benefits do not occur immediately, a discount rate is applied to take into account the point in time at which they accrue: it is argued that individuals are impatient and have a time preference for immediate gains in well-being over postponement to a future occasion. Where the net present value (NPV) (the aggregated benefits minus the aggregated costs) is positive, a policy or project is viewed as socially worthwhile. In principle, the impact of a project or policy should be economically efficient or 'Pareto optimal': the effect of an intervention should increase the welfare of all, without reducing any particular individual's utility. However, in practice there are always 'losers' and CBA actually operates in terms of potential Pareto optimality: that is, taking into account all costs and benefits, there should be an overall gain in social welfare. The criterion of *potential* Pareto optimality is also known as the Kaldor–Hicks compensation test. If the total social welfare is increased, those negatively affected by the intervention could *in principle* be compensated by those who gain. The theoretical nature of this potential compensation indicates that conventional CBA tends not to be particularly concerned with distributional issues.

This sort of economic analysis of government interventions has become central to liberal democratic decision making (see, for example, HM Treasury, 1991; DOE, 1991a). There is a clear preference and tendency towards the inclusion of all costs and benefits in an economic form, and this includes environmental effects. In the UK (and elsewhere), the work of David Pearce and his colleagues has been particularly influential in this move towards the economic valuation of environmental values, particularly since the publication of *Blueprint for a Green Economy* (1989),[2] originally a report commissioned by the then Minister for the Environment, Chris Patten. This directly influenced the Department of the Environment's *Policy Appraisal and the Environment* (1991a), one of the central aims of which is to promote the monetary valuation of environmental effects of policy options within economic decision procedures such as CBA.[3]

Monetary valuation: internalising environmental costs and benefits

All human activity has an impact on the environment, either positively or negatively. However, the prices of goods bought and sold in markets tend not to include environmental costs and benefits, for instance the pollution costs of production. Where the market price fails to take into account such costs and benefits, they are termed 'externalities'.[4] A seminal article by Ronald Coase (1960) argued that externalities could be internalised through a strict system of property rights, although for complex environmental problems such as air and water pollution such an option seems far from practicable.[5] As we saw in Chapter 5, states have responded to environmental externalities through the introduction of policy instruments such as direct legal regulation or indirect control through taxes and charges on environmental degradation. In this chapter we shall initially focus on how decision makers have attempted to internalise environmental externalities within extended CBAs of policies and projects by calculating monetary valuations of environmental impacts.

Traditionally, the environmental costs and benefits of projects and policies have not appeared in CBA calculations and have had to be balanced against the NPV at the point of judgement. Many commentators have noted that decision makers tend to be swayed more by a positive NPV – a high *economic* benefit – than by a description of potential environmental impacts. As the environmental economist Ian Bateman contends: 'In general planners may well be familiar with the monetary rather than the qualitative assessments and critics have seen this as promoting a bias against the latter' (Bateman, 1991, p. 19). Certain projects and policies might not have been taken forward if environmental values had been included within an extended-CBA. Environmental economists argue that this can be done by valuing environmental impacts in monetary terms and entering them into the cost/benefit streams. For instance, Jean-Phillipe Barde and David Pearce argue that had the CBA for the motorway extension through Twyford Down included the economic valuation of the aesthetic worth of the area, the road cutting would never have been allowed to progress (Barde and Pearce, 1991, pp. 1–2).[6] The developing field of environmental economics bears witness to this drive to internalise environmental costs and benefits through, for instance, the calculation of individuals' willingness to pay (WTP) for environmental improvements or their willingness to accept (WTA) compensation for a loss in environmental quality. A number of the assumptions and practices of environmental economic valuation have proved controversial and we shall evaluate the criticisms after an investigation of the environmental values that economists aim to reveal and some of the techniques they use.

The economic value of the environment

As in other areas of environmental thinking, there is some disagreement over terminology within the field of environmental economics. For this discussion we shall be using the typology found in the work of David Pearce and his colleagues (Pearce *et al.*, 1989; Pearce and Turner, 1990, pp. 129–40), where:

Total Economic Value = Actual Use Value + Option Value + Existence Value
(Pearce and Turner, 1990, p. 131)

Actual use value is relatively obvious – the quantification of the benefits derived by those who make use of the environment directly, for instance farmers, industrialists, anglers and walkers. Option value includes a number of different aspects: first, it takes into account the willingness to pay for the preservation of an entity in the likelihood that the individual may make use of it in the future; second, it includes the preference to conserve the environment for future generations (often referred to as bequest value); third, it also incorporates the pleasure secured in the knowledge that others derive a value from the entity in question. Existence value includes 'concern for, sympathy with, respect for the rights or welfare of non-human beings', the values of which are unrelated to human welfare (ibid., p. 130). Environmental economists are attempting to calculate monetary values for the different types of environmental values discussed in Chapter 1.

Environmental valuation techniques

Techniques for valuation can be roughly divided into two approaches, direct and indirect.[7] Direct valuation techniques utilise either revealed or expressed preferences in market situations and aim to derive individuals' willingness to pay (WTP) or accept (WTA) compensation for particular environmental conditions. The revealed preference or surrogate market approach attempts to derive the monetary value of environmental benefits or costs through individual behaviour in actual markets. For instance, air quality or a beautiful landscape has an influence on house prices; employees will accept a premium to work in an environmentally-risky workplace; and people are willing to incur travel costs to visit environmental amenities. Expressed preference or experimental techniques aim to create hypothetical market conditions where the WTP or WTA for particular environmental conditions are elicited from individuals. Indirect techniques, as the name suggests, do not derive economic values directly from market conditions; rather, there is a two-stage approach. Initially a 'dose–response' relationship between a form of pollution and an effect is scientifically calculated (for instance acid rain on forests and buildings or pollutants on human health); only then is the economic value of that effect assigned a value by using the appropriate direct valuation technique.

Direct approaches

Hedonic pricing method

The property value method aims to isolate the value of environmental amenities, such as landscape, noise or pollution levels, by comparing prices of similar properties in different locations. Environmental quality is only one of the variables involved in determining relative prices and the technique is therefore statistically complex. A second approach focuses on wage differentials where the premium paid to workers exposed to environmental risks can be used 'to estimate the implicit values that workers place on the risk of death from workplace accidents' (Winpenny, 1991, p. 53) and health risks from pollution. Both of these techniques share the contested assumption that both the property and labour markets function freely and individuals are fully informed and in an economic position to respond to environmental conditions.

Travel cost method

This technique is used predominantly to reveal the value of recreational sites that typically have no entrance fee, such as national parks and lakes. The value of the time spent and the cost of travelling to the site is taken to be representative of the willingness to pay for such an amenity. Complications include the possible pleasure of travel itself – it may not be viewed as a cost by those travelling – or the fact that trips may be multi-purpose. Further, the value of the site to those individuals who have chosen to live close by because they value it highly will be understated in terms of travel cost. For those individuals who do not or cannot visit the amenity but still value its existence, their valuations will be ignored.

Contingent valuation method (CVM)

The revealed preference techniques discussed thus far derive preferences from individuals' existing behaviour in markets. However, in many cases economists have noted that no market information exists and so hypothetical markets have been created by directly interviewing individuals. By making 'bids', individuals express their willingness to pay (WTP) for environmental improvement or willingness to accept (WTA) compensation for a loss of environmental quality. CVM is receiving a great deal of attention within environmental economics, both because it has potentially wide applicability over many areas of environmental concern, and also because it is the only technique available that enables economists to distinguish between aspects of the total economic value of environmental entities (use, option and existence values). However, there are concerns about the nature of the values derived from these surveys since much will depend on, for instance, the structure of the questions asked, how many issues are raised and the information provided. The accuracy of CVM depends crucially on the ability of economists to eliminate these practical and methodological biases.[8]

Sources of bias within CVM

Strategic	Incentive to 'free-ride'.
Design	(a) starting point bias – any example of possible 'bids' affects the individual's response.
	(b) vehicle bias – instruments of payment, such as taxation or entrance fees, affects responses.
	(c) informational bias – amount and quality of information affects response.
Hypothetical	Are bids in hypothetical markets different to actual market bids? Why should they be?
Operational	Are hypothetical markets genuinely comparable with existing markets in which actual choices are made?

(expanded from Pearce and Turner, 1990, p. 149)

A familiar problem for economic analysis that appears in CVM is 'strategic bias': the temptation to free-ride. Many environmental problems facing decision makers involve the use (or abuse) of public goods where individuals may be tempted to bid a lower WTP in the expectation that others will cover the cost of provision. The methodology of welfare economics focuses simply on the *private* preferences of individuals, treating the collective as merely the aggregate of these preferences. As we argued in Chapter 4, the provision of public goods, by its very nature, requires us to think beyond purely private self-interest and towards a political, collective response.

Some of the most striking problems that CVM faces concern survey design, in particular, when, how much and what sort of information is provided to the respondents. In most surveys it is the interviewer who offers the initial 'bid' to which individuals respond. 'Starting point bias' has been frequently documented in which this initial bid affects the respondent's final choice. Further, there is a 'vehicle bias' with respect to the instrument of payment, for instance taxation, entrance fee, surcharge, or higher prices. Respondents are far from neutral in respect of these payment strategies. Both of these biases could be included within a wider 'information bias' which takes into account the type of information offered during the decision-making process. What information is relevant and in what form should it be presented?

The hypothetical nature of the exercise would also seem to offer problems. What is the relation between the hypothetical nature of the transactions of a CVM survey and actual market conditions? A 'hypothetical bias' can result from the difference between the nature of the survey and actual markets. 'Operational bias' may result from the unfamiliarity of treating the good in question as a market commodity. Why should we assume that bids in a hypothetical market accurately represent actual market conditions? After all, most of the respondents will have no experience of paying for the environment in these terms.

It has been found that WTA compensation is consistently several times higher than WTP for environmental improvement. A number of explanations for this have been forthcoming. It is often argued, for example, that individuals place a higher value on those things with which they are familiar than on those of which they have no experience; or, again, that the discrepancy could also be explained by 'the fact that willingness to pay is constrained by ability to pay, while willingness to accept compensation is unconstrained' (Adams, 1995, p. 5). Alternatively, the higher WTA 'may be . . . the only way non-monetary, non-preference based valuations can be expressed within the confines of the exercise' (Jacobs, 1994, p. 80); it is an expression of a moral dimension to our valuation of public goods. This differential can have a significant effect on policy decisions, since economic theory assumes that WTP and WTA are equivalent and techniques for deriving environmental values tend to be based on WTP – consistently the lower of the two valuations. As Jack Knetsch argues:

> [I]t is likely that, among other implications, losses are understated, standards are set at inappropriate levels, policy selections are biased, too many environmentally-degrading activities are encouraged, and too few mitigation efforts are undertaken. . . . The conventional assertion that values attached to gains and commensurate losses are equivalent, and the advice that 'practically speaking' it does not appear to make much difference which definition is accepted, seem now to be incorrect for a large class of environmental and other

values. . . . [T]he continued reluctance to modify the assertion of symmetry appears to be increasingly costly.

(Knetsch, 1990, pp. 227 and 236)

Aside from this discrepancy, it is often the case that respondents lodge high protest bids or refuse to take part in the valuation exercise. Frequently economists will overlook such responses, treating them as 'errors'. For some commentators, however, such a reaction is illuminating since it may show that people balk at the idea of the 'commodification' of aspects of the environment. As John O'Neill argues:

The existence of protest bids shows individuals to have a healthy commitment to certain goods and an understanding of the limits of markets. Protests reveal neither irrationality nor strategic rationality, but decent ethical commitments.

(O'Neill, 1993, p. 120)

Indirect approaches

We do not need to pay too much attention to indirect techniques, since, after the initial stage of scientific investigation of a particular environmental effect, the actual monetary valuation proceeds using one of the direct techniques discussed above.

Examples of indirect valuation techniques

- **Effect on production**: Physical effects on the environment are scientifically determined and then the monetary value of the impact is estimated, e.g. effect of overfishing on fish stocks; air pollution on vegetation.
- **Human capital**: This method focuses on the link between environmental pollution and health problems and calculates loss of productive time and health care costs.
- **Replacement cost**: The cost of replacing or restoring the environment to its original condition is estimated, e.g. cost of cleaning a building soiled by acid rain; achieving bathing water objectives.
- **Preventative expenditure**: This method relates to the money spent by individuals to mitigate the effect of environmental impacts, e.g. insulation to mitigate noise pollution.

Indirect methods not only suffer from the monetary valuation problems associated with direct valuation techniques, but also from the scientific uncertainties inescapable in the early stages of isolating the particular effect in question. For instance, in the case of the effect of air pollution on human health, it can be extremely difficult to isolate the specific impact of, say, traffic exhaust fumes. Other pollutants from other sources may be present; there may be reactions between pollutants from alternative sources; or something else may prove to be the trigger for respiratory problems with exhaust fumes simply exacerbating the situation.

Criticisms of economic decision-making procedures

As Pearce states in an introductory text on CBA, the procedure has the 'fundamental attraction of reducing a complex problem to something less complex and more manageable' (Pearce, 1983, p. 21). This is undoubtedly the case in that the various costs and benefits of a project or policy are weighed in terms of a single criterion, namely monetary value. Eventually a single figure, the net present value (NPV) of the proposed intervention, is produced. But what is lost in this reduction of complexity? What does that net present value represent, particularly if environmental valuations are incorporated? We have already discussed some of the limitations and biases inherent within particular valuation techniques such as CVM and hedonic pricing, but the central question at issue here is whether economic analysis per se distorts the values it claims to represent, particularly those we associate with the non-human world. In this section we shall briefly introduce a range of criticisms that are frequently aimed at these forms of economic decision making, which range from the use of individual preferences through to the potential political misuse of economic figures.

Individual preferences, commensurability and environmental values

In welfare economic theory, individuals are taken to be calculating, utility maximisers with given and immutable preferences. It is assumed that individuals have both full information and are rational – rational in the sense that given full information about a state of affairs they will calculate and choose that option which will maximise their utility function. According to welfare economists, the welfare function of an individual can be discovered through their behaviour in market situations, through revealed preferences. As we noted earlier, where revealed preference techniques (hedonic pricing and travel cost) have had limited application, environmental economists have turned to contingent valuation methods (CVM) – the use of direct interview techniques to create hypothetical markets from which values can be derived. But are individuals best understood as utility maximisers? Does this picture of human character really correspond to the ways in which we value the non-human world? There are at least two problems with this account of individual choice and decision making: first, the availability of information and our sense of what is possible, and second, the impact of values aside from utility.

In the practical world, information is scarce. However, if individuals are not fully informed, in what way can their behaviour be taken to be rational in the economic sense? We have already shown that there is an information bias in CVM and similarly, with respect to revealed preference techniques, the preferences derived will be affected by the knowledge of the particular individual in question and the information available to them. Further, and in many ways associated with this problem of information deficit, social and economic constraints would appear to affect decisions. An individual may not be in an economic or social position to act on information given (such possibilities were raised earlier with respect to the limitations of hedonic

195

pricing techniques) or their sense of what is possible may be restricted. As Bernard Williams argues:

> What one wants, or is capable of wanting, is itself the function of numerous social forces, and importantly rests on a sense of what is possible. Many a potential desire fails to become an express preference because the thought is absent that it would ever be possible to achieve.
>
> (Williams, 1973, p. 147)

Along similar lines, Cass Sunstein contends that taking market behaviour as a guide to preferences is highly problematic since people will adapt themselves 'to undue limitations in current practices and opportunities' (Sunstein, 1991, p. 21). He emphasises that: 'Poverty itself is perhaps the most severe obstacle to the free development of preferences and beliefs' (ibid., p. 23).

Information deficit and individuals' sense of what is possible are two aspects of the world that raise uncomfortable questions for economic analysis. But the relationship between revealed preference and welfare can be further challenged if we take into account other values aside from utility that may be appealed to in individual decisions. As Amartya Sen argues, 'choice may reflect a compromise among a variety of considerations of which personal welfare may be just one' (Sen, 1977, p. 324). The preference schedule derived from revealed preference techniques in many situations is likely to be affected by our commitments, goals and values, many of which are associated with the non-human world. This can affect results in two ways: first, commitments can reduce utility functions – for example, my behaviour in choosing not to visit a particular environmentally-sensitive area because I believe it should be preserved rather than opened to tourists would not be recorded in travel cost assessments; and second, behavioural analysis may overlook and disregard commitments and other values. An example of the latter occurrence can be seen in the Department of Transport's quantification of travel cost savings in their CBA for potential road developments which we discussed in the case study in Chapter 5. It is assumed that all road users have a preference for quicker journeys. The fact that specific individuals may 'prefer' environmental protection over a new road scheme is not regarded as relevant. As Sen argues: 'Commitment . . . drives a wedge between personal choice and personal welfare' (Sen, 1977, p. 329).

Contingent valuation methods are designed to overcome these objections and have been used and supported because, unlike revealed preference techniques, they aim to isolate such commitments and represent them in valuations. However, this raises a further question of whether the plurality of values that we associate with the environment can be represented by the single measure of money. The assumption that it can is fundamental to welfare and environmental economics and, as the Department of the Environment stated, 'a monetary standard is a convenient means of expressing the relative values which society places on different uses of resources' (DOE, 1991a, p. 23).

A monetary standard may be 'convenient', but does the view that there can be a single standard against which the relative worth of all other values can be judged stand up to critical scrutiny? Advocates of CVM argue that they can isolate and compare the different aspects of the total economic value of the environment. The actual use value of the environment may seem relatively uncontroversial, although even here questions of information and the sense of what is possible can be raised, as can problems associated with the valuation of public goods. But where environmental economists seek to determine a monetary value for option and existence values there would seem to be even more scope for dispute. The purpose of seeking these valuations is to represent our duties to future generations and to non-human nature 'unrelated to human use' (Pearce and Turner, 1990, p. 130) within the CBA. Is it acceptable to attempt to value such commitments using the same criterion that we use to represent economic preferences? Are they not qualitatively different types of things (Keat, 1997)? Here we might reflect on what the economic value of a duty to future generations or of the commitment to the preservation of aspects of the non-human world actually means. That economists have generated a monetary value is unquestionable; what precisely that value represents is another matter. Obligations, duties and commitments are understood and judged against criteria other than utility. They refer to different aspects of the human condition and as such are not necessarily reducible to one another. They are probably best understood as incommensurable in the sense that, when we reason about the environment, we do so by employing a range of criteria which are neither reducible to one another nor clearly rankable in a scale of relative worth.[9]

At this point it would appear that economists are straying into an area where their methodology becomes meaningless. Either they need to make the strong claim that all values, commitments and beliefs are ultimately reducible to the single value of utility maximisation or they should recognise that there are values which cannot be adequately represented by CBA valuation techniques and that therefore their calculations are an extremely partial representation of our relations with the non-human world. The reduction of all environmental values to commodity values and the focus on individual preference satisfaction necessarily fails to account for many of the features of our relations with the non-human world. As Tim Hayward comments, 'environmental economists can by definition recognise no sources of value in nature other than those which assume the form of human preferences' (Hayward, 1995, p. 104). Representing the aesthetic and ethical dimensions of environmental values in terms of individual preferences distorts the significance of such values. For Mark Sagoff, there is a 'category mistake' in employing economic techniques (Sagoff, 1988, pp. 92–4). Environmental goods such as beautiful landscapes and rare species 'are not "commodities", since they are not traded in markets, and they are not consumed individually – their value is appreciated collectively' (Jacobs, 1991, p. 212). Questions concerning these goods ought to be the subject of deliberation among citizens and not reduced to a simple aggregate of consumer preferences.

Aggregation and discounting

A central issue for any technique that claims to aid decision making concerns the question of *whose* values count and *by how much*. Thus, two further features of CBA are open to criticism: the procedure of aggregation and the discounting of future values. Whose values are to be included in the decision-making process? What is the decision-making constituency? For instance, with respect to the loss of an area such as Twyford Down, whose preferences should count? The drivers who will have a faster route? The local community who may have less traffic passing through their town or may lose an important cultural landscape? Or wider still, to all those who value such areas? And what of the values of future generations? Again, the recognition of values beyond pure 'use' or 'resource' values begins to raise distinct problems for economists and decision makers.

It is far from clear that the community of concern is, or should be, a particular geographical location. Our emotions, attitudes and preferences can be shaped and transformed by aspects of the environment which are physically distant, but close to us in the sense that they constitute a significant aspect of our thoughts and actions. Perhaps the most obvious example are the values that people in Europe associate with the rainforests of Borneo, Brazil and the like. Where is the 'cut-off point' for the inclusion of such values in any decision-making process that affects such aspects of the environment?

Related to both the 'who' and the 'by how much' questions is the practice of discounting – that is, the issue of how are we to deal with future costs and benefits. Discounting is a familiar practice within resource management where we are 'simply' dealing with purely economic values. However, even here, there is a serious debate concerning the level of the discount rate. A high rate often militates against environ-mental projects with a long-term return (for instance sustainable forestry) and can result in an economic argument for resource depletion. In the literature we find calls for lower or even negative discount rates for particular types of policies and projects as well as concerns as to what differential rates might mean for comparison between options (Pearce and Turner, 1990, pp. 211ff). The DOE is itself well aware of such problems:

> [W]here there is a risk of losing an environmental benefit for all time, the appraisal should be sure to recognise both present and future perceptions of environmental values. Rising expectations about environmental quality, coupled with a diminishing stock of relatively untouched environmental assets, may mean that the value to society of certain resources will increase over time. Therefore, even though the loss of an environmental amenity may not seem to be of major importance now, that same amenity may be more highly valued in the future.
>
> (DOE, 1991a, p. 6)

Rather than tampering with the discount rate, however, the DOE, in line with the practice of most environmental economists, argues that the values incorporated into the CBA should be adjusted *prior* to discounting and that option values are the quantification of this future worth (ibid., p. 32). The interests, preferences and beliefs of future persons are therefore dependent on each currently-existing individuals' awareness of such values: the welfare and agency of future peoples is reliant upon the recognition of their needs in the economic behaviour of individuals acting in the present. To ensure that the interests of future generations are met, many environmental economists argue for the introduction of 'sustainability constraints' which would stop non-sustainable depletion of 'critical natural capital'. We shall consider the question of such constraints and interpretations of weak and strong sustainability from which they are derived in the case study at the end of the chapter. For the time being, though, the recognition that such constraints are necessary constitutes a further indication of the limits of the economic paradigm.

> The view implicit in conventional CBA is that future generations are provided for by maximising the productivity of present investments so far as to bequeath them the largest possible stock of economic and financial wealth. However, this attitude will not safeguard the future if it is accompanied by the loss of vital natural capital which cannot be replaced or substituted.
>
> (Winpenny, 1991, p. 67)

Relating back to the question of commensurability, there is an assumption that all the values derived by economists are related to the future in the same manner, a manner similar to the valuation of commodities in a market. But is this how we understand the aesthetic, moral, cultural or scientific values that economic techniques claim to distinguish? Does our aesthetic or moral sensibility relate to the future in the same way as an economic valuation of a natural resource? Are we impatient aesthetically and morally for immediate gratification and what would 'gratification' mean in these terms? Different values and modes of association with the non-human world have different temporal features. There are grounds for challenging not only the assumption that qualitatively different values can be represented by a monetary value but also that they then should be treated in the same manner as economic commodities when compared over time.

Finally, there is a range of criticisms that relate to the practice of aggregation and specifically to the Kaldor–Hicks compensation test. If, as we have argued, the economic assumption that differing values are commensurable is questioned, any simple aggregation across individuals becomes problematic. However, even if we overlook this issue there is still the standing of potential Pareto optimality to consider. Sen argues that the compensation criteria within potential Pareto optimality 'are either *unconvincing* or *redundant*': redundant if compensation is in fact paid since the decision can then be said to be Pareto efficient; unconvincing if not paid since this would be ethically questionable – the losers in CBA calculations, Sen contends, are frequently 'the most miserable in society, and it is little consolation to be told that it is possible to compensate them fully, but ("good God!") no actual plan exists to do so' (Sen, 1987, p. 33). This raises the issue of exactly *who* the losers and the gainers are – the distribution of costs and benefits. It raises questions of social justice. Pareto optimality is a criterion of economic or allocational efficiency; it does not consider, for instance, the distribution of effects. But why should we give priority to economic efficiency when we are considering environmental effects?

Uncertainty, risk and irreversibility

How are uncertainty, risk and irreversibility to be incorporated within the monetary evaluation of environmental impacts? A significant number of our interventions in the natural world are shrouded in a high level of uncertainty and risk. We are ignorant of many of the functions of

---

continued

ecological systems, such as the extent to which oceans operate as a sink for carbon dioxide, or the potential medical value of undiscovered plants in threatened rainforests.

Once an ecosystem is destroyed it is often difficult, if not impossible, to regenerate or replace. The extinction of a species is irreversible. Environmental economists are sensitive to a number of these problems and some have argued that CBA needs to be modified through the inclusion of sustainability constraints in order to ensure that critical aspects of the non-human world are maintained at sustainable levels. This theme is taken up in the case study at the end of the chapter.

What future for environmental valuation and extended-CBA?

While recognising the problems involved with the monetary valuation of environmental goods, a number of environmentalists have supported the use of extended CBA on pragmatic grounds. Decision making is typically 'dominated by concerns over "value for money" in public expenditure. In this context a measure that purports to show cash returns from public investment has a greater influence on decision-makers' (Atkins, 1990, p. 7). Thus, it is better to have some valuations of environmental costs and benefits in CBAs, even recognising that they are partial and inaccurate. R. Kerry Turner and his colleagues push the pragmatic line:

> [E]conomic (monetary) valuation of non-market environmental assets may be more or less imperfect given the particular asset together with its environmental and valuation contexts; but, invariably, some valuation explicitly laid out for scrutiny by policy-makers and the public, is better than none, because none can mean some implicit valuation shrouded from public scrutiny.
>
> (Turner *et al.*, 1994, p. 109)

Such a position is problematic on a number of counts. It may be the case that specific projects, such as the cutting through Twyford Down, might not have gone ahead, but this will not always be the case. If support has been given to the use of an extended-CBA, and the decision favours an environmentally-destructive option, the legitimacy of any challenge to the decision is reduced and environmentalists would be implicated in legitimising a distorted decision-making process. Further, contrary to the views of Turner and his colleagues, valuation is far from 'explicitly laid out' in CBA. All that normally faces the decision maker is a row of figures representing the valuation of environmental and other impacts. The judgement of their worth has already been made by the economist. CBA leads to values and assumptions being shrouded from public scrutiny with only the economist being granted privileged access.

There is an intuitive appeal to thinking about and weighing the costs and benefits of proposed interventions, but the idea that it can be achieved in such a quasi-scientific manner appears to be over-stretching the intuition. Economic evaluation of environmental values over-extends economists' area of competence and brings the apparent 'expert' authority and status of economists into question. Behind the shroud of expertise, environmental economists are offering advice on the basis of valuation techniques which distort the very values they aim to weigh. Simplification leads to misrepresentation. Political conflict is reduced to questions of aggregating preference intensities.

Environmental impact assessment

Environmental impacts do need to be weighed against other forms of costs and benefits. If we accept that monetary valuation of environmental entities is in some way mistaken, then how are environmental aspects of development to be taken into account? How are they to be presented in such a way as to be accessible to decision makers? In this section it is argued that environmental impact assessment (EIA) may offer an alternative, although it places more explicit emphasis on the role of sound political judgement. Decision makers are not faced simply with the numerical result of an economic calculation – the NPV of an intervention – but instead are required to balance a range of qualitatively different economic, social and environmental factors.

> EIA can be described as a process for identifying the likely consequences for the biogeophysical environment and for man's health and welfare of implementing particular activities and for conveying this information, at a stage when it can materially affect their decision, to those responsible for sanctioning the proposals.
>
> (Wathern, 1988, p. 6)

Since the 1970s, environmental impact assessment (EIA) has been increasingly turned to as a method of collating and presenting the significant environmental and social impacts of proposed projects. In June 1985, EC Directive 85/337 instructed all member states to enact legislation within three years that would require an EIA for certain large-scale and potentially damaging projects.[10]

The aim of the EIA process is to present, in as unbiased manner as possible, a systematic analysis of the significant impacts of a proposed development as an aid to decision makers. Consultation with statutory agencies (such as government departments or pollution-control agencies) and non-statutory groups (such as voluntary conservation organisations) is seen as central to the process of information gathering, as is a period of consultation with agencies and the public after the environmental impact statement is published. Such consultation should mean that the best sources of information are accessed and can often lead to project redesign and mitigation of impacts. These comments, along with the environmental impact statement, feed into the decision-making process where they are balanced against other material considerations.

Minimum content of environmental impact statements

(to conform with EC Directive 85/337)

1 An outline of the main alternatives to the chosen project which have been investigated by the developer and the main reasons for the preferred choice, taking their respective likely environmental effects into consideration.
2 A description of the main features of the chosen project which may cause significant impacts, including estimates of the residues and wastes it may create.
3 A description of the base-line condition of those aspects of the environment likely to be significantly affected by the chosen project.
4 An assessment of the likely significant impacts of a project, including its likely compatibility with existing and proposed environmental regulations and land use plans.
5 A description of any ameliorating measures which are proposed (or which have already been incorporated into the project design) to reduce the potentially harmful effects of the project on the environment.
6 A non-technical summary of the total assessment.

(Lee, 1989, p. 19)

The EIA study should incorporate all significant effects, both positive and negative, direct and indirect on:

- human beings, buildings and man-made features;
- flora, fauna and geology;
- land;
- water;
- air and climate;
- other indirect and secondary effects associated with the project.

(DOE, 1989, pp. 39–40)

A number of problems have arisen, most specifically concerning the definition of 'significant impact'. It is the developer who is generally charged with producing the environmental impact statement and it may well be in their best interest to downplay the significance of potential environmental effects. For this reason the quality of many environmental impact statements in the UK has been questioned, resulting in calls for an independent body to review practice. Consultation and participation are seen as essential if the EIA process is to work well, and for many commentators and practitioners the earlier consultation occurs the more likely agreement over the impact of a development is achieved. EIA is still in its relative infancy but already its potential as an aid to decision makers is being widely recognised.

Further questions have been raised as to the timing of any environmental impact assessment. Although EIA does provide a method of bringing environmental considerations into authorisation processes for developments and projects, it may be that in many cases it is too late in the decision-making process to have any profound effect. Focus on the environmental impact of projects does not entail analysis of the policy, plan or programme from which the project was developed. This has the effect of limiting the possible alternatives at the project stage. For instance, 'the use of an alternative transportation mode will not be considered in the EIA of a road link, because the alternative is no longer realistic' (Wood and Dejeddour, 1992, p. 6). Further, EIAs of projects tend to focus on the impact of the specific development and not on the cumulative impacts that are produced in combination with existing and future schemes. If environmental considerations are to substantially alter our practices, as environmentalists advocate, assessments need to be carried out at the earliest possible opportunity – hence the development of strategic environmental assessment (SEA).

Strategic environmental assessment (SEA)

Alternative approaches, cumulative impacts and synergistic impacts (which may be cross-sectorial in nature), ancillary impacts, regional or global impacts and non-project impacts may be better assessed initially at the policy, plan or programme level, rather than at the project level.

(Wood and Dejeddour, 1992, p. 3)

Compared to project-based EIA, strategic environmental assessment has had an even shorter history (Therivel et al., 1996). Strategic environmental assessment follows the same basic methodology as EIA although it focuses on policies, plans and programmes rather than on individual projects. A number of countries utilise strategic environmental assessment to a limited extent, particularly on land-use plans, although in Western Europe this will become more formalised with the ratification of the recent EU directive 2001/42, 'The assessment of the effects of certain plans and programmes on the environment'. Perhaps the most interesting development however is the commitment in Canada for all Cabinet policy decisions to undergo environmental assessment (Lee and Walsh, 1992, p. 128).

Strategic environmental assessment offers the possibility of overcoming the deficiencies of project-specific EIA and institutionalising the kind of analysis advocated by those who promote sustainable development – the integration of environmental concerns at all levels of decision making. Clearly the accuracy and detail of strategic environmental assessments will differ from EIAs, as will the time-scales involved. This however is simply a feature of any policy assessment when compared with project assessments.

EIA or extended-CBA?

What is the best way of proceeding with the assessment of the environmental effects of interventions, from policy level through to project level? Is it a straight choice between cost–benefit analysis or environmental impact assessment? Could we not use both? If the EIA procedure is thought to have merit, then it follows that monetary valuations of environmental costs and benefits should not form part of an extended-CBA for the same project or policy; otherwise we would be in the awkward position of double counting these environmental effects. This in turn would bias any decision made. Perhaps, in the end, the question needs to be recast in terms of the openness of any decision and the view that is taken as to the accuracy and commensurability of monetary valuation. Any detailed monetary valuation will actually initially require a full-scale EIA or SEA. The question then is whether political judgement is better served by the economic valuation of environmental and social impacts or through a more explicit process of weighing the significant effects of any intervention. We have argued that the move from a description of the environmental effects to a monetary valuation may alter the character of any decision. Further, there are numerous contested assumptions implicit within monetary valuations which are 'hidden' once the calculations enter the cost–benefit streams. The making of accountable political judgements requires these assumptions to be as open to scrutiny, deliberation and challenge as the policy or project under assessment. If not, then it may appear that political questions are being surrendered to the authority of economic analysis and the values we associate with the non-human world will be distorted.

Measuring sustainable development

In Chapter 2, we discussed the relationship between the environment, society and the economy centred around the concept of sustainable development. The idea that there may be ecological and social limits to growth is seen as a fundamental critical standpoint for environmentalists – if the earth is a finite planet, economies cannot continue to grow exponentially without permanent ecological damage and social disintegration. In this section we shall continue the discussion by focusing on the measurement of economic growth. The popular view, perpetrated particularly by economists and politicians, is that economic growth is always 'a good thing'. This view assumes that 'the more growth the better' and that a continued increase in economic performance can be directly translated into an increase in human welfare. It is this widely-assumed correlation between economic growth and human development that critics of a growth-centred orientation reject. In recent years an increasing amount of work has focused on the inadequacies and inconsistencies of government economic statistics that incorporate such a correlation.[11] Initially we shall focus on the environmental and social critique of national income accounting (NIA) used by states and international economic institutions and then turn our attention to possible alternatives.

National income accounting

National income accounting produces statistics such as gross national product (GNP) and gross domestic product (GDP), consistently used by economists and politicians to indicate the state of national economies and the well-being of its citizens. It is in light of such statistics that comparative analysis of the standing of nations is made and in terms of which national and international agencies make investment decisions. For instance, the success or failure of development projects or economic restructuring instigated by the World Bank or the International Monetary Fund (IMF) is frequently measured in terms of changes in GNP or GDP. If these do not adequately reflect the environmental or social impacts, then the wisdom of such interventions may be challenged.

National income accounting

Gross domestic product (GDP) is the total monetary value of goods and services produced within a country.

Gross national product (GNP) is the total income of all residents of a country.

GNP is **GDP** plus rents and dividends flowing into a country from abroad, minus rents, interests, profits, and dividends paid out to people in other countries. **GNP** depends on where the owners are located; **GDP** depends on where the economic activity is located.

GDP or **GNP per capita** is often referred to as the 'average standard of living'.

So what is wrong with such statistics? Critics argue that national income accounting only takes into account a limited set of economic factors which tell us nothing about the social and environmental conditions central to an adequate conception of well-being. This mirrors the earlier criticism that economic analysis is based on an impoverished conception of well-being as utility maximisation; from this it follows that even if GNP per capita is regarded as an accurate measure of economic welfare, it is only a partial representation of total well-being. It is conceivable that an increase in economic welfare so measured could be associated with a corresponding decrease in environmental and social conditions. NIA fails to account for a wide variety of environmental and social issues and incorporates a number of contradictions.

What is wrong with national income accounting?

NIA does not take into account:
- unpaid domestic labour (usually carried out by women), non-monetary transactions and voluntary work;
- the distribution of income across society and the marginal utility of money – an increase in income is worth relatively more to the poor than the rich;
- defensive expenditure – purchases to offset worsening social and environmental conditions; rather, this is counted as a benefit to the economy;
- unstable exchange rates used for international comparisons;
- the benefits of conservation over exploitation of resources – rapid throughput of transactions shows up more favourably than durability and re-use;
- long-term environmental damage, particularly to critical natural assets.
              (adapted from Anderson, 1991; Daly and Cobb, 1990; Ekins, 1986)

Taking these different factors into consideration, the conventional view that there is a direct correlation between per capita GNP and economic welfare begins to look rather suspect. GNP appears to provide an inaccurate and misleading approximation of our quality of life and the state of the environment. So what alternatives have critics proposed?

The Index of Sustainable Economic Welfare

In response to the perceived weaknesses of national income accounting, Herman Daly and John Cobb developed the Index of Sustainable Economic Welfare (Daly and Cobb, 1990, pp. 401–56). The Index adjusts GNP to take into account the contradictions inherent within conventional economic measures. An index of this sort is based on the recognition that a single figure can be useful in making broad comparisons of welfare over time. The Index has been applied to both the US (ibid.) and the UK economy (Mayo, 1994, pp. 6–7) over the period 1950 to 1986. In both cases sustainable economic welfare rose broadly in line with GNP up until the mid-1970s. However, this was purely a contingent relationship because since then the measure of sustainable welfare has levelled off and begun to decline, most strikingly in the UK. Both studies highlight three interconnected factors which have caused this drop: the deepening of economic inequality within society; the exhaustion of natural resources; and the failure to invest in sustainable future practices.

Although the Index provides a critical standpoint from which to analyse the cogency of national income accounting, questions again need to be raised as to the accuracy of the monetary valuations of environmental and social factors used in the Index, in particular with respect to long-term environmental damage. Equally, the Index includes contested assumptions concerning the weighting of income distribution factors. But, even given these methodological problems, the Index provides additional evidence that conventional measurements of economic growth are poor measures of the quality of life within a particular society.[12]

Quality of life indicators

GNP focuses attention on one particular form of progress, which even in its own terms appears to be a miscalculation. The Index of Sustainable Economic Welfare attempts to take into account the wider social and environmental context that GNP ignores, although it still depends on the economic valuations of such aspects of well-being. If the accuracy of these valuations is questionable, what other options are left? Perhaps one of the most interesting developments in recent years has been in the area of alternative quality of life indicators.

Victor Anderson has been at the forefront of arguing for the need to develop a range of indicators that take into account a wider understanding of well-being and correspond to our social and environmental situations. He isolates three aspects of welfare where indicators are necessary – financial, social and the relationship with the natural world (Anderson, 1991, pp. 42–7). Clearly, it is the social and environmental aspects that have been predominantly overlooked in contemporary society. Anderson argues that social indicators need to be developed that take into account such factors as education and literacy, work and unemployment, consumption, distribution of income and wealth, and health. Similarly, environmental indicators need to take into account significant and critical factors such as deforestation, climate change, population pressures, nuclear threats and energy consumption. Various criteria for a good indicator are offered, particularly the need for readily accessible information and ease of understanding. Further they should allow comparison between regions and nations while at the same time allowing for cultural specificity. With both social and environmental issues it is important that they are easily measurable and understandable and that only a small number of significant factors are measured for ease of comparison.

Alternative social and environmental indicators

Human and social indicators

1   Net primary school enrolment ratio for girls.
2   Net primary school enrolment ratio for boys.
3   Female illiteracy rate.
4   Male illiteracy rate.
5   The rate of unemployment.
6   Average calorie supply as a percentage of requirements.
7   Percentage of population with access to safe drinking water.
8   Telephones per thousand people.
9   Household income received by the top 20 per cent of households divided by that received by the bottom 20 per cent.
10   Infant mortality rate.
11   Under-five mortality rate.

Environmental indicators

12   Deforestation in square kilometres per year.
13   Carbon dioxide emissions from fossil fuel use, in millions of metric tons per year.
14   Average annual percentage rate of increase in population.
15   Number of operable nuclear reactors.
16   Energy consumption (in tons of oil equivalent) per million dollars of GDP.

(In addition, there is an urgent need for more comprehensive data both on rates of species loss and rates of desertification.)

(adapted from Anderson, 1991, pp. 55–74)

Using these indicators, a comparative analysis of a number of nations indicates that GNP obscures a number of important differences in well-being and the standard of living.[13] What is most striking (although unsurprising) is the gap between the nations of the North and South. The division occurs across almost all the factors represented by each indicator. From his survey, Anderson draws the following conclusions:

1 Social conditions are generally improving, and in the short term, this is likely to continue.

2 In the medium term, environmental deterioration threatens to put these social improvements into reverse. For example, growing desertification threatens current improvements in calorie supply: pollution will threaten current improvements in health.

3 In the long term, the outcome depends on whether the current improvements in environmental 'cause indicators' (such as energy intensity and rate of population growth) continue and are sufficiently big scale to put the environmental 'effects indicators' into reverse. This would allow the social indicators to resume their past trend of general improvement.

(Anderson, 1991, p. 91)

There is growing recognition that such indicators provide a broader understanding of the relationship between the economy, society and the natural world and that they could form the basis of more efficacious decisions. This recognition has led a number of non-governmental organisations to develop similar quality of life indicators in an attempt to influence decision makers. For instance, the Environmental Challenge Group, an initiative supported by a group of British non-governmental organisations, developed a range of environmental indicators in order to push its case for higher levels of environmental protection in Whitehall. The study seems to indicate that the UK's environment is deteriorating. Some of the most interesting work in this area is taking place at the local level. In Seattle, for instance, a community-based initiative – Sustainable Seattle – has achieved widespread local support in a process of generating economic, social and environmental indicators for the city. Public participation has been central to the development of the indicators and Sustainable Seattle argues that only when such information is fully available will citizens be able to judge how sustainable Seattle actually is and to generate initiatives to alter environmentally- and socially-destructive practices (Lawrence, 1994; Sustainable Seattle, 1993; International Institute for Sustainable Development, 1997). This project is discussed in more detail in the case study in Chapter 10. A number of local authorities, national governments and international agencies have begun to experiment with similar broad indicators of quality of life (LGMB, 1995b; DETR, 1999; IISD, 1997; UNDP, 2001). The approach taken by the UK government is discussed in Chapter 9.

Although such indicators do not offer a single figure such as in national income accounting, they do make the trade-offs inherent in decisions explicit and offer ongoing data for monitoring the effect of policies. They also lead to a recognition that financial factors are but one aspect of political judgements. Political decisions may be more difficult to make with respect to such a range of information, but at least they will be made with a recognition of the range of significant factors involved. After all, what is the economy there to achieve – the creation of more economic wealth or the development of the quality of life, in the broadest sense?

Conclusion

We can draw at least two conclusions from our discussion of the economic analysis of environmental values and goods. First, decision makers appear to be seduced by the apparent technical simplicity of quasi-scientific economic calculations. Both CBA and GNP provide a single figure with which simple comparisons can be made between alternative projects, policies or even national economies. Our investigations have shown that such figures may well conceal a range of assumptions and simplifications which misrepresent the human condition and specifically our relationship with the non-human world. To what extent should we accept political decisions based on such simplification and distortion?

Second, it is perhaps not surprising that such measures underpin the logic of capitalist patterns of economic growth. Individuals are taken to be utility maximisers and their economic preferences the only aspect of the human condition that is of interest. Rethinking the way we assess interventions and economies as a whole requires us to reassess what we believe is important about humanity and the natural world. Closing off such a critical endeavour by shrouding politically-sensitive assumptions in economic analysis will simply mean more of the same, including continued environmental and social degradation. The relationship between the economy, society and the natural world needs to be articulated in all decisions – EIA and indicators offer methods by which this goal might be achievable.

Case study: weak and strong sustainability

CBA can only provide information about the relative economic value of different policy or project options – it cannot tell us whether a policy or project is sustainable. A commitment to sustainable development, with its requirement to take into account the needs of present and future generations, would appear to place certain requirements, if not constraints, on development projects. Conventional economic analytical tools, such as CBA, are often far from useful when questions turn to the optimal size of the economy or the minimum physical levels of certain stocks of environmental goods; they can help with optimal allocation but not with optimal size or distribution.

Where environmental economists have attempted to respond to the obligations implicit within sustainable development, they have taken it to entail a duty to pass on to future generations the equivalent 'stock of wealth' (Pearce et al., 1989, pp. 34ff). But, is this constant stock of wealth to be a mix of man-made and natural capital? Can manufactured goods be seen as substitutable for natural entities? Further, how is such a stock of wealth to be calculated? It is on such questions of the relationship between different forms of capital stock that distinctions between competing interpretations of sustainable development can be made, specifically between weak and strong sustainability.[14]

Three types of capital are commonly distinguished:

- Human-made: consumer goods, buildings, machinery;
- Human: labour, skills, knowledge, creativity;
- Natural: natural resources.

continued

Advocates of weak sustainability hold that the three different types of capital are substitutable; the loss of a particular aspect of the environment can be substituted by the equivalent value of human-made or human capital. What we bequest to future generations should be the equivalent total stock of all three types of capital. Clearly, holding such a position would sanction any level of environmental degradation, resource depletion or species loss, so long as the equivalent value of human or human-made capital is substituted in its place. The monetary valuation of environmental entities becomes central to the weak sustainability argument since substitution requires a common measure in order that equivalent amounts of what are qualitatively different entities can be weighed against one another. In this sense, it is the economic value of human-made, human and natural capital that is to remain constant. To advocate weak sustainability requires the acceptance of the principles of economic valuation discussed earlier.

On the other hand, advocates of strong sustainability deny the direct substitutability of different types of capital, arguing that there is a common misinterpretation among economists as to the nature of natural capital. Paul Ekins highlights three different functions of natural capital:

- Provision of resources for human activity;
- Absorption of wastes from human activity;
- Provision of environmental services independently of or interdependently with human activity.

(Ekins, 1995, p. 183)

The first two functions, although frequently neglected (particularly the waste assimilation function), can be incorporated in traditional economic modelling. It is the third function that is perhaps the most important and is neglected by advocates of weak sustainability. Not only does the environment provide the basic materials for production and the assimilation of humanity's waste products, but it is also the milieu in which human activity takes place. The natural world provides fundamental survival and amenity services (Ekins, 1995, p. 185) that appear to be far from substitutable. These include examples such as the ozone layer, the climate-regulating functions of the oceans and rainforests, the stability of ecosystems, as well as more aesthetic properties associated with, for instance, wilderness or other beautiful landscapes. Not only do such functions appear to be non-substitutable, but there is uncertainty concerning the consequences of depleting or degrading certain natural entities and losing the apparent resilience of diverse ecological systems; degradation is frequently irreversible and unjust in respect of the distribution of effects (Beder, 1996, pp. 145–52).

In response to the assertion that forms of capital are substitutable, strong sustainability holds that human-made/human capital and natural capital are better viewed as complements (Daly, 1995, p. 49; Jacobs, 1995c, p. 59). In the contemporary world, natural capital needs to be understood as the limiting factor for development and constraints must be placed on certain environmentally-destructive types of activity. Sustainable development requires the recognition of certain duties to future generations. These can be fulfilled to a certain extent by the preservation of a constant stock of *natural* capital.

> Strong sustainability as a constraint is a way of implicitly providing property rights in the resource base to future generations. It says that they have ownership claims to as much natural capital as the present – i.e. the rule is to keep natural capital intact.
>
> (Daly, 1995, p. 53)

Generally, advocates of strong sustainability are critical of the idea of ecological modernisation, in which economic growth and environmental protection are taken to be complementary (see Chapter 2). For instance, Herman Daly (1992) has consistently argued that we require a 'steady-state' economy,[15] one where there is not only an unaltered reserve of natural wealth (strong sustainability) but this is also tied to a constant population; zero economic and population growth. The earth and its finite resources cannot provide the panacea of constant growth; rather humanity must concentrate its efforts and creativity on alternative forms of human development. Far more radical than Daly is the group of bioeconomists, including Nicholas Georgescu-Roegen and Juan Martinez-Alier, who share his view that processes of economic growth and accumulation degrade the natural system, returning waste products at a higher level of entropy and unfit for human use.[16] In their view, conventional economics pays little attention to the moral and physical aspects of the economy, focusing mainly on added value as if the current economic system were the end of the historical process of development. The contemporary capitalist economic system is open and linear rather than closed and circular and the dissipation of energy is irreversible. Such a situation requires not zero growth but a reduction in the scale of the economy that will have regard to the physical and moral aspects of development.

More conventional environmental economists, who accept the distinction between the different types of capital, tend to accept the substitutability thesis, but with the caveat that there clearly are some forms of critical natural capital that cannot be substituted. Such a position is somewhere between the two poles of weak and strong sustainability. It accepts the argument that the natural world provides certain types of capital which we cannot replace (such as the ozone layer, oceans, etc.) but that other types of natural capital can be replaced by human-made substitutes. Within environmental economics this is perhaps the dominant interpretation of sustainable development and tends to form part of the ecological modernisation stream of thought. It would be wrong however to claim that there is consensus within neo-liberal welfare economics as to the usefulness of the concept of sustainable development; Wilfred Beckerman, for instance, argues that unless we hold the strong interpretation, which he finds 'morally unacceptable and totally impracticable', the weak interpretation is nothing more than welfare maximisation and the principle of optimality. The concept of sustainable development cannot generate measurable criteria and is therefore redundant. The power of human creativity to discover and introduce substitutes and alternatives to natural resources should not be hampered by restricting market transactions and constraining economic analysis techniques such as CBA (Beckerman, 1994, pp. 191ff).[17] Within this debate there is a mirroring of some of the divisions in green thinking discussed in Part I of this book. Advocates of strong anthropocentrism or technical optimism tend to support a version of weak sustainability; those who subscribe to a weak or enlightened anthropocentrism tend towards a strong interpretation of sustainability.

Whichever position one takes on this (unless of course one does not accept the need to constrain policies in the name of sustainable development at all) there still remains the issue of how the level of natural capital is to be calculated. Is it the physical amount or a financial valuation of natural capital that needs to be taken into account? For environmental economists the answer is invariably the latter and this brings in the whole question of the economic valuation of environmental entities with which the above chapter engaged.

> It is . . . a moot point whether we should be concerned with passing on a constant physical level of capital, or one that preserves its value on economic terms. As resources become

continued

scarce they become more economically valuable. The last piece of coal mined on earth will no doubt have a high rarity value, but that is no consolation to people dependent on burning coal.

(Winpenny, 1991, p. 3)

Taking sustainability into account has certain implications for the development of projects and policies. First, it places a restriction on policies that impact on critical natural assets. Second, it points towards the inclusion of shadow projects or at least financial compensation within developments. For instance, the destruction of woodlands for housing might require the developer to plant the equivalent tree coverage elsewhere. Third, renewable natural capital such as fisheries or woodlands should be exploited only up to sustainable levels, that is, not beyond the point at which they are no longer able to regenerate. Clearly, however, many environmental assets are neither critical nor renewable and can be used only once, for instance oil and coal reserves. Sustainable development points towards the use of such resources in a prudent manner with emphasis being put on the search for alternatives. We cannot stop intervening in the environment for our own sustenance – it is quite simply a question of what form of development we aim to achieve and *how* we are to utilise the natural world in its fulfilment.

Suggestions for further reading

The seminal text defending the approach of environmental economics is David Pearce, Anil Markandya and Edward B. Barbier *Blueprint for a Green Economy*, originally commissioned by the Department of the Environment. A *Blueprint* series aiming to capture the economic value of a variety of different environmental impacts followed. Pearce and Barbier have updated their work in *Blueprint for a Sustainable Economy*. *Environmental Economics* by R. Kerry Turner, David Pearce and Ian Bateman is an accessible introduction to the subject. Michael Jacobs in *The Green Economy* offers a number of critical reflections on this neo-classical approach, as does the collection *Valuing Nature* edited by John Foster. Peter Wathern's edited collection *Environmental Impact Assessment* is a useful guide written by both practitioners and academics. For assessment at policy level, *Strategic Environmental Assessment* by Riki Therivel and colleagues offers a useful introduction. Victor Anderson *Alternative Economic Indicators* raises the profile of the debate on the limits of national accounting.

Notes

1   For a detailed discussion of the rationale behind cost–benefit analysis see Mishan (1988) or Pearce (1983).

2   This book has proved so popular that Pearce and his colleagues have developed a series of *Blueprint* texts on different aspects of economic valuation of environmental issues, from global environmental change to the cost of transport.

3   Where policies and projects are constrained by the need to fulfil environmental targets or objectives, such as air or water quality standards, the decision-making tool is known as cost-effectiveness analysis (CEA). See DOE (1991a, p. 19).

4   The concept of externalities was originally developed by A.C. Pigou (1932).

5   However, representatives of the neo-liberal school of free-market economics (discussed in Chapters 2 and 5) attempt to follow through Coase's argument to its logical end by introducing the idea of property rights for the atmosphere and the oceans; see for instance Anderson and Leal (1991).

6   The circumstances surrounding the development of the road scheme and the subsequent protests at Twyford Down are discussed in the case study at the end of Chapter 3.

7   Not all commentators use exactly the same typology although that need not concern us here. For a more detailed discussion of direct and indirect techniques see Winpenny (1991, pp. 42–72), Pearce and Turner (1990, pp. 141–59) and OECD (1989, pp. 25–58).

8   For more detailed discussions of the biases inherent within CVM, see, for example, Pearce and Turner (1990, pp. 149–53), Winpenny (1991, pp. 59–61) and Jacobs (1991, pp. 205ff). There are also numerous articles in the *Journal of Environmental Economics and Management* devoted to the results and refinement of CVM and other valuation techniques.

9   For a discussion of the different meanings of commensurability see O'Neill (1993, pp. 110ff).

10   For more on the nature and impact of European Union environmental policy, see Chapter 8.

11   See in particular the work supported by the New Economics Foundation. Its newspaper *News from the New Economy* and other publications provide a wealth of information.

12   Friends of the Earth (UK) has an interactive guide to the Index of Sustainable Economic Welfare on its website www.foe.co.uk/campaigns/sustainable_development/progress/.

13   Fourteen countries were selected – the USA, Canada, Japan, France, West Germany, Italy, the UK, China, India, USSR, Indonesia, Brazil, Nigeria and Bangladesh. Together these nations represent 66 per cent of the world's population (Anderson, 1991, p. 75).

14   For alternative distinctions between conceptions of sustainable development, see Baker *et al.*'s 'ladder of sustainable development' (1997) and Dobson's three conceptions of environmental sustainability (1998).

15   As mentioned in Chapter 2, the origins of steady-state economics can be traced back to the nineteenth century and the writings of John Stuart Mill (1909, pp. 746–51).

16   Bioeconomists frequently refer to the second law of thermodynamics which holds that useful low entropy energy always eventually dissipates into an inaccessible high entropic state. Bioeconomists argue that traditional forms of economic theory abstract to such an extent from physical and social reality that their theories are almost worthless and, in many cases, potentially dangerous. They aim to forge theories that are multidisciplinary, working with physicists, biologists and the like. See for example Georgescu-Roegen (1971).

17   For a taste of the ongoing debate around weak and strong sustainability see the entertaining and somewhat polemical exchanges in *Environmental Values* between Beckerman (1994, 1995b), Daly (1995) and Jacobs (1995c).

Part III

ENVIRONMENTAL GOVERNANCE: GLOBAL TO LOCAL

International dimensions

> Can a fragmented and often highly conflictual political system made up of over 170 sovereign states and numerous other actors achieve the high (and historically unprecedented) levels of cooperation and policy coordination needed to manage environmental problems on a global scale?
>
> (Hurrell and Kingsbury, 1992, p. 1)

Since the early 1970s there has been a growing recognition that many environmental problems, in particular those of a transboundary nature, cannot be successfully tackled solely at the national level. A nation state can no longer act alone to solve many of the environmental problems that it faces. States have responded by creating international 'regimes' in an attempt to tackle problems ranging from ozone depletion and climate change to biodiversity loss and toxic-waste export. A regime is typically defined as a set of 'implicit or explicit principles, norms, rules and decision-making procedures around which actors' expectations converge in a given area of inter-national relations' (Krasner, 1983, p. 2).[1] However, some regimes are stronger than others and one of the aims of this chapter is to analyse why that should be so. For example, the ozone-depletion regime is taken to be one of the most effective, with the 1990 amendment to the Montreal Protocol requiring the phasing out of CFCs and other ozone-depleting chemicals by 2000. By comparison, the forestry regime is only held together by a weak set of principles initially agreed at the Rio Earth Summit in 1992. In the development of regimes difficulties arise from all sorts of directions. These include the basic definition of the environmental problem; disagreements over scientific and economic impacts; the actions of states who are willing to veto agreements that appear to conflict with their perceived interests; the vagueness of commitments and soft obligations embodied in many agreements; and problems with implementation and compliance. It is simply not possible to discuss here the development of each environmental regime and all the different factors alluded to above.[2] Instead, the chapter will examine two factors which seem to militate against the creation of effective environmental regimes: the nature of the international political and economic systems. Sovereignty and the logic of capital accumulation are often seen as inimical to the development of adequate responses to global environmental problems. However, there have been over sixty multilateral environmental treaties signed in the last three decades and, in some areas, regimes are proving to be effective. To begin to understand why this might be the case it is necessary to focus on the activities of two different types of international actors and the role they play in global environmental politics: international organisations (IOs) such as the United Nations Environment Programme (UNEP) and international non-governmental organisations (NGOs). In seeking to understand the nature of international environmental politics, it is not enough to simply focus on the actions of states and the multilateral agreements they sign.

In the final section of this chapter, the discussion will turn from the generation of regimes in response to isolated environmental problems to the international response to sustainable development. The growing recognition that patterns of development and environmental degradation are linked achieved its greatest political expression to date at the United Nations Conference on Environment and Development (UNCED), held in Rio in June 1992. The genesis of the 'Earth Summit' can be located in two earlier events. The first is the United Nations Conference on the Human Environment held in Stockholm in 1972 where the global nature of environmental degradation received initial recognition. The second is the publication in 1987 of *Our Common Future*, the report of the World Commission on Environment and Development (the Brundtland Report), which capitalised on the political space created as the Cold War came to an end. The principles and implications of sustainable development can challenge the very structures of the global political and economic systems far more than the environmental regimes developing in response to separate problems. It is not surprising, then, that the agreements produced at Rio fell far short of what many environmentalists desired. It is a hotly debated question as to whether the Earth Summit and the processes and institutions it spawned can be described as a success. The chapter will end with a case study on the global politics of climate change.

The international political and economic systems

The international politics of the environment is marked by a series of related conflicts and tensions between Northern and Southern nations around issues such as the nature of the global economy, population and resource consumption and the significance of sovereignty. These disagreements in many ways structure the debates during the creation and evolution of regimes and will be continuing themes that resurface throughout this chapter. The manner in which environmental problems are understood has implications for questions of *responsibility* and international justice.

One of the fundamental disputes surrounds the nature of the economic system. Typically, Northern nations (which benefit from existing economic arrangements) tend to conceive of environmental problems as separate from the nature of economic relations. Environmental problems are viewed as technical issues which can be tackled without altering the structures of the global economic system; without challenging free-market principles and the logic of capital accumulation. For most Southern states economic reform is taken as essential, but typically the language of capital accumulation is not challenged. Rather, trade rules need to be restructured so that the South can enjoy the development opportunities that the North has achieved. States in the North and the South share the view that economic growth and environmental protection are reconcilable; a vision of sustainable development as ecological modernisation dominates (Weale, 1992; see Chapter 2). For many greens such analyses are flawed in that the global environment cannot sustain ever-increasing economic development. In their view both the North and the South will have to radically restructure their economies, with the North reducing its levels of consumption and the South developing in a manner which is both sustainable and provides for the needs of its populations. Greens are also aware that the focus on national development and the North–South dynamic of much of the international debate fails to acknowledge the effect of capitalist development on local communities and traditional practices and forms of knowledge. The dominant discourse of ecological modernisation is seen to favour the interests of political and economic elites in both the North and the South, with little regard for other communities. An adequate response to environmental problems means a radical reappraisal of what is understood by 'development'.

A related area of contention is the relative impact on the global environment of resource consumption and increasing population levels. Northern countries tend to emphasise the increase in sheer numbers in the South, pointing to the impact that existing levels have on resources and asking what the global effect of an increased population might be. The world's population currently stands at around 6 billion and, although earlier estimates that it will double by 2050 have recently been brought into question, levels in the South are still increasing, putting further pressure on resources (Brown *et al.*, 1996, p. 88). The current estimate is that global population will increase by 50 per cent to nine billion by the middle of the twenty-first century. Projections of increased population growth have fuelled resurgences in neo-Malthusian theories, many influenced by the Club of Rome's *The Limits to Growth* (see Chapter 2). Concerns are frequently aired as to the pressures that such numbers will have on resources such as agricultural land, water supplies and the like. Organisations such as the World Health Organisation argue that the sheer pressure of numbers leads to millions of deaths each year 'largely owing to their own con-tamination of water, soil and air' (Thomas, 1993, p. 22). However, studies of the impact of sheer numbers on natural resources are often seen by Southern states as an attempt to deflect attention away from the North's consumption rates and its responsibility for the creation of many contemporary environmental problems. Take for example the issue of use of fossil fuels: 'There are great disparities in fossil carbon *per capita* emissions. The US emits approximately 5.7 tonnes of carbon per person per year, while India (for example) emits approximately 0.4 tonnes' (Paterson, 1996, p. 14). In a similar manner, Richard Falk highlights the fact that 85 per cent of the world's income is enjoyed by only 23 per cent of the world's population living in the North, whereas the other 77 per cent of the population in the South are left with only 23 per cent of the wealth (Falk, 1995, pp. 57–8; UNDP, 2001, p. 19).[3] In particular, the plight of Sub-Saharan Africa has worsened dramatically, 'per capita income, around 1/9 of that in high-income OECD in 1960, deteriorated to around 1/18 in 1998' (UNDP, 2001, p. 16). Focusing on the question of consumption levels empha-sises the role that the North has played and is still playing in global environmental degradation.

Challenges to human development

Developing countries

Health

> 968 million people without access to improved water sources.
> 2.4 billion people without access to basic sanitation.
> 3.4 million people living with HIV/AIDS.
> 2.2 million people dying annually from indoor air pollution.

Education

854 million illiterate adults, 543 million of them women.
325 million children out of school at the primary and secondary levels, 183 million of them girls.

Income poverty

1.2 billion people living on less than $1 a day, 2.8 billion on less than $2 a day.

Children

163 million underweight children under the age of five.
11 million children under five dying annually from preventable causes.

OECD countries

15 per cent of adults lacking functional literacy skills.
130 million people in income poverty (with less than 50 per cent of median income).
8 million undernourished people.
1.5 milion people living with HIV/AIDS.

(UNDP, 2001, p. 9)

A final area of conflict is over the issue of sovereignty. For example, Southern states view population issues as a matter of domestic concern and see attempts by Northern countries to establish demographic regimes as attempts to override their sovereignty. Equally, they see pressure put on them to stem their development and to take the environment into account as further attempts to undermine their sovereignty; a form of 'ecocolonialism' (Salih, 1997, pp. 124ff). Environmental concern is taken to be an obstacle erected to halt development in the South. One of the reasons that the regime on forests is so weak is that there is a fundamental disagreement as to the status of tropical forests. Attempts to view forests as global commons or the 'common heritage of mankind' is seen by many Southern nations as legitimising the North's right to interfere with their management of their own resources. A similar disagreement can be seen over the issue of biodiversity. It is with this question of sovereignty that we begin our analysis of the international political system.

Sovereignty and the international political system

Sovereignty is at the heart of what can be termed the 'settled norms' of the contemporary international order: 'national self-determination, non-aggression and respect for international law combined with support for the principles of sovereignty' (Brown, 1997, p. 31). Take, for example, Principle 2 of the Rio Declaration on Environment and Development:

States have, in accordance with the Charter of the United Nations and the principles of international law, the sovereign right to exploit their own resources pursuant to their own environmental and developmental policies, and the responsibility to ensure that activities within their jurisdiction or control do not cause damage to the environment of other States or of areas beyond the limits of jurisdiction.

As has already been intimated, environmental problems can be seen as a challenge to this principle of sovereignty, particularly as it embodies the idea of complete *dominion* over the resources within a state's territory rather than the idea of *stewardship* so central to green thinking (see Chapter 1). However, Southern states are far from happy with any weakening of the principle given that they see this as an attempt by Northern nations to control their development patterns.

The idea of sovereignty is central to much international relations theory, as is the idea of the state of anarchy that is said to exist at the international level – there is no formal system of government or authority above the level of the state.[4] The state is taken to have sovereign authority over its territory and its legitimacy to rest on its ability to achieve internal and external security and to provide for the well-being of its citizens. How, then, are states with apparently divergent interests able to cooperate in a manner that is effective in responding to international environmental problems? Typically, the development of international environmental regimes is taken to provide an excellent example of the problem of collective action which we discussed in some depth in Chapter 4. The two dominant theories of international relations, neo-realism and neo-institutionalism, can be understood as competing variants on rational choice theory.[5]

Neo-realism stresses that states should be understood as self-interested egoists whose actions are determined by attempts to maximise their welfare relative to other states. Under such conditions it is no surprise that there is difficulty in achieving international cooperation, as the actions of states are always to be interpreted as an attempt to exercise power over others: to gain an advantage over other states. We are left with the collective action problem writ large – with no supranational organisation that can claim authority over states, any attempt to develop environmental regimes flounders in the face of the logic of the tragedy of the commons – in theory, free-riding and non-cooperation should be rife. However, despite this, international cooperation does occur and therefore needs to be explained.

Neo-liberal institutionalists argue that it is possible to overcome collective action problems and to develop stable regimes. The basic realist assumptions of international anarchy and rational egoism are accepted, but it is argued that particularly strong states – hegemons – are willing to accept the costs of establishing regimes. Such hegemonic states recognise that it is in their own interests that cooperation should occur, their interests being defined in terms of absolute improvements in the state's welfare rather than improvements relative to other states. Typically, the USA is viewed as the hegemonic power. This goes some way to explaining why environmental problems have been cast in language that does not doubt free-market assumptions and why those affecting the interests of industrialised nations have been tackled most effectively. However, in the environmental arena, the USA appears to be a declining influence as a hegemon. Whether this is because of a lack of willingness or ability (read power) on the part of the US administration is not always clear. Despite strong support from within Bill Clinton's administration, the USA failed to sign up to the Kyoto process because of the opposition of the Republican-dominated Senate; under

George Bush, Jnr., the USA has chosen to take a unilateral, isolationist stance against the emerging regime (see case study). As Gareth Porter and Janet Brown argue:

> When the United States has taken the lead, as it did in the Montreal Protocol on ozone depletion, whaling, or the African elephant, the result has been a stronger regime than would otherwise have been established. But when it has been a veto state, as in the sulfur dioxide protocol to the acid rain convention, the hazardous waste trade convention, and the climate convention, the result has been a significantly weaker regime.
>
> (Porter and Brown, 1996, p. 106)

But, liberal institutionalists argue that even in the absence of a hegemon or where a hegemon is in decline, cooperation can still occur, although normally at a sub-optimal level. Formalised agreements and a supportive context that promotes the exchange of knowledge and information increase the likelihood of stable regimes. Cooperation is fostered through the development of institutions; sets of norms which guide behaviour and provide an incentive for states to cooperate.

The analysis of international politics as the politics of collective action does offer certain insights into some of the problems facing the development of international environmental regimes. However, the basic assumptions of such an analysis are somewhat limited, specifically the accounts of sovereignty and international anarchy. With respect to sovereignty, it is important to recognise that the term can be understood in different ways. Perhaps the most important differentiation here is between the understanding of sovereignty as a *judicial* status and as a *political* concept (Brown, 1997, pp. 125–7). The identification of the state system as one of 'anarchy' implies that under international law, states have judicial sovereignty. This form of sovereignty is unqualified – there is no legal authority above the state. However, the second aspect of sovereignty, understood as a political concept, is far from unqualified. The political understanding of sovereignty highlights the fact that states have differential powers and capacities. What follows from this?

First, for states to retain their legitimacy, understood in terms of the provision of welfare for their citizens, it may be necessary for states to cooperate, to 'pool' their sovereignty and as such increase their (collective) capacities and powers. For instance, no single state has it within its sole power to protect its citizens from the effects of hazardous ultra-violet radiation caused by the degradation of the ozone layer. Only the pooling of sovereignty, the institutionalisation of a ban on production of CFCs, can achieve that. As Chris Brown notes: 'The bundle of powers that a state possesses as a "sovereign" body is thereby simultaneously diminished *and* enhanced' (ibid., p. 126) – each state is able to protect itself from certain forms of ultra-violet radiation, but only by giving up certain capacities in agreeing to abide by the rules of the ozone regime. As Brown reflects, 'although the world lacks government, because states have been unwilling to surrender their *judicial* status as sovereign, their attempts to rule effectively and exercise their *political* sovereignty have created extensive networks of global "governance"' (ibid., p. 128). Environmental regimes are an aspect of these networks of governance.

Second, it is important to recognise the differing abilities of states to realise their desired ends and to influence other states. Legal authority over a given territory does not necessarily mean that states are immune from the actions and behaviour of others; neither does it mean that a state will confine its power and influence within its own borders. Reflecting on the dimensions of power discussed in Chapter 4, we can understand how dominant states, such as the United States, can exercise power over other states in a number of ways: overtly by simply threatening military action or trade sanctions; covertly by keeping certain environmental issues off the political agenda (non-decision making); or perhaps even structurally in continually reaffirming that the legitimacy of states rests on capital accumulation. As we shall see below, the structure of the international economy is most definitely in the interests of certain nations over others. What is interesting about international environmental politics is that the capacity for some Southern nations to exercise power is likely to increase as the global reach of environmental problems is further recognised. States such as India, Brazil and China have threatened to veto agreements in areas such as ozone depletion if issues of technical transfer and financial assistance are not strengthened. More fundamentally, it is important to recognise that environmental politics can be seen as challenging dominant understandings of sovereignty as the legitimacy of states understood in terms of their ability to secure continued capital accumulation is itself challenged. Such accumulation does not necessarily defend citizens from the harms of global environmental degradation.

The rational choice assumptions of neo-realism and neo-institutionalism can be further challenged by recalling arguments developed in earlier chapters concerning how we consider preference and interest formation. To what extent should the preferences and interests of states be taken as given and immutable? We have already begun to suggest that stable regimes may provide the conditions for actors to exchange information and understandings of environmental problems. As such, social learning is promoted. We must be alive to the way in which preferences and interests are formed: they are not simply given, but can be transformed. Environmental regimes and forms of governance need therefore to attend to the process of preference formation. Stable regimes can promote trust, mutual learning and the transformation of preferences when states are exposed to alternative interpretations of environmental problems, and pool their knowledge and information. It is thus necessary to begin to look beyond the actions of states alone and to analyse the roles played by other international actors. It should not be surprising that the central focus of international relations is the actions of states, but this downplays and disregards the importance of other actors. For instance, the existence of the United Nations system, although not having any legal priority over state sovereignty, has helped to accelerate the institutionalisation of functional cooperation, particularly in the environmental arena. Here we can point to actors such as the United Nations Environment Programme (UNEP) and more recently the Commission on Sustainable Development (CSD) which have been crucial in bringing together states and creating the conditions for the development of stable expectations and relations of trust so essential for mutual understanding that underpins the development of successful regimes. Again, non-governmental organisations (NGOs) play an important role in lobbying states and international organisations; raising environmental issues and offering potential policy options. Of course, not all NGOs have such a positive impact, and we have only to reflect on the role of the business lobby in challenging the Kyoto climate change process to understand the power and influence of 'anti-environment' actors. International organisations and NGOs will be returned to later in the chapter, but for now it is enough to recognise that the conception of international politics based on the anarchical nature of inter-state relations is too restricted. As Brown argues: 'The *anarchy problematic* . . . does not simply serve the interests of rich and powerful states by legitimising certain ways of exercising power, it also sets in place a particular conception of politics which privileges *all* states' (Brown, 1997, p. 120). We must recognise the role that other (non-state) actors play in the development of environmental regimes and forms of global governance.

What is clear is that issues thrown up by environmental politics challenge the position of certain dominant interests. In the next section we shall focus on the actors and interests in the economic arena, but to conclude this discussion of the challenge environmental politics poses to standard notions of sovereignty, we return to the question of security. National security has been seen as the fundamental concern of states, built into the very logic of the anarchical nature of the global system. It is well understood that this creates a 'security dilemma' in that increasing the military capacity to defend national security causes insecurity in other states which then increase their own military capacity, thus ironically creating further instability in the system. This results in the emergence of incredibly powerful political-military interests, particularly in the most industrialised and wealthy nation, the USA. An alternative interpretation of international security emerges from reflections on the nature of contemporary environmental problems, one that challenges established political-military interests. The end of the Cold War has opened the space for the development of new understandings of security beyond traditional military interpretations. Within this space, the common nature of global threats is emphasised, in particular the possibility of environmental and nuclear catastrophe. This 'comprehensive' or 'common security' agenda was vociferously championed by Mikhail Gorbachev, former leader of the USSR, and Boutros Boutros-Ghali, former Secretary-General of the UN (Thomas, 1993, pp. 6–9; Boutros-Ghali, 1992; Brown, 1997, pp. 231ff). The new security agenda is highly critical of global militarism and the traditional security view based almost solely on the protection of national territory. Unsurprisingly, such a position finds strong resistance from powerful vested political-military interests. Moves by the UN to link militarism with environmental degradation have been vehemently opposed by the USA, UK and France (Porter and Brown, 1996, p. 29). Again, though, we can see that the demands of environmental politics challenge traditional interpretations of the nature of international politics.

The global economy

The global economic system is built on neo-liberal free-market principles. The dominant capitalist economic paradigm holds that the well-being of states is increased as the sphere of free trade is increased and as such is sceptical of any environmental regulation which might inhibit the free movement of goods and services. However, just as the nature of the international political system and international security is challenged by environmental politics, so also is the dominant economic paradigm. Typically, it is the economically powerful nations that support and shape the rules of the present structures: their political power stems in large part from their economic dominance.[6] At the same time we are witnessing the rise of powerful transnational corporations (TNCs)[7] which have become the target of much green analysis and rhetoric. The activities of these relatively new economic actors and the nature of the economic system itself create further barriers to the development of effective environmental regimes.

The current global economic system has its roots in the Bretton Woods Conference held in the United States in 1944. As the end of the Second World War approached, the USA and other nations, including the UK, looked towards the development of a new world economic order based on free-market principles. The Bretton Woods System was to be regulated by three institutions: the World Trade Organisation (WTO), World Bank, and International Monetary Fund (IMF).

The Bretton Woods institutions

The **WTO** was established in 1995 to administer global trade rules agreed after seven years of international negotiations dominated by the major economically-developed nations.[8] The new rules have increased world competition in areas such as service industries (for instance, banking and insurance) which is seen to favour highly efficient Northern industries able to capitalise on improved access to the markets of developing nations. It has been criticised by many NGOs for lacking effective environmental or labour standards, although future negotiations under the auspices of the WTO may attend to such standards as well as the further lowering of trade barriers.

The **IMF** is the central organisation that deals with balance-of-payments crises. Its long-term loans to low-GDP countries are almost always conditional upon the recipient applying Structural Adjustment Programmes (SAPs). 'SAPs include exchange-rate devaluation, restraints on government spending, controls on wage increases to public- and private-sector workers, improved regulatory environments for private-sector economic actors, liberalisation of trade and encouragement for export-orientated economic activities' (Devlin and Yap, 1993, p. 67). Critics argue that SAPs fail to consider environmental consequences and that their 'limited government'/free-trade approach exacerbates poverty and environmental degradation.

The **World Bank** provides loans to Southern states for specific development projects in such areas as agriculture, energy and transport infrastructure. In recent years, following growing pressure by NGOs, the World Bank has begun to alter its lending principles through the introduction of environmental impact assessments on all large-scale development projects. However, the Bank is still frequently criticised for a lack of transparency and democratic accountability and its failure to consult with local communities affected by development proposals.[9]

The ability of nation states to influence these global economic institutions is tied directly to economic power – unlike the UN General Assembly it is not 'one member, one vote'; rather, the boards are appointed according to the relative economic strength of states. This immediately raises questions as to their neutrality in regulation and their democratic legitimacy and accountability, a theme that recurs in much green writing on international institutions. Hence there have been major disagreements over the location of the Global Environment Facility. Southern nations were far from happy that a fund to assist the development of environmentally-sensitive practices should be located in the World Bank, an institution whose practices are perceived as biased against their interests and lacking in any transparency (Paterson, 1996, p. 76).[10] The central role envisioned for the Bretton Woods institutions after the war was thrown into question in the 1970s when the international system of fixed exchange rates was abandoned. The contemporary global economic context is completely different and, although the Bretton Woods institutions still have an important role to play, it is now also necessary to take into account the activities of TNCs and global financial markets.[11]

A question mark hangs over the Bretton Woods institutions' ability to respond to the growing recognition of links between trade, development, poverty and environmental degradation. Any changes seem to be on the periphery of the structure of the global trade system which continues to produce unsustainable patterns of production and consumption in the North and the adoption of unsuitable develop-ment patterns in the South. The logic of free market economics permeates the trade rules and the lending policies of these institutions. The system has provided enormous economic growth in the Northern nations, but the supposed 'trickle down' of wealth to the South has not always been apparent. Crippled by the debt crisis of the 1980s, repayment conditions and structural adjustment policies, the gap between the rich and the poor nations has grown dramatically.[12] As such, natural resources in the South have been consistently exploited to aid balance-of-payments deficits. The gap between the rich and the poor is growing: looking at incomes, the gap between the richest and poorest 20 per cent of the world's population has more than doubled in the last thirty years. It is too simplistic to say that this is just a gap between the North and the South – there are elites in the South who benefit to a great degree from the structure of the present economic system, just as there are many who suffer in the more industrialised nations. Such figures need to be treated with some caution – they do not expose the growing gap *within* the North and the South (Thomas, 1997, pp. 2–4; see also UNDP, 2001, pp. 17–18).[13] Any discussion of global distributive justice must thus not only be seen as justice *between* states, but also *within* states. Hence, the growing concern in green writings about the impact of the global economic system on local communities and practices.

The economic system is subject to a wide range of green criticisms and we can only hope to touch on some of these. One that we have already discussed and which takes us back to the concept of power is the differential influence that states have on the institutions that 'police' the economic system. We have already pointed out that states are represented in the Bretton Woods institutions in proportion to their economic strength. This raises a question about the 'neutrality' of these institutions in regulating the free-market system; it raises a shadow over whether the system can be understood as 'free' at all. For instance, it has been argued that the conditions of trade which are the outcome of the Uruguay Round of negotiations have been designed to open up markets in those areas where the North is most competitive and where it has most to gain; and that the WTO presides over an elaborate set of rules which protects Northern economies, while removing trade barriers in the South. For example, the South unsuccessfully opposed the inclusion of Trade Related

Investment Measures (TRIMS) and Trade Related Property Rights (TRIPS). TRIMS open up the world's financial and insurance sectors, sensitive economic sectors where Northern companies are in a position to dominate; whereas TRIPS allow companies to take out patents on various biological materials. As Peter Wilkin argues: 'TRIPS enabled Northern transnational corporations (TNCs) to take out patents on a range of genetic, agricultural and pharmaceutical materials that have their origins in the historical practices of Southern farmers, communities, and so on. Having secured the patent, Northern-based TNCs will then be free to sell these commodities back to Southern states at profitable prices' (Wilkin, 1997, p. 30). Not surprisingly, environmentalists have seen such moves as attempts by the North to exert even more control over the South (Goldsmith and Mander, 2001).

A further aspect of the free-trade rhetoric which greens challenge is the theory of competitive advantage upon which such trade is supposed to be based. This theory holds that under a system of free trade it is economically more effective for nations to develop and specialise in the production of particular goods. To a certain degree, we can see such patterns of specialisation in national economies. However, critics are quick to point out two basic problems. The first challenges one of its underlying assumptions that capital movements are bound to a great extent by national borders. Deregulation and the globalisation of capital movements means that this assumption may no longer be relevant (Lang and Hines, 1993, pp. 20–3; Daly and Cobb, 1990, pp. 209ff). Second, it is argued that even if we accept the basic thrust of the theory, we need to examine closely the kinds of goods that states have specialised in producing and the impact this has on domestic economies. Typically, the economies of the South are based on primary products – food and raw materials. For example, the economy of Uganda is almost entirely dependent on coffee production and Nigeria on crude petroleum. It is argued that, first, the demand for such goods is limited compared with the demand for manufactured goods mainly produced in the North, and, second, that an economy based to such an extent on a single primary product has few defences against the vagaries of the market (Brown, 1997, pp. 189–90). Falls in commodity prices put pressure on resources and the environment as Southern states are forced to increase production and exports as they struggle to repay debt. As Porter and Brown state:

> Falling commodity prices devastated the economies of those countries that were heavily dependent on commodity exports. Between 1980 and 1991, the weighted index for thirty-three primary commodities exported by developing countries . . . declined by 46 per cent. And heavy debt burdens, taken on at a time when commodity prices were high and Northern banks were freely lending dollars from Arab oil revenues, siphoned off much of the foreign exchange of many developing countries. At the beginning of the 1990s, no less than forty severely indebted countries were spending the equivalent of 30 per cent or more of their export income on debt repayments – well beyond what capital markets normally regard as the threshold of a financial crisis.
> (Porter and Brown, 1996, p. 109)

Tied in with criticisms of the logic of the capitalist system is the attention given to the activities of transnational corporations (TNCs). The relative wealth of TNCs brings into question the ability of states to control global capital flows. As Caroline Thomas argues:

> Their influence is clear when we consider that the largest 500 (which incidentally generate more than half the greenhouse gas produced annually) control about 70 per cent of world trade, 80 per cent of foreign investment, and 30 per cent of world GDP (about US $300 billion per annum).
>
> (Thomas, 1993, p. 19)

The United Nations Conference on Trade and Development (UNCTAD) in its *World Investment Report 1995* highlighted the growing influence of TNCs, with over two-thirds of global transactions in goods and services taking place either within or between TNCs. This means, as Chakravarthi Raghavan argues, 'only one-third of world trade in goods and services operates according to free-market-free-trade theories of arm's-length transactions' (Raghavan, 1996, p. 31) leading to an enormous potential for TNCs to manipulate markets. There is some contention as to how much control states have on the activities of TNCs and the level of political influence these firms enjoy. There is also some disagreement as to how mobile their activities actually are. In the case of raw materials such as oil, TNCs have little choice about location and there is evidence of corporations such as Shell helping to prop up the military dictatorship in Nigeria in order to access resources. In the sphere of manufacturing, by comparison, TNCs are able to be more selective about their location and have frequently been charged with locating where there is weak or non-existent environmental legislation and where the state in question is desperate for any form of investment.

The financial muscle of TNCs is often convertible into political power: the only UN agency formally charged to investigate their activities, the United Nations Commission on Transnational Corporations (UNCTC), has been disbanded. At Rio, TNCs financed the Summit and were able to exercise their influence so that the only mention of TNCs in Agenda 21 is that they should be self-monitoring; and during the Kyoto process on climate change the Global Climate Coalition, an industrial lobby group led by most of the major oil companies, obstructed the development of an effective regime (see case study). UNCTC's final report stressed the ability of TNCs to influence and at times control the economic and social performances of many countries, but its calls for regulation went unheeded.

The 'myth' of the free market thus needs to be challenged. Industrialised nations impose protectionist measures in areas where the South is competitive to defend their economic advantage, whilst pushing for those nations to open up their own domestic markets to international competition. The role that protectionism actually plays in the so-called free market needs to be recognised. We only have to look at the rise of the 'tiger' economies in East Asia to see the role that protectionist measures and state intervention can play in development. This runs completely counter to the rhetoric of free trade and economic liberalisation (Thomas, 1997, p. 11). Similarly, we need to be aware that according to certain accounts of global-isation, economic liberalisation is taken as the only possible mode of development – the state has been marginalised as a major actor and can do little in the face of the power of global financial markets and movements of goods and services.[14] Greens need to be wary of such rhetoric as it acts as an apology for current distributions of production and consumption. As Wilkin rightly contends: 'The idea that all governments are necessarily powerless to control the forces of capitalism serves only to mystify and mythologise the workings of the capitalist world-system and to reify the restructuring that has taken place. As is well recognised, it is the people of the South that have suffered most severely from this global discipline' (Wilkin, 1997, pp. 24–5). The role of the state has changed in the contemporary capitalist system, but there is political space to act, to restructure the system: the critical question is whether states, and particularly those in the North, are willing to act to change a system that without doubt is of benefit (in economic terms) to themselves. Calls by greens for new forms of protectionism to defend local economies (Lang and Hines, 1993; Goldsmith and Mander, 2001) and the restructuring of existing forms of property rights and ownership (*The Ecologist*, 1993) are a clear challenge to existing economic relations.

What should be clear from this discussion of the global economic system is that the logic of global capitalism is having a detrimental effect on those living in poverty and on the environment. But the logic is deeply ingrained. Capital accumulation is seen as the fundamental goal of the state. As Matthew Paterson contends, global capitalism operates at a deep level, 'structuring states in certain ways – in particular by making promotion of capital accumulation central to their identity, something which they cannot avoid in decisions and still maintain their legitimacy either domestically (to electorates) or internationally (with international financial institutions)' (Paterson, 1996, pp. 180–1). If global environmental concerns are to be taken seriously, the actions needed will often conflict with the accumulative logic of capitalism. Increased growth in GDP can no longer be an indicator of success. The logic of sustainable development is based on different values from those central to capitalist models of development. Green values of self-reliance and local self-determination are in conflict with the logic of global capitalism and capital accumulation. However, although the Western model of economic development cannot be universalised – the global environment could simply not cope with the impact of such a level of industrialisation – this must not be taken as an excuse to abandon those in the South to ever-more disastrous levels of poverty and environmental degradation. Global environmental politics should not be allowed to degenerate into a form of protectionism that allows the North to continue to enjoy lifestyles which are based on the subjection of the South. Global justice and security demands a more effective international response. Later in the chapter we shall look at how far international politics has responded to the need to develop new patterns of *sustainable* development, patterns that are sensitive to the uneven development of the contemporary economic system. Before we move on to such issues, however, it is necessary to turn our attention to other international actors that have been central to the development of environmental regimes.

Agents of change: international organisations and non-governmental organisations

So far, much of our discussion of the international political and economic systems has, from an environmentalist's perspective, looked fairly bleak. The 'logics' of sovereignty and of capital accumulation would appear to structure international relations so as to ensure that environmental problems are both marginalised and responded to ineffectively. To a certain degree such a pessimistic attitude is not misplaced in that, by and large, there has been an insufficient response to contemporary environmental problems. But nonetheless there *has* been a response, as the number of treaties and agreements forged in the last two decades indicates. But given the emphasis on sovereignty and the 'settled norms' of international relations, how are we to explain the emergence of environmental regimes? As we have already intimated, the traditional 'state-centric' approaches to international relations tend to ignore or misrepresent the impact of other actors. In the discussion of the international economy, for instance, it was shown that any meaningful understanding of the system must have regard to international organisations such as the World Bank, IMF and WTO and to other actors such as TNCs. This is not to say that the role of the state is meaningless, but rather that any analysis must be tempered by a recognition that other actors besides states affect international politics. In this vein, this section will focus on two types of actors that have a central role in the development and success of environmental regimes. The first are international organisations (IOs) which facilitate the generation of environmental regimes. After a brief discussion of the roles that such organisations play, the work of one particular institution, the United Nations Environment Programme (UNEP), will be highlighted.[15] The second agents of change are international environment and development non-governmental organisations (NGOs) whose emergence and influence have been relatively recent. Both IOs and NGOs have been fundamental in creating the conditions where the 'implicit or explicit principles, norms, rules and decision-making procedures around which actors' expectations converge' (Krasner, 1983, p. 2) have emerged in response to environmental problems.

International organisations

> Is it possible to mitigate environmental problems without abrogating state sovereignty? . . . If judging by standards of budgets and authority, inter-governmental organisations and rules are extremely weak. The impact of international institutions lies in their performance of three catalytic functions: increasing governmental concern, enhancing the contractual environment, and increasing national political and administrative capacity.
>
> (Levy *et al.*, 1993, p. 424)

If states are going to cooperate in response to environmental problems, international organisations such as UNEP have an essential role to play in creating the conditions for that cooperation. In the first instance, they play a central role in building scientific consensus. For instance UNEP, along with the World Meteorological Convention (WMO), was pivotal in setting up the Intergovernmental Panel on Climate Change (IPCC). The IPCC's first report produced in 1990 was essential in setting the agenda for future climate negotiations.[16] Such scientific consensus is important to provide the cognitive basis upon which political negotiations take place. A number of commentators have pointed to the emergence of 'epistemic communities' (Haas,

1989) as the basic reason why there has been collective action on particular environmental issues. The emergence of scientific consensus, a dominant interpretation of the cause of environmental degradation, is seen as a central condition for establishing effective environmental regimes.[17]

It is clear that scientific consensus can have a definite impact. Take for instance the issue of ozone depletion. In November 1987, under the Montreal Protocol, industrialised countries pledged to reduce the production of CFCs by 50 per cent by 1990. A complete ban on production had been vetoed by the EC which claimed that there was not enough scientific evidence to warrant a total ban. Within months their opposition had crumbled with the discovery of the infamous 'ozone hole' by the British Antarctica Expedition. In the follow-up meeting in London, an agreement to completely phase out CFC production by 2000 was signed.

But it is not enough simply to produce scientific evidence, and international organisations involved in environmental regime building play an important role in creating the conditions in which states and other actors are able to develop relations of trust and to increase their knowledge of environmental problems. We have already argued that traditional models of international relations typically assume that states' interests are given and immutable. But this has been challenged and international organisations can be seen as providing the conditions for states to transform their preferences and interests and to develop institutional arrangements through which resources – whether knowledge, technology or financial assistance – can be shared or transferred. This is not to say that this is in any way easy as any analysis of technological and financial transfer would highlight. However, international organisations provide stability in negotiations and thereby make cooperation and mutual learning more likely. As this analysis shows, the process and informal aspects of regime building in international environmental politics can be as important as the documentation and agreements produced.

United Nations Environment Programme (UNEP)

UNEP was established in the follow-up to the United Nations Conference on the Human Environment by the UN General Assembly on 15 December 1972. It was set up specifically to address environmental issues although not as a large-scale direct operational agency. It plays a vital role in monitoring and coordinating international action and its role is often described as that of a 'catalyst' – in almost every area of global environmental concern UNEP has played a consciousness-raising role, often cooperating with other organisations to define issues and promote conferences, research and negotiations. Returning to the issue of ozone depletion, for example, it was UNEP which was instrumental in establishing expert scientific, technological and environmental effects and economics panels (Parson, 1993, p. 47) and acting as a secretariat for the negotiations. The then Executive Director, Dr Mostafa Tolba, exploited UNEP's position to push aggressively for an effective treaty (ibid., p. 65). Much of this work in regime building goes unnoticed, but it is quite incredible how much influence UNEP has asserted when taking into account the meagre and unreliable funding with which it has been provided: in comparison to UNEP's annual budget of only $60 million dollars and a professional staff of 240, the World Bank has a staff of over 6,000, lending billions of dollars annually (Porter and Brown, 1996, p. 41).

UNEP has its headquarters in Nairobi and although this can prove isolating – the majority of UN organisations are located in Europe and North America – it has at times been useful in relations with Southern nations which often feel removed from the agenda-setting process. Fifty-eight states have places on UNEP's principal decision-making body, the General Council, which reports through the Economic and Social Council (ECOSOC) to the UN General Assembly. Its annual budget is based mainly on voluntary donations which can make planning very difficult. UNEP has had only four directors: Maurice Strong from Canada (1973–5),[18] Dr Mostafa Tolba from Egypt (1976–93), Elizabeth Dowdeswell also from Canada (1993–8) and now Dr Klaus Töpfer from Germany.[19] It was the charismatic Tolba who tried to champion the causes of the South, although he was often forced to compromise his position because of the influence of the Group of Seven (G7) – the seven leading industrialised nations – whose funding is essential to UNEP's work. Although the General Council officially holds a broad holistic view of the environmental crisis, most attention has been focused on issues affecting the North such as ozone depletion, climate change and biological diversity. UNEP has attempted to raise issues such as desertification and fresh water supply, but since these problems mainly affect the South, little attention has been given to them by the Northern industrialised nations.

The work of UNEP has been widely praised, in particular in the Brundtland Report, and in the late 1980s the UN General Assembly raised the profile of UNEP. It has been credited with creating much of existing environmental law, including the Vienna Convention on Ozone Depletion, the Basel Convention on the Control of Transboundary Movements of Hazardous Wastes and their Disposal, the Convention on International Trade in Endangered Species of Wild Fauna and Flora (CITES) and the Convention on Migratory Species (CMS) (Dodds, 2001, p. 321). However, UNEP's current role has become ambiguous since the Rio Earth Summit and the establishment of new international organisations such as the United Nations Commission on Sustainable Development (CSD)[20] in areas where UNEP had previously taken the lead. On the positive side, the CSD has taken over some of the coordinating responsibilites that UNEP had played within the UN. Given its lack of funding and staff, the removal of this burdensome function should allow UNEP to target its limited resources to awareness raising, monitoring and improving its links with financially more robust organisations such as the United Nations Development Programme (UNDP). However, the loss of this responsibility and others, such as the secretariat for the UN Framework Convention on Climate Change (UNFCCC), may have the effect of further marginalising UNEP.

International non-governmental organisations

Wherever power is exercised, interest groups will mobilise. Given that much political and economic power has gradually been transferred to international forums (including multi-lateral economic institutions such as the World Bank, IMF and the WTO), environmental NGOs have been forced to organise at this level.[21] Recent years have witnessed the emergence of a range of different groups, including well-known multinational, multi-million-dollar organisations such as Greenpeace International, less recognised, but influential think-tanks such as the World Resource Institute (WRI) and Southern-based NGOs such as the Third World Network. Given the difficulties of organising at the international level, environment and development NGOs have established a number of ad hoc and more permanent coalitions and networks in an attempt to share the burden of organisation and to exchange resources and information (Bichsel, 1996).

A wide range of tactics and actions are employed by NGOs. Most people are aware of the visually stunning actions of Greenpeace activists that are often timed to coincide with important international negotiations. Again, much influence has been gained through publicity and consumer boycotts. For instance, the global CFC boycott launched by FOE International helped to persuade many industries to stop the use of ozone depleters in production processes and influenced governments to support stronger agreements. Similarly the boycott of Icelandic fish products, coordinated by a coalition of environmental and animal welfare groups in 1988, helped force Iceland to halt its violation of the global moratorium on whaling (Porter and Brown, 1996, p. 79).

However, the most interesting development has been the direct influence of NGOs on international conferences and negotiations and the activities of international organisations. Often NGOs will run parallel events that can at times generate as much interest as the official negotiations. The Global Forum in Rio was attended by some 30,000 NGO representatives; The Other Economic Summit (TOES) organised by a network of environmental and social justice groups accompanies the major G7 meetings. But it is the activities of NGOs *within* the negotiations that is changing most rapidly. Not only are NGOs active in lobbying their own national governments, but they have stepped up their activities at major conferences and preparatory negotiations and are generally afforded official observer status. Many NGOs, such as Greenpeace and Oxfam, not only claim to be legitimately expressing citizens' concerns, but also include scientists, economists and legal experts within their delegations and thus have access to sophisticated information and knowledge. Often their research and information is much more accurate and up-to-date and they have been able to hold states to account over their environment and development policies and practices and also supply them with precious data that can influence the outcome of negotiations. NGOs play key roles as independent bargainers and as agents of social learning (Princen and Finger, 1994, p. 217). At times this can promote substantial changes in the bargaining positions of states and NGOs have played an increasingly important role in setting the international agenda. The establishment of the Commission on Sustainable Development (CSD), created in the wake of Rio, has raised the profile of NGOs further. Whereas NGOs have typically only been afforded observer status, accredited NGOs are much more active participants in the workings of the CSD. As well as reviewing nation states' progress towards sustainable development, the Commission also accepts reports from NGOs (see later). Again, NGOs are often deeply involved in the drafting of agreements and proposals and, as in the case of the International Tropical Timber Organisation's (ITTO) 1990 Action Plan, are 'frequently cited as key actors for implementation' (Princen and Finger, 1994, p. 5).

The focus of environment and development NGO activity is not simply on international environmental negotiations, conferences and organisations. The multi-lateral economic institutions – the World Bank, the IMF and WTO – have also found themselves subject to ever-increasing pressure from NGOs. Gradually all three institutions have been forced to respond to the growing environmental pressure, although the limited reforms are far from satisfactory from the perspective of NGOs. Although the dominant neo-liberal thinking at the heart of these institutions has yet to be systematically challenged, nonetheless they have felt the need to engage with NGOs in order to legitimise their agenda in the eyes of the wider public. The World Bank, in particular, has also found it necessary to develop good working relationships with NGOs in order successfully to implement development programmes and projects. This engagement also points to the limits of any understanding of global environmental politics that simply focuses on states. NGOs have 'side-stepped' states and engaged directly with multi-lateral economic institutions (O'Brien *et al.*, 2000).

The increasing activity of NGOs at the international level has led some commentators to describe the emergence of a 'global civil society'. This characterisation seems problematic on a number of counts, not least because in reality NGO activity tends to be dominated by a relatively small number of Northern-based groups such as the international arms of Greenpeace, FOE and WWF. Southern NGOs do not have the resource base of their Northern counterparts and thus tend to find themselves marginalised in both the process of setting the agenda for the international environmental movement and access to international conferences and organisations. Southern NGOs have been critical of the sometimes patronising attitude of the dominant NGOs and the manner in which they conceptualise environmental problems that may have specific impacts on the South. The more resource-rich groups have begun to recognise this problem and have attempted to provide resources to help Southern organisations mobilise more effectively within existing coalitions and networks.

Another interesting development has been the recent emergence of mass mobilisations at international economic and political negotiations, beginning with the demonstrations at Seattle in 1999. Just at the point when established NGOs have achieved unprecedented levels of access, marginalised and radical groups who feel that their agendas are not being recognised have taken to direct action. The international environmental movement seems to be mirroring what has happened at the national level (see Chapter 3). For many of these activist groups, the more established NGOs have been blinded by power and co-opted by national government and international organisations.

Rio and beyond: sustainable development and international politics

So far in this chapter, discussion of environmental regimes has tended to focus on the development of formal and informal relations around a single issue, be it ozone depletion, climate change or forestry. However, as we have made clear in earlier chapters, focusing on single environmental problems may not provide an effective enough response to environmental degradation: responding to environmental problems requires a consideration of the connections between the economy, society and the environment. Since the late 1980s, there has been growing international attention given to the idea of sustainable development and this manifested itself most prominently in 1992 at the United Nations Conference on Environment and Development (UNCED), also known as the Rio 'Earth Summit'. Sustainable development requires states to negotiate the difficult terrain around high consumption levels in the North, the South's need to respond to dramatic levels of poverty and the desire for industrial development, and the environmental and social impact of these trends. But, as has been made clear earlier in this book, sustainable development is an 'essentially contested concept' and, as such, a number of different interpretations are given as to what it entails in practice. These range from proposals for ecological modernisation, a largely technical response to environmental problems and the inclusion of environmental costs in economic decision making (Weale, 1992; see Chapter 2), through to calls for radical changes in economic and political structures that would leave control of resources in the hands of local communities (Sachs, 1993; *The Ecologist*, 1993; Goldsmith and Mander, 2001). At one end of the spectrum we find a defence of the existing economic order; at the other a radical restructuring of political and economic arrangements and organisations. Given the primacy of states in the international arena, it should be no surprise that radical proposals that suggest a diminution of state influence tend to have little effect on the agenda of international relations. Where Southern states challenge the dominant economic system, it is typically on the grounds that they do not enjoy the same levels of economic development as the North. The logic of capital accumulation is rarely challenged; rather the injustice of present uneven development patterns. That this would require a reform of the present system is undeniable; whether it is anything close to a 'sustainable' response is a moot question.

1972 – the birth of a new agenda?

The year 1972 is a highly significant date for environmental politics. *The Limits to Growth*, published in that year, argued that the post-war rate of economic expansion and population growth cannot be sustained without exhaustion of global natural resources, irreparable environmental damage and an increase in poverty and malnutrition (see Chapter 2).

In the same year, the United Nations Conference on the Human Environment, held in Stockholm, provided the first major international opportunity for the South to highlight the links between the prevailing international economic system, environmental degradation and poverty. Not surprisingly, there was a lack of consensus on the way forward – Stockholm witnessed major disagreements between the North and South over the causes of global environmental degradation and poverty. Conflicts over the relative impact of population levels and consumption that emerged at this conference have raged on ever since. Only a broad set of sometimes contradictory principles were forthcoming. However, the Stockholm conference allowed the issues to be aired for the first time in an international context and it opened possibilities for further developments, in particular the emergence of UNEP and the legitimisation of environment and development NGOs.

The Brundtland Report

During the 1970s and 1980s, the focus of the international community was very much on the international security concerns generated by the Cold War. Where the South had looked as if it was beginning to gain increased influence in global politics in the 1970s, the 1980s saw many of these nations plunged into financial crisis as commodity prices fell and debt levels increased. The majority of national economies, particularly in the South, found themselves in recession; the plight of a large percentage of the world's population worsened and increased pressure was placed on natural resources.

In 1983, against this background of a growing security dilemma and increased environmental degradation and poverty, the UN Secretary-General called upon Gro Harlem Brundtland, former Prime Minister of Norway, to set up and chair an independent commission to assess and address environment and development pressures. The World Commission on Environment and Development (WCED) presented its highly influential report, *Our Common Future*, to the UN General Assembly in 1987. The significance of the Brundtland Report cannot be understated in that it introduced the concept of sustainable development into common usage. The report advocated an interpretation of sustainable development that has become almost a mantra within environmental politics: 'development that meets the needs of the present without compromising the ability of future generations to meet their own needs' (WCED, 1987, p. 8).

Main recommendations of the Brundtland Report

In February 1987 the final meeting of the Commission was held in Tokyo. The members called upon 'all nations of the World, both jointly and individually, to integrate sustainable development into their goals and to adopt the following principles to guide their policy actions':
- revive growth;
- change the quality of growth;
- conserve and enhance the resource base;
- ensure a sustainable level of population;
- reorientate technology and manage risk;
- integrate environment and economics in decision making;
- reform international economic relations;
- strengthen international cooperation.

(WCED, 1987, pp. 4–5)

Brundtland's interpretation of sustainable development emphasised the mutual reinforcing of economic growth, social development and environmental protection, putting a forceful case forward for a higher level of multilateral cooperation and the need to reform economic practices such as trade, finance and aid. These recommendations found widespread support among many states and multilateral economic institutions since the report stressed that effective environmental protection rested on continued economic growth. The report was also generally well received by NGOs, although those campaigners who did not accept the primacy given to economic growth and believed the development patterns outlined by Brundtland would result in the loss of traditionally sustainable practices were further marginalised (de la Court, 1990).

Although the Brundtland Report raised the profile of the environment and sustainable development in international politics, its message has been somewhat corrupted. The mutual reinforcing of economic growth and environmental protection has tended to dominate debates – the conception of sustainable development understood as ecological modernisation (see Chapter 2). However, the third aspect of Brundtland's analysis – social development – has not been given equivalent weight. The integration of environmental considerations within economic decision making will not necessarily lead to poverty reduction and social development. An environmentally-sustainable global economy could well rest on an unjust global division of wealth and opportunity. The relative marginalisation of social aspects of sustainable development highlights the dominance of Northern nations which benefit considerably from the current development patterns. The Brundtland conception of sustainable development may have disappointed more radical greens in that primacy was given to economic growth; however, its vision of a more just form of sustainable development is more challenging than the current dominant conception of ecological modernisation.

The United Nations Conference on Environment and Development

The Brundtland Report galvanised international support around the idea of sustainable development and was instrumental in the launch of the United Nations Conference on Environment and Development (UNCED) by the UN General Assembly in 1989. Maurice Strong, the first Executive Director of UNEP, was appointed Secretary-General of UNCED and a series of 'prep-coms' (preparatory committees) and conferences followed over the next two years as the agenda of UNCED was fought over. In some ways the debate appeared not to have moved on since Stockholm two decades earlier. The industrialised nations of the North were looking to focus on environmental degradation as a short-term, technically solvable issue; in response, the South argued that such an approach only tackled the symptoms of the crisis and avoided the background issues which they believed desperately needed tackling, namely unfair trading rules, debt, SAPs, the role of TNCs, and financial and technical transfers.

UNCED, held in Rio in June 1992, was unprecedented for an international environmental event – 176 national delegations attended and the level of media and public attention was quite staggering. A parallel event, the Global Forum, attracted some 30,000 NGO representatives from all over the world. Five agreements were signed:

- Rio Declaration
- Agenda 21
- Declaration on Forest Principles

- Convention on Climate Change
- Convention on Biological Diversity

Strictly speaking, the Conventions on Climate Change and Biological Diversity were not really part of the Rio process – they emerged from separate negotiations and were opened for signature at the Summit. Again they are examples of international responses to individual environmental problems rather than an attempt to respond to the interconnectedness of environmental and developmental pressures.[22] This interconnection was recognised within the Rio Declaration and, more importantly, Agenda 21.

The Rio Declaration on Environment and Development

This builds on a similar declaration produced two decades earlier in Stockholm. It is a set of guiding principles for national and international environmental behaviour. The declaration endorses the polluter pays principle (PPP) and the precautionary principle as well as the need for access to environmental information, increased public participation, and environmental impact assessment of development schemes. The declaration also explicitly makes the link between poverty and environmental degradation and the different responsibility of states: 'States have common but differentiated responsibilities. The developed countries acknowledge the responsibility that they bear in the international pursuit of sustainable development in view of the pressures their societies place on the global environment and of the technologies and financial resources they command' (Principle 7). Although such principles have no legal status, Southern nations believe that it was an important step for the North to acknowledge its particular responsibility for present environmental conditions.

Agenda 21

Agenda 21 is arguably the most significant outcome of the Earth Summit. It is the most thorough and ambitious attempt at the international level to specify what actions are necessary if development is to be reconciled with global environmental concerns. With its adoption by all the nations represented at UNCED, it is intended to guide all nations towards sustainable development into the twenty-first century.

The document is the result of long and protracted negotiations between virtually all political, social and economic interest groups in the run-up to UNCED and at the conference itself. The text is often contradictory because of the need to find compromises acceptable to the different interests. Areas fought over included population control (offensive to the Vatican), reduction of fossil fuel usage (against the commercial interests of the oil-producing states) and the nature of North–South debt. It is not surprising that the final text did not appear until September 1992 – four months after the conference.

Agenda 21

Agenda 21 consists of 4 sections:

1 **Social and economic dimensions**: highlights the interconnectedness of environmental problems with poverty, health, trade, debt, consumption and population.

2 **Conservation and management of resources for development**: emphasises the need to manage physical resources such as land, seas, energy and wastes to further sustainable development.

3 **Strengthening the role of major social groups**: stresses the need for partnership with women, indigenous populations, local authorities, NGOs, workers and trade unions, business and industry, scientists and farmers.

4 **Means of implementation**: discusses the role of governments and non-governmental agencies in funding and technical transfer.

Criticisms of Rio

> I had low expectations, and all of them were met.
> (Jonathan Porritt, environmentalist and former director of FOE)

The significance of the Rio process divides greens – some argue that it should be seen as an important turning point in the move towards more sustainable practices, others that it was simply 'greenwash' and that the conference actually subverted the environmental movement and reinforced existing political and economic relations. Where does the truth lie? How are we to judge the impact of the Earth Summit?

Critics point to the fact that there were no firm commitments on important issues such as debt, SAPs, population, and financial and technological transfer, and that fundamental questions about the structure of the capitalist system, the role of TNCs and global militarism were completely ignored (Third World Network, 1992; Thomas, 1993; Chatterjee and Finger, 1994). Given that the logic of ecological modernisation underpinned much of the negotiations, this should not be so much of a surprise. There may have been reference to differential consumption levels in Agenda 21, but where are the targets and action plans to actually reduce these levels? One Third World diplomat famously remarked: 'What was unsaid at UNCED eclipsed what was said.'

Although the relationship between debt and poverty was recognised in Agenda 21, most of the text celebrated the free market; much of the debate and final documentation was based on free-market ideals. This highlights the continued international domination of the North and the Bretton Woods institutions. The dominant vision was the ecological modernisation model with the emphasis on the necessity of continued economic growth. Other visions of development were marginalised and any minor concessions made to alternative ideas will be swamped by the force of recent trade agreements. After all, how are the non-binding proposals in Agenda 21 going to fare against the WTO's trade regulations?

Many Southern states were looking to Rio as an opportunity to begin to regulate the activities of TNCs. However, the international industrial and business lobby proved too powerful. In the run-up to the conference, many of the leading TNCs came together under the banner of the Business Council for Sustainable Development (BCSD) whose Chair, the Swiss billionaire Stephen Schmidheiny, became a prominent advisor to Maurice Strong. Compared with environment and development NGOs, such an alliance was well resourced and was able to put forward a unified and coherent position. At the same time, the TNCs 'bank-rolled' the conference and the Global Forum – much of the finance came from the business sector – and many of the world's business leaders were part of national delegations. It should be no surprise then that at the same time as the only UN agency that monitored the activities of TNCs – the United Nations Commission on Transnational Corporations (UNCTC) – was disbanded, TNCs were able to raise their profile as 'pro-environment' actors. Rather than the threatened limiting of operations, the business lobby successfully negotiated a self-monitoring role for themselves. The only mention of TNCs in Agenda 21 is in a positive light, as a major social group whose role needs to be strengthened – as a 'partner'. For many environmentalists this was simply too much and exposed the Rio process as a sham (Chatterjee and Finger, 1994, pp. 109ff).

Questions also remain over the issue of funding and financial assistance for the South. It has been estimated by the UN that around $600 billion per annum would be needed for the developing countries if they are to begin the process of moving towards a more sustainable future. In the event only about 1 per cent of that total was forthcoming at UNCED – the largest pledges coming from Japan (Young, 1993, p. 46). Not only were donations thin on the ground, but the industrialised nations did not even agree to provide immediately the 0.7 per cent GNP that the UN had previously advised should be allocated to aid and development projects. All this even though Agenda 21 has a chapter dedicated specifically to the interconnections of debt and environmental degradation. At the same time, Southern nations were far from satisfied with the funding mechanism, the Global Environment Facility (GEF), which is attached to the World Bank. The Bank has a poor reputation and the South wanted to see an independent fund established, separate from existing financial institutions that they believe to be heavily influenced by Northern economic interests. Since Rio, however, Southern nations have been relatively successful in reforming the GEF.

The Global Environment Facility

The GEF is the primary international institution through which financial assistance is provided to the South for sustainable development projects. It was established in 1991 by the leading industrialised nations (without the input of the G77[23]) originally as a three-year pilot project to support financial transfers within environmental regimes, such as climate change, biodiversity, etc. The GEF is housed within the World Bank with UNEP and UNDP acting as advisory bodies. It is this relationship with the World Bank and the fact that control was relative

continued

to financial contributions that made Southern nations suspicious of the GEF. Their grievances were ignored at Rio when the South's alternative proposal for a new environment fund controlled on the more democratic basis of one-country-one-vote was rejected by Northern countries who were only willing to recognise the GEF. At the time this seemed a substantial defeat for the South. Since Rio, however, the South has managed to win some important concessions. As the reputation of the World Bank continued to diminish, with continued exposure of poor environmental lending practices and its lack of openness and accountability, the G77 collaborated with Northern NGOs to persuade the Clinton administration that the decision-making structures of the GEF needed to be reformed. The new Council of the GEF is now made up of 16 developing nations, 14 developed nations and 2 members from Central and Eastern Europe and the Soviet Union. Decisions are also no longer left purely to the World Bank: the Council has the final approval on all projects. The funds available to the GEF are relatively meagre in global terms and do not compensate for reductions over the last decade in overseas development aid by most Northern governments. However, the concessions gained by the South are important since 'the GEF represented the first major North–South battle over the governance of a global environmental institution' (Porter and Brown, 1996, p. 142).[24]

Two other aspects of the Rio process are often raised by critical commentators. The first is the manner in which the USA used its hegemonic status to defend the existing political and economic relations.

> The Bush administration's strategy for UNCED negotiations, based on the assumption that UNCED represented a potential threat to US interests, was aimed at averting any initiatives that would limit US freedom of economic action worldwide. The United States was prepared to veto any initiative that could be viewed as redistributing economic power at the global level, that would create new institutions, or that would require additional budgetary resources, technology transfers, or changes in domestic US policies.
>
> (Porter and Brown, 1996, pp. 117–18)

In many ways the actions of the USA seem to fulfil the prophecies of the realist account of international relations discussed earlier in the chapter. Its behaviour in the subsequent Kyoto climate change negotiations simply reinforces such a position (see case study). With the dominant world power viewing its interests as conflicting with global environmental protection, critics question just how far any moves towards sustainable development can go. It is an interesting question as to how far the emergence of the European Union as an international political actor will affect international environmental politics. It is certainly more sympathetic to environmental issues than the US administration.

Finally, did Rio see the neutralisation of the green movement itself? Unquestionably, environment and development NGOs achieved previously unknown levels of access to negotiations. However, critics contend that access should not be conflated with influence (see Chapter 4). As Pretap Chatterjee and Matthias Finger argue:

[T]he mobilisation of peoples and NGOs to participate actively in the UNCED process, while not letting them influence the outcome, has led to an overall legitimation of a process that is ultimately destructive of the very forces that were mobilised.

(Chatterjee and Finger, 1994, p. 103)

In their view, NGO participation could simply be viewed as a public relations exercise by the organisers of the conference and any democratic principles that Agenda 21 might embody will be subverted by national and international institutions. Few truly grassroots community groups were either willing or able to attend the UNCED negotiations and the international NGOs that were involved have now been co-opted into supporting the international political processes that they are supposed to be challenging. There is simply no way that NGOs can compete in terms of lobbying or resources with the business and industrial community (ibid., p. 113). If this is an accurate analysis, then green politics at the international level is facing serious dilemmas.

Agenda 21 as a move towards sustainable practices?

Without wishing to discount or ignore these criticisms of the UNCED process, can a positive light be shed on the Earth Summit? Have some greens been too enthusiastic in damning UNCED? Certainly most greens did not achieve all that they desired, but should we write off everything that happened? There are at least two areas where greens might draw some comfort: the nature of many of the guiding principles of Agenda 21; and the recognition that Rio is part of an ongoing process, in particular a process that has positive institutional implications.

It is true that generally UNCED reinforced many of the 'settled norms' of the international order – earlier we noted that Principle 2 of the Rio Declaration defends a strong interpretation of sovereignty. But what else would we expect from a set of negotiations between states? The state is, and will for some time remain, a dominant actor in international politics – green thinking needs to recognise this fact. However, given the continued existence of the state, Agenda 21 and the Rio Declaration stress important themes that greens should support and reinforce: themes such as differential responsibilities for environmental damage and future action; the need for improved cooperation between states and other actors; the defence of equal rights, empowerment and education of individuals and communities; the need for increasing the capacity of institutions to manage change; and the need for increased financial and technological assistance for the South. These are all fundamental principles within environmental politics and can all be found in Agenda 21. For instance, given the criticisms of the Earth Summit itself and the fact that the final version of Agenda 21 is the result of long and protracted negotiations, it is perhaps surprising that such a strong theme of democratic renewal runs through the document. At all levels of governance, local to international, the development of new institutional forms that increase participation by all major groups is taken to be fundamental (Roddick and Dodds, 1993).

Critical to the effective implementation of the objectives, policies and mechanisms agreed by Governments in all programme areas of Agenda 21 will be the commitment and genuine involvement of all social groups. . . . *One of the fundamental prerequisites for the achievement of sustainable development is broad public participation in decision-making.* Furthermore, in the more specific context of environment and development, *the need for new forms of participation has emerged.*

(UNCED, 1992, Chapter 23: emphasis added)

The third section of the document, 'Strengthening the Role of Major Social Groups', argues the case for the involvement and participation of all social groups within decision-making processes. The theme of inclusiveness and participation is taken to be fundamental to the restructuring of political institutions and the creation of new forms of dialogue: 'The overall objective is to improve or restructure the decision-making process so that consideration of socio-economic and environmental issues is fully integrated and a broader range of public participation assured' (UNCED, 1992, Chapter 8).

Agenda 21 does not simply promote the principle of basic rights to, for instance, health, shelter, clean food and a safe environment. Its reach is far more radical and participatory – all groups have the right to articulate their perspectives in decision-making processes.

Its concern is more than charitable and welfare-related. It also sees disadvantaged groups as having the same rights to a voice in decisions about the path that development should take, and as having their own contribution – of traditional knowledge, values, life experience or place in a broader society or culture – to make to its achievement. Agenda 21 is thus profoundly democratic and egalitarian in its outlook.

(LGMB, 1992, pp. 4–5)

We have argued in Chapter 2 and elsewhere that new forms of democratic engagement are necessary for the development of sustainable practices and in many ways Agenda 21 embodies such ideals. The whole Rio process should not be discounted simply because conflicts remain: greens need to take what they can from the process and advocate those themes and principles which accord with their own visions of a sustainable society.

The Aarhus Convention

In 1998 the members of the regional United Nations Economic Commission for Europe (UNECE) signed the *Convention on access to information, public participation in decision-making and access to justice in environmental matters*, otherwise known as the Aarhus Convention after the Danish City where it was signed. This regional convention explicitly draws on Principle 10 of the *Rio Declaration on Environment and Development* which stresses that transparency, public participation and access to justice are preconditions for achieving sustainable development.

The convention recognises 'that every person has the right to live in an environment adequate to his or her health and well-being, and the duty, both individually and in association with others, to protect and improve the environment for the benefit of present and future generations.' But the primary focus of the convention is how this right and duty might be exercised. It not only recognises that 'citizens must have access to information, be entitled to participate in decision-making and have access to justice in environmental matters', but also acknowledges that 'citizens may need assistance in order to exercise their rights'. Enhancing the transparency and accountability of public authorities is seen as fundamental; equally the capacity of institutions to promote participation needs to be developed. In line with the theoretical arguments on ecological democratisation discussed in Chapter 2, the convention argues that environmental benefits will flow from increased participation:

[I]n the field of the environment, improved access to information and public participation in decision-making enhance the quality and the implementation of decisions, contribute to public awareness of environmental issues, give the public the opportunity to express its concerns and enable public authorities to take due account of such concerns.

The Aarhus Convention came into force in October 2001 and the first meeting of the parties takes place in October 2002. It is unclear how much force the convention will have in practice. However, Kofi Annan, the UN Secretary-General, argues that:

The Aarhus Convention is the most ambitious venture in environmental democracy undertaken under the auspices of the United Nations. Its adoption was a remarkable step forward in the development of international law.

(DEFRA, 2002, p. 133)[25]

Beyond principles, we also need to recognise that Rio is part of an on-going process; not a one-off event. One of the most significant outcomes from Rio was the establishment of the United Nations Commission on Sustainable Development (CSD) created in 1993 as envisaged in Chapter 38 of Agenda 21. According to its mandate, the CSD's role is to act as a forum for international dialogue on sustainable development: 'To monitor progress on the implementation of Agenda 21 and activities related to the integration of environmental and developmental goals' (Mensah, 1996, p. 28). The CSD is not itself a decision-making body – it can only provide advice and recommendations to the General Assembly through the Economic and Social Council (ECOSOC). The CSD's primary role is thus to act as an independent body monitoring the progress of nations in the implementation of Agenda 21 and, as such, it has developed a rolling programme to tackle all the issues raised within the action plan.[26] In its own right, the monitoring of states is a massive task, but the CSD has also inherited a number of UNEP's coordinating tasks; the Commission is also required to oversee the environmental activities of 'all relevant organs, organisations, programmes and institutions of the UN dealing with various issues of environment and development, including those related to finance' (Hurrell, 1993, p. 277). Critics have argued that these coordination and facilitation functions will blunt its immediate effectiveness (Imber, 1993; Thomas, 1993; Henry, 1996). The CSD functions in a similar way to the UN Commission on Human Rights in that it will have no legal powers over states to fulfil their obligations. However, it will be a 'much needed forum for publicising progress (or lack of it) of states towards sustainable development – if only through moral persuasion and public criticism' (Hurrell, 1993, p. 278).

The activities of the CSD have been praised on at least two grounds. The first is that it has proved to be a forum within which controversial issues within Agenda 21 have been raised and debated. The CSD's rolling programme has included topics such as sustainable consumption and production and sustainable forestry; both issues typically kept off the political agenda by Northern states and powerful interest groups.

Second, the CSD has proved to be controversial in another area: access for NGOs. The CSD mandate states that one of its functions should be:

> To receive and analyse relevant input from competent NGOs, including the scientific and private sector, in the context of the overall implementation of Agenda 21; to enhance the dialogue, within the framework of the United Nations, with NGOs and the independent sector.
>
> (Mensah, 1996, p. 29)

After a protracted battle with more conservative nations, the CSD allows accredited NGOs to move beyond the usual observer status and to provide evidence and take part in on-going deliberations: 'it has come to be seen as a testing ground for new ways of involving non-governmental organisations in UN processes' (Bigg and Dodds, 1997, p. 17). The inclusion of representatives other than state delegates leads to a democratic potential far beyond that of many existing international institutions. New forms of international negotiation are developing. For instance: 'None of the sessions is now closed – even the small working groups are held open for major group representatives to attend and in many cases speak. Their increased involvement in implementing the UN Conference agreements has also meant increased involvement in framing them in the first place' (ibid., p. 31). This has taken some getting used to on the part of professional diplomats. However, it is still the case that Northern NGOs have the resources to engage effectively with the CSD while those from the South do not: there is a clear under-representation of NGOs from the South (Khor, 1994).

Even though, at times, the operations of the CSD have been compared to an 'international beauty contest' and concerns have been raised that it diverts attention from more important forums such as the Bretton Woods institutions and the G7 (Bigg and Mucke, 1996, p. 5), critics have admitted that it 'has acted as a spur for change' (Sandbrook, 1996, p. 5). Tom Bigg sees the potential of the CSD lying in its 'ability to hold governments responsible to their peers, and to their citizens, for progress achieved'. But, as he continues: 'There are obvious problems with this, not least the difficulty of persuading governments to lay themselves open to such criticism and accountability. It also presupposes that the impetus for change is a good deal more forceful than at present' (Bigg, 1994, p. 18).

The ongoing work of the CSD highlights that Agenda 21 was intended as a catalyst for action towards sustainable development; and for a number of nations and localities this has been the case. As we shall see in Chapters 9 and 10, national governments have produced sustainable development strategies of varying quality and, at the local level, many different groups have been inspired to collaborate with their local authorities in the development of Local Agenda 21s. It is too easy to be critical of the non-binding nature of much of the output of the Earth Summit – to focus solely on the documents is to neglect the impact of the event on public and governmental consciousness. The level of media coverage, the high level of the delegations and the tough negotiating stance of many nations at UNCED and beyond bears testimony to the importance placed on environment and development issues, even if many states still view short-term domestic issues as a higher priority.

The Earth Summit also provided an opportunity for further networking for NGOs. As Martin Khor of the Third World Network argues, although the documentation and commitments from the Earth Summit were disappointing, the activities of NGOs in and around the UNCED process has led to important contacts and opportunities for mutual learning:

> The UNCED process forged new and stronger links between Northern and Southern groups, between development and environmental activists. It would now be difficult for environmentalists to stick to wildlife issues or population, without simultaneously addressing international equity and global power structures. A major step forward has been the increasing involvement of Northern-based environment groups like Greenpeace, WWF, and Friends of the Earth in economic issues such as trade, debt, and aid.
>
> (Khor, quoted in Chatterjee and Finger, 1994, p. 99)

Rio also spawned a follow-up process including conferences and reviews on population, social development and human settlements.

International conferences and reviews since Rio

1994 Conference on Population and Development (Cairo)
1994 Conference on Small Island Developing States (Barbados)
1995 World Summit on Social Development (Copenhagen)
1995 Fourth Conference on Women and Development (Beijing)
1996 Habitat II – Conference on Human Settlements (Istanbul)
1996 Food Summit (Vienna)
1997 UN General Assembly Review of Implementation of Agenda 21
1999 UN General Assembly Review of Cairo
1999 UN General Assembly Review of Barbados Plan of Action

(Dodds, 2001, p. 320)

Although not always in the media or political spotlight, international engagement around these issues continues. However, the commitment to sustainable development remains patchy on the part of most states. Thus the five-year UN General Assembly Special Session to review implementation of Agenda 21 was widely viewed as a disappointment, with little in the way of notable progress. Even the UN resolution from the Session did not hide the lack of global achievement:

Five years after the United Nations Conference on Environment and Development, the state of the global environment has continued to deteriorate . . . and significant environmental problems remain deeply embedded in the socio-economic fabric of countries in all regions. Some progress has been made in terms of institutional development, international consensus-building, public participation and private sector actions, and, as result, a number of countries have succeeded in curbing pollution and slowing the rate of resource degradation. Overall, however, trends are worsening.

The year 2002 will witness the second Earth Summit in Johannesburg – the World Summit on Sustainable Development. According to critics, the decade since Rio has exposed the hypocrisy of the North, in that few of the commitments made at the first Earth Summit have been forthcoming. The South is right to be disappointed by the lack of international resolve. The continuing globalisation of the world economy and the lack of willingness on the part of the North to restructure economic relations has undermined any positive results of the Rio process. The 'spirit of Rio' has been lost as the volume of aid has dropped further; no real progress has occurred in technology transfer; environment and development concerns in the North have been downgraded while the South continues to suffer from environmental degradation and development problems (Khor, 1997, pp. 5ff). Have the critics of the Rio process been proved right?

Conclusion

There was a 'spirit of Rio' and environmental regimes have developed quite considerably over the past two decades. However, the agenda has been dominated by the interests of Northern states – particularly the G7 – and those international and domestic institutions that share similar short-term economic and political interests. This means that issues directly affecting the highly-industrialised, high-consumption nations are normally given priority and those of more concern to Southern nations often lack international attention and funding. This Northern hegemony also means that environmental issues tend to be viewed both as isolated phenomena and also as merely technical problems admitting of technical solutions. They are considered in an isolated fashion because it is not in the short-term interest of the North to tackle wider structural issues such as the nature of the international economy and political-military interests; they are considered as merely technical problems that allows highly industrialised nations to sidestep issues of global justice.

If this was all that could be said then it would seem that the North will continue its dominance of the international agenda and patterns of development and environmental degradation will continue to be at the expense of the South. However, this does not necessarily have to be the case. As the importance of successfully implementing environmental treaties is understood, the bargaining power of the South will increase. If it is fully appreciated that a more concerted approach to issues such as climate change is necessary and that environmental impacts will affect all nations regardless of wealth or political status, Southern nations will be able to apply more pressure for technical and financial transfers and reassessment of the structure of the international political and economic system. Whether there is a will to challenge the hegemony of values associated with capital accumulation and free-market rhetoric is a moot point. Perhaps, then, we are left with two possible scenarios. The first is desperate, with continued deterioration of the planet and increasing economic, social and environmental differentials between the North and the South. Environmental issues and international policy forums are used to provide domestic publicity stunts for political leaders. Empty speeches and hollow promises are made.

An alternative scenario would see the embrace of the democratic and cooperative principles of Agenda 21 together with a recognition that sustainable development requires a reassessment of uneven patterns of development, consumption levels and poverty. Ecological modernisation could be seen as a first step – a stepping stone – to much more sustainable patterns of development and environmental protection and new forms of global governance. Whether states and other international actors are able to truly grasp this agenda is another question.

Case study: the politics of climate change

The greenhouse effect is a natural phenomenon: a number of atmospheric gases, including carbon dioxide, absorb radiation reflecting back from the Earth's surface, thereby trapping heat in the atmosphere and providing suitable conditions for the sustenance of life. The problem is that human activities, such as the burning of fossil fuels and increasing deforestation, are enhancing this greenhouse effect, leading to an acceleration of climate change. The Intergovernmental Panel on Climate Change (IPCC), established in 1988 by UNEP, and the World Meteorological Organisation (WMO) has taken a lead in developing a broad scientific consensus on the nature and implications of climate change. The modelling involved is highly complex, but the reports produced by IPCC have increasingly supported the view that evidence is strong for human-induced impacts on the climate and that harmful effects are likely to include:

- a general reduction in crop yields in most tropical and sub-tropical regions;
- decreased water availability in many water-scarce regions;
- an increase in the number of people vulnerable to vector-borne diseases such as malaria and water-borne diseases such as cholera;
- flooding of many human settlements from increased rain and sea level rise.[27]

However, to understand the complexity of climate change politics, it is important to recognise two characteristics of the problems highlighted by the IPCC. First, although globally, more people are likely to be harmed than helped by changes in the climate, there will be *differential impacts*: harms are not distributed evenly across the globe. It is not obvious that everyone will be adversely affected. Some countries will get hotter and benefit from a longer growing season; some will suffer a reduction in crop yields, shortage of water and an increase in disease; others may even get colder because of the local impacts of the changes to world weather patterns. Some countries – especially small island states and Bangladesh – will be quickly and adversely affected by the rise in sea levels. These countries are both sensitive (affected by the problem) and vulnerable (unable to adapt or respond adequately or quickly enough) when compared to richer, low-lying, industrialised nations such as The Netherlands.

continued

Second, we find *differential responsibility* for climate change. Highly-industrialised, high-consumption societies have achieved their current levels of 'development' on the back of fossil-fuel economies. Climate change is a direct consequence of industrialisation. Hence we are in a situation where the USA, which has 4 per cent of the world's population, is responsible for approaching 25 per cent of all global greenhouse gas emissions. This is eleven times more per capita than China, twenty more than India and 300 times more than Mozambique. Even comparing high-consumption societies there are significant differences in contributions: annual per capita emissions of carbon dioxide in the USA is 20 tonnes; in Sweden it is 6.5 tonnes.

But what do these differential effects and responsibilities mean for climate change politics? First, climate change raises fundamental questions about justice. If climate predictions are correct, future generations are going to be faced with severe environmental problems which could have been reduced by actions in the present. Equally, there will be differential impacts across the same generation – some will suffer more than others. The recognition of differential responsibility appears to place a double obligation on highly-industrialised, high-consumption societies: they are required to both reduce their emissions of greenhouse gases and to transfer finance and technology to less economically-developed nations so that they can develop in a more environmentally-sensitive direction.

Second, given that the atmosphere is a global commons, we have a collective action problem, but one which has some highly problematic features. A number of nations do not perceive climate change as directly harmful to their own (typically economic) interests: responding to climate change, in terms of changing patterns of energy use, may be a costly affair which does not bring with it tangible benefits. This is the position in the USA. And the problem here is that the USA is the largest polluter. As Todd Sandler notes, 'successful collective action requires that all participants perceive a net benefit. This simple realization is often forgotten' (Sandler, 1997, p. 14). Given the way that the USA perceives its own interests, there are good reasons for it to avoid cooperation and action. From the perspective of justice, the nation with the most responsibility has the least incentive to engage in building an effective climate regime.[28]

Climate negotiations

The first climate conference took place in the late 1970s as scientific concern about the impact of human activities increased. The establishment of the IPCC in 1988 and the growing scientific consensus paved the way for the creation of the United Nations Framework Convention on Climate Change (UNFCCC) which was signed by over 150 nations at the Rio Earth Summit in 1992.[29] At this point, no fixed targets were established and no firm commitments were made for financial and technological transfer to the South, although the Global Environment Facility (GEF) was established as the main funding mechanism (see earlier in the chapter) (Paterson, 1996). Since 1992, there have been seven Conferences of the Parties (COP) to the Convention. COP3, held in Kyoto in 1997, is arguably the most well known, given that it produced the Kyoto Protocol which included legally-binding targets for highly-industrialised (referred to as Annex I) nations.

The Kyoto Protocol

The Kyoto Protocol requires Annex I nations collectively to reduce their collective emissions of greenhouse gases by an average of 5.2 per cent below 1990 levels in the period 2008–12

(Newell, 1998, p. 156). In recognition of differential capacities and forms of energy stocks, not all nations have the same targets, for example:

- the EU (as a whole) is required to reduce its emissions by 8 per cent; the USA by 7 per cent; Canada and Japan by 6 per cent;
- Russia, New Zealand and Ukraine are expected to stabilise their emissions;
- Norway is allowed to increase its emissions by 1 per cent; Australia by 8 per cent; Iceland by 10 per cent.

The EU has established a 'bubble' of 8 per cent, within which some member states are making significant reductions in emissions (e.g. 21 per cent in Denmark and Germany; 12.5 per cent in the UK), others are required to stabilise (e.g. France and Finland) and the remainder are allowed to increase emissions (e.g. 27 per cent in Portugal; 25 per cent in Greece; 15 per cent in Spain; 13 per cent in Ireland).[30]

The Protocol also provides for flexible mechanisms: the establishment of an international emissions-trading system between Annex I nations; the clean development mechanism (CDM) which would allow Annex I nations to receive credit for financing emissions-reduction projects in less-industrialised states; and joint implementation (JIM) which would allow joint agreements on emissions savings or carbon-sink development projects between Annex I nations.

The negotiations running up to and including Kyoto witnessed the emergence of a number of different 'blocs' each with different agendas. USA, Canada, Australia, Japan, New Zealand (referred to collectively as JUSCANZ) sought to hold back or veto agreements. They insisted that developing countries in the South should be required to limit their emissions if the highly-industrialised nations were being asked to limit theirs. At the same time they were arguing for increased opportunities to develop alternative approaches beyond simple emissions limits. For example, they argued for the development of:

- an emissions-trading system that would allow states to purchase emission credits from nations that were able to meet their targets (for example Russia which is likely to easily achieve its targets because of the collapse of many of its highly-polluting industries);
- mechanisms (such as CDM) that would allow states to offset reductions against projects that provided clean technology to the South;
- a system to include 'carbon sinks', for example the management and development of forests, that would allow states to offset emissions.

JUSCANZ found themselves in direct opposition with the EU which was arguing for serious and substantial cuts. The EU and its member states accused these nations of attempting to shed their global responsibilities. Although agreement was reached to include alternative mechanisms, the EU consistently argued that these should be viewed as supplementary to domestic action; not a replacement for action. What is interesting, then, about climate change politics is that it is not simply North versus South. High-consumption, highly-industrialised nations find themselves in opposition, with the EU adopting a (relatively) strong pro-environment position.

continued

The Kyoto negotiations did not only include the high-consumption countries (although at times it appeared that way). The G77 and China consistently appealed to the principle of justice, arguing that it was the primary responsibility of highly-industrialised nations to act and to act quickly. Most vociferous were the Association of Small Island States (AOSIS), comprising those countries most immediately sensitive and vulnerable to changes in sea level. Unsurprisingly, the Organisation of Petroleum-Exporting Countries (OPEC) started as they meant to go on, by doing all they could to oppose any agreement which they viewed as a threat to their economies.

Infamously, the USA announced after COP6 in The Hague in 2000 that it intended to withdraw from the Kyoto process and that it would not ratify the Protocol. While it was still a party to the negotiations the USA led attempts to water down the impact of targets by insisting on the inclusion of carbon sinks and trading of carbon credits. Now that these have been included within the agreement, it has pulled out of the negotiations, thereby weakening the regime twice over. Given the significant level of US emissions, this means that the effectiveness of a ratified agreement will be much less.

COP7 was held in Bonn in 2001 and completed in Marrakesh later in the same year. A common view was that the talks (the first to take place after the withdrawal of the USA from the Kyoto agreement) succeeded, but only at the expense of making major concessions to countries such as Japan, Canada and Russia (now known as the Umbrella Group), 'which used the threatened collapse of the negotiations in the face of US hostility to milk as much national advantage as they could' (ENDS, 2001d, p. 49). The veto power of these remaining nations was enhanced by the fact of US withdrawal: these countries need to ratify the Protocol if it is to come into force, and they can use the other participants' knowledge of this as a mechanism to gain advantage. In particular they were able to gain concessions from the EU on the use of carbon sinks in forests and agricultural land that provides a way for industrialised nations to avoid actual emission reductions. The Kyoto Protocol may still be ratified by the requisite number of states, but it is a weakened agreement, both in structure and with the US free-riding.

Why would the USA not ratify?

Reflecting on the difficulties in achieving collective action on climate change, Paul Harris makes the point that:

[E]ach country's position in the climate change negotiations is driven by a variety of factors. Among those that are most important are: perceptions of national interests (usually *economics* for most countries); geography (location, land forms, water systems, soil types, etc.); and existing national and international political coalitions, blocs and friendships. Climate change impacts – more accurately, assessments and expectations of them – combine with domestic and international politics to shape the course of the international climate change deliberations.

(Harris, 2001, p. 17)

Thus, as we have already noted, we find divergent positions taken by highly-industrialised nations and differences emerging between the perceived interests of states in the North and South. Central to the US position on climate change is a perception that it will adversely affect the national (economic) interest. However, many commentators were surprised that an agreement was not reached during the Clinton administration which was perceived as pro-environment. This is to neglect forces at play in domestic US politics.

First, even if the Clinton administration had come to an agreement at COP6, the division of powers in the US political system requires any international convention to be agreed by the US Senate. At the time this was controlled by the Republicans who perceived the Kyoto process as a threat to national interest.

Second, there is a reluctance on the part of US citizens to curb their high-consumption, high-pollution lifestyles. As President Bush famously stated at the Rio Earth Summit, 'the American lifestyle is non-negotiable'. The USA is locked into a pattern of production, consumption and transport from which it is politically and socially difficult to escape. The USA is

> the second largest oil producer, the second largest natural gas producer and the largest coal producer in the world. It has developed with the benefit of cheap and abundant energy supplies, and correspondingly low prices. As a result, a 'gas-guzzler' culture has emerged which makes it very difficult culturally for the US to contemplate restrictions on energy use.
>
> (Paterson, 1996, p. 80)

Third, the strength of the energy production and motoring lobbies in the USA acts as a serious impediment to the development of environmental policy. US business interests mounted a phenomenal campaign against the Kyoto process, attacking the scientific basis of the regime and raising fears about its effect on the economy if countries such as China were exempt from the process. These interests formed a highly successful lobbying organisation, the Global Climate Coalition, which was active at both domestic and international levels.[31] Given the intimate relationship between the oil industry and his administration, it is no surprise that George Bush, Jnr has taken such an oppositional stance towards Kyoto. His questioning of the science behind the agreements mirrors the position of the Global Climate Coalition, even though respected and independent scientific organisations in the USA support the IPCC. So, even though the USA is one of the most energy-inefficient nations and thus has a huge potential for rapid and cheap reductions in emissions of carbon dioxide, the US administration is unwilling to act (Ward *et al.*, 2001, p. 452).

Compared to the USA, the EU has not developed the same kind of energy economy, is politically less in thrall to large energy lobbies (most EU members are oil importers) and has a significant and effective green lobby. Over the years the EU has developed an environmental policy characterised by a precautionary approach (see Chapter 8) which means that it is more sensitive to the issue of climate change, and in this, contrasts sharply with the US approach. Further, there is a recognition of the potential and opportunity for technological leadership in energy-saving technology (Ward *et al.*, 2001, p. 439). There is a growing gap between the USA and the EU, with the latter beginning to assert itself in international environmental politics. As the French environment minister stated at the end of COP6, it is not just about climate change:

> In her final remark to the COP, French environment minister Voynet put her finger on the root of a much bigger problem that has recently become increasingly obvious, not just in climate politics, but on a growing portfolio of friction points from recent trade disputes (for

continued

example, banana wars, genetically-modified foods) to nuclear missile defence systems. She said the breakdown of the climate talks reflected a significant cultural gap between the US and Europe in how they approach economic and social policies. Voynet said the US places much of its faith in free-market methods that in France would be deemed 'the law of the jungle'. In other words, we are facing a global governance crisis.

(Dessai, 2001, p. 143)

The search for a just solution

From the position of the South, climate change is typically considered to be a matter of economic justice. The industrialised countries have benefited from unrestricted free access to the atmosphere and display a lack of commitment to reduce their impact. At the same time, Northern states such as the USA argue that *all* states should be required to reduce their emissions. Given differential responsibility for the current situation, it is no surprise that Southern nations view this as double standards and demand their equal share of the global atmospheric commons. The claim is that the rich North owes an ecological debt to the poor South.

The Global Commons Institute has attempted to develop a plan – 'contraction and convergence': contraction of overall emissions and convergence of Northern and Southern emissions. The proposal (which in many ways is a return to, and development of, the principles of the original UNFCCC) is built on the recognition of differential responsibility and embraces two principles: first, that every person in the world should have (in the long run) an equal emission quota; and second, that all emissions quotas would be marketable – but only within a stringent global emissions limit. In other words, global tradeable permits are proposed, but not as a way of relieving individual countries of their responsibilities. Rich countries who wish to continue with more than their share will have to pay for the privilege, thereby generating resources for countries who need them (Meyer, 2000). The contraction and convergence approach counters the US approach which has rejected stringent limits and opposed the adoption of per capita emissions quotas. It has been adopted as a policy goal by India, China and many African countries; although it is not yet official EU policy it has been approved by the Parliament (Layton, 2001, p. 15).[32]

Conclusion

Cooperation in climate politics has been difficult to secure. At the same time as the USA has unilaterally withdrawn from the process, the small island state Tuvalu is in negotiations with New Zealand to transfer its population. The Kyoto protocol is likely to be ratified and come into force, but in the absence of the USA it will remain in a precarious state. Not only are there disagreements among the remaining Northern countries, but the task of gradually drawing Southern nations into a broader process will surely be made even more difficult in the face of the absence of commitment by the USA. Why should they cooperate when the USA most palpably will not?

Suggestions for further reading

Lorraine Elliot *The Global Politics of the Environment* (second edition) is a highly accessible introduction to the sub-discipline. Gareth Porter and Janet Walsh Brown *Global Environmental Politics* (third edition) provides an excellent survey of international regimes and institutions. The essays in Caroline Thomas's edited collection *Rio: Unravelling the Consequences* (originally a special edition of *Environmental Politics*) investigate the immediate impact of UNCED, while Felix Dodds's edited collection *Earth Summit 2002* provides an agenda for action for the Johannesburg conference. The more radical wing of environmental thinking is well represented by Wolfgang Sachs's collection *Global Ecology* and Edward Goldsmith and Jerry Mander's edited volume *The Case Against the Global Economy*. A well-documented analysis of the impact of the environmental movement on the World Bank, IMF and WTO can be found in Robert O'Brien *et al. Contesting Global Governance*. For a comprehensive and theoretically informed analysis of the politics of climate change, see Matthew Paterson *Global Warming and Global Politics* and Peter Newell *Climate for Change*. Contemporary reviews of the state of theories of international environmental politics can be found in Eric Laferrière and Peter Stoett *International Relations Theory and Ecological Thought* and Matthew Paterson *Understanding Global Environmental Politics*. The journals *Global Environmental Change* and *Environmental Politics* both publish relevant articles. Finally, *Third World Resurgence*, published monthly by the Third World Network, includes regular articles on environment and development issues from the perspective of Southern NGOs.

Useful websites

United Nations Development Programme: www.undp. org
United Nations Environment Programme: www.unep. org
United Nations Commission on Sustainable Development:
  www.un.org/esa/ sustdev/csd.htm
World Summit on Sustainable Development (Earth Summit II):
  www.johannesburgsummit.org
Global Environment Facility: www.gefweb.org
United Nations Framework Convention on Climate Change: www.unfccc.org
Global Commons Institute: www.gci.org.uk
Greenpeace International: www.greenpeace.org
Friends of the Earth International: www.foei.org
World Resources Institute: www.wri.org
International Institute for Sustainable Development: www.iisd.org
Third World Network: www.twnside.org.sg

Notes

1 Some writers such as Gareth Porter and Janet Walsh Brown argue that the system of norms and rules that underpin regimes should be 'specified by a multilateral

agreement among the relevant states' (Porter and Brown, 1996, p. 16). This has the merit of allowing us explicitly to identify the existence of regimes, although it fails to appreciate the informal aspects of many regimes – the informal development of norms through which actors (be they states and/or other organisations) develop mutual understanding and relations of trust (Paterson, 1996, pp. 182–3).

2   For a more detailed analysis of the state of a number of environmental regimes, see Porter and Brown (2000). There are a number of collections that cover a range of environmental issues (some are listed in the bibliography) and a growing number of texts on the international politics of particular problems, for example, Matthew Paterson's *Global Warming and Global Politics* (1996).

3   As we shall emphasise later, this figure tells us nothing of the distribution of wealth *within* the North or the South.

4   Clearly the European Union (EU) is a special case in that it is a supranational institution. We shall have more to say about the EU in Chapter 8, but for the purpose of this analysis it can be ignored.

5   This is only a brief discussion of international relations theory. For a much more sophisticated introduction to traditional and contemporary theories, see Brown (1997). For an analysis of international relations theory in light of global climate politics, see Paterson (1996) and for a more general collection of essays, see Vogler and Imber (1996).

6   In one of the more sophisticated analyses of power in international politics, Susan Strange argues that there are four sources of structural power: security, production, financial and knowledge structures (Strange, 1988, pp. 29ff). According to this account, the USA is still by far the dominant nation in terms of structural power, even if it is unwilling to take a leadership role in international environmental regimes.

7   Also known as multinational corporations (MNCs).

8   This was the final (Uruguay) round of negotiations of the General Agreement on Tariffs and Trade (GATT) which had been set up in the 1940s as a precursor of the WTO. However, the WTO was only finally created five decades later.

9   O'Brien *et al.* (2000) provide a systematic analysis of the impact of global social movements (including the environmental movement) on the policies and practices of the Bretton Woods institutions.

10 We shall have more to say about the Global Environment Facility later in this chapter.

11 It is perhaps a fair criticism of green international political economy that the role of the financial markets is under-theorised and researched.

12 For a disturbing account of the economic plight of Africa in the face of growing debt, see Mihevc (1995) and de la Court (1990).

13 We need to be aware of 'the existence of a growing "South" in the "North"' (Thomas, 1997, p. 3) and similarly, a growing 'North' in the 'South'.

14 On the emerging debates over 'globalisation', see Held *et al.* (1999), Held and McGrew (2000) and Hirst and Thompson (1999).

15 A more complete analysis would also look at the work of international organisations such as the United Nations Development Programme (UNDP), the Food and Agriculture Organisation (FAO) and the World Health Organisation (WHO) among others.

16 For a comprehensive discussion of the IPPC and its findings, see Paterson (1996, pp. 40ff).

17 Questions have been raised about the nature and significance of 'epistemic communities'. For instance, they are only likely to be effective in so far as they do not challenge the core interests of the state (Brown, 1997, p. 234) and as such their role in bringing into question the very structures of the international political and economic systems is limited. This ties in with the recognition that science and politics are intimately linked in international negotiations and that, as we discussed briefly in Chapter 4, it is difficult to separate out the manner in which scientific investigation is

taken forward and the political ends to which it is used. For an extended discussion of the limits of the epistemic communities approach, see Paterson (1996, pp. 134–56).

18   Maurice Strong was the chair of the 1972 United Nations Conference on the Human Environment and was Secretary-General of UNCED two decades later.

19   Dr Töpfer also serves as Director of Habitat at the UN Centre for Human Settlement also based in Nairobi.

20   The workings of the CSD are discussed later in this chapter.

21   Environmental pressure groups are often described as NGOs in the literature on international relations.

22   For more on the politics of climate change, see the case study at the end of the chapter.

23   The G77, formed in the 1970s, is a coalition of Southern states pressing for North–South economic reform.

24   For a more detailed discussion of the political negotiations surrounding the GEF, see Porter and Brown (1996, pp. 141–4) and Chatterjee and Finger (1994, pp. 151–7).

25   Further details of the Aarhus Convention can be found at www.unece.org.

26   For a summary of the first four annual sessions of the CSD, see Bigg and Dodds (1997, pp. 23–9). A new five-year programme of work for the CSD (1988–2002) was agreed at the five-year review of Rio (Bigg, 1997). See also Dodds (2001, pp. 322ff).

27   The IPCC reports can be found at www.ipcc.ch.

28   Interesting analyses of negotiations in terms of rational choice and game theory can be found in Harris (2001), Ward et al. (2001) and Sandler (1997).

29   For details of the UNFCCC and the Kyoto process, see www.unfccc.int.

30   For more on the national approaches of high-consumption societies to tackling climate change, see Lafferty and Meadowcroft (2000).

31   Not all industrial interests sided with the Global Climate Coalition. For example, BP and Shell left the Coalition because of its opposition to the negotiations, and the insurance industry, especially in Europe and Japan (but also in the USA), is concerned that climate change could bankrupt them and therefore are in favour of action to prevent climate change (Ward et al., 2001, p. 452; Salt, 1998).

32   Details of contraction and convergence can be found at www.gci.org.uk.

European integration

> The EU is one of the most significant of the new international regimes
> and organizations that have been established to manage areas of
> transnational activity, including environmental policy. Its significance
> lies in the fact that its powers reach further than any other kind of
> international organization by virtue of its rights to make laws which can
> be imposed on member-states.
>
> (Baker, 1996, p. 215)

The European Union (EU)[1] has emerged over the past two decades as a major source
of environmental action and law making. On the global stage it enters into
negotiations in its own right: for example, it is the only supranational organisation that
is a signatory to the Earth Summit documents and took a strong pro-environment
stance in the Kyoto climate change negotiations in direct opposition to the USA. For
an organisation whose original rationale was the creation of the conditions for
sustained economic growth for its member states, the transformation into a leading
promoter of environmental innovation and change needs some investigation. Despite
the EU's emergence as an important policy maker and international actor in the
environmental sphere, it has nonetheless attracted criticism. For example, it has
been reproached for lacking an adequate monitoring and enforcement machinery,
for depressing environmental standards within Europe to the lowest common
denominator and for supposing that it can pursue an effective environmental policy
while giving higher priority to promoting economic growth and increased trade.

This chapter will examine how and why the EU adopted an environmental
role. Initially, it is necessary to briefly describe the institutional arrangements of the
EU, as a number of different institutions have an input into policy making. The
development of comprehensive European environmental policy can be seen as an
incremental process and the chapter will focus on the political and administrative
aspects of its evolution. In the final section, the two most recent Environmental Action
Programmes (the fifth and sixth) will be discussed. The title of the fifth action
programme is *Towards Sustainability*: to what extent has this been achieved? The
case study focuses on the creation and development of the European Environment
Agency (EEA), an institution over which there has been much political disagreement.
Does the EU require a supranational environmental inspectorate, or would that be
an unaccepable infringement of national sovereignty? As we shall see, conflicts such
as this are at the heart of the emerging European project and environmental policy
is a creature of such tensions.

The structure and operation of the European Union

The EU is a supranational organisation. This entails not only that member states are
committed to work together, but that (in contrast to other international organisations)
there are formal constraints on the actions of its members. The EU has a quite
distinctive structure and set of practices. For example, it creates a body of law
which takes precedence over national law (much of the British concern over 'loss of
parliamentary sovereignty' arises from this) and its network of institutions, most
of which are located in Brussels, compose a political and administrative structure

quite unlike any national arrangement. Its actions and judgements penetrate the politics of member states to an extent beyond that of any other international organisation.

The European Economic Community (EEC) was initially established, as its name indicates, to promote and secure the economic well-being of its member states. Article 2 of the 1957 Treaty of Rome originally defined its purpose:[2]

> The Community shall have as its task, by establishing a common market and progressively approximating the economic policies of Member States, to promote throughout the Community a harmonious development of economic activities, a continuous and balanced expansion, an increase in stability, an accelerated raising of the standard of living and closer relations between the States belonging to it.

The primary rationale of the Community was, therefore, not only directly economic in intention, but also, it might be argued, anti-environmental in practice in the sense that it gave a clear priority to the promotion of economic growth. Subsequently the Treaty of Rome has been supplemented and modified in a number of ways, the most important being the 1987 Single European Act (SEA) and the 1993 Maastricht Treaty on European Union (TEU) which together enhanced the powers of the European Parliament, developed the principle of subsidiarity, moved the European Community towards an integrated European Union with enhanced powers, and established a firm legal basis for environmental policy. These moves have now been modified and confirmed by the Treaty of Amsterdam (1997) which amended Article 2 to include the EU's commitment 'to promote . . . a harmonious, balanced and sustainable development of economic activities' and 'a high level of protection and improvement of the quality of the environment'.

Since 1957, the organisation has grown in size from the original six (France, West Germany, Italy, Luxembourg, Belgium, Netherlands) in 1957, to nine in 1973 (with the accession of the UK, the Republic of Ireland and Denmark). Greece joined in 1981, Spain and Portugal in 1986, Austria, Finland and Sweden in 1995. Hence the European Union currently comprises fifteen members. Further expansion through the incorporation of Central and Eastern European Countries (CEECS), such as Hungary, Poland and the Czech Republic, is currently being negotiated. The inclusion of up to fifteen new members will alter the profile of the EU; the new Union of perhaps 28 countries will increase its population by a further 170 million with a 58 per cent increase in land area.

The institutions

The EU comprises a number of bodies such as the European Commission, the Council of Ministers and the European Parliament which have varying powers and capabilities and which interact with one another in an often complicated and opaque manner. The key institutions are:

- European Commission
- Council of Ministers

- European Council
- European Parliament
- European Court of Justice.

To describe the European Commission as the EU's equivalent of the 'civil service' would be to underestimate its degree of autonomy. Its role is not simply to administrate, but also to initiate policy, and in particular to initiate policy that 'transcends' a limited notion of the national self-interest of its member states. As such it is an activist organisation and often finds itself in conflict with national governments and other institutions within the EU. The Commission consists of a number of commissioners appointed by each member state.[3] Margot Wallström, the Swedish commissioner, is responsible for environmental matters. These commissioners are serviced by officials grouped into a number of directorates each charged with specific responsibility for a particular policy area. The Environment Directorate General (EDG) was originally created as DG XI in 1981 to cover the environment, consumer protection and nuclear safety. It now comprises five directorates covering general and international affairs, integration policy, nuclear safety and civil protection, environmental quality and natural resources, and industry and the environment (McCormick, 2001, p. 102). The Commission initiates and drafts policy (including Environmental Action Programmes) and draws up proposals for the Council of Ministers to approve. It also has responsibility for implementing EU policies and for policing and enforcing EU law.

The Council of Ministers is the main decision-making body of the EU and is made up of one representative from each member state. It is an avowedly political body, unlike the Commission. Although formally the Council of Ministers comprises only foreign ministers, in practice representatives are usually the relevant ministers from each member state according to the nature of the decision being taken. Thus, for example, environmental ministers will decide on environmental policy, agricultural ministers on agricultural policy, and so on. These decisions are later formally ratified by a full Council meeting. Decisions are made in the Council of Ministers using different voting procedures. For some measures unanimity is required, but for an increasing number of decisions a qualified majority is sufficient.[4] Before the introduction of the SEA in 1987, all environmental policy required a unanimous decision; the SEA modified this. Following the Maastricht TEU in 1993, qualified majority voting was adopted for most (but not all) environmental policy. The removal of the de facto veto means that it is now easier to push through environmental legislation. The Council's area of competence also covers the work of the Committee of Permanent Representatives (COREPER) which comprises national officials from member states who discuss proposals emanating from the Commission and explore possible areas of agreement and conflict.

The European Council (at times referred to as the European Summit) typically meets twice a year and consists of heads of government from each member state. Its purpose is to resolve any issues which have proven intractable to the normal decision-making procedures of the EU. The introduction of European Council meetings to some extent represented a move away from *supranational* decision making and towards *intergovernmental* decision making. A supranational body is one which has powers over and above the powers of its members and which is (at least to some extent) an actor in its own right in international politics; an intergovernmental body is a forum for debate and common action between states, with no additional powers. The EU contains elements of both supranationalism and intergovernmentalism – whether it acts in one or the other way depends on circumstances and the issues concerned. In practice it often appears to be a hybrid of the two.

The EU as an independent international actor

It is important to recognise that the EU can act in its own right as an international actor. On these occasions it is more than an intergovernmental body; it is a supranational actor. This brings into question the 'settled norm' of national sovereignty at the international level (see Chapter 7). The EU is a party to the Convention on International Trade in Endangered Species of Wild Flora and Fauna (CITES) and a signatory to the Geneva Convention on Long-range Transboundary Air Pollution (1981) and the Montreal Protocol on Ozone Depleting Substances (1987). In 1992 it was one of the signatories to the Framework Convention on Climate Change agreed at Rio, and in the 1997 negotiations in Kyoto it committed itself to an 8 per cent reduction in carbon dioxide emissions by the year 2010. It proposed the idea of a European 'bubble' in which it was the overall emissions of the EU which were to be measured.[5] Within this bubble individual member states could be permitted different emission levels. For example, Germany and the UK are committed to reductions while Portugal (as a less-industrialised member) is to be allowed to increase its emissions for the immediate future (see case study in Chapter 7). The emergence of the EU as a strong pro-environment actor raises the possibility that it may replace the more isolationist USA as the hegemonic power within international environmental politics.

The European Parliament is composed of 626 directly elected representatives – Members of the European Parliament (MEPs) – from each member state. These representatives are not grouped by national origin, but by political affinity, including the Group of the Greens (see later). Although the Parliament has gained powers in the course of the EU's development, it does not possess the extensive powers of the Council of Ministers or the European Commission. In large part it is a body limited to a consultation and advisory role, although following the introduction of direct elections in 1979, and the ratification of the SEA and the TEU, it is gradually acquiring new powers which perhaps go some way towards remedying the 'democratic deficit' which many have identified in the decision-making processes of the EU. The Parliament cannot, as such, reject a piece of legislation, but consultation with the assembly has always been a requirement without which a piece of EU legislation will be void. In addition, following the ratification of the SEA, the Parliament can delay matters by withholding its opinion on a piece of legislation, and in respect of legislation subject to qualified majority voting, it can reject or propose amendments. It also has the power to withhold its assent to some parts of the Union budget. This gives it some important powers and capabilities, which, given its general willingness to embrace environmental issues, means that environmental policies continue to have a platform in the EU even when they may have dropped down the broader political agenda of other institutions and member states. Although the Treaty of Amsterdam continued the slow process of extending the Parliament's limited powers by granting it rights of co-decision over certain objectives of environmental policy, 'MEPs will have to work hard to ensure the greening of the European Union' (Duff, 1997, p. 77).

Other key institutions include the European Court of Justice (ECJ) which has supreme authority on matters relating to EU law. It is responsible for interpreting EU law and for ensuring that it is properly implemented. As such, its major concern is to ensure uniformity in application of the law across member states. Article 169 gives the Commission power to bring enforcement proceedings against a member state which has not properly transposed a directive into national law or ensured practical compliance with it. However, procedures are begun in only a very small proportion of breaches of environmental law. As Ludwig Krämer remarks:

> [I]t is increasingly recognised that the effective application of environmental measures is the most serious existing problem of environmental law. The numerous environmental provisions . . . are frequently either not transposed at all into national law, or not properly applied in practice.
>
> (Krämer, 1997, p. 300)[6]

Other notable European institutional arrangements include the Economic and Social Committee (ECOSOC), a consultative committee comprising members representing employers, trade unions and consumers. It produces opinions on policy proposals. Finally, the Committee of the Regions, created by the Maastricht Treaty in 1993, is likely to become increasingly important as the application of the principle of subsidiarity devolves decision-making power to regional and local level. The majority of states within Europe allow for a degree of regional autonomy. Where regional government is strong they are able to take advantage of EU funding channelled through the Committee of the Regions.[7]

The instruments of EU legislation

The most important legislative instruments employed by the EU are regulations and directives. Other available instruments are decisions, recommendations and opinions. The bulk of EU environmental law is made in the form of directives.

European Union legislation

Regulations have general application. They are binding in their entirety and directly applicable in all member states. There are very few regulations in EU environmental policy.

Directives bind member states to achieving specified outcomes; but leave the choice of method to each national authority. Most EU environmental legislation takes the form of directives; they are well suited to this as they leave some flexibility in the choice of

---

how best to implement policy to each member state. Increasingly *framework directives* are being used in EU environmental legislation. These are general directives laying down a strategic framework to achieve specified aims; more detailed 'daughter' directives follow, dealing with particular issues to achieve the aims. Framework directives currently exist for discharge of pollutants into water, waste, the restriction and use of chemicals, and for air pollution. Although sometimes criticised for diluting legislation, they have the advantage that they provide a clear strategic statement: 'definitions, adaptation procedures and other mechanisms are established in the basic or mother directive, to which other directives then refer' (Krämer, 1997, p. 121).

Decisions are not general but specific to the member state concerned. They are rare in EU environmental policy.

Recommendations and **Opinions** have recommendatory or persuasive force, but are not binding.

Regulations are directly applicable: once a regulation is adopted it automatically becomes part of the national legal system of all of the EU's member states without any need for further legislative or administrative implementation. Directives, on the other hand, are more flexible in that it is left to member states to choose the most appropriate method of implementation. Accordingly, member states vary in the ways they enact EU directives. They can be enacted through primary legislation (very often a composite bill such as the UK's 1990 Environmental Protection Act which consisted largely of measures required under a whole range of EU directives); they can be enacted through statutory instruments;[8] they can also be implemented by means of administrative circulars. Given that directives explicitly admit of flexibility in their interpretation and execution (setting, as they do, the ends, but leaving the means to national discretion) there is sometimes a danger that member states will interpret them more liberally than the EU intended. However, it would be a mistake to suppose that the difference between regulations and directives is always sharp; very often it is a matter of degree, and as EU law has developed, the difference has been further eroded with the emergence of the principle of 'direct effect'. Legislation which has direct effect gives rights to citizens of member states on which they can rely in a national court in challenging lax implementation. All regulations are directly effective, and directives may also be directly effective in cases where they are clear, unambiguous and unconditional.

Monitoring and implementation

In complying with EU legislation, member states have both a positive and a negative duty. Positively they are required to implement a directive fully and within the specified time limit; negatively they are required to repeal any previous law incompatible with the directive. But EU environmental legislation suffers from one obvious drawback: monitoring is largely, and implementation is solely, in the hands of the member states themselves. Each member state is normally required to file a compliance letter with the Commission indicating the action or actions they have taken to implement the relevant legislation. In the past this procedure has been neither uniformly nor rigorously followed. Directive 91/692 on the standardisation and rationalisation of implementation reports for environmental directives seeks to remedy this unsatisfactory situation. Reports will be made through the use of questionnaires covering a policy sector, be it water, air, or waste. National reports by member states and an EU-wide report by the Commission will be presented every three years. It is hoped that this new procedure will avoid unnecessary infringement procedures against member states. Further, the European Environment Agency (EEA) should also enhance the ability of the Commission to detect non-compliance on the part of member states (see case study). Where the Commission takes the view that an infringement has occurred, it will deliver a formal notice to the member state concerned. Following a formal reply it will issue a reasoned opinion setting out the grounds for its belief that the member state has not complied; this opinion must also set out the steps to be taken by the member state, together with a timetable for action. Ultimately, if the state still does not comply, the case will be taken to the ECJ which, if it finds against the member state, may impose a penalty payment.

However, the Commission has no independent method for checking and monitoring implementation: its responses are largely based on information supplied by member states themselves. This means that very often the countries which are most assiduous in monitoring and issuing reports are the ones which are reprimanded by the Commission, simply because they are supplying the evidence on which it bases its judgement. Although it is a disadvantage for the EU to have no independent means of checking, the story does not end there, because the implementation of EU policy by any member state can be challenged by individuals and groups and reports made to the Commission. This was strengthened by the Fifth Environmental Action Programme (5EAP) which encouraged citizens of member states to engage in 'shared responsibility' for the environment. Citizens can act as a complainant and in this they are aided by legislation such as Directive 90/313 on Free Access to Environmental Information which came into force in 1992. This directive allows for any individual in any member state to request, without having to show an interest, environmental information covering the activities of any member state. This directive, especially if exploited by environmental groups, might have an important impact on environmental policy, especially in those countries which are relatively lax in monitoring and implementing environmental policy. There are, nonetheless, drawbacks. Although most enforcement proceedings are initiated in response to complaints made by citizens, the procedure under Article 169 is time consuming and unwieldy. In addition, the dispute is regarded as being between the Commission and the defaulting state. The complainant is not a party and hence has no legal right to be informed of progress or to have access to copies of the formal notice or the reasoned opinion: this limits the ability of the complainant to force the issue and exert pressure (Kunzlik, 1994, pp. 115–16). Despite these limitations, there is clearly scope for action on the part of concerned groups and individuals, and this scope may be enhanced further by the current emphasis on joint responsibility for the environment.

The role of active environmental pressure groups in ensuring that states (particularly the UK) implement EU environmental legislation properly is well illustrated by Nigel Haigh and Chris Lanigan:

More and more information reached the Commission from British citizens and pressure groups as they became aware of the possibility that Commission action could challenge both past and present government policies which threatened the environment. By 1990, one third of individual complaints made to the Commission about breaches of environmental directives were coming from Britain, and pressure groups were setting up their own monitoring systems to provide the Commission with information on breaches they could otherwise never have known about. Given that DG XI was more accustomed to EC states providing too little monitoring data with which to identify offences to prosecute, it is hardly surprising that enthusiastic action against Britain should have resulted.

(Haigh and Lanigan, 1995, p. 26)

The corollary is, of course, that member states without an active environmental movement may be (and often are) relatively lax in both their interpretation and their implementation of environmental policy.

The UK stands third (behind Spain and France) in the table of suspected infringements of EU environmental policy. This gives some credence to the frequent characterisation of the UK as the 'dirty man of Europe'. But this is perhaps overstated and to some degree unfair. First, by comparison with the EU average, it has a better record than most in persuading the Commission that suspected infringements are not real and in correcting breaches when threatened with legal action (ENDS, 1996c, p. 39). Second, the UK was instrumental, for example, in the European push for lead-free petrol and has been a vociferous (and at times isolated) voice in debates on reform of the Common Agricultural Policy, animal welfare and overconsumption of fish stocks. Nonetheless, it is certainly true that the UK has on occasion frustrated or delayed a number of European environmental initiatives. The previous Conservative administration refused for many years to accept the link between sulphur dioxide emissions, acid rain and destruction of forests in Europe, and vociferously fought the directive on large combustion plants (88/609). At other times, the UK has been forced to implement directives on issues where it would have otherwise delayed or even neglected action. The content of the Wildlife and Countryside Act (1981) and the Environmental Protection Act (1990) is, for the most part, the necessary national implementation of relevant EU directives. Further, the ECJ has found the UK to be in breach of directives on two occasions. But the picture is a complex one and, ironically, one in which the UK is to some extent a victim of its own good practice. It has a good record of reporting on its compliance with directives[9] and it also has an active environmental movement. These two facts taken together mean that the UK is likely to be taken to task quicker and more readily than other member states whose environmental inactivity may be relatively invisible to the Commission. Countries whose environmental record is worse than the UK's may appear to have a better record simply because their reporting is poorer.

From policies to policy?

The European Economic Community was not originally set up with the intention of promoting environmental policy. Despite this, by 1967 the Community had begun to issue directives concerning environmental matters; and by 1973 it had developed environmental policy explicitly stated in the form of the First Environmental Action Programme. Subsequently there have been five other action programmes: the Fifth Environmental Action Programme (5EAP) ran from 1993 to 2000; the Sixth will run from 2001 to 2010. Hence an organisation which originally emerged with a purely economic mandate has metamorphosed not only into the European Union, but also into an organisation which is increasingly seen as an important agent of environmental protection. How did this come about?

The incidental nature of environmental policy

As the European Community grew and developed, it became impossible in practice to separate environmental issues from the other issues to which it was dedicated. At the barest minimum (that is, leaving aside environmental concern for its own sake) the establishment of the common market, and later the single European market, required that standards within and between countries be comparable so as to ensure equality of competition. A framework was needed in which no member state was advantaged or disadvantaged by unfair competition arising from local conditions. In economic terms this is often referred to as the maintenance of a 'level playing field'. For instance, if environmental standards were lower in one country, firms operating there would have a competitive advantage because their costs of waste disposal or emission control would be lower. This would be an unfair advantage, which might also have the effect of encouraging firms to move their operations to locations where environmental standards were relatively lax.[10] Thus legislation in these matters was necessary, not directly for environmental protection per se, but to secure protection of the primary purpose of the Community, that is, the achievement of an economic common market. Environmental concern was contingent on the primary rationale of the Community.

Despite its secondary or incidental origin, European environmental legislation began to take on a life of its own as environmental concern increasingly became a focus of governmental activity in general in the 1970s. The EC matched the mood of the times in formulating its first Environmental Action Programme in the wake of the publication of *The Limits to Growth* (Meadows *et al.*, 1972). Thus the EC became concerned with environmental issues, but faced the problem that there was no explicit provision for the making of environmental policy within the Treaty of Rome. All legislation at the European level has to be sanctioned by reference to specific articles in the Treaty and its relevance justified in relation to the primary purpose of the EC. Environmental legislation had thus to be 'smuggled' into the Community's legislative processes on the back of non-environmental concerns, through a reinterpretation of Article 2 of the Treaty of Rome. Recalling Article 2, we noted the emphasis on 'an accelerated raising of the standard of living'. Despite the context of the promotion of economic growth, such a statement could nonetheless be interpreted as including environmental protection as environmental quality was increasingly coming to be seen as an essential part of what constituted 'a good standard of living' (Marin, 1997, p. 575).

However, a comprehensive turn towards environmental protection ultimately required more than this: it required an independent legal basis. Prior to the SEA, environmental policy was given such a basis under article 100 dealing with the approximation of laws and article 235 relating to the EC's general powers. The wording of these articles indicated clearly that, first, the Council had to act unanimously in the making of environmental policy, and, second, that environmental policy had no independent status within the Treaty. Hence, there were distinct practical problems as all states had the power of veto, thereby making it difficult to ensure high standards of environmental protection and maximising the chances that any unanimously agreed policy would operate at the level of the lowest common denominator. Despite these restrictions, the EC was nonetheless passing environmental legislation, and developing a positive environmental policy expressed through its environmental action programmes.

Some examples of environmental directives

- Bathing Waters (1975)
- Lead in Petrol (1978/1985)
- Sulphur Dioxide and Suspended Particulates (1980)
- Lead in Air (1982)
- Emission of Pollutants from Industrial Plants (1984)
- Environmental Impact Assessment (1985)
- Large Combustion Plants (1988)
- Framework Directive on Waste (1991)
- Conservation of Natural Habitats and of Wild Fauna and Flora (1992)
- Integrated Pollution Prevention and Control (1996)
- Framework Directive on Ambient Air Quality (1996)
- Framework Directive on Water (2000)
- Assessment of Effects of Plans and Programmes on the Environment (2001)

The third programme (1982–6) was succeeded in 1987 by the SEA which revised the Treaty of Rome in a number of important respects, particularly in the creation of the unified internal market. The SEA was particularly important for European environmental policy making because it established for the first time the principle that environmental policy should be one of the direct concerns of the Community itself. Indeed, it is one of the four policy areas – together with consumer protection, culture and health – recognised as a component in all other EU policy making. To that end, a new title was inserted into the modified treaty and new articles were added which legitimised the position of environmental actions. In addition, DG XI of the Commission was given explicit responsibility for environmental policy. Title VII of the Treaty included the new articles 130r, 130s and 130t which introduced explicit powers for making environmental law. From this point on, environmental policy had a secure place within the structures and purposes of the Community, a place which was confirmed and strengthened by the Treaty of Maastricht in 1993. This Treaty increased the integration of environmental concerns into the EU by further modifying these articles. It recognised that 'a policy in the sphere of the environment' should be one of the EU's main activities and replaced the original

Article 2 of the Treaty of Rome with a new version which referred to promoting 'a harmonious and balanced development of economic activities' and 'sustainable and non-inflationary growth respecting the environment'. Increasingly decisions were being taken by qualified majority voting, and policy promoted to a greater degree by the European Parliament, a body sympathetic to environmental issues. The Treaty explicitly states that decisions should be taken by qualified majority voting, with the Parliament able to amend but not to veto. Under the Treaty of Amsterdam, the co-decision procedure was both extended to more environmental issues; where this procedure is used the Parliament now has the right to propose amendments to legislation. This has increased its power in the formulation of environmental policy.

The purpose of the environmental action programmes is to lay down basic principles of environmental policy and thereby to act as a framework within which specific legislation will be enacted. They also assert current priorities and commitments and plan future action. The first two action plans (1973–6 and 1977–81) focused on pollution control and remedial measures, and also stated the basic principles of emerging EC environmental policy. The third and fourth (1982–6 and 1987–92) emphasised preventative measures and the integration of environmental protection into other policies. The 5EAP (1993–2000) went beyond these objectives through an explicit commitment to sustainable development, as did its successor (see below). EU environmental policy has been *incremental* in approach, each action programme building on its predecessors, although the principles enunciated in the first programme have been common to all later environmental policy making. As we saw in Chapter 4, incremental development can give rise to large-scale changes over time, and certainly that is a fair assessment of the way incidental policies have developed and increasingly converged on a coherent policy approach. Perhaps the best summary of the development of EU environmnental policy is given by John McCormick when he states that 'while the EU lacks a comprehensive environmental policy, it has developed an increasingly coherent set of policies in a growing variety of areas that come under the general rubric of the "environment"' (McCormick, 2001, p. 39).

Principles of EU environmental policy

The principles of EU environmental policy are clearly stated in the first action programme. This indicates that although environmental policy still largely consisted of relatively ad hoc legislation responding to issues as they arose, there was none-theless a desire to go further and to develop comprehensive and even holistic environmental policy. Although these principles have been modified to a certain extent by subsequent developments, they are largely still operative. They state that:

- Pollution and nuisance should be prevented at source.
- Decision making should take account of environmental effects as early as possible.
- Exploitation of natural resources which causes significant damage to the ecological balance should be avoided.
- Scientific knowledge should be improved and research encouraged.

- The cost of preventing and eliminating nuisances should be borne by the polluter.
- Activities carried out in one member state should not cause environmental deterioration in another.
- The effects of environmental policy should take account of the interests of developing countries.
- The Community and its member states should act together to promote international environmental policy.
- The public should be informed and educated about environmental protection.
- Action should be taken at the appropriate level.
- National environmental policies should be coordinated and harmonized.

(summarised from Johnson and Corcelle, 1995, pp. 14–15)

Following the ratification of the SEA and TEU, some of these principles have been formally included in the Treaty of Rome. These include the polluter pays principle, the preventative principle, the precautionary principle and the principle of integration. The Treaty now states that:

> Community policy on the environment shall aim at a high level of protection taking into account the diversity of situations in the various regions of the Community. It shall be based on the precautionary principle and on the principles that preventative action should be taken, that environmental damage should as a priority be rectified at source and that the polluter should pay. Environmental protection requirements must be integrated into the definition and implementation of other Community policies.

(Article 174)

The preventative principle

Rather than seeking only to remedy environmental damage after the event, EU policy is to be based in part on the principle that preventative action should be taken. Damage should, where possible, be avoided at source. The importance of this principle is reflected by the fact that it was listed as the first of eleven policy principles enunciated in the First Environmental Action Programme:

> The best environmental policy consists in preventing the creation of nuisances at source, rather than subsequently trying to counteract their effects. To this end, technical progress must be conceived and devised so as to take into account the concern for protection of the environment and for the improvement of the quality of life at the lowest cost to the Community . . .

The First Action Programme conceived of the preventative principle as primarily concerned with the development of technological solutions to avoid or reduce pollution at source. The need to encourage the development of new 'clean technologies' remains an important part of EU policy, and one of the key functions of the EEA is to support research and development projects in this field (see case study).

The preventative principle can be activated in a number of ways: an example is the 1985 directive on environmental impact assessment (85/337) which provides common rules for the prior evaluation of the environmental effects of certain private and public projects (see Chapter 6). The information required includes a technical description of the project; details of likely significant effects on the environment; details of alternatives explored by the developer; details of measures taken to avoid or reduce any negative effects on the environment. In addition, a non-technical summary has to be made available. All of these have to be provided to the relevant planning authority. Projects covered include: oil refineries, power stations, radioactive waste storage and disposal facilities, iron and steel works, asbestos facilities, chemical installations, motorways, long-distance railway lines, large airports, ports and toxic-waste-disposal installations. This approach has now been adapted to the policy and planning level under directive 2001/42 (see Chapter 6).

Again, direct help and finance can be given to help enact the principle. For example, in 1984 a Regulation on action by the Community relating to the environment (ACE) created a fund for financing environment projects (1872/84). The driving force behind this was the preventative principle. The rationale was to provide support to projects aimed at creating clean technologies, developing new techniques and methods for measuring and monitoring the quality of the natural environment and maintaining or re-establishing the habitat of endangered species of birds. Later ACE was given a wider remit including recycling and locating and restoring sites contaminated by hazardous wastes. It was replaced in 1992 by Regulation 1973/92 which established a financial instrument for the environment (LIFE). Like its predecessor, this is used to finance projects which have as their objective the definition and implementation of environmental policies. LIFE is an integral part of the 5EAP. LIFE II came into being in 1996 with almost half of its budget devoted to nature-protection projects; in 1999 funding was extended to East European countries.

The precautionary principle

The TEU amended article 130r by stating that environmental policy should be based on the precautionary principle (see Chapter 4). Although this appears similar to the preventative principle, it goes further in that it implies that action should be taken even before a definite causal link has been established between an activity and any consequent harm to the environment or human health; reasonable evidence of an environmental threat is enough. This approach is similar to that adopted by the US Clean Air Act in 1982.

The precautionary principle is not defined by either the Treaty or by the 5EAP, but its meaning can be interpreted from international agreements to which the EU is a party. For example, the UN Framework Convention on Climate Change provides that the parties should

> take precautionary measures to anticipate, prevent or minimise the causes of climate change and mitigate its adverse effects. Where there are threats of serious or irreversible damage, lack of full scientific certainty should not be used as a reason for postponing such measures.
>
> (quoted in Kunzlik, 1994, p. 26)

Recently there has been some progress on providing a working definiton of the precautionary principle. A new regulation (178/2002) concerning food safety states that where the possibility of harmful effects on health have been identified, but scientific uncertainty persists, 'risk management measures . . . may be adopted, pending further scientific information for a more comprehensive risk assessment'. This move, together with the Commission's recent proposals for making sustainable development a 'core concern' of all EU policies, is a promising development.

Integration of environmental policy

If environmental policy is to be effective, environmental protection cannot be seen as a separate item or policy area among other discrete policy areas. Rather it must penetrate all areas of policy. The First Environmental Action Programme stated that effects on the environment should be taken into account at the earliest possible stage in all the technical planning and decision-making processes and that:

> The environment cannot be considered as external surroundings by which man is harassed and assailed; it must be considered as an essential factor in the organization and promotion of human progress. It is therefore necessary to evaluate the effects on the quality of life and on the natural environment of any measure that is adopted at national or Community level and is liable to affect these factors.

The SEA reinforced the principle of integration explicitly by stating that: 'Environmental protection requirements shall be a component of the Community's other policies.' This article was further modified by the TEU and now reads: 'Environmental protection requirements must be integrated into the definition and implementation of other Community policies' (Article 174). This formulation is clearly stronger than the original in that it emphasises that environmental protection should not only be part of the framing of other policies, but also of their implementation. It follows that integration is no longer merely a matter of the way policy is formulated within the EU itself: implementation of policy imposes direct responsibilities on member states.

Ensuring genuine integration of environmental policy is no easy matter (see Chapter 4). One problem is that it will almost inevitably require a shift in focus away from the environmentally-active Environment Directorate General (EDG). This is inevitable if environmental policy is not to be seen as a mere add-on or separate policy area, but as integral to all policy areas. The problem is that EDG is known to be assiduous in its environmental concern; it is less obvious that other DGs will be equally attentive, and even where they might intend to be, there is a danger that environmental policy will come second to their traditional primary priorities and remit. Proposals to make an initial step towards better integration include the setting up of an Integration Unit within EDG, the appointment of an Integration Correspondent for each DG and subjecting all policy proposals with significant environmental effects to an environmental appraisal. In addition it is proposed that each DG carry out an annual evaluation of its environmental performance and that a code of conduct be drawn up for the Commission itself (Wilkinson, 1997, p. 160).

These are all important proposals, but implementing them will be far from straight-forward. The effects of trying to secure integration are potentially far-reaching and valuable, but there is an associated danger of a loss of focus and a dilution of corporate effort. The dilemma is brought out by David Wilkinson:

> Successful integration entails a fundamental redefinition of the role of the environment departments, and some loss of control over environmental policy. The dilemma this poses is that the focus for advancing integration across the activities of government may consequently become less distinct.
>
> (ibid., p. 165)

Maintaining standards

Some EU members, in particular the environmental 'lead' nations of Germany, Sweden, and the Netherlands, have consistently argued that they should not be prevented from going further than the minimum environmental standards agreed by the EU. Despite the common claim that EU environmental policy sets standards at too low a level because of the need to secure agreement, Article 175 states that protective measures adopted under its aegis 'shall not prevent any member state from maintaining or introducing more stringent protective measures compatible with this Treaty'. Together with the move towards qualified majority voting on environ-mental legislation, extra pressure from relatively new member states such as Sweden and Finland should go some way towards revitalising EU environmental policy. However, there is clearly a danger on the horizon: when the EU is further enlarged to include countries from the former Communist bloc there may be pressure for the dilution of environmental initiatives in favour of economic development (see below).

A related issue is the type of pollution standard adopted in EU environmental legislation. Although there is a variety of approaches and standards available for pollution control (see Chapters 5 and 9), debate at the European level has tended to centre on two approaches often seen as mutually exclusive: emission standards and environmental quality standards. There is a widespread impression that the Commission and countries such as Germany have a particular preference for uniform emission standards, while the UK has an equal and opposite preference for setting emission standards individually in relation to environmental quality. This may be an accurate description of views expressed in the negotiations over Directive 76/464 on dangerous substances in water, but it is an inaccurate and over-simplified view of national approaches to pollution control as such. In fact, for the most part, the two approaches are not necessarily opposed. Each has arguments in its favour reflecting the best way to ensure administrative efficiency and whether it makes sense only to worry about a pollutant which is known to be actively causing harm, or to minimise emissions of anything with harmful potential even where no actual harm has or is likely to be incurred.

The argument for environmental quality standards is based on the assumption that the purpose of pollution control is for ambient pollution to remain below a certain level and therefore that it makes sense to monitor and control at the point of impact. However, it may be accepted that it is often more practicable to control and monitor nearer the point of emission. Emission standards are thus viewed as a means to the end of achieving quality objectives designed to protect identified environments, and they do not need to be any more stringent than necessary to meet those objectives. It follows from this that emission standards might therefore justifiably vary from place to place. The counter argument holds that the emission of polluting substances should be reduced as far as technically possible, even if at a particular concentration they have no known effect. This could be seen as a strict interpretation of the prin-ciples of prevention and precaution. The best place to control and monitor is taken to be the point of emission, and controls should be as stringent as possible. Uniform, fixed emission standards are taken as the best way to proceed.

Haigh points out that these contrasting views are not always made explicit and applied uniformly. In the UK, for example, air-pollution control has been based on the uniform standards view while water-pollution control has been based on achieving defined quality objectives through the setting of local emission standards (Haigh, 1989, p. 21). There may be good reasons for these different approaches: the issue becomes that of acceptable levels of emissions and the most effective and efficient means of monitoring and controlling them. Should permitted emission levels reflect the ability of the local environment to disperse or absorb the pollutant, with the corollary that what might be acceptable in one place is not necessarily acceptable elsewhere; or is it always best to insist on reducing emissions to the absolute minimum technically possible? The uniform-emissions-standards approach has the practical advantage that monitoring is relatively easy and it is easy to assess compliance; it also contains a built-in presumption of improvement in standards – the better the technology the further the reduction in emissions. Monitoring and control are more difficult where ambient environmental conditions have also to be taken into account. Emissions standards have the advantage of seeking to minimise within an overall acceptable level of emissions; but quality standards can allow flexibility according to local circumstances. For example, the UK has relatively short, fast-running rivers and is surrounded by sea. There is therefore an obvious argument against applying emission standards for water set by reference to what is necessary to protect, say, the Rhine, which drains many industrial areas and which is used as an important source of drinking water by the Germans and the Dutch. Controls can and should be applied most stringently where the environment is most vulnerable (ibid., p. 22).

The challenge for the EU is to allow member states flexibility in implementation of policy without sacrificing local environments to the mercies of those governments whose approach to the environment perhaps reflects not a considered and reasonable preference for one policy approach over another, but an indifference to environment policy and issues as such.

Contemporary issues in EU environmental policy

The fact that the EU has adopted environmental policy making as one of its main activities should not lead to complacency. There are a number of reasons for this. The first is that although the EU has moved on from its primary concern being purely economic objectives, nonetheless these objectives still constitute a major thrust of its activities and therefore there is always likely to be conflict between environmental and economic considerations. The revised Article 2 may refer to environmental considerations, but at the same time it explicitly requires a balance to be struck between economic and environmental issues and this is likely to constrain radical environmental policy making in the EU. Second, there is always going to be a problem of enforcement. There is currently no effective enforcement machinery (see case study on the EEA). The implementation of policy is largely at the mercy of individual member states and therefore subject to their willingness (or otherwise) to implement and promote environmental policy. Third, there are clashes between environmental policy and other policy areas such as agriculture and fisheries: environmental policy can be negated by other EU policy areas, not only by economic objectives. Fourth, it is not clear that EU environmental policy will always improve standards; in many cases a levelling down may be required to ensure a level economic playing field. These are all pertinent concerns for the future development of environmental policy and have already been touched on in this chapter; we will now briefly attend to three other areas which impinge on the efficacy of European environmental policy: the principle of subsidiarity and deregulation, the entry of new member states, and the impact of green parties in the European Parliament.

The impact of subsidiarity and deregulation

Maastricht put subsidiarity at the top of the European political agenda. It is a concept which is interpreted in different ways. Some member states hope to use it to curb the power of the EU itself (the UK under Conservative administrations and Denmark); others see it as a way of safeguarding the power of their regions (Germany and Spain). Again, others, such as the Netherlands, support the principle of subsidiarity because it is seen as a way of preserving their different regulatory traditions. The principle of subsidiarity was stated in the First Environmental Action Programme and later incorporated into the Treaty of Rome through the SEA. When it was first introduced it referred solely to environmental policy. Article 130r stated: 'The Community shall take action relating to the environment to the extent to which the objectives . . . can be attained better at Community level than at the level of the individual Member States.' The political and legal meaning of the principle is still a matter of dispute, despite its more general application in the TEU where the principle was extended to cover all the EU's activities. Whether it should act as a constraint on coordinated EU policy, as some member states suggest, is at the very least disputable. However, the principle of subsidiarity – sometimes expressed as 'do less but do it better' – in principle leaves the EU free to legislate principally for issues of a cross-border nature and at the same time to increase the enforcement of compliance.

In a positive environmental light, the principle of subsidiarity can be seen as lying at the heart of the green idea of appropriate scale – appropriate action at the appropriate level – which is central to sustainable development (see Chapter 2). Subsidiarity, along with increased deregulation, could lead to a flexible approach to environmental protection that is sensitive to local environmental conditions – perhaps to an increase in the effective use of market-based instruments and genuine self-regulation. Again, if subsidiarity leads to decisions being taken as close to the citizens as possible and with their increased participation, this can only be seen as positive from a green perspective.

However, sceptics see the challenge to European-level environmental policy making in a different light. If individual governments are left to their own devices, not only might this compromise the idea of a single market, but also subsidiarity (and deregulation) may become an excuse for not taking action and also raises issues of the enforcement of environmental directives. The unhappy truth is that many EU member states are unlikely to take environmental action in the absence of EU legislation, and that the concept of subsidiarity can be used as a justification for their inaction. The principle of subsidiarity can be exploited in the narrower interests of national sovereignty and the idea of deregulation can degenerate into unenforced self-regulation by industry and business. The various interpretations of subsidiarity make environmental policy vulnerable, as not only do member states legitimately differ on their interpretation, but, given their reluctance to take environmental action in the absence of EU legislation, perhaps deliberately use ambiguity as a cover for inaction (Collier, 1997, p. 3). Although the principle of subsidiarity can be used to legitimise EU environmental action on the one hand or to strengthen the role of sub-national actors on the other,[11] its effect in practice has tended to be a down-grading of environmental proposals in which a greater scope is left for national interpretations. It has led to repatriation of proposed measures and there has also been a move away from the use of directives towards weaker framework directives and recommendations.

New member states

The fourth enlargement of the EU occurred in 1995 when Sweden, Finland and Austria joined. This is generally expected to have a positive impact on the environmental policy of the EU as both Sweden and Finland have high domestic environmental standards and concerns and will now join the green lead states – The Netherlands, Germany and Denmark. Given the increasing amount of environmental policy being enacted through qualified majority voting, and the relative isolation of these lead states, the addition of the new members means that environmental policy should receive an easier passage; it also means that these countries can together form a 'blocking minority' and thereby act to prevent environmental policy being over-ridden, ignored or weakened. The new member states will also affect the type of policy instruments employed. For example, both Sweden and Finland are strong advocates of the use of economic instruments and this enthusiasm is likely to carry over into promoting a new direction in EU environmental policy.

However, what will be the effect of further enlargement? It is clear that the primary concern of Central and Eastern European countries is economic regeneration and there is a widely-held belief that they will not be able to adhere to the relatively strict European standards on environmental protection. In this they will be helped by the Cohesion Fund which allocates funds for the improvement of transport and environmental infrastructure. Equally, there is some concern that these nations could become part of a larger blocking vote which could hamper the further development of European-wide environmental policy. At present, this is simply speculation, but enlargement of the EU is a political priority and whatever else happens, this will undoubtably have some effect on environmental initiatives. One concern is not only the prospect that environmental policy might be weakened with the accession of member states whose priorities lie in rapid economic development rather than in environmental protection (here there is a significant contrast with the 1995 enlargement), but also whether the enlarged EU will lead to a widening rather than a deepening of the Union. Opinions differ, but it is by no means obvious that larger necessarily means shallower; on the contrary, decision making will have to take place mostly by qualified majority voting and this will reduce the opportunities for individual members to veto proposals. In this context it is not surprising that there has been extended discussion concerning the number of weighted votes each member will have in the Council of Ministers.

Green parties in Europe

Greens first entered the European Parliament after the 1984 European elections when 11 were elected from three member states. In the 1989 elections, 28 Greens from six different countries were elected. Following the 1994 elections the group had 22 members, by 1999 this had increased to 37 from eleven member states, including two from the UK which for the first time used proportional representation for the election. At present, Green MEPs form the Group of the Greens; this is allied with the European Free Alliance made up of other sympathetic parties and the coalition currently totals 45 members. Within the Parliament we can find a considerable body of green opinion. However, given their commitments to democratic renewal and openness in decision making, membership of the Parliament is fraught with tensions for Green MEPs: the EU itself is frequently charged with violating these basic principles. So, on the one hand, the EU allows access to influence on decision making; while on the other the institution is, in the eyes of many greens, basically flawed, characterised in their view by technocratic policy making, remote decision-making bodies and the dominance of intergovernmental influence and the politics of national self-interest.

Despite their misgivings about the democratic deficit in the EU, the Group of the Greens have now largely adopted a policy of working within the institutions. For example, Green MEPs are able to force environmental concerns on to the agenda by submitting written questions to the Council and Commission. These questions have to be answered in either written or oral form. They can also introduce new issues through 'urgency resolutions'. If the subject matter is genuinely urgent, these resolutions will receive immediate attention from committees and be directed to the Council, Commission, member state or appropriate international body. Green members have, through these means, introduced resolutions on nuclear waste and protection of the North Sea, among other issues. They are also active in arranging conferences and seminars on environmental and related concerns. Despite these successes, greens are hampered both by their own rooted objections to the structures they have to work within, and the palpable way in which those structures flagrantly violate what they see as elementary democratic and participatory principles. As Elizabeth Bomberg asks: 'how can greens achieve "green" goals through structures that are deeply implicated in the *status quo* they seek to shift?' (Bomberg, 1996, pp. 329–30).

In Bomberg's opinion, three complications exacerbate the green paradox. The first is that in the Green Group's view, the subordinate position of the Parliament highlights the democratic deficit in the EU. The European Parliament is the EU's only directly-elected body, and yet it wields the least amount of authority in a policy-making process dominated by the Commission and Council. Of course, many besides greens are concerned about the EU's democratic deficit, but most other groups do not share their radical emphasis on open democratic structures and grassroots participation. Second, policy making in the EU is technocratic, bureaucratic, and largely centralised. It is centralised because it relies on interaction between national and EU bureaucracies to formulate and enact policies. This is perhaps inevitable given the task of coordinating policy across Europe; but the result, nonetheless, appears to be an EU run by an unaccountable technocracy. Green MEPs, therefore, by comparison with MEPs from traditional parties, have to face the dilemma of pushing for decentralised politics within the often centralised structures of the EU. Third, Green MEPs face the difficulty of separation and distance from those they represent. This makes it especially problematic as they are committed to grassroots participation, the possibility of which is denied by geographical isolation and remoteness (ibid., p. 330).

Perhaps these are impossible challenges and maybe the greens, who have their own national and ideological divisions, are not yet in a position to conjure up a common view of a 'green Europe'. Despite this they have had successes and cooperated on issues such as anti-nuclear protest and biotechnology and, as Bomberg argues, 'whether or not they alter fundamentally the course of EU policies, they at least offer a refreshing critique of the EU, and raise important questions concerning European policies, practices and democracy' (ibid., p. 330).[12]

Towards sustainability? The EU's Fifth and Sixth Environmental Action Programmes

EU environmental action from 1973 to 1992 was largely prescriptive and top down. It typically consisted of the imposition of environmental legislation from the centre in response to what it perceived to be current pressing environmental concerns. The Fifth Environmental Action Programme (5EAP), covering the years 1993–2000, sought to change this. As its extended title, *Towards Sustainability – A Community programme of policy and action in relation to the environment and sustainable development* indicates, sustainable development is identified as the main objective of environmental policy. This requires 'a policy and strategy for continued economic and social development without detriment to the environment and the natural resources on the quality of which continued human activity and further development depend' (OJ, 1993, p. 18). The Sixth Environmental Action Programme (6EAP), *Environment 2010: Our Future, Our Choice* builds on this objective.

Fifth EAP

The 5EAP was adopted in 1992 and approved by a Council Resolution in 1993. It was thus adopted only a few months before the Rio Earth Summit and, moreover, it was prepared in parallel with the main Rio agreements so that it shares most of their strategic objectives and principles (Wilkinson, 1997, p. 158). The 5EAP has been chosen as the main European vehicle for the implementation of Agenda 21 and other UNCED agreements. It is important in that it marks a change of direction in EU environmental policy. Previously programmes tended to be lists of proposed legislation. The focus of the 5EAP, by contrast, is anticipatory and committed to long-term sustainability

The 5EAP also signals a move away from traditional command-and-control legislation; there is a more explicit recognition of the concept of subsidiarity, and there is a move towards de-regulation and market-based policies – using different policy instruments such as economic incentives and disincentives, taxation, and voluntary agreements with industry. In addition, an emergent key theme of the 5EAP is that of integration: the need to integrate the environment into the development and implementation of other policies. This integration is seen as a fundamental prerequisite for the achievement of sustainable development. However, this objective is hampered by the fact that the programme is not binding on EU member states nor in practice on individual DGs in the Commission.

Issues and policy sectors

The first part of the 5EAP comprises a review of the state of the European environment and an assessment of the causes of environmental degradation in a number of areas: air, water, soil, waste, quality of life, high-risk activities, and biological diversity. The second section, entitled *Towards Sustainability*, sets the objectives, policy and implementation programmes for the environment for 1993–2000. The report goes on to consider the five key sectors where integrated approaches to sustainable development are necessary. These sectors are: agriculture, energy, industry, transport, and tourism.

In addition to the target sectors there are also a number of priority issues identified in the programme. These are climate change, acidification, nature and biodiversity, water resources, the urban environment, coastal zones, and waste.

Principles and procedures

The 5EAP is based on the principle of subsidiarity and shared responsibility. It also recognises the EU's international obligations. Measures within the programme identify which level is responsible for implementation and provide target dates for implementation. Attention is also paid to enforcement. The success of the 5EAP is understood as depending on the contributions of public authorities, public and private enterprise and the general public. For example, it is estimated by the EU that some 40 per cent of the 5EAP is the implementation responsibility of local government

Table 8.1 Key sectors in the 5EAP

Sector	Policies
Agriculture	Reform of Common Agricultural Policy (CAP). Reduction of phosphate and pesticide use. Promotion of new forests. Establishment of agriculture/environment zones. Exchange of good practice between regions.
Energy	Moves to reduce energy demand and to control emissions. Use of economic instruments to ensure that the real cost of energy consumption is passed on to the consumer. Promotion of new technologies and use of renewable energy.
Industry	Implementation of strategic environmental impact assessment. Promotion of eco-audit; life-cycle analysis; BATNEEC. Introduction of eco-labelling. Promotion of self-regulation. Control of waste management. Increased public information.
Transport	Move towards sustainable mobility. Commitment to developing the Trans-European Network. Reduction of pollution and energy consumption. Promotion of integrated public transport. Reduced use of cars.
Tourism	Reconciling tourism with development. Protection of natural assets left to member states, regional and local authorities, the tourist industry and individual tourists – an application of the principles of shared responsibility and subsidiarity.

(LGMB, 1993a, p. 28). The programme goes beyond the traditional legislative approach by advocating the use of market-based measures such as charges, fiscal incentives, state aids, environmental auditing and an environmental liability regime. It also promotes the use of 'horizontal, supporting instruments' (for example, education, training, improvement of data and LIFE) which aim to increase the capacity of actors to exercise their 'shared responsibility'. In addition, environmental impact assessment is seen as necessary, not only for specific developments, but also in relation to the framing of structural policies themselves. Hence there is support for the introduction of strategic environmental assessment (see Chapter 6).

Article 130r (amended by the TEU) requires the EU to promote international cooperation in dealing with environmental problems. Accordingly, the 5EAP states that already existing international activity should be furthered and supplemented. Hence there is added legitimacy for the participation of the EU as an independent actor in international regimes. This role has been played effectively in the UNCED process and recent climate change negotiations. It could even be argued that the EU may evolve into the hegemonic international environmental actor that so many international relations theorists believe is necessary for effective regime building (see Chapter 7).

To improve policy making and implementation, the 5EAP established three 'dialogue groups'. The General Consultative Forum on the Environment (renamed the European Consultative Forum on the Environment and Sustainable Development in 1997) comprises representatives of trade and industry, trade unions, environment and consumer organisations, local and regional government. Members do not represent their organisation but speak for themselves. The Implementation Network is made up of national and Commission officials involved in implementing environmental policy and is concerned with information exchange and experience, and developing common approaches to implementation. The Environmental Policy Review Group comprises senior officials from member states and the Commission and is designed to facilitate understanding and the exchange of views on environmental policy and measures independently of specific proposals and infringement proceedings.

Towards what sort of sustainability?

Previous environmental programmes had taken the form of lists of proposed legislation, often selected in relation to specific events. This has been successful in many ways: for instance, over 200 pieces of legislation have been introduced. In comparison, the 5EAP attempts to address the fundamental causes of environmental degradation as a means of creating a more sustainable economy and society: it states that the principle of sustainable development should be incorporated into all other EU policies. However, what is clear is that its approach to sustainability is redolent of Brundtland – the rhetoric of ecological modernisation and weak sustainability is dominant (see Chapters 2 and 6). As Susan Baker argues: 'What is especially noticeable in the Fifth Action Programme is the centrality given to breaking the perception that there is a trade-off between environmental protection and economic development' (Baker, 1997, p. 97).

The Maastricht Treaty talks of sustainable progress, development and growth, using the terms interchangeably; thus, although the 5EAP contains the EU's most explicit commitment to sustainable development, it is a commitment to a weak rather than a strong conception. Why has the EU adopted such a weak view of sustainable development? The short answer is that it did so because of the context within which its environmental policies evolved and the extent to which EU policy making as a whole is incremental in character.

> Incrementalism makes the chances of successful translation of the commitment to sustainable development into actual policy dependent upon the extent to which the required policy changes can be fitted with existing policy commitments. Policy proposals that fit with the strategy of environmental quality management stand a greater chance of acceptance, while policies that fit more closely with the second, more radical, pattern have little, if any, chance of success. The concept of sustainable development has been interpreted by the Union (and its member-states) to fit within the confines of managerial as opposed to radical policy solutions.
>
> (Baker, 1997, p. 102)

However, even if the dominant understanding of sustainable development is ecological modernisation, this must be seen as progress given that the original EEC had absolutely no reference to environmental concerns. Even though it may not go far enough for many greens it may provide a critical standpoint from which to judge the continuing development of the EU. For example, the principles and policies within the 5EAP could be used to combat the tendency for member states to interpret the subsidiarity principle in a negative way and it may begin a move towards integration of environmental policy across policy sectors. However, as already noted, integration can imply a loss of control over environmental policy. No longer is it the exclusive reserve of the EDG but something which has to be encompassed by all DGs and is therefore subject to their discretion, interpretation and judgement.

DG XI's 1995 progress report on the 5EAP states that:

> The measures so far have had limited impact . . . progress has varied according to sectors, but the message of the Fifth Programme has not been sufficiently integrated in operational terms within the Commission. The process depends on persuasion and influence and will take time. In the longer term, change is likely to take place through increased education, training and changes of attitude. It will require continued adequate resources and sustained commitment.
>
> (quoted in Wilkinson, 1997, p. 164)

The achievement of sustainable development is in the balance. Much depends on interpretation of the term; on how the principles of subsidiarity and integration are interpreted and acted upon; on the activities of EDG, the European Parliament and the leadership of the Council of Ministers; and the enthusiasm and enterprise of the member states in promoting environmental policy.

When originally introduced, the 5EAP was considered to be binding neither on the Commission nor the member states, as the Council had approved only the 'general approach and strategy of the programme' and not its detailed targets and timetables. This approval was given in the form of a non-binding resolution (Wilkinson, 1997, p. 169). However, under the provisions of the Maastricht Treaty a new legal status was given to general action programmes on the environment (Article 175). This implies that future action programmes will be legally binding and also that the 5EAP will be interpreted in a stricter form than its formal status suggests. Further, the programme's promotion of sustainable development has recently been strengthened by the signing of the Treaty of Amsterdam. This contains a stronger and less equivocal commitment to sustainable development than any previous statement. In the new Article 2 it calls for 'a harmonious, balanced and sustainable development of economic activities' and the new provision in Article 6 states that 'environmental protection requirements must be integrated into the definition and implementation of Community policies and activities . . . in particular with a view to promoting sustainable development'. In a declaration attached to the Treaty, the Commission has also promised to prepare 'environmental impact assessment studies when making proposals which may have significant environmental implications'. The European Environmental Bureau (EEB), an umbrella organisation representing environmental groups in Brussels,[13] described this as 'a radical change of course after forty years of placing economic growth at the top of the EC's political priorities' (ENDS, 1997a, p. 45). There may still be scope for optimism.

Sixth EAP

The 6EAP emerged out of consultation following the publication in November 1999 of an assessment of the 5EAP, 'Europe's Environment: what directions for the future?'. This in turn was based on the EEA's major report 'Environment in the European Union at the turn of the century'. The 6EAP, entitled *Environment 2010: Our Future, Our Choice*, runs from 2001 to 2010. In many ways it built on its predecessor, continuing to pursue many of its targets. However, it is intended to go further by adopting a more strategic approach. The assessment of the 5EAP had shown that there was a deficiency in the implementation of environmental policy in the EU and a weak ownership of environmental policy by the member states. Thus there is now to be a greater emphasis on better implementation of existing environmental laws and policies. The Commission has announced that it will bring increased pressure to bear on member states by making implementation failures better known. Another theme running through the programme is that of working with business and consumers to achieve greener forms of production and consumption and, in general, greening the market. An important enabling theme is that of enhanced environmental information. One striking feature is that the 6EAP embraces the ideals of ecological modernisation (see Chapter 2). A central goal is the de-coupling of economic growth from environmental damage:

> to ensure the consumption of renewable and non-renewable resources does not exceed the carrying capacity of the environment. To achieve a de-coupling of resource use from economic growth through significantly improved resource efficiency, dematerialisation of the economy, and waste prevention.

Table 8.2 Four priority areas in the 6EAP

Area	Policies
Climate change	Ratification and implementation of the Kyoto Protocol to cut greenhouse gas emissions by 8 per cent over 1990 levels by 2008–12. This is the first step to the long-term target of a 70 per cent cut.
Nature and biodiversity	Preservation of valuable environmental areas and the protection of species and their habitats through the Natura 2000 programme. This includes a deeper and more effective integration of environment and biodiversity into agriculture, landscape, forestry and marine policies together with a new soil strategy for Europe.
Environment and health	An overhaul of the EU's system for managing risks from chemicals, in particular, a strategy for reducing risks from pesticides. Water quality will be addressed through the implementation of the water framework directive (2000).
Natural resources and waste	Increased use of recycling will be promoted and an integrated product policy to promote waste prevention introduced.

Like its predecessor, the 6EAP is also committed to extending the range of policy instruments employed, including extending the range of voluntary agreements. The current environment commissioner, Margot Wallström, is firmly committed to this approach and the 6EAP itself frequently speaks of promoting, encouraging and supporting action by business. As we saw in Chapter 5, in this ambition the EU is firmly in line with important developments in environmental policy. But this relationship with business creates suspicions. For example, recently a draft directive on environmental liability which was nine years in the making has now been watered down as a result of business pressure (ENDS, 2002a, pp. 40–1; ENDS, 2001e, pp. 42–4).

It is, of course, far too soon to make any comment on an action programme that is only at the beginning of its life. However, commentators have argued that the 6EAP tends to be stronger on rhetoric than on substance. They suggest that it is thin on specific commitments or timetables for achieving its environmental objectives, and that those objectives are themselves expressed in extremely general terms (ENDS, 2001a, pp. 46–7).

Conclusion

EU environmental policy is based on a notion of weak sustainable development; a conception of ecological modernisation. This should not be surprising. Although environmental policy now has an assured place, the origins of the EU as a community dedicated to promoting economic growth and prosperity limit the extent to which environmental policy can escape from or challenge that primary rationale. Despite the best efforts of the EDG, the tensions between its environmental concerns and the concerns of the policy makers in the Commission as a whole and in the Council of Ministers is always likely to limit its effectiveness in mounting a radical challenge to the status quo. It also means that to some extent the EU is always likely to lag behind the environmentally-committed position of some of its member states which regard its policy as weak and ineffective. But this should all be placed in a broader perspective. We have already seen in this book that it is notoriously difficult to achieve agreement and action in environmental policy: perhaps we should therefore give credit to the EU for achieving what it has. In addition, the EU's adoption of sustainable development as a policy target (whatever their own interpretation of the term) provides a criterion against which its success or failure can be judged in the future. Whichever way we look at it, a European Union originally dedicated to economic growth and prosperity has become a major source of environmental policy, commitment and concern.

But before we get complacent it is important to recognise that the task has only just really got fully under way and there is much to be done. The 1995 European Environmental Agency report on the 5EAP stated that:

> The European Union is making progress in reducing certain pressures on the environment, though this is not enough to improve the general quality of the environment and even less to progress towards sustainability. Without accelerated policies, pressures on the environment will continue to exceed

human health standards and the often limited carrying capacity of the environment.

(quoted in Collier, 1997, p. 2)

Since this judgement was made, important new legislation has been passed and the 6EAP published; further, the Commission has recently been considering proposals for a comprehensive sustainable development strategy which aims to place it at the centre of all EU policies. This strategy proposes making sustainable development a 'core concern' of all policies (ENDS, 2001c, p. 47). But the caution still holds. In a European Union now facing the new political and economic challenges of assimilating new members, developing its constitution and ensuring the success of economic and monetary union, it is more important than ever to ensure that the environmental dimension of EU policy maintains the status and importance it spent so long acquiring.

Case study: the role of the European Environment Agency

The Fourth Environmental Action Programme suggested that the Commission should set up an environmental inspectorate. This suggestion was greeted with suspicion and some hostility, principally because few member states had sound enough environmental records to relish the prospect of its being overseen by a central EU inspectorate (ENDS, 1995b, p. 20). Despite this concern, in 1990 environment ministers adopted a regulation establishing the European Environment Agency (EEA). After further political disagreements as to its location, the EEA's headquarters in Copenhagen was eventually opened in November 1994. It began its substantive work in 1995 and now has a staff of around 70 and an annual budget of 17m Euros. One important feature of the EEA is that it is open to all nations which share its objectives. It currently has 29 member countries: the 15 EU member states, Iceland, Norway and Liechtenstein (members of the European Economic Area), and 11 of the 13 countries seeking accession to the EU – Bulgaria, Cyprus, the Czech Republic, Estonia, Hungary, Latvia, Lithuania, Malta, Romania, Slovenia and the Slovak Republic. The EEA is the first EU body to take in the candidate countries; it is likely that the two remaining candidate countries, Poland and Turkey, will also join shortly.

One of the key debates in the run-up to the formation of the EEA was whether it should have the powers of an inspectorate. ECOSOC and the European Parliament argued that it should have rights of inspection and of assessing compliance with legislation. They failed to achieve this, but the Parliament was successful in forcing the inclusion of uniform assessment criteria for the collection of environmental data by all member states (Collins and Earnshaw, 1993, p. 239). In the final version of the EEA regulation, the tasks of monitoring compliance and enforcing environmental law via inspectorates were specifically not included. There were three reasons for this: first, it was viewed primarily as an information gatherer; second, the view was taken that adding an inspectorate role at the outset would be too great a burden; third, there was a concern that it would not be able to sustain the contrasting roles of mediator and enforcer (Bailey, 1997, p. 149).

Although the EEA might be said to have limited powers, it is at the same time important not to underestimate the extent to which reliable information has a vital role to play in ensuring full and uniform compliance with environmental legislation. As we saw above, some countries such as the UK suffer at the hands of the Commission simply because their environmental reporting is better than that of other member states. Hence the UK supported the formation of the EEA:

> The fledgeling EEA could improve this situation and remove the UK's vulnerability to being singled out by information-starved DG XI officials. Other EU states are likely to be revealed as more serious transgressors of Directives.
>
> (Haigh and Lanigan, 1995, p. 29)

The executive director, Señor Domingo Jiménez-Beltrán, described the EEA as forming the tip of an iceberg made up of national information networks. In his view the problem lay not in securing information as such; it lay in securing good information. Accordingly he saw his primary task as establishing the EEA as an independent source of reliable data and knowledge as to the state of the European environment.

Europe's environment

The Agency's first Report *Europe's Environment (The Dobris Assessment)* was published in 1995. This provides a base-line picture of the state of Europe's (not merely the EU) environment and the pressures on it. It highlighted twelve issues as particularly important for the attainment of sustainability: climate change; stratospheric ozone depletion; loss of biodiversity; major accidents; acidification; tropospheric ozone and other photo-chemical oxidants; management of fresh water; forest degradation; coastal zone threats and management; waste reduction and management; urban stress; and chemical risks (Osborn, 1997, p. 256). The second report, *Europe's Environment (The Second Assessment)* was published in 1998. The EEA also publishes many other reports and prepares briefing papers for Environment Council and European Council meetings. For the past few years it has been producing an annual indicator-based assessment of major environmental trends; the latest, *Environmental Signals 2002*, shows that, for example, emissions of greenhouse gases are not yet meeting targets and that the renewables share of energy consumption is showing only a slight increase.

European Environment Agency

Objective

To provide EC institutions and member states with information to enable them to take measures to protect the environment, assess the results of such measures, and ensure that the public is properly informed about the state of the environment and the pressures on it.

Key tasks

- To establish and coordinate an Environmental Information and Observation Network (EIONET).
- To provide Community institutions and member states with the information they need to frame and implement sound and effective environmental policies.

continued

- To collect and analyse data on the state of the environment and to provide uniform assessment criteria for the collection of data by member states which the Commission will use to determine compliance with EC legislation.
- To ensure environmental data are comparable and to encourage the harmonisation of monitoring methodologies.
- To ensure the broad dissemination of reliable environmental information, and in particular, publish a report on the state of Europe's environment every three years.
- To promote application of environmental forecasting techniques and preventive measures.
- To stimulate the development of methods to assess the costs of damage to the environment, prevention, protection and restoration.
- To stimulate information exchange on best available technologies.

(ENDS, 1995b, p. 22)

The first formal review of the Agency's mandate was published in 1997. This showed that it is having some difficulties in persuading national networks to deliver information (ENDS, 1997b, p. 40). In building an environmental information network, the Agency designated European Topic Centres. Each was to be a system of cooperating institutions led by a recognised national institute. The intention was to link experts in member states together (Jiménez-Beltrán, 1995, p. 267). However, of the eight planned topic centres, only those on air quality and atmospheric emissions have made a real impact. Others covering inland waters, soil quality, nature conservation, the marine and coastal environment, and land cover are just beginning to produce useful data. The waste management centre was only set up in 1997. Because the Agency was having these difficulties in its information-gathering role, the Commission decided in its review that it would be inappropriate and premature to add major new tasks to the EEA's remit at that point (ENDS, 1997b, p. 40). A recent EEA report, *Reporting on Environmental Measures: are we being effective?* (2001), showed that information gathering is still a live issue and addresses not only the comprehensiveness of the data collected on the state of the environment, but also the *type* of data the EEA has been collecting. The report asked fundamental questions concerning the extent of the influence of EU environmental legislation on member states. Nigel Haigh, in his Foreword, claimed that the report challenges both the EEA and the Commission:

It is not just a question of what information we need in order to evaluate effectiveness, or of how to do it, but also of who does it. . . . The Commission has not been systematically evaluating the effectiveness of EU legislation, and the data it has is incomplete to enable it to do so. The Agency has concentrated on collecting information about the state of the environment, and has not been encouraged to collect other relevant data such as on institutional arrangements within Member States and what they do to make the legislation work. Yet such data on 'state of action on the environment' is as necessary as that on 'state of the environment'.

(EEA, 2001, p. 4)

There is perhaps a concern on the part of the Commission that collection of this sort of data is a little too close to policy making, which is not the role of the EEA. However, Haigh's riposte to this is to emphasise that 'it cannot . . . be repeated too often that evaluating effectiveness is not the same as making new policy' (ibid., p. 4). This debate serves to show that the status and purpose of the EEA has not yet been entirely settled.

New roles for the EEA?

From its inception, there has been a debate about what the EEA's role should be. Although it was established primarily as an information-gathering agency, it is possible that at a later stage it could assume some sort of inspectorate role. Broadly speaking there are three possibilities. The first is the status quo: the EEA would remain as it is, a data-gathering and information service; the second is that it could become an 'inspectorate of the inspectorates', auditing the actions of national inspectorates such as the UK Environment Agency (see Chapter 9); the third is that it could become an inspectorate in its own right.

Could the EEA develop from being a passive recipient of information towards a stronger role in the coordination of environmental measurement and inspection in member states? Such a move would require it to have an oversight or audit function, inspecting the methods employed by national regulatory authorities (Collins and Earnshaw, 1993, p. 239). In 1995, the UK House of Lords Select Committee Report on the EEA took the view that while the work of the EEA would help by making the environmental action or inaction of member states more transparent, it would be of rather less help in securing enforcement. It concluded that an inspectorate of national inspectorates would eventually need to be formed. Such an inspectorate, in its role as auditor, would be allowed to visit a member state to take samples and to verify methods of data collection, compilation and analysis. It accepted that this was unlikely in the near future but that it should be established if patterns of persistent non-compliance are noted (Bailey, 1997, p. 150). Such a role would actively seek the cooperation of member states:

> While some analysts support the idea of an inspectorate, an inspectorate in the strict sense of the word may not be the best way to achieve compliance. Instead, the EEA could develop an inspectorate which works in conjunction with environmental ministries and enforcement bodies of the member states, thus operating in a more cooperative manner. In this way, the policies of the administrations of the member states can be used to affect implementation.
>
> (ibid.)

Could the EEA go further and become a full inspectorate? There are broadly two schools of thought here. On the one hand, the access to Europe-wide environmental information that it is developing would put it in a good position to do the job objectively; but on the other, because it is dependent on the goodwill of member states for the success of its existing projects and information gathering, it could jeopardise this relationship by becoming an inspectorate. A key issue is whether it could sustain the contrasting roles of mediator and enforcer (Bailey, 1997, p. 149; ENDS, 1995b, p. 22; Barnes and Barnes, 1999, p. 113). In addition it is often thought (as the 1997 report stated) that it is simply too soon for the Agency to extend its activities. In 1992, the House of Lords Select Committee on the European Communities proposed that an environmental inspectorate should be established if the EEA discovered that member states are failing to comply. It would require powers to make spot checks on data collected by national authorities. However, such a move is now regarded as inappropriate given the 'current political

continued

mood in the member states' concerning the powers of EU institutions and a more incremental approach is now suggested. The EEA should recommend standards for data collection, sampling and analysis, publish annual reports on compliance, and if it finds persistent non-compliance, an inspectorate with the power to make spot checks should be brought into being (ENDS, 1995d, p. 31). More recently the environment commissioner Margot Wallström, who has laid great emphasis on the issue of implementation, has warned that if national environmental enforcement agencies fail in their task, she would propose the creation of an environmental inspectorate (McCormick, 2001, p151).

Future prospects for the EEA

Clearly, discussion about the role of the EEA goes beyond the narrow remit of environmental policy itself: it touches on and reflects broader issues concerning the nature of the EU, national sovereignty and the principle of subsidiarity. For example, it is often argued that member states would not accept an EU level inspectorate because it would have the power to intervene in national monitoring and policy (Collins and Earnshaw, 1993, pp. 238–9). However, such an inspectorate within the EU would not be unique:

> A common argument against inspectorates is that the sovereignty of the member states must be respected. But in reality, various forms of inspectorate can be found in other areas of the Community, such as competition policy, agricultural policies and fisheries management. Thus, an environmental inspectorate which audits both collection methods and methods of analysis would hardly intrude further on member states' sovereignty. Nonetheless, member states are always resentful of any perceived intrusions on their sovereignty; creating an environmental inspectorate at Community level will certainly be difficult.
>
> (Bailey, 1997, p. 150)

A further set of arguments centres not so much on whether there ought to be an EU-wide inspectorate, but whether if there is to be one, should, or even could, the task be assigned to the EEA.

> The Commission might only give qualified support to the idea of the EEA taking on an audit inspectorate function. During the negotiations over the creation of the EEA the Commission was reluctant to assign monitoring or inspection functions to the EEA. Apart from the difficulty that it would have faced winning support in Council for such a development, the Commission also sought to defend its own role. It wanted to ensure that functions envisaged for the EEA were clearly distinct from, even if complementary to, its own role. The Commission emphasised that the treaties give it specific responsibilities and prerogatives for the implementation and enforcement of EC environment legislation. In view of this it is also doubtful that the Commission was in a position in any case to sanction what could amount to a transfer of power to a new body.
>
> (Collins and Earnshaw, 1993, pp. 239–40)

In May 1996, a European Parliament hearing on implementation and enforcement debated the issue of the desirability of an EU-level body to oversee the work of inspectorates. Three candidates were considered for the role: IMPEL (Network for the Implementation and Enforcement of Environmental Law – an informal network of pollution inspectorates), the EEA and the Commission. IMPEL does not consider itself ready to take on the role and MEPs were opposed to this idea as it is regarded as a secretive talking shop. The Agency itself is wary, taking the view that an inspectorate role could jeopardise relationships with member states which are crucial for obtaining information. However, the EEA could monitor member states' inspection arrangements and thus be a natural institutional location for IMPEL. The Director General of DG XI insisted that the duty of ensuring compliance lay with the Commission. But the Commission itself regarded it as premature to set up an EU inspectorate when some member states still needed to build up their own inspectorate capacity (ENDS, 1996a, pp. 44–5); many national inspectorates are still undeveloped and, with the accession of new member states, the problem is likely to become more acute.

Resolution of these debates is clearly still some way off; but, whatever the final outcome, it is worth heeding the remarks made by the chair of the European Parliament Environment Committee, Ken Collins, that 'it is increasingly clear that without a well-resourced independent inspection and enforcement agency the job will never be done effectively' (ENDS, 1996a, p. 45).

Suggestions for further reading

John McCormick *Environmental Policy in the European Union* provides an excellent and comprehensive account of this area; this is well complemented by Pamela and Ian Barnes *Environmental Policy in the European Union.* David Judge's edited collection *A Green Dimension for the European Community* (originally a special edition of *Environmental Politics*) is a valuable source on the incorporation of environmental issues within European policy. *The Politics of Sustainable Development* edited by Susan Baker and colleagues is a useful collection of essays on theoretical and practical considerations, relating EU policy to national and local actions. Philip Lowe and Stephen Ward provide an interesting analysis of the relationship between the EU and Britain in their edited collection *British Environmental Policy and Europe.* Elizabeth Bomberg considers the role of green parties in *Green Parties and Politics in the European Union.* Dorothy Gillies *A Guide to EC Environmental Law* is useful as a reference source. Articles with a EU focus can often be found in *Environmental Politics.* The monthly report from Environmental Data Services (ENDS) provides up-to-date reportage and analysis on developments in EU policy.

Useful websites

Europa: the EU online: www.europa.eu.int
European Environment Agency: www.eea.eu.int

Notes

1 In 1957, the organisation was known as the European Economic Community (EEC). In 1967, a number of European organisations merged to form the European Community (EC). When the Treaty on European Union (Maastricht Treaty) came into effect in 1993, the name changed again to the European Union (EU). In this chapter we shall use all three terms depending upon the time period referred to.

2 A new numbering system was introduced by the Treaty of Amsterdam in 1997 (which came into force in 1999). The new numbers will be used except where the old system is more appropriate to the context.

3 The five larger states appoint two commissioners each.

4 Qualified majority voting is a weighted voting system that gives larger member states a higher value vote. Thus the UK, France, Italy and Germany currently have ten votes while Luxembourg has only two. For approval, a minimum of sixty-two out of eighty-seven votes is required and therefore, although the large states are dominant, it is possible for coalitions of small states to combine block legislation. Under the Treaty of Nice (2000), the overall number of votes allocated to each state will increase and the five largest states will have a greater share. This will make it easier for the largest member states to block proposals. From 2005 a proposal will need to achieve 169 votes out of a possible 237 to be passed. This will be progressively reviewed as enlargement takes place.

5 The idea of a European bubble was not new to these negotiations. Nigel Haigh points out that agreement on the Large Combustion Plant Directive (which concerned emissions of sulphur dioxide and other contributors to acid rain) required the acceptance of different national targets within an overall 'bubble' (Haigh, 1989, p. 227).

6 For instance, there is not a single member state which has fully complied with the requirements of the Directive on Drinking Water Quality (80/778) (Krämer, 1997, p. 17). The Commission acted against the UK for non-compliance and found it to be in breach of the directive in a ruling by the ECJ in 1992; the UK was also found in breach of Directive 76/160 on Bathing Waters in 1993 (Bell, 1997, p. 91).

7 The role of the UK regions on the Committee of the Regions is likely be increased given that the Labour administration supports increased regionalisation of policy making and implementation. The most obvious practical instantiation of this is the devolution of power to a Scottish Parliament and Welsh Assembly. At present the regional institutions in England are only indirectly elected through local councils.

8 The use of statutory instruments is the most common mechanism for introducing EU legislation into UK national law. Many Acts of Parliament contain clauses which empower the minister to issue directives and regulations (statutory instruments) at a later time. Much EU environmental policy is thus enacted through delegated rather than primary legislation.

9 Ludwig Krämer of DG XI estimates that out of forty-seven pieces of environmental legislation, compliance is as low as about 25 per cent. To date, the UK and Denmark have the most impressive implementation records (Haigh and Lanigan, 1995, p. 29).

10 This mirrors the concern expressed in Chapter 7 that TNCs will often relocate production for competitive advantage in Southern nations where environmental standards are low.

11 As we shall see in Chapter 10, the UK government has tended to support subsidiarity down to the level of the nation state, but not below that level to local authorities.

12 Some of the dilemmas and difficulties faced by green parties were addressed in general terms in Chapter 3.

13 In 2000 the EEB had 130 NGO members from twenty-four countries representing 14,000 organisations (McCormick, 2001, p. 117).

National responses

> There is sufficient evidence of institutional innovation occurring in the UK to be confident that there is a cautious shift towards addressing sustainable development beyond the rhetoric. Building on this capacity so that previously neglected policy areas and interests are included in a coherent transition is the current and continuing challenge.
>
> (Voisey and O'Riordan, 1997, p. 49)

This chapter will focus on national attempts to respond to the environmental and sustainable development agendas. There are obvious differences in the policy responses of nation states and initially we will analyse some of the factors that might explain why some states have responded enthusiastically while others have been hostile to the emerging policy agendas. In comparing nations we must be alive to the different political structures, culture and policy styles and the commitment of political leaders. However, we must also recognise that nation states act within a broader context of governance. Not only should we consider relations with other levels of government, including the EU and local government, but also the role of international organisations, private corporations and other pressure groups. Nation states do not act in a vacuum. These different factors will be kept in mind when we progress to an analysis of one particular policy area, pollution control in the UK. The traditional British approach of consensual and secretive negotiations between industry and various agencies has been transformed into a much more standardised and integrated regime bearing a closer resemblance to other European traditions.

Achieving integrated pollution control is but one aspect of policy for sustainable development. At a more strategic level it is necessary to develop a coordinated strategy or plan that integrates national environmental, social and economic policy. By again focusing on the UK, which during the 1980s was ideologically opposed to economic planning, we can see just how far the green agenda has been addressed at the national level. A case study on the much praised Dutch *National Environmental Policy Plan* (NEPP) affords the opportunity to compare the fortunes of two contrasting European liberal democracies.

Factors affecting national environmental policy making

Policy making in nation states differs according to factors such as political structure, political culture and policy style. So, for example, we might expect to find differences between nations with a relatively unitary and centralised political system and those with a more federal structure. Although federal systems offer the opportunity for environmental groups to access political elites at different levels and for federal units to respond to local differences in environmental conditions, it may be more difficult to coordinate effectively environmental policy across different power centres. Again, the political culture of nation states may well affect policy making. Certain nations have a more consensual approach (or style) to policy making, with the policy process being relatively open to environmental (and other) pressure groups. The nature of the electoral system may have a significant impact here: in the UK, for example, the plurality (or first-past-the-post) system means that, typically, one party controls the executive and parliament and feels no necessity to include other parties and organisations in discussions or decision making. In nations with more proportional systems the government (probably a coalition) is more likely to adopt a consensus-orientated approach. At a deeper level, we would expect diverse national traditions of environmental management and control to affect the formulation of environmental policy. Different cultures display different attitudes to different environmental issues. It should be no surprise that the concern in North America, Australia and New Zealand over wilderness protection is not exactly replicated in more densely-populated European nations. Even within Europe itself, Germany and the Scandinavian countries display a broader conception of well-being (extending to environmental quality) in their language and practices. Again, differences between European nations over attitudes to intensive animal-farming practices vary, with the UK having a long tradition in animal welfare, whereas France, Spain and other Southern European nations appear to lack such sentiments.

As political control moves from one political party to another we would expect that both the conceptualisation and commitment to environmental issues and sustainable development will also affect the nature of environmental policy. A good example of this is the UK Conservative government's ideological opposition during the 1980s to the development of a comprehensive environmental policy, which it saw as an impediment to economic development.[1] A clear distinction can be drawn between the ideological perspective of the Thatcher government and the current Labour administration; the latter more vigorously promoting the equity aspect of sustainable development. At the same time as she was engaged in marginalising environmental concerns, Margaret Thatcher was vehemently opposed to the inclusion of pressure groups within the policy-making process. Environmental NGOs found themselves in a most inhospitable political climate. The United States suffered a similar period of ideological opposition to environmental policy in the 1980s under Ronald Reagan and then George Bush. After a more constructive phase under Bill Clinton, the administration of George W. Bush has witnessed a return to a hostile and sceptical attitude towards environmental issues. However, the Thatcher government is also a prime example of how national governments are to some extent creatures of public opinion and the issue–attention cycle. The 'greening of Thatcher' in 1989 can thus be seen as a shrewd political manoeuvre given growing public concern over the environment and the Green Party's success in the European election, rather than as a deep political rethink (McCormick, 1991, 1993).

The pioneers

In a number of studies, the Netherlands, Norway and Sweden have emerged as nation states that have been consistent 'pioneers' and innovators in environmental policy and the implementation of sustainable development (see, for example, Lafferty and Meadowcroft, 2000; Andersen and Liefferink, 1997; Jänicke and Weidner, 1997). William Lafferty and James Meadowcroft identify three general factors of recent history and political culture that have affected this supportive policy climate towards sustainable

---

continued

> development. First, all three states are highly supportive of 'international organisations, multilateral cooperation and structures of world governance'. Second, the countries 'share a relatively dominant social-democratic and/or consensual political culture, that places significant emphasis upon equity, social planning, state intervention in the pursuit of common ends, and which involves neo-corporatist or negotiated modes of decision making'. Third, 'each country has established traditions of solidarity with the poorer countries of the world, manifest most clearly in disproportionately large development-assistance budgets' (Lafferty and Meadowcroft, 2000, pp. 424–5). This active international orientation may be partially explained by the small size and relative lack of international economic and political power. From this a recognition of interdependence emerges. Such a finding is reinforced when we consider that, among high consumption nations, it is the United States that has consistently failed to engage constructively with the sustainable development agenda (Bryner, 2000).

So far, in highlighting factors affecting policy making, we have tended to treat the state as a single actor. As we argued in Chapter 4, this is an oversimplification: it is important to recognise the fact of institutional pluralism within the state itself. This is vital to a proper understanding of the fate of environmental policy and the development of a coordinated response to sustainable development. All states approach the business of governing by compartmentalising issues into discrete ministries or departments. Environment is generally one among many departments, for example, finance, foreign affairs, agriculture, transport, industry, social security, education, health, etc. The creation of environment ministries can be seen as a positive development in that it gives the environment a discernible champion in government. However, in practice there have been problems. Typically the political profile of the environment ministry is low because politicians are drawn to the higher-profile and large-spending ministries. Environment is often seen as a political backwater or a stepping-stone to 'better things' for up-and-coming ministers. Additionally the environment ministry will often deal with other issues beyond 'the environment' – as the issue–attention cycle progresses, environmental concerns may not even be at the top of the ministry's own agenda. Equally other ministries, such as agriculture, industry and most obviously finance, will be responsible for policies that directly impinge on the environment. In such a fragmented departmental context, the environment can easily become compartmentalised and marginalised and the cross-departmental working necessary for achieving sustainable development difficult to coordinate.

Taking the UK as an example: although the Department of the Environment (DOE), created in 1970, was the first cabinet-level department of its kind, its title was a misnomer in that much of its focus has historically been on local government, urban regeneration and housing policy. As Neil Carter and Philip Lowe stress:

> [T]he DOE addresses policies for planning and regional development, local government, new towns, housing, construction, inner cities, environmental protection, water, the countryside, conservation, and the management of government-owned land and property. . . . It has been estimated that only 10 per

cent of the DOE's staff actually deal with environmental issues and several of its key environmental responsibilities, e.g. for industrial pollution, water quality, and nature and landscape conservation, are discharged by separate quangos. . . . In short, environmental issues often struggle to reach the top of even the DOE's political agenda.

(Carter and Lowe, 1998, pp. 22–3)

Under Thatcher, the DOE spent much of its time and energy attempting to restructure local government, with the environment a relatively peripheral concern.

At the same time, the DOE's ability to coordinate policy on environmental issues was severely limited by the activities of other departments and agencies, for instance, the Department of Transport (DOT) tended to prioritise road construction; the Ministry of Agriculture, Fisheries and Food (MAFF) emphasised food production rather than conservation issues; and the Treasury prioritised economic growth. The rare ability of the DOE to set the political agenda typically coincided with political support from the Prime Minister. So, for example, the relatively influential environment minister, Chris Patten, was able to produce the White Paper, *This Common Inheritance* (DOE, 1990), in the wake of the 'greening of Thatcher'. In comparison, the most committed of Conservative environment ministers, John Gummer, typically found himself isolated.

The election of Labour in 1997 heralded a re-structuring of government departments, with John Prescott, the Deputy Prime Minister, heading the Department of the Environment, Transport and the Regions (DETR).[2] From a green perspective this was in principle a positive step: first, transport policy had for too long failed to address its environmental impact; and, second, the promotion of sustainable development became an objective of the DETR and the new Regional Development Agencies. However, in practice, the environment once again took a back seat as Prescott's attention became fixed on transport policy and, in particular, the future of the privatised rail industry. Following the 2001 election, a second restructuring occurred with environment becoming part of a new ministry, the Department of the Environment, Food and Rural Affairs (DEFRA). This offers an excellent opportunity for environmental considerations to be at the heart of agricultural policy after the BSE and foot-and-mouth policy disasters, although whether the broad sustainability picture will once again be lost in the rush for immediate results is an open question. Certainly the presence of an environment ministry does not, on its own, ensure coordination. We shall have more to say on this theme as the chapter progresses.

Beyond the problems created within the state by institutional pluralism, national policy making occurs within the context of multi-level governance. Thus we need to recognise the impact of, for example, international organisations, the European Union, local government and other non-governmental actors such as environmental pressure groups.

The growing number of international environmental agreements (see Chapter 7) creates a framework within which national environmental policy is formulated. Some of these agreements are legally binding, forcing a national response on issues such as carbon dioxide emission reductions or endangered species protection. The very existence of international environmental regimes structures the way that nations approach environmental policy. In a positive sense, such regimes can be understood as creating the conditions for social learning – they provide an opportunity for states to gather information about environmental problems and possible solutions. On a more negative note, this learning is often done within a limited understanding of the nature of environmental problems and sustainable development. Typically, the prevailing economic orthodoxy is left unchallenged. Obviously not all international agreements and regimes result in positive environmental and developmental actions. Particularly for many Southern nations, attempts at developing effective environmental policies have often been overridden by the requirements of the structural adjustment policies imposed by the IMF or by the more immediate demands of widespread poverty and, in extreme cases, famine and war. A further major difficulty here is that the World Trade Organisation is entitled to act against any unilateral national imposition of high environmental standards in the name of free-market international competition.

For member states, the expansion of the EU's competence into environmental policy (see Chapter 8) is perhaps the largest single influence on the direction of national environmental policy making. As the only currently existing supra-national institution with legislative powers, its influence on member states has been quite profound (Lowe and Ward, 1998). Much of the content of UK environmental legislation over the past two decades – for instance, the Wildlife and Countryside Act (1981) and the Environmental Protection Act (1990) – was predominantly the legally required national implementation of relevant EU directives. It is questionable whether some of these environmental protection laws would have ever reached the statute book without the existence of the EU. As we shall see below, the EU's influence on the emerging UK pollution-control regime has been profound and indicates the influence of more environmentally forward-thinking states such as Germany.[3]

Below the national level, the activities of local government also affect the policy process. As we shall discuss in Chapter 10, local political structures and competence vary throughout liberal democracies. The relative autonomy of local government is an important factor in environmental governance and local authorities need to be seen as agents for environmental change in their own right.

Finally, the strength and activities of national green movements is a significant factor in understanding the development of environmental policy (see Chapter 3). In certain states, environmental organisations are actively engaged in the policy process. This is certainly the case in the pioneer states such as the Netherlands, Norway and Sweden. Even where the political opportunity structure of a nation state is closed and inhospitable and national policy communities are exclusionary, the multi-level nature of environmental governance means that environmental organisations can actively affect policy through engagement at other levels. Certainly, during Thatcher's administration, characterised as it was by hostility to environmental pressure groups, many of the well-resourced organisations focused their campaigning attention on the European and international levels.

This is by no means an exhaustive account of the factors that influence national-level environmental policy making. Rather, it is an attempt to stress that it is not enough to simply analyse the substance of environmental policy alone – a variety of issues come into play and create the conditions within which environmental policy is generated and the direction of its development. It is worth bearing these types of factors in mind as the chapter progresses. Just as environmental problems cross political borders, we must recognise that the governance of the environment is not simply the responsibility of a single actor, the nation state.

Towards integrated pollution control (IPC)

> Environmental protection goes to the heart of the relationship between state and economy. . . . At the centre of these conflicting forces stand the pollution inspectorates. They have the day-to-day task of enforcing environmental legislation upon emitters and the longer-term task of evolving standards of environmental protection.
>
> (O'Riordan and Weale, 1989, pp. 277–8)

IPC: a definition

Environmental problems are by their very nature complex. It is rare for a discharge from an industrial process to impact on one medium alone, be it air, water or land; more likely the impact will to some extent affect all media. Hence, it is no real answer to deal with pollution through analysing and licensing discharges to one medium only. Such a response may lead to reductions and acceptable levels in that specific medium, but often only at the expense of increased impacts to the others. Integrated pollution control (IPC) comprehends the holistic nature of pollution episodes and seeks systems of control that take into account all impacts to all media: it aims to anticipate and prevent pollution rather than simply reacting to pollution incidents. Typically such control is stronger if a single permitting authority is responsible for all factors.

Integrated pollution control (IPC)

A system of pollution control would lack integration if:

- it is reactive rather than anticipatory in its policy making;
- it ignores problems of cross-media pollution;
- it fails to consider a sufficiently wide range of alternative solutions to problems;
- it displaces pollution across time and space;
- it fails to integrate environmental concerns with other areas of public policy.

(Weale et al., 1991, p. xiv)

In the UK, the creation of Her Majesty's Inspectorate of Pollution (HMIP) in 1987, the introduction of the Environmental Protection Act (1990) and, more recently, the establishment of the integrated Environment Agency in 1996 have all led to the UK taking a relatively large step towards the implementation of effective IPC practices. An analysis of the traditional approach to pollution control will show how both the structure and style have altered quite radically over a relatively short period of time.[4]

Traditional pollution control methods in the UK

Compared with the ideal of IPC, the organisation and structure of pollution control in Britain has traditionally been fragmented. Pollution control authorities have tended to focus on a single medium, irrespective of impacts outside their competence and jurisdiction. These authorities were built up over a period of time, often in response to contingent problems – beginning with the Alkali Inspectorate in 1863. This led to an unacceptable situation in which there was a variety of different agencies, incoherent structures and often overlapping responsibilities.[5] This not only had detrimental environmental consequences, but caused problems for industry, since it had to deal with more than one agency, some interested in specific aspects of plant operation, others only concerned with 'end-of-pipe' emission levels.

As with policy formulation affecting economic and industrial interests across all sectors of government, pollution control in the UK has tended to be 'discretionary, collaborative and secretive' (Jordan, 1993, p. 407). The norm has been close, confidential collaboration between public officials and representatives from industry resulting in 'negotiated consents' based on very loose national guidelines and the principle of best practicable methods (BPMs) to reduce or modify total wastes produced. The close relationship between regulator and regulated occurred in part because most inspectors of industrial processes have an engineering background – the same intellectual and social background as the industrialists they regulate.[6]

BPM was never adequately defined in court, in legislation or by the enforcement agencies and its vague nature suited the style of regulation. The stress on 'practicable' conformed to the discretionary style of control negotiations in that it required interpretation of a range of factors including the nature and state of the technology, the costs to the operator and wider environmental and social conditions. Without rigid standards and based on a philosophy of 'partnership' between the regulator and industry, very few prosecutions occurred. The traditional politics of pollution control in many ways mirrored the rest of British political culture, with a close and often unspecified relationship between government and its agencies and the industrial sector. As Andrew Jordan argues: 'The only way that this culture of collaboration, trusting co-operation and voluntary compliance could be sustained was on the basis of confidential dealings between regulators and the regulated' (ibid., p. 408).

Integrated pollution control in Sweden

Sweden has one of the most integrated systems of pollution control, dating back to the 1969 Environmental Protection Act. Even though its organisation might be considered highly fragmented, its success is in large part down to the Swedish corporatist political culture which takes consensus, cooperation and non-adversarial problem solving to

---

be of prime importance. Integrated pollution control was reinforced in 1999 with the introduction of the Environmental Code: framework legislation that integrated fifteen existing national environmental laws, thus promoting a more coordinated and holistic approach. There are four major institutions in the Swedish pollution-control system:

- **Ministry of Environment**: coordinates environmental policy and prepares legislation;
- **Environmental Protection Agency**: sets national guidelines and coordinates policy implementation;
- **Franchise Board for Environmental Protection**: grants licences for processes under court-like procedures;
- **Local Authorities**: 289 municipalities monitor and enforce licences.

Regulation is not based on uniform emission standards, but weighs environmental protection with economic feasibility and best available technology. Central to the Swedish system is a high level of public scrutiny and decentralisation, with the involvement of municipalities and opportunities for public participation in licensing and recourse to legal challenges. However, there have been complaints by environmental, consumer and health pressure groups that they are poorly represented on the (corporatist) boards of the EPA in comparison with industry, business and union organisations.[7]

Criticisms of traditional UK methods

This approach to pollution control in the UK was widely criticised for failing adequately to address environmental considerations in licensing procedures. Its fragmented structure led to a failure to consider the environment as a whole. For instance, in the control of atmospheric pollution there was much confusion, with agencies having overlapping powers; in other aspects of the environment there would be no control whatsoever. To add to these structural inconsistencies, the discretionary nature of control and a lack of public accountability meant that both industry and the enforcement agencies were discredited by a distrustful and ever more environmentally-aware public.

One of the earliest and most insightful systematic criticisms of the UK's traditional system was the influential Royal Commission on Environmental Pollution's (RCEP) *Fifth Report: Air Pollution Control – An Integrated Approach* published in 1976.[8] As the title of the report suggests, the Commission proposed the creation of a unified pollution inspectorate, 'able to tackle in a comprehensive manner the waste of complex industrial processes' (O'Riordan and Weale, 1989, p. 284). It made clear the need to regulate not only the effect of, for instance, air pollution, but the overall environmental impact of industrial processes. To this end, the RCEP proposed the introduction of best practicable environmental option (BPEO) to supplement BPM. BPEO was again not clearly defined and possibly the most detailed definition did not appear until over a decade later, in the RCEP's twelfth report:

A BPEO is the outcome of a systematic consultative and decision-making procedure which emphasises the protection of the environment across land, air and water. The BPEO procedure establishes, for a given set of objectives, the option that provides the most benefit or least damage to the environment as a whole, at acceptable cost, in the long as well as the short term.

(RCEP, 1988, para 2.5)

Although the Commission had proposed quite radical changes to the structure of the regulating authorities, it was reasonably supportive of the style and process of regulation, re-emphasising the important role that the consensual relationship between powerful and established interested parties – typically economic rather than environmental – played in British politics.

Vorsorgeprinzip: the German precautionary principle

Since the early 1970s, pollution control in Germany has explicitly evolved around the principle of precaution, the *Vorsorgeprinzip*.[9]

> [T]he principle of precaution is the notion that environmental policy should not be based simply upon dealing with known and certain problems, but should also be concerned with future and uncertain problems.
>
> (Weale *et al.*, 1991, p. 116)

Vorsorgeprinzip incorporates two basic ideas that refer to environmental quality and the nature of technology. First, any impact from a process should not have adverse effects on long-term environmental quality. Second, emission standards should be set at as strict a level as possible bearing in mind the current state of available technology (i.e. best available technology). The German uniform and formal technology-based approach to standard setting contrasts strongly with the British appeal to discretion and negotiation. A further general principle of German administrative law, the principle of proportionality, also has to be taken into account. This states that a balance between environmental improvement and costs is necessary. This interpretation of *Vorsorgeprinzip* formed the basis of the EU Directive on Atmospheric Emissions from Industrial Plants (84/360) where the phrase 'best available technology not entailing excessive cost' (BATNEEC) first appeared. A version of BATNEEC was to become one of the foundational principles in the development of IPC in Britain.

Her Majesty's Inspectorate of Pollution (HMIP)

Even by the standards of Whitehall, the response to the RCEP's 1976 report was slow in the extreme. After equivocating for a decade, the government announced its decision to create a unified inspectorate and in 1987 HMIP emerged. HMIP, an agency answerable to the DOE, was a merger of four inspectorates that dealt with industrial air pollution, hazardous waste, radio chemicals and water quality. There were a number of reasons for this delay that reflect the issues raised at the beginning of the chapter. In the decade following the publication of the RCEP report, environmental issues had a relatively low political priority and this coincided with the Thatcherite aversion to institutional reform and industrial regulation. At the same time, any possible momentum for change was lost as internal disputes deepened within Whitehall over the departmental location and powers of any amalgamated organisation.

In the late 1980s, however, the issue–attention cycle had moved on and the environment once again became a top political priority as public concern grew. The need for a unified inspectorate was taken up by the influential environment minister, William Waldegrave. His position was reinforced by the incompetent reaction of the existing pollution-control agencies to a radioactive discharge at Sellafield in 1983 (O'Riordan and Weale, 1989, pp. 283–4). At the same time, the UK was under pressure from the European Community to alter its enforcement practices as it wished to develop a common, Community-wide pollution-control process. However, the HMIP had to wait for the 1990 Environmental Protection Act to provide its legislative basis. It was not until April 1991, with the implementation of Part 1 of the Act, that the new agency was able to operationalise a version of IPC. Almost two decades after the RCEP's report, some of the first operators received IPC authorisations.

Environmental Protection Act (1990)

The Environmental Protection Act was Britain's legislative response to a number of EU directives, in particular Directives 84/360 (emissions from industrial plants) and 88/609 (large combustion plants). From 1 April 1991, all new or substantially-altered industrial processes required IPC authorisation – a fundamental shift in British pollution-control philosophy. A rolling programme was set up to authorise existing processes, industrial sector by sector.

A successful IPC application requires prospective operators to prove in substantial detail that the process selected meets the objectives of the Act. This requires the operator to use the best available technology not entailing excessive costs (BATNEEC)[10] to prevent, minimise or render harmless substances released and to control any releases with regard to the best practicable environmental option (BPEO), considering the environment as a whole. The operator must also comply with any relevant national or international environmental objectives. The procedure is rigorous and once an application is received it can take up to four months for a decision to be forthcoming. This time allows both statutory bodies and the public to make comments.

The Environmental Protection Act introduces a number of features that are novel to the UK. Embracing the principle of public access to information, local authorities are required to hold a register of the authorisations. Along with this, the public can comment on proposed licences and are able to take both the pollution control agency and the company to court if they believe the IPC authorisations are being ignored. The Act also introduces stricter emission standards and higher penalties for offending operators.

The programme of IPC authorisation was somewhat delayed for a number of reasons. First, the HMIP inspectors had to adapt to completely new working practices and more formal working relations with industry. There was an enormous workload with over 5,000 prescribed processes requiring IPC authorisation and few new resources or staff to fulfil the original 1996 deadline. Second, industry itself often found the exercise problematic and costly. At the beginning of the authorisation programme there was a lack of knowledge and expertise in IPC on the part of industry and many of the initial applications for authorisation were rejected because of lack of detail. Additionally, not only was there a charging system in operation for the first time, but also the stricter guidelines in some cases entail expensive new plant. Third, a number of companies appealed to the Secretary of State for the Environment who has enormous discretionary powers under the Act to determine standards, resolve disputes and decide what information is to be in the public domain – it is a common claim that too much public information on pollution standards will expose trade secrets.

For many commentators, the creation of HMIP, and the introduction of the Environmental Protection Act, were the foundation stone of an IPC system: 'For the first time there is in place a mechanism and a legal basis for looking at the impact which a process *as a whole* has on the environment *as a whole*, and for balancing the imperative of protecting the environment against the reality that the protection has a financial cost' (Slater, 1994, p. 4). Clearly there was a definite move away from traditional UK methods and towards a more integrated, formal approach. The structure of HMIP had been envisaged in the 1976 RCEP report; its style and procedures were being influenced through growing European pressures. However, the question remains: could such an arrangement be truly classified as IPC?

Two problems emerged. First, although the IPC authorisation process was intended to be more formal, actual practice witnessed a partial return to the UK's traditional regulatory style of cooperative relationship with industry. As Jim Skea and Adrian Smith argue: 'A multiplicity of factors – scant regulatory information, organisational constraints, industry opposition, and lack of political support – therefore forced HMIP to abandon its arm's length approach' (Skea and Smith, 1998, p. 274).

Second, the Environmental Protection Act did not make HMIP the sole permitting authority. The majority of more straightforward and less-polluting processes were still authorised by local authorities' environmental health officers who continued to operate a single-medium approach: their concern was only with atmospheric emissions. Of more importance though was that HMIP had little authority over discharge to water. Here the agency had to cooperate with the National Rivers Authority (NRA). The privatisation of the state water industry had exposed the UK government's poor record on pollution control and Thatcher's attempt to give the water companies a self-monitoring role was deemed illegal by the EU. The independent NRA was therefore established under the Water Act (1989). Under this legislation and the Water Resources Act (1991), the NRA was charged with safeguarding and improving the national water environment. This function was not only with reference to pollution control, but also to flood defence, regulation of rivers and ground water, protection and improvement of water stocks and promotion of water-based activities – a unique combination of pollution control, river management and conservation roles. By comparison with HMIP, the NRA exhibited a much more zealous enforcement philosophy. Certainly it achieved a larger number of prose-cutions, with the courts becoming more inclined to hand down stiffer penalties to persistent polluters. One of the largest of these was handed down to Shell (UK), which in February 1990 was fined and required to pay compensation of several million pounds for an oil spillage in the Mersey. The more arm's-length approach to pollution control was in part a result of the NRA being a completely new inspectorate and not an amalgamation with inherited practices and associations with industry. Also its focus on water quality and what is discharged into water courses meant it had little interest and specialist engineering knowledge of the processes themselves: NRA inspectors did not necessarily share the technical sympathies that HMIP often had with operators.

Although explictly mentioned within the Environmental Protection Act (1990), the concepts of BATNEEC and BPEO still require a large degree of interpretation. 'Not entailing excessive cost' is more explicit than BPM; however, it has still not been satisfactorily defined. What relative weight should be given to economic, social and environmental costs? How are they to be accounted for? As Jordan argues: 'Ultimately, the fate of many jobs, millions of pounds worth of investment and the welfare of people living in close proximity to industrial plant may ride on HMIP's interpretation of BATNEEC in any one case' (Jordan, 1993, p. 418). Again, with BPEO, which was fundamental in HMIP authorisations, similar problems can be exposed. Neither HMIP nor the RCEP developed a successful method by which the impact of emissions to different media can be balanced. The modelling required would necessarily include the carrying capacity or critical loading of the local environment, a notoriously difficult measure to determine.[11]

Overall, however, the creation of HMIP and the legislative framework of the Environmental Protection Act signalled a move towards a more formalised and open process and a certain level of transparency was instituted. Further, polluters were being charged a growing proportion of the costs of HMIP's services – although this remained far from the polluter pays principle (PPP) – and there was higher public scrutiny and possibilities for recourse through the Courts.

The Environment Act (1995) and a unified environmental agency

The Environment Act (1995) finally put in place the legislative framework for a unified Environment Agency which had been a commitment in the Conservative election manifesto of 1992. The Environment Agency and its Scottish equivalent, the Scottish Environmental Protection Agency (SEPA), came into existence in April 1996. The Agency is an amalgamation of the functions of the NRA, HMIP and local govern-ment's Waste Regulation Authorities (WRAs)[12] and is one of the largest organisations of its kind in the world, employing over 10,000 staff with a budget of around £650m a year, much of it raised from charges on industry, commerce and anglers. Simply by virtue of being one large body instead of many smaller ones, environmental protection should be improved as it will allow a comprehensive, holistic approach to the regulation of industrial pollution, making possible overall assessments about net damage to air, land and water, rather than defending just one domain. That is, its introduction finally facilitates IPC. For industry, the Environment Agency has the advantage of providing a single consistent licensing and inspection regime. As Carter and Lowe argue, the creation of the Environment Agency

> marked a significant departure not only in indicating a gathering consensus over the need for major reform, but also in breaking with a strong tradition of institutional pragmatism in Britain whereby machinery and measures were devised to address the problem to hand rather than by reference to more general principles.
>
> (Carter and Lowe, 1995, pp. 43–4)

Although there was broad agreement across a variety of interests and policy networks that a unified agency should be established, the delay in the creation of the new Environment Agency can again be traced to intense Whitehall battles over its size, structure and remit. For instance, MAFF laid a claim to a number of the operating functions of the NRA, in particular its conservation responsibilities; and the Department of Trade and Industry saw the process as an opportunity to reduce and narrow the regulatory remit of any new authority. Under pressure from NGOs, the NRA itself, and sympathetic MPs and Peers, the Act was not weakened and retained most of the existing legislative responsibilities of the amalgamating inspectorates. However, the DTI and Treasury did force through a new requirement for the Agency to carry out a cost–benefit analysis (CBA) of all its policies and practices. NGOs were joined by the RCEP and the Chairs of the Environment Agency Advisory Committee and the Panel on Sustainable Development (see below) in raising concerns that such a principle 'may expose the Agency unduly to judicial review, bog it down in bureaucracy, and stir up distracting disputes about valuation methodologies' (ENDS, 1995e, p. 2). Certainly there is no uncontroversial method of valuing many environmental costs and benefits (see Chapter 6). Further, there is some concern that any emphasis on CBA will mean that priority is given to the principle of cost-effectiveness rather than precaution or prevention.

If there is scepticism about this specification of CBA, the requirement (under the 1995 Environment Act) for the Environment Agency to concern itself with the achievement of sustainable development is an important recognition of the potential role of pollution-control agencies. Given the differing functional responsibilities of HMIP, NRA and WRAs, the statutory responsibilities of the Environment Agency are wide ranging, from an obvious role in the prevention and minimisation of pollution, the regulation of radioactive waste and improvement of water quality, through to an advisory role in the development of national and local air-quality strategies and plans and the maintenance of fish stocks. However, beyond these functions the Agency has the more holistic general duty of promoting sustainable development. The Act states: 'in discharging its functions the Agency is required so to protect or enhance the environment, taken as a whole, as to make the contribution that Ministers consider appropriate towards achieving sustainable development'.[13] Beyond its day-to-day functions, the Agency is proving to be a consistent, and at times politically controversial, champion of sustainable development.

In practice, there has been some criticism of the low number of prosecutions and the level of fines imposed. In 1999 only one company was fined over £100,000;

this was the Milford Haven Port Authority, fined £750,000. It is frequently and plausibly argued that low-level fines will not act as a deterrent to large companies. This is not actually a criticism of the Environment Agency; rather there is a widespread view that magistrates and judges need to use their discretion and push the general level of fines upwards to act as a deterrent. Although prosecution levels appear to be low, there are two reasons for this. First, there is a funding deficit: although its budget appears large, the Agency has a wide range of functions to fulfil. Second, the Agency argues that it has adopted a 'two-track approach', providing guidance to those companies it believes genuinely wish to improve their environmental performance, and prosecuting those which blatantly disregard their responsibilities.[14] This could be interpreted as a return to the previous cosy relationship with industry or, alternatively, as a pragmatic approach that attempts to steer companies in the right direction. Further, there is clearly a wish not to alienate industry unnecessarily, since if inspectors are to assess whether a company is satisfying the principles of BATNEEC and BPEO, they will need to know the level of emissions, the nature of existing pollution-abatement technology and financial information about the company. This knowledge is all in the hands of the industrial operator. So, even if the Environment Agency wished to, it could never completely regulate at arm's length. The consequence of this is that even with a radical reorientation of pollution-control methods in the last decade, the Agency has been forced to allow companies back into a closer, more participative role in setting standards – although this time without the veil of secrecy that characterised the traditional approach to pollution control.

The US Environmental Protection Agency

When the US Environmental Protection Agency (EPA) was established in 1970 (as perhaps the earliest unified pollution-control inspectorate) its mandate was based on taking a cross-media approach to regulation and enforcement. However, in terms of organisation and legislation the EPA has been unable to live up to the principles of integrated pollution control. In what may be seen as a lesson for the new UK Environment Agency, the EPA was founded on an amalgamation of existing agencies, each bringing their own traditions and styles, which it has never been able to overcome adequately. Rather than developing new integrated management structures and administrative processes, the Agency was required to enforce a new wave of legislation responding to the heightened environmental awareness of the early 1970s. The fragmented structure of the EPA was reinforced by legislation, such as the Clean Air and Water Acts, which tended to focus on specific media. As Albert Weale argues: 'Since there is less political momentum in the US for consolidating legislation than for highly visible attacks on single-issue problems, it is perhaps not surprising that the organisational capacity of the EPA is hamstrung by its legislative mandate' (Weale, 1992, p. 102).

Environmental legislation has tended to legislate for comparatively strict environmental standards, the complexity of which often overwhelm the under-resourced EPA. Along with this, a further feature of the US political system has acted against the effectiveness of the Agency, namely the culture of litigation and appeal. The implementation and enforcement of much environmental legislation has been delayed by industry appealing in the courts, to Congress or

continued

to state legislatures, against strict standards and interpretations of legislation. Finally, the success of the EPA has often been influenced to a large degree by the attitude to environmental issues of the President at any particular time. The Head of the EPA is a highly-politicised appointment and the Agency had a rough decade under the Ronald Reagan and George Bush administrations where deregulation of industry was of central concern. Given the political orientation of the current incumbent, George W. Bush, the environmentally-hostile context of the 1980s is likely to reappear.

The next step: Integrated Pollution Prevention and Control (IPPC)

Just as the process of change in the UK's methods of pollution control appeared to be coming to a conclusion with the unification of the major agencies in 1996, a further development at the EU level emerged. Based on a 1996 EU Directive, the Integrated Pollution Prevention and Control (IPPC) Act (1999) heralds a new approach to pollution control. It moves one step beyond IPC with a shift in focus away from emission standards and towards waste and pollution prevention. The objective of IPPC is to prevent or solve pollution problems rather than transferring them from one part of the environment to another.

The creation of the European IPPC regime appears to signal a more constructive relationship between the UK and EU. Rather than being seen as a laggard, out of step with other EU nations, Skea and Smith suggest that 'the UK found itself quite close to the "centre of gravity" in the IPPC negotiations' (Skea and Smith, 1998, p. 278). The UK had recently established its IPC regime and the EU drew on this experience, seconding a British pollution-control expert to help draw up the directive. At one extreme, Germany continued to argue for uniform technology-based standards (Best Available Technology), while at the other, Spain argued that such standards could be relaxed as long as ambient environmental quality was sustained. The IPPC regime represents a compromise much closer to the British procedural approach: Best Available Technique is the guiding concept, with the directive explicitly requiring consideration of economic and technical costs and local environmental conditions (ibid., pp. 274–81). The Directive legitimates site-specific discretion and greater contact between regulator and industry, thus creating a hybrid between the more pragmatic, traditional UK philosophy and a more formal objective-led European approach. However, in practice, implementation of the new IPPC regime has further stretched the Environment Agency's capabilities. The number of industrial inspections has fallen to the lowest in decades as it struggles to cope with the transition (ENDS, 2002d, p. 6).

Even though there are still criticisms from the green movement, there has definitely been a fundamental shift in the UK's approach to pollution control in the last two decades. As O'Riordan and Weale noted as early as 1989:

Prominent features of this transition include the shift in emphasis from confidential flexibility towards greater openness and information, from single-medium discharge control to multi-media waste management, from focus on end-of-pipe treatment towards a more comprehensive approach to good management practice, and from paternalism to a more structured accountability.

(O'Riordan and Weale, 1989, p. 278)

A number of factors have been at play in this process and some – although by no means all – have been touched on here. Clearly the debate in Europe and the ensuing directives have been integral in forcing Britain's hand, particularly with the EU's emphasis on the need to prevent pollution rather than taking remedial action; the enforcement of strict standards and rules; and public access to information. At the same time, domestically, there is a growing aversion to, and distrust of, state secrecy, as well as the realisation that well-being is tied up with levels of pollution and environmental quality.

Sustainable development and the nation state

Just as the traditional policy approach to pollution control was ad hoc – dealing with problems in isolation as they arose – governments have typically responded in the same manner to the emerging sustainable development agenda. The tasks of governments are subdivided into discrete departments with new bits of 'machinery of government' added as new problems arise. Thus 'the environment' is the concern of the environment ministry. However, the sustainable development discourse offers new challenges to government. First, its concerns are holistic and thus subvert departmental compartmentalisation. The recognition of the economic, social and environmental dimensions of sustainable development challenge the very structure and processes of policy making in contemporary governments. Second, the comprehensive nature of sustainable development means that an ad hoc, reactive response to individual problems is not enough. Sustainable development demands a coordinated, anticipatory and preventative approach. This has been recognised to different degrees by governments and, since the publication of the Brundtland Report, *Our Common Future* in 1987, we have witnessed the emergence of national sustainability plans and strategies, often explicitly inspired by the Brundtland Report and Agenda 21 (see Chapter 7). In this section we shall focus on the UK's developing approach to sustainability planning. This will be followed by a case study on the much lauded Dutch *National Environmental Policy Plan* (NEPP).[15]

The story of the UK's response to the challenges of sustainable development can be told with reference to three documents produced since the publication of the Brundtland Report. The first two, *This Common Inheritance* (DOE, 1990) and *Sustainable Development: The UK Strategy* (DOE, 1994b), were the product of Conservative administrations; the most recent, *A Better Quality of Life: A Strategy for Sustainable Development for the United Kingdom* (DETR, 1999), was produced by the first Labour administration for two decades.

Environmental policy prior to Rio: **This Common Inheritance**

It was not until 1990, in the wake of the 'greening of Thatcher', and over a decade after the party first took office, that a Conservative administration produced its first white paper on the environment, *This Common Inheritance* (DOE, 1990). Although it was steered through by the sustained leadership of a strong and environmentally sympathetic minister, Chris Patten, the document did little more than summarise the ad hoc policies already being undertaken in the environmental arena and included no action plan for change.

Although Patten was a strong environment minister, his personal influence and that of his department across government was limited. So, for example, his more radical ideas on economic instruments and green taxation were relegated to an Annex,[16] and his specific proposal for a carbon tax was opposed by the energy minister on the grounds that increased prices would adversely affect the forthcoming electricity privatisation, by the Treasury because it might create inflationary pressures, and by the transport ministry as it would raise the cost of road haulage and motoring. At the same time, the issue–attention cycle had moved on, environmental concern appeared to be waning as recession set in, and Thatcher's contingent support for environmental issues became increasingly apparent. As a consummate politician she had tapped into the wave of public concern on such issues as pollution, but her true interest lay in short-term economic issues such as inflation, and with the reduction of industrial regulation and promotion of privatisation. Again, the Conservative administration showed itself to be closer to the established interests of the business and industrial lobby than to the environmental movement.

One of the few 'new' and potentially important initiatives that emerged from *This Common Inheritance* was the introduction of two structural changes to the machinery of government aimed at developing a more coordinated approach to environmental issues across Whitehall: the creation of 'green ministers' in each department to take responsibility for environmental issues in their area of competence and the formation of a cabinet-level environment committee. However, the lack of transparency within Whitehall meant that it was difficult to judge the effectiveness of these changes. The suspicion that the green ministers were having little impact on decision making was confirmed when it was revealed that the ministers had met only seven times in the five years from 1992 to 1996 (ENDS, 1996e, p. 24). Similarly, the details of the frequency, agenda or outcomes of the cabinet committee meetings were deemed not for public consumption. Regardless of their effectiveness at the time, the establishment of new machinery of government was important in that mechanisms were in place through which environmental issues could be debated. Also, on a more informal level, the very process of developing the strategy drew in civil servants from across Whitehall and thus saw the emergence of a sustainable development policy network that stretched into local government, prominent NGOs and industry (Young, 2000, p. 248). Overall, though, the final form of *This Common Inheritance* and its yearly updates exposed the lack of understanding of the challenging nature of environmental problems among the majority of civil servants and ministers in Whitehall and further exposed the entrenched interests and strengths of established departments. This context was far from ideal for dealing with the challenges that emerged in the form of Agenda 21 at the Rio Earth Summit.

Post-Rio: The UK Strategy

Between the publication of *This Common Inheritance* and the Rio Earth Summit, Thatcher had been replaced as Prime Minister by the more pragmatic John Major. He was active in his support for the Rio process and shortly after his return from the Summit he made a commitment to publish a national plan to implement Agenda 21 by the end of 1993. He was also instrumental in persuading other G7 and EU countries to follow suit in order that the United Nations Commission on Sustainable Development (CSD) would be able to fulfil its functions (see Chapter 7).[17] On 25 January 1994, the UK government formally responded to the agreements signed at UNCED, publishing four white papers on sustainable development, climate change, biodiversity and sustainable forestry. Of central concern here is *Sustainable Development: The UK Strategy*, the government's direct response to Agenda 21.

Throughout 1993, the government undertook an impressive consultation exercise inside and outside Whitehall, inviting agencies, local authorities, NGOs, businesses, individuals and any other interested parties to comment on a wide-ranging consultative paper (DOE, 1993b). The strategy that eventually appeared considered sustainable development over a twenty-year period, providing a review of the state of the UK environment, an analysis of the potential contribution of the different sectors of the economy, potential trends and problems, and the various actors and instruments that could promote sustainable development. Although more comprehensive in its approach than *This Common Inheritance*, the strategy was widely criticised for lacking any strong commitment to new policies, objectives and targets for the problems it highlighted. It was argued that without such targets progress towards sustainable development could not be measured. The document hardly deserved the title 'strategy' at all. Beyond the lack of targets, the strategy was also criticised for having a limited understanding of sustainable development. Although policy-making principles such as the polluter pays principle and the precautionary principle were highlighted, the broad understanding of sustainable development was very much 'environment-focused'. Its sectoral analysis of the economy took into account environmental impacts, but had next to nothing to say about questions of social justice.

The sectoral approach did however highlight evidence of the growing relative strength of the DOE and the influence of the sustainable development policy network: the principle of demand management in areas such as energy, water, minerals and transport was accepted. This had been the cause of bitter inter-departmental conflict and can be seen as an integral part of the pressure that was developing in the DOT to rethink its demand-led policy on road building and private and commercial road transport.[18] The strategy sets out starkly the consequences for sustainable development if increased traffic generation and road building is not tackled, despite the DOT's attempt to edit this out.

Where the DOE still clearly lacked influence however was in relation to the Treasury. The sectoral approach meant that the broad macro-economic and fiscal policy of the Treasury was not directly considered. This was either a terrible oversight or, more likely, an acknowledgement of the Treasury's power and influence. The House of Lords Select Committee on Sustainable Development, set up in March 1994, called the Treasury to account for their apparent lack of interest in sustainable development. This, it seems, was 'the first occasion on which the Treasury had sent a team to defend its contribution to environmental protection before a parliamentary committee' (ENDS, 1995c, p. 29) – a telling fact in its own right. Its response showed that action on developing new fiscal policies to protect the environment had been almost negligible, because it took the view that such policy should be developed by the DOE. This ran firmly against the supposed cross-departmental nature of the strategy, exposed the lack of understanding and interest from the Treasury (the strongest of all Whitehall departments), and highlighted the enormous task ahead of the green movement if it is to persuade the UK government to adopt coordinated policies across all sectors of the economy and wider society.

In an interesting development, the strategy again introduced new machinery of government, this time external to Whitehall. Two new advisory bodies were created – the British Government Panel on Sustainable Development and the UK Round Table on Sustainable Development – and a citizens' environmental awareness initiative (*Going for Green*) was launched. The Panel comprised a group of five prominent and highly-experienced individuals, appointed by the Prime Minister, whose role was to provide authoritative and independent advice on strategic issues and priorities for attaining sustainable development. Its convenor, Sir Crispin Tickell, had already publicly intervened in the debate surrounding the remit of the recently formed Environment Agency and the Panel included two members of the Royal Commission on Environmental Pollution. The Panel's yearly reports contain detailed work and submissions in areas where it contends that the government lacks a coordinated approach, including: environmental pricing and economic instruments; environmental education; depletion of fish stocks; ozone depletion; reform of the Common Agricultural Policy; environmental accounting; biotechnology; and disposal of radioactive waste. In agreement with the critics of *The UK Strategy*, the Panel's first report recommended a more strategic and comprehensive approach, arguing that 'the Government should give higher priority to its environmental objectives and targets and how it intends to meet them' (British Government Panel on Sustainable Development, 1995, p. 11). The Panel endorsed the use of economic instruments and argued for a radical shift in taxation policy away from labour and capital and onto pollution and resource use.

The Round Table embodied a 'stakeholder' philosophy, attempting to include the most significant organisations in the sustainable development debate from all sectors – an approach promoted within Agenda 21 (see Chapter 7). This included representatives of central and local government, the business and industrial sector, voluntary groups and the scientific and academic community.[19] The stakeholder structure was seen as important in order

> to encourage discussion on major issues of sustainable development between people who approach them from different positions and who have different responsibilities. Members will be able to compare notes on what is being done in different sectors, to develop a better understanding of the problems faced by others, and to see how far a common perspective might be developed on various issues.
>
> (DOE, 1994b, p. 235)

Consensus on difficult issues was seen as the goal.[20] The Round Table produced a large number of reports and an annual summary, some of which attracted significant short-term media and government attention, although its status within broader policy-making processes remained ambiguous. At times the Round Table was openly critical of government responses to its work.[21]

Although *The UK Strategy* has been rightly criticised as lacking any vision, inspiration and long-term objectives, set against this was the deeper thinking about sustainable development that the process of preparation provoked across Whitehall. This may seem only a small advance but its significance should not be overlooked – for instance, it helped provoke a rethink in transport policy and forced civil servants and ministers to consider environment and development issues. At the same time, the process increased the standing and influence of the DOE. The creation of bodies such as the new Panel on Sustainable Development and Round Table could only help strengthen its emerging powerbase.

The yearly updates of the strategy turned out to be low-key events and added little to existing policies and practices. However, one or two interesting developments, important in the process of embedding a more fully-integrated approach to sustainable development, emerged towards the end of the Conservative administration. As we have already seen, the creation of the unified Environment Agency in 1996 ensures a powerful voice for environmental protection: the promotion of sustainable development is seen as one of its fundamental objectives. In the same year, the government published *Indicators of Sustainable Development for the United Kingdom* (DOE, 1996b) which contained 118 indicators of resource use, pollution levels, species and habitats, human health and the like. This preliminary report was broadly welcomed by the environmental movement although the sheer number of indicators meant that it was difficult to get a clear sense of current conditions. The last Conservative Secretary of State, John Gummer, proved a vociferous champion of environment and sustainable development issues, but was in reality marginalised within a government that had little interest in that agenda.

New Labour: new (sustainable development) agenda?

When Labour returned to power in 1997 there was renewed hope that the sustainable development agenda would be embraced by government. In opposition, the Labour Party's policy document *In Trust for Tomorrow* (1994) had been well received by environmental organisations and a number of senior figures within the Labour administration, such as Robin Cook and Chris Smith, were known to have strong pro-environment views. Within months of winning the election, the Prime Minister, Tony Blair, had given widely publicised pro-environment speeches at both the UNGASS Rio+5 and G7 meetings, challenging the USA to take the Kyoto climate process more seriously and offering support for the Local Agenda 21 initiative (see Chapter 10). Again, his Deputy Prime Minister, John Prescott, was widely praised for his determined approach at the Kyoto negotiations.

The Labour administration lost no time in reforming and restructuring the machinery of government. Most obviously Blair created a new 'superministry', the Department of the Environment, Transport and the Regions (DETR) under the control of Prescott. At the core of its aims was the promotion of sustainable development and ensuring that environmental considerations were at the heart of transport and regional and local government decision making. Environmental groups were supportive of the reorganisation and Prescott's desire to create an integrated transport system. Under the 'Greening Government Initiative', the Cabinet Committee on the Environment (ENV) and the Green Ministers network were relaunched, and the DETR created the Sustainable Development Unit (SDU) with the objective of overseeing implementation of sustainable development across government. At the parliamentary level, a select committee, the House of Commons Environmental Audit Committee (EAC), was established with the primary purpose of monitoring and auditing the extent to which government departments and agencies contribute to sustainable development. The Treasury began to take more interest in the idea of environmental taxation and the DETR was able to exert enough pressure for the Treasury to accept that future congestion charges on motor vehicles could be hypothecated and ploughed back into public transport initiatives. The environmental agenda appeared to be on the rise and within the first year of the administration the DETR had produced a guidance document for policy making in departments *Policy Appraisal and the Environment* (DETR, 1998d). The DETR further developed the Conservative administration's work on indicators and began a widespread consultation exercise both within and outside Whitehall to revise the previous government's sustainable development strategy.

A Better Quality of Life: A Strategy for Sustainable Development for the United Kingdom emerged in 1999. The most obvious differences with preceding documents lay in the wider interpretation of sustainable development. Whereas the Conservatives typically concentrated on the environment alone, Labour's objectives also included a commitment to social justice, a commitment more acceptable to a centre-left party. The objectives thus combine economic, social and environmental considerations:

- social progress which recognises the needs of everyone;
- effective protection of the environment;
- prudent use of natural resources;
- maintenance of high and stable levels of economic growth and employment.

(DETR, 1999, p. 8)

These objectives are to be integrated into government policy by taking into account ten guiding principles:

- putting people at the centre;
- taking a long-term perspective;
- taking account of costs and benefits;
- creating an open and supportive economic system;
- combating poverty and social exclusion;
- respecting environmental limits;
- the precautionary principle;
- using scientific knowledge;

- transparency, information, participation and access to justice;
- making the polluter pay.

(DETR, 1999, pp. 22–3)

A number of these principles are familiar within the environmental policy literature (see Chapter 4), and it is again clear that the conception of sustainable development is broad, reflecting key themes in the *Rio Declaration on Environment and Development*. However, it is far from obvious which principles are to take priority where there are conflicts; this is an important consideration as there will not always be a comfortable synergy between economic, social and environmental objectives.

The strongest feature of the strategy is arguably the manner in which objectives, priorities and guiding principles are laid out and related to headline quality of life indicators. Again, a broad notion of sustainable development is embraced: the UK's sustainable development priorities not only include economic development and obvious environmental concerns such as transport, agriculture and wildlife, energy efficiency and waste, but also clear commitments to reducing the level of social exclusion, refocusing urban regeneration and an activist international orientation. The importance of the social (justice) dimension of sustainable development is further reinforced in chapters solely devoted to the themes of building sustainable communities and international cooperation and development.

Headline indicators

- total output of the economy (GDP)
- investment in public, business and private assets
- proportion of people of working age who are in work
- qualifications at age 19
- expected years of healthy life
- homes judged unfit to live in
- level of crime
- emissions of greenhouse gases

- days when air pollution is moderate or high
- road traffic
- rivers of good or fair quality
- populations of wild birds
- new homes built on previously developed land
- waste arisings and management
- satisfaction with quality of life (to be developed)

(DETR, 1999, p. 21)

The strategy also re-affirmed the importance of the structural changes to the machinery of government introduced in the first two years of the administration (see above) and announced that the British Government Panel on Sustainable Development and the UK Round Table on Sustainable Development would be merged into the UK Sustainable Development Commission (SDC), again drawing its membership from a range of backgrounds. Jonathan Porritt, the well-known environmentalist, was announced as the first chair of the Commission. In what may prove to be an important development, the SDC is sponsored by the Cabinet Office and reports to the Prime Minister and the First Minister or Secretary of the three devolved assemblies. Direct sponsorship of the Commission by the core executive may prove significant in moving sustainable development to the mainstream of government. The strategy also relaunched the environmental awareness campaign under the title *Are You Doing Your Bit?*, involving celebrities in an attempt to raise the consciousness of citizens.

The environmental machinery of government

Institutional apparatus includes:

- Department of the Environment, Transport and the Regions (DETR), reorganised in 2001 into the Department of the Environment, Food and Rural Affairs (DEFRA)
- Cabinet Committee on the Environment (ENV)
- Green Ministers network
- House of Commons Environmental Audit Committee
- Environment Agency
- Sustainable Development Commission
- Royal Commission on Environmental Pollution
- *Are you Doing Your Bit?* environmental information campaign

Policy appraisal tools include:

- Departmental strategies for improving environmental performance
- Policy guidance *Policy Appraisal and the Environment*
- Integrated system of impact assessment promised in *Modernising Government* (March 1999)
- Headline quality of life indicators

Although the strategy included clear objectives, policy principles and indicators and a number of broad commitments, it was still criticised for lacking detailed targets and deadlines – no detailed action plan for change emerged. The strategy was seen as good on rhetoric, but poor on specific timetables. However, environmental organisations will be able to use the headline quality of life indicators to challenge the government: these should present a clear scorecard showing where performance and practice is poor.

The other main criticism was that the strategy (like its predecessor) was very quickly forgotten and its annual progress reports have had little political impact (DETR, 2001; DEFRA, 2002). Within months Labour was faced with a series of policy problems that had clear implications for sustainable development. These included challenges to the government's policy on the trial planting of genetically-modified organisms (GMOs), its much vaunted integrated transport policy and the industrial energy tax. The administration appeared completely wrong-footed by the public outcry on GMOs, initially siding with agri-chemical corporations, misunderstanding public perceptions of risk and ignoring the precautionary principle. In relation to transport, electoral sensitivities meant that the emerging policy failed to tackle effectively the ever-increasing levels of car ownership and usage. Finally, the industrial energy tax was watered down as the Department of Trade and Industry and sectional industrial interest groups put pressure on the Treasury. Electoral concerns and the interests of established industrial pressure groups took precedence over many of the principles laid out in the sustainable development strategy.

Problems also began to emerge with some of the reforms of the environmental machinery of government. On a day-to-day basis Prescott was preoccupied with transport and the modernisation of local government. Although widely respected by the environmental movement, the environment minister, Michael Meacher, was not a cabinet-level appointment. It was thus felt that the environment had no consistent and effective voice in core government decision-making forums. In many ways this may help explain the lack of environmental sensitivity in the handling of, for example, the GMO fiasco. Again, the effectiveness of other institutional changes was also questioned. The House of Commons Environmental Audit Committee quickly found that it could not fulfil its scrutiny function without improved resourcing – just as the work of the Public Accounts Select Committee is supported by the National Audit Office, an equivalent environmental auditing office is needed for the EAC (Ross, 2000; EAC, 2001). The EAC itself was critical of both the Cabinet Committee on the Environment (ENV) and the green ministers. The former had failed to provide leadership and remained shrouded in secrecy (a criticism of its predecessor under the Conservatives); the latter comprised only junior ministers who had little political influence and who had to balance their environmental commitments with their own departmental obligations. The impact of the Greening Government Initiative was widely seen as disappointing, reflected in the fact that few policy appraisals were taking place outside the DETR (ENDS, 1999, 2000). The discourse of sustainable development had clearly not caught the imagination of Blair: whereas policy priorities such as social exclusion were embodied in the form of special units within the Cabinet Office itself (for example, the Social Exclusion Unit), the Sustainable Development Unit remained within the DETR, marginalised from the core executive. The Labour government has developed some potentially significant mechanisms for internalising and coordinating environmental concerns within decision making; however, sufficient resources and sustained high-level support from the Prime Minister are still lacking.

Michael Jacobs has offered an interesting assessment of why New Labour, and Blair in particular, has failed to fully embrace the sustainable development agenda. The lack of environmental sensibility is perhaps a surprise given that Anthony Giddens (a close advisor to Tony Blair) views the environment and ecological risk as a key element of 'third way' philosophy (Giddens, 1998, pp. 54–64)[22] and the emerging ecological modernisation discourse (see Chapter 2) in many ways chimes with Blair's modernisation zeal. However, Jacobs argues that New Labour remains fundamentally suspicious of environmentalism because it understands green concerns as 'basically anti-modern, a worldview fundamentally uncomfortable with the thrust of change in contemporary societies' (Jacobs, 1999b, p. 10). Greens are taken to be a sectional interest that is anti-aspirational, anti-poor and would add to the 'burdens of business'. In contrast, Jacobs argues that the New Labour government could easily embrace what he terms 'environmental modernisation' within its existing philosophical worldview. Such a worldview stresses the need for higher environmental productivity; quality of life based on more environmentally-benign consumption; risk management; the need to challenge environmental exclusion and injustice; and a central role for science and technology in policy making. In contrast to the 'gloom and doom' discourse of radical ecologism, environmental (or ecological) modernisation 'sees the future as essentially optimistic, and environmental problems as solvable' (Jacobs, 1999b, p. 29).

In many ways Blair seems to have picked up this particular line of argument with his more recent set-piece speeches in 2000 and 2001 addressing environmental issues within a broader modernisation framework.[23] Again, he has committed himself to attending the Rio+10 Conference in South Africa in 2002. The timing of Blair's return to environmental issues so close to a general election raised some suggestions that this was pure electoral pragmatism; others have suggested that, faced with policy disasters such as GMOs, public transport and foot-and-mouth disease, he has recognised the salience of coordinated environmental governance. Certainly the agriculture policy network was shaken when, after Labour's return to office in 2001, the DETR was reorganised and environmental responsibilities were transferred into a new Department of the Environment, Food and Rural Affairs (DEFRA). The effect of this restructuring is difficult to judge. From a positive perspective, it is a recognition that a sustainable agricultural policy is needed; one where environmental concerns are as important as producer interests. However, there is some disquiet among many environmentalists. The creation of DEFRA is seen as knee-jerk reaction to the agricultural crisis. In the long term the reorganisation may well damage environmental governance – the DETR was a prestige ministry which offered meaningful opportunities to integrate environmental concerns into transport, regional and local government and land-use planning policy. Rather than being secure in the heart of government, the environment is being moved around Whitehall like a hot potato. The danger is that the environment and sustainable development become further marginalised.

Conclusion

In this chapter we have focused primarily on the practice and policies of the UK government, although in the case study that follows we shall turn our attention to the Netherlands. Over the last two decades or so, the UK government has often been castigated for not giving enough attention to issues such as environmental protection and sustainable development. In many ways this is not surprising given the dominant ideological outlook of the Conservative administrations between 1979 and 1997. But even in such a hostile political environment, it must be acknowledged that there were significant advances made on the environmental front: our discussions of pollution control and sustainable development planning bear this out. It may have taken many years for the unified Environment Agency to be established, but it is now in place and operates a control regime which is a long way from the (much criticised) traditional, secretive approach. And it was a Conservative administration that published the UK's first sustainable development strategy. The election of a Labour administration in 1997 paved the way for a more comprehensive strategy and the strengthening of the environmental machinery of government, although the long-term impact of the recent reorganisation of Whitehall departments is far from clear.

A number of important insights have emerged from the foregoing analysis of pollution control and sustainable development strategies. The first of these is the recognition that nation states do not operate in isolation. Multi-level governance is a reality. So, for example, much of the regulatory regime for pollution control emerges at a European level; the Brundtland Commission and the Rio Earth Summit set the tone for the progression of the sustainable development agenda at national level. And successful governance entails engagement with actors beyond government: the Environment Agency has a level of discretion and independence from Whitehall and must develop effective relations with the industries it regulates; the Sustainable Development Commission draws its membership from all sectors, including business and environmental pressure groups. Governments must learn to operate in a complex political environment. Second, it should be recognised that, given the complex policy-making context, coordination is vital. The establishment of the Environment Agency as the single pollution-control authority tasked with regulating pollution across all media was a large step forward from the traditional, fragmented and ad hoc approach to environmental problems. The significance of the environmental machinery of government must be recognised. In an attempt to internalise environmental concerns across Whitehall, the government has established a series of different mechanisms, including the Cabinet Committee on the Environment, the Green Ministers network, the Environmental Audit Committee and the Sustainable Development Commission and policy-appraisal procedures. The importance of establishing such machinery is that even when sustainable development is not high on the political and public agenda, mechanisms are in place for raising environmental concerns. However, even with improved coordination within Whitehall, between different levels of government and across different sectors, one lesson is clear from our analysis: sustained political leadership is a key element in the progression of the sustainable development agenda. It is also clear that although some progress has occurred, at present the challenge of environmental protection and sustainable development has yet to sufficiently capture the political imagination of either political elites or the public.

Case study: the Dutch *National Environmental Policy Plan: to choose or to lose?*

The Dutch *National Environmental Policy Plan* (NEPP) is frequently held up as by far the most impressive attempt to date to plan *nationally* for sustainable development. Certainly, the Dutch government responded with apparent urgency to the 1987 Brundtland Report, *Our Common Future* (see Chapter 7), with the NEPP being presented to the Second Chamber of the States General as early as May 1989. Obligations to future generations were taken seriously, with a commitment to achieve environmental sustainability within a single generation. A major factor here was the publication of *Concern for Tomorrow* by the National Institute of Public Health and Environmental Protection which raised public awareness of the limitations of existing environmental measures. The Ministry of Housing, Physical Planning and Environment (VROM) was able to take advantage of the high levels of environmental consciousness among both the public and elites, drawing other government departments into the development of a comprehensive sustainable development strategy. The Dutch government has a strong tradition of planning; prior to the NEPP, beginning in 1984, a series of *Indicative Multi-Year Plans* had been brought forward that attempted to coordinate environmental regulation and policy. By

continued

comparison, the UK does not share the same level of enthusiasm for detailed planning. The NEPP is much more detailed and systematic than its UK equivalents, although interestingly it suffers from similar problems, including a lack of attention to implementation strategies and policy instruments.

There are at least two areas in particular that illustrate why the NEPP has been seen by many as ground-breaking. The first is its comprehensive and detailed analysis of environmental problems and how they might be managed. The second is the detailed costing of alternative environmental policy scenarios and the defence of a relatively vigorous vision of the measures necessary to move towards a sustainable future.

Understanding sustainable development

The NEPP contains perhaps the most sophisticated analysis of sustainable development within a national strategy. It recognises the differences in scale – local to global – of environmental problems as well as their multiple sources. The interconnected nature of environmental, social and economic factors is fully appreciated, and so too is the inconsistent nature of previous responses to environmental problems in which impacts were too often treated in an isolated fashion. Such treatment of environmental problems was seriously misguided as displacement could lead to even more deleterious effects in some other part of the environmental–social system. Commenting on the NEPP, Albert Weale states:

> The natural and social worlds are seen as a large, complex, interlinked system in which disturbance at one point can cause malfunction at another. To the extent to which we can understand the system we should seek to rectify the malfunctioning not at the point of effects but at sources. This means modifying or eliminating the human activities that are responsible ultimately, as sources, for environmental degradation.
>
> (Weale, 1992, p. 128)

Action needs to focus on the initial cause of problems – the objective of policy ought to be preventative rather than reactive. *Source-orientated* rather than *effect-orientated* measures must be given preference.

The NEPP's case for source-orientated measures

Source-orientated measures are to be preferred to effect-orientated ones because the possibility of control is greatest at the source; one source may cause more than one effect; uncertainties about the cause–effect chain can exist; irreversible effects can occur; and it generally costs less to intervene at the source.

Source-orientated measures can be divided into:

- emission-orientated measures: add-on technology which reduces emissions and waste streams without changing the processes of production and consumption;
- volume-orientated measures: legal and organisational measures which reduce the volumes of raw materials and products without changing production and consumption processes as such;

- structure-orientated measures: structural changes of a technological or other nature which change the processes of production. (Structural measures will also result in changes in volumes and emissions.)

Effect-orientated measures are only taken if:

- environmental quality has already been damaged by past developments or calamities, but the effects can still be mitigated;
- there are prospects for structure-orientated measures, but they cannot be taken at short notice;
- effect-orientated measures have significantly lower social costs and do not impede structural measures for other environmental problems.

(Ministry of Housing *et al.*, 1989, p. 13)

Possible scenarios and a vision for change

As well as promoting a widely-respected, sophisticated theoretical analysis of the concept of sustainable development, the NEPP also provides a long, detailed list of policies and actions that need to be taken within the planning period 1990–4 if a sustainable future is to be achieved within twenty years. These measures were chosen from an analysis of the environmental and economic impacts of three policy scenarios.

NEPP scenarios

I   a package of measures reflecting the continuation of current policy;
II a package of measures reflecting maximum utilisation of currently-known emission-orientated measures;
III a package of measures reflecting a mix of emission-orientated and structural source-orientated measures such as:

- extended energy conservation in the household and business sector;
- shifts from private car use to public transport;
- more efficient use of minerals in agriculture;
- recovery of raw materials from waste streams;
- large-scale application of process-integrated clean technology.

(ibid., p. 19)

The three scenarios were then compared with the necessary emissions reductions the Netherlands needs in order to achieve sustainable development. These reductions are extremely strict with, for instance, emissions of sulphur dioxide, nitrogen oxides, ammonia, hydrocarbons, discharges to the Rhine and North Sea, waste dumping, noise and odour all required to be

continued

decreased by somewhere between 70 and 90 per cent. It is made clear that Scenario I cannot achieve such reductions. In Scenario II, an ever-increasing investment and share of GNP would be required to achieve ever-smaller environmental gains. Further, this emission-orientated approach can never lead to the required emission reductions. Such an end-goal requires much more radical policies, including structural changes. The measures outlined in Scenario III do achieve the required reductions in some areas, in others they come close. Interestingly, the calculations drawn up by the Central Planning Bureau 'demonstrate that even severe measures and strict norms will not have a significant effect on macro-economic variables' (Straaten, 1992, p. 58) – the economic case against the radical policies needed to achieve sustainable development appear not to hold. In the light of these results the NEPP argues for a gradual transition from the second to the third scenario – 'the reason for this choice is that Scenario III requires major technological and social adjustments which will take time to realise' (Ministry of Housing *et al.*, 1990, p. 15).

Problems of implementation

Although the NEPP offered a comprehensive analysis of the policy requirements for sustainable development, it faced a number of problems in its implementation. We shall briefly discuss three issues: leadership; policy instruments; and cooperation.

Despite being co-presented by the Ministers of Economic Affairs, Agriculture and Fisheries, and Transport and Public Works, the NEPP was driven mainly by the strong leadership of the Minister of Housing, Physical Planning and Environment, E.H.T.M. Nijpels, with the support of the Dutch Prime Minister. Nijpels was able to keep control of the emission-reduction targets and thus the radical nature of the plan was secured. However, the right-wing Liberal Party, a minority member of the Christian Democrat-led coalition government, was not prepared to support a number of the financial measures that the NEPP sought to impose, in particular abolishing tax-reductions for commuters and tax increases for home-owners – the constituency of its core supporters. The Liberals forced an election (perhaps the first time that a government has fallen over an environmental policy?) but had mistaken the mood of the electorate and the Christian Democrats were able to form a new governing coalition with the Social Democrats. Although this coalition supported strong policy planning, Nijpels's leadership of the NEPP was lost as, being a Liberal, he lost office.

Even with its radical vision, the NEPP tended to be rather conservative in relation to policy instruments. In particular, its proposed use of economic instruments was somewhat limited. It appears that (as in the UK) the Ministry of Economic Affairs and Finance was not prepared to sanction their widespread use. As well as the Ministry's concern as to their effect on the economy, many within the business and industrial sector proved vociferous opponents of their introduction (Straaten, 1992, pp. 66–7; Bressers and Plettenburg, 1997, p. 115). A large number of the responses to the NEPP, particularly from NGOs, saw this political marginalisation of economic instruments as its major weakness (Ministry of Housing *et al.*, 1990, pp. 54–73).

Where the NEPP had been applauded for focusing policy implementation on different 'target groups', such as agriculture, industry and refineries, traffic and transport, etc., it was also criticised for failing to engage with other levels of government and non-governmental groups in the *formulation* of policy. Provinces and municipalities complained that the process was too 'top-down': targets and timetables had been set at a national level; collaboration was only promoted in relation to *implementation* (van Muijen, 2000, p. 154). Resistance from the provinces and municipalities emerged as local authorities found themselves presented with strict requirements from central government. Although an emphasis was placed on the necessity of cooperation in achieving sustainable development, production of the NEPP itself involved only consensus among the Ministries. Developing consensus on the way forward with other actors outside central government was lacking. However impressive the document, barriers to implementation emerged.

Revising the NEPP

The NEPP has gone through a series of revisions since 1989, although the broad analysis of the degree of reform and restructuring necessary to achieve sustainable development remains. Where most change has been witnessed is in relation to implementation. The mutual dependency between different levels of government and non-government actors (for example, industry, environmental organisations and citizens) has been recognised. Later versions of the NEPP stress the importance of public–private collaboration in the generation of targets and timescales for different target groups. Self-regulation through the use of covenants and similar policy instruments was promoted (see Chapter 5) in an attempt to build wider support for change, internalise environmental responsibility across all sectors of society and draw on different forms of expertise in the hope of generating more creative solutions. As Marie-Louise van Muijen states in a discussion of NEPP II:

> The key role for the authorities then is to bring different agencies and individuals together. NEPP II therefore offered – at least on paper – the foundation for an incentive structure which encouraged (and required) all groups in society to make decisions that will reduce adverse environmental impacts. Consultation and negotiation are central to mobilising this co-operative effort because it leads to a greater sense of involvement and commitment by all parties. The chances of achieving policy objectives are further improved if implementation procedures are shaped by those who are responsible for carrying them out.
>
> (van Muijen, 2000, p. 155)

Recent studies suggest that levels of pollution in many key areas have declined since the implementation of the NEPP process (Jänicke and Jörgens, 1998; Bressers and Plettenburg, 1997) and the Dutch government's stated aim is to 'achieve an *absolute decoupling* of environmental pressure and economic growth' (VROM, 1997, quoted in van Muijen, 2000, p. 162). Both the rhetoric and the practice of ecological modernisation appear to have been self-consciously embraced. But problems still exist. For example, the government is engaged in a difficult balancing act with different types of policy instruments: regulation, economic and voluntary. Although there has been some success in the use of voluntary covenants, there is concern that certain industries and other actors are avoiding their responsibilities. A more sensitive and effective use of different types of instruments to cover different policy areas and actors needs to emerge. Successful development of covenants is especially difficult when the target group is diffuse: a collective action problem emerges. This is particularly true for target groups such as households, farmers, car drivers, retailers and other small firms (Bressers and

continued

Plettenburg, 1997, p. 120). Finally, the Dutch may be suffering from the 'law of diminishing environmental returns' (van Muijen, 2000, p. 171). Many of the cost-effective changes have been made: future environmental reforms are likely to be more expensive and challenge established practices of consumers and householders. At the same time, public support for environmental issues is no longer as high as it was when the NEPP process began. The lack of public support is likely to act as a brake on further government action.

Divergent traditions: comparing the UK and the Netherlands

Why is it that, compared with the UK's sustainable development strategies, the NEPP and its successors reveal a much more sophisticated conception of sustainable development together with the necessary measures required to move towards it? Why was the Dutch government able to set comparatively stringent targets, objectives and timetables, cost the relevant policies and provide a clear vision of a sustainable future? There appear to be a number of possible reasons.

First, there is clearly a different attitude towards policy planning in the Netherlands. With its particular geographical and social situation – much of the Netherlands is below sea-level and it has a dense population – land-use and development planning are well established. In the UK, the Thatcherite government was ideologically opposed to strict planning and it has only been in the last few years that the land-use planning system in the UK has been strengthened again (see Chapter 10).

Second, the more sophisticated understanding of sustainable development and the reasonably broad support for the NEPP may stem from the consensual and collective style characteristic of Dutch politics. One element in this is long experience of coalition governments produced by proportional representation. Policy formulation appears more collaborative and debate among divergent interests, often beyond central government, is well established. More effective multi-level environmental governance emerges. By comparison, the first-past-the-post system in the UK tends to lead to a single political party holding power that is able to use its majority in Parliament to push through policies with little debate and opportunity for social learning.

Third, Dutch politics seems to embody a wider conception of well-being and a stronger conception of citizenship. The Dutch people appear to be more politically aware and have a more developed sense of their responsibility towards the environment. Again this could well be traced back to the consensual and collective nature of Dutch politics and to their geographical location. The idea of environmentally responsible citizenship is a central theme in the NEPP. In contrast, it is often a more economic conception of well-being that dominates political debate in the UK and this is reinforced with the frequent portrayal of the electorate as individual consumers rather than citizens.

Suggestions for further reading

For a collection of essays looking at different areas of British environmental policy, see Tim Gray *UK Environmental Policy in the 1990s*. Philip Lowe and Stephen Ward's edited collection *British Environmental Policy and Europe* offers an analysis of the important relationship between Britain and the EU. A number of collections comparing the national responses of liberal democracies to sustainable development have emerged in recent years. The most comprehensive is probably William Lafferty and James Meadowcroft *Implementing Sustainable Development* which includes chapters on European nations (including the Netherlands and UK), the United States, Canada, Japan and the European Union. Two other useful comparative collections are Martin Jänicke and Helmut Weidner *National Environmental Policies* and Tim O'Riordan and Heather Voisey *Sustainable Development in Western Europe: Coming to Terms with Agenda 21* (originally a special edition of *Environmental Politics*). Albert Weale *The New Politics of Pollution* provides a sophisticated analysis of pollution contol and sustainability policy, including an evaluation of the NEPP. Wolfgang Rüdig's edited collection *Environmental Policy* contains a number of classic articles on national environmental policy approaches. *Environmental Politics* is an authoritative source for up-to-date and relevant articles. The monthly report from Environmental Data Services (ENDS) provides up-to-date reportage and analysis on developments in the UK.

Useful websites

Department of the Environment, Food and Rural Affairs (DEFRA): www.defra.gov.uk
Royal Commission on Environmental Pollution: www.rcep. org.uk
UK Sustainable Development Commission: www.sd-commission.gov.uk

Notes

1   Historically, however, Britain can be seen as an innovator in the environmental field, with policies often instigated by earlier Conservative administrations. Britain was responsible for the world's first piece of anti-pollution legislation in 1273 (a decree prohibiting the burning of sea coal); the first government environment agency, the Alkali Inspectorate, established in 1863; the first private environmental group, the Commons, Open Spaces and Footpaths Preservation Society, founded in 1865; the first comprehensive air-pollution-control Act, the Clean Air Act of 1956; and the first cabinet-level environment department created in 1970 (McCormick, 1991, p. 9).

2   In many ways this was reminiscent of the original 1970 DOE which included transport policy in its remit. A fully independent (and environmentally-insensitive) DOT was created in 1976.

3   Germany's status as an environmental lead nation in Europe was affected by German reunification. The environment slipped down the political agenda as the economic redevelopment of former East Germany took priority.

4   For a comparative analysis of progress towards IPC in Europe and North America, see Haigh and Irwin (1990).

5   For a description of the variety of pollution-control agencies and their responsibilities prior to the creation of HMIP, see O'Riordan and Weale (1989, p. 282).

6   A similar argument is made by Hamer in his study of the relationship between the roads lobby and the DOT, *Wheels Within Wheels.* He argues that the emphasis on road building can partly be traced to the fact that the road lobbyists and civil servants tend to have similar backgrounds – 'overwhelmingly male and middle-class . . . share the seemingly trivial details of social conditioning – a car, a house with a garden in the suburbs – that are so important in prejudicing attitudes in transport policy' (Hamer, 1987, p. 112).

7   For more on the Swedish Environmental Protection Agency and the objectives and structure of environmental policy, see www.internat.environ.se/index.php3.

8   The Royal Commission on Environmental Pollution was established in 1970 as an independent advisory body. The RCEP has produced over twenty reports on various environmental issues based on authoritative scientific evidence. Although not bound by their conclusions, the Secretary of State for the Environment is responsible for producing the government's response to RCEP reports. See www.rcep. org.uk.

9   The precautionary principle is discussed in Chapter 4.

10   Note that the UK government reinterpreted BATNEEC – 'technology' was replaced with 'technique', reflecting a broader British concern with procedure and management (Skea and Smith, 1998, p. 271).

11   There may be a tension in the heart of pollution-control philosophy given that at the same time as there is a move towards formalised, national standards, BPEO and BATNEEC require sensitivity to local environmental conditions.

12   Unlike its English and Welsh counterpart, SEPA also includes the local authority environmental health officers who previously dealt with pollution control. The separation of waste regulation, disposal and collection functions within local authorities is discussed briefly in Chapter 10.

13   The current objectives, policies and practice of the Environment Agency can be found on its website www.environment-agency.gov.uk.

14   Much of what is said in this paragraph is taken from an interview with Ed Gallagher, the agency's then Chief Executive, on *File on Four*, Radio 4, December 1997.

15   A number of texts are available that compare national approaches to sustainable development. See, for example, O'Riordan and Voisey (1997b), Lafferty and Meadowcroft (2000) and Jänicke and Weidner (1997).

16   This Annex was based on a report by the environmental economist David Pearce which was published in 1989 as *Blueprint for a Green Economy* (see Chapter 6). The DOE continued to promote the use of economic instruments. See, for example, *Making Markets Work for the Environment* (DOE, 1993a).

17   The UK was 'one of only 13 countries that had submitted a national report for 1996 to the CSD by the end of January 1996' (Voisey and O'Riordan, 1997, p. 48).

18   It was this demand-led approach to road building that was at the heart of *Roads for Prosperity* (DOT, 1989) – the policy challenged by the anti-roads direct-action movement in the 1990s (see case study in Chapter 3).

19   For a full list of the members of the UK Round Table on Sustainable Development see its *Second Annual Report* (1997). In order to work efficiently, the Round Table broke up into smaller sub-groups to develop its recommendations, often co-opting expert advisers and other interested parties.

20   To avoid charges of partiality and co-option, the Round Table was originally co-chaired by the Secretary of State for the Environment and Richard Southwood, former Chairman of the Royal Commission on Environmental Pollution. Under the new Labour administration, Southwood became the sole chair, with John Prescott being afforded the role of President.

21   The reports of the British Government Panel on Sustainable Development and the UK Round Table on Sustainable Development can be found on the Sustainable Development Commission website www.sd-commission.gov.uk.

22   Giddens is generally accepted to be one of the leading influences on Blair's views on political philosophy.

23   The two speeches were presented at conferences organised by the WWF and by the CBI and Green Alliance. Transcripts can be found on the Prime Minister's Office website, www.number-10.gov.uk and the Labour Party website, www.labour.org.uk.

Local authorities and local democracy

> Whether it is identified as subsidiarity, decentralisation, empowerment or participation, some component of democratisation is widely viewed as being integral to the achievement of an environmentally sustainable future.
>
> (Agyeman and Evans, 1994, p. 14)

The preceding chapters have focused attention on global, European and national pressures for change and the differing reactions to the developing environment and sustainable development agendas at these different levels. Much of the policy framework generated at these levels of political organisation requires implementation at a local level and thus local government is often at the forefront of this process. However, to view local action as solely consisting of the implementation of policy generated from above would be to underestimate the practices and influence of local authorities. In many countries the experience of local government in fashioning policies and actions and the day-to-day environmental problems that they face has driven them to adopt innovative practices and partnerships with other sectors of the community. Their experiences, and the perceived inadequacies of the policy and resource framework at global, European and national levels, has meant that local authorities are often in the forefront of developing a more coherent approach to environmental issues. Local authorities and their representative organisations have often taken a lead in pressurising and lobbying other levels of government, international organisations and other public- and private-sector bodies to develop sustainable policies.

The constitutional status, structure and powers of local government vary considerably across nations and this chapter will focus in particular on the experience of local government in the UK. The first part of this chapter will discuss the emerging pressure for the reinvigoration of local democracy. Without doubt, greens stand alongside such a political programme, believing that enhanced public participation at the local level is a key element in achieving environmental sustainability. However, a tension is frequently apparent between this democratic vision for localities and the drive for economic efficiency that manifests itself in tight fiscal discipline and fragmentation of responsibilities. Nowhere was this more the case than in the UK in the 1980s, where the reforming zeal of the Thatcher governments was driven by the desire for economic efficiency in local service delivery and the liberalisation of the local planning system, rather than by the desire to enhance the democratic potential of local government. In the 1990s it was recognised that such fragmentation and liberalisation was a significant barrier to sustainable development. In particular, the Labour administration's modernisation agenda has attempted to reinvigorate the democratic and leadership function of local government within a broader context of local governance. This appears to be a more sympathetic political context from an environmental perspective.

The final section of the chapter focuses on the emergence of the Local Agenda 21 process, perhaps the most important recent development in local environmental politics. Faced with a national government that showed little commitment to sustainable development, enlightened local authorities in the UK used the Rio process as an opportunity to stimulate innovations in local participation in environmental decision making. The chapter ends with a case study on Sustainable Seattle, a series of initiatives, including a much-vaunted community-indicators project, that inspired many local authorities and community organisations in the early 1990s.

The case for local democracy

Greens frequently celebrate 'the local' as a site of environmental action and appropriate democratic arrangements and engagement: one only has to reflect on the most famous of green slogans, 'think globally, act locally'. Green politics can be seen as part of a wider project of democratisation, and more specifically *local* democratisation. Clearly, any study of local democratisation needs to attend to the role of local government. In the UK, unlike many other liberal democracies, the democratic and political features of local government have often been sidelined or ignored. The dominant strand in thinking about local government has emphasised its role in the efficient delivery of services: 'the national political consensus was that local government was more an agency administering welfare functions than an entrenched institution of the democratic polity' (John, 1997, p. 254). Under the New Right Conservative administrations of the 1980s, the focus on efficiency in service delivery reached new heights with the introduction of market and quasi-market mechanisms in many areas of local government competence. Here the rationale was to provide 'a more effective way of achieving efficiency. Competition between producers and choice for the consumer were to be the crucial weapons of reform' (Stoker, 1996b, p. 190). William Waldegrave, a vociferous defender of local government management reforms, argued that: 'The key point . . . is not whether those who run our public services are elected, but whether they are producer-responsive or consumer-responsive' (ibid., pp. 190–1). Local government in other liberal democracies may also have undergone processes of reform, but in comparison to the UK, local democratic political principles and the idea of subsidiarity – taking decisions at the appropriate political level – remained fundamental and broadly stayed intact. We shall have more to say about the nature and effect of these reforms and the response of more recent national administrations later in the chapter. For now it is enough to recognise that calls for greater local democracy have gained added urgency in the light of shifts in local government thinking over recent decades and challenge the orthodoxy that local government should simply concern itself with local service delivery.

Local government in liberal democracies

Two aspects of the British experience of local government separate it from the practice of other liberal democracies.[1] The first is the preoccupation with service delivery; the second is its constitutional status. In the UK, local government is a creature of statute – it has only a limited legal and political status. Local government in the rest of Europe and the United States, on the other hand, has formal constitutional status. Within the rest of Europe, local authorities can be divided into two categories related to differing political traditions. First there is the 'Franco' model with a tradition of strong centralised administration, but where local areas enjoy

---

continued

fundamental political status. The second is that typical of 'Northern and Middle Europe' where the principle of subsidiarity is embraced and a high value is placed on local self-government. Here local autonomy and financial independence are relatively important and local self-government has a constitutional status. By comparison with the UK, local authorities in the rest of Europe enjoy a much higher level of influence in the affairs of state and are seen as important political actors in their own right (Goldsmith, 1996; Batley, 1991). In the USA, local government operates in a formal constitutional context based on traditional American values of localism and local autonomy. Here individual rights and checks and balances on centralised power are fundamental concerns (Wolman, 1996). Looking at the capacity of local government to respond to contemporary environmental problems, UK local authorities are relatively powerless. If we take control over greenhouse gas emissions as an example, we find that in North America and Northern Europe local authorities typically have the capacity to develop more effective energy-efficiency policies as they have some influence over energy production, distribution and consumption in their localities. In the UK, by contrast, the energy market is highly liberalised and local authorities lack any meaningful control (Nijkamp and Perrels, 1994). In all liberal democracies tensions emerge between local democracy and efficiency and between local autonomy and centralisation. The interesting issue is the manner in which different traditions interpret and resolve these tensions.

Arguments for enhanced local democracy have a number of justifications.[2] First we find arguments based around the idea of 'localism'; the view that local problems are best dealt with by local decision-making processes. Local government is taken to have a sensitivity to local needs, interests, demands and conditions: its legitimacy rests on local knowledge and its responsiveness to the individuals and communities to which it is democratically accountable. Often this localist argument is linked with a claim about efficiency in service delivery: local government is best placed to provide efficient and effective services because of its local knowledge and ability to react to changing conditions. Such a position is often at the heart of arguments for subsidiarity. In a European context, recent Conservative administrations enthusiastically promoted the principle of subsidiarity, but only down to the level of the nation state; not below that to the level of local government.

A second defence of local democratic arrangements is the prudential argument that the enhancement of local democracy guards against the over-centralisation of power. In the UK it is a common argument that there need to be increased checks and balances on the powers of Whitehall and Westminster. In many ways the diminution in the power and authority of local democracy can be traced to the lack of embedded constitutional status for local government in Britain.

A third set of arguments revolves around the celebration of public participation. Again this could be tied into arguments for diffusion of power. Increased opportunity for participation is taken as a way of transforming both the nature of politics and transforming the way in which people act and think. On this view, political participation is regarded as a transformative and educative process and local government is taken to be the 'most accessible avenue of public participation' (Phillips, 1996, p. 26). Given that there is widespread dissatisfaction, cynicism and apathy among citizens (and even among councillors and officers) with the workings of existing representative structures (Gyford, 1991),[3] the forms of participation proposed are understood to require far more than periodic voting or standing for election as a councillor. Suggestions include developing the wider use of institutional arrangements such as public meetings, referendums, citizens' juries and electronic democracy (Stewart, 1996b; New Economics Foundation, no date). Local government is thus seen as having the potential to create the conditions within which divergent local interests can reveal and express their concerns and come to an understanding of competing claims.

These considerations by no means exhaust the justification for enhanced local democracy, but they do provide a flavour of the current debates on the topic. Greens draw on similar arguments. As we have already seen in Chapter 2, decentralisation is fundamental to much green political thinking. Local communities, particularly in anarchist streams of thinking, are taken to be the most appropriate level for political, social and economic relations, as well as relations with the non-human world.

Green arguments for local democracy

- Decentralisation is related to a shift towards a green consciousness.
- The corrosive effect of self-interest as displayed in the 'tragedy of the commons' is best controlled by community-level political processes.
- Smaller-scale economic processes have a lower environmental impact.
- Grassroots democracy is a necessary condition for sustainability.

(adapted from Ward, 1996)

Some green arguments for local democracy allow no place for local *government*. This view draws on anarchist principles which regard relations of hierarchical authority as essentially implicated in both human and non-human subjugation. In Chapter 2 we rehearsed a number of problems with the eco-anarchist position, including the potential for parochialism, the lack of coordination between localities, and the fact that the local is not always the most appropriate scale for economic, social and political action. Questions of distribution of resources and, as such, social justice, require government-type structures (not that the arrangements necessarily have to mirror current political arrangements and institutions). So, if we are to talk about government, greens take local authorities to be a prime site for political participation and action. Thus the environmental and local democratisation agendas converge, offering a new basis of legitimacy for local government (Ward, 1996, p. 131).

A combination of these arguments for enhanced local democracy can be found at the heart of the Local Government Management Board's (LGMB) *A Statement to UNCED* published in the run-up to the Rio Earth Summit. The concepts of subsidiarity and political participation are strongly affirmed in the light of contemporary environmental problems.

[T]he potential of local government in applying the principle of subsidiarity ... rests upon the following essential characteristics:

- closeness to the issue;
- a capacity for learning;
- 'local choice and local voice';
- local differences, local diversity, local innovation;
- the basis for citizen participation;
- an understanding of local interactions and impacts;
- the starting point for actions leading to sustainable development within the community;
- the ability to set conditions for local action;
- a partner for global action across districts, regions and countries and a key player in the local economy.

(Hams, 1994, pp. 31–2)

Tensions frequently emerge between arguments for enhanced local democracy (whether on the grounds of responsiveness to local needs, diffusion of power, or political participation and education) and arguments for economic efficiency in allocation and service provision which typically rest on the achievement of national standards. Again, tensions emerge when critics of localism argue that a strong centralised state is necessary in order to promote social justice, equity and comprehensive environmental protection. How are we to negotiate clashes between values such as 'democracy' and 'efficiency'; 'localism' and 'centralisation'? Potential resolutions of these tensions mirror alternative visions of local government and democracy. As this chapter develops, it will become clear that local government has become just one of a number of organisations operative at the local level. Thus any conception of local democracy requires us to attend to the relationships between these different public, private and voluntary organisations and to recognise that local authorities have become one element in networks of *local governance*. Green arguments for enhanced participation need to be sensitive to these new conditions. Local democracy cannot and should not simply be equated with the actions of local government alone.

The structure and practice of local government

Under the Conservative administrations of the 1980s, local government became one of the key sites of ideological confrontation. The reforms of local government led to fragmentation and a differentiated pattern of structure, management and service provision. Local government often seemed to be under constant reform and reorganisation and the degree of change was in many ways unprecedented. The election of a Labour government in 1997 brought with it a modernisation programme for local authorities. This did not return local government to its pre-Thatcher structure and functions, but rather offered a different vision; one based on community leadership and partnership. These changing visions of local politics have had ramifications for the capacity of local authorities to promote sustainable development.

Structure

The 1972 Local Government Act created a fairly consistent two-tier system throughout England and Wales – forty-seven shire county councils and 333 district councils; and six metropolitan county councils and thirty-six metropolitan districts. A similar structure was introduced in Scotland in 1975 with a two-tier system of regional and district authorities. The 1980s witnessed increased ideological conflict between the Conservative central government and Labour-controlled urban authorities. The so-called 'militant' left-wing metropolitan county councils, such as the Greater London Council (GLC) and Greater Manchester Council, were abolished in 1986 and their functions transferred to the lower tiers (metropolitan districts) and joint planning boards. From a green perspective, these changes were criticised on the grounds that the large cities now lacked the capacity for strategic planning in areas such as environmental protection, transport, economic development and education and that there was a 'democratic deficit' at the heart of the UK's largest urban areas: small metropolitan districts simply did not have the capacity to respond to many of the city-wide environmental, social and economic pressures.

A further reorganisation of local government began in 1992, led in England and Wales by the Local Government Commission. Government guidance for the Commission stressed the potentially contradictory criteria of efficiency, account-ability, responsibility and localness. Although the Conservative administration originally favoured the creation of a single tier of local government, the final outcome was a 'patchwork' of unitary and two-tier authorities – often Whitehall ignored the Commission's advice on the grounds of political expediency and opportunism. Further, a number of problems have been noted with the Commission's terms of reference: for instance, it was not given the option of promoting regional authorities or rearranging political boundaries so that unitary city authorities would include their conurbations; and the fate of metropolitan areas was left out of its remit (Leach, 1996a, pp. 164–5). At the same time, the review process led to increased animosity between councils, particularly between districts and counties vying for control of each other's functions. Working relationships on cross-authority issues such as the environment became increasingly soured. Second, funding and political support for long-term environmental policy found itself squeezed by short-term publicity and marketing campaigns by authorities hoping to impress the Commission. Third, the review criteria did not refer explicitly to environmental-management issues but primarily to financial and social concerns. Against this antagonistic and often highly competitive backdrop it is perhaps a surprise that the environmental agenda moved forward at all.

On coming into power in 1997, the Labour administration did not undo these boundary changes to any great degree, preferring to focus its attention on the powers, functions and practices of local government (see below). The lack of strategic planning capacity in London was remedied through the establishment of a London Mayor and the Greater London Assembly (GLA).[4] Responsibility for local authorities was passed to the devolved assemblies established in Scotland, Wales and more recently Northern Ireland. Labour also displayed a degree of enthusiasm and commitment to regional policy within England, establishing Regional Development Agencies and, more recently, Regional Chambers. At present these assemblies comprise members from local authorities, although there is a commitment to the establishment of directly elected assemblies in regions where there is widespread support for such an institution. This is not a political priority of the current government, although there is a recognition that some form of regional governance is an essential element of the political system, particularly for planning purposes.

Three models of local government: 'provider', 'enabler' and 'community governance'

The traditional model of local government in the UK is the all-purpose administrative unit, directly delivering services. In many ways this remains the primary under-standing of the role of local authorities, with citizens typically blaming councils for poor-quality local service provision (even when it is not the local authority's respon-sibility!). However, this direct service-provision model was severely challenged in the 1980s and early 1990s by the reforms of the Conservative central governments. These reforms also had a negative impact on the democratic credentials of local authorities. Local government found it increasingly difficult to coordinate effectively local activities as central-government control over finance and revenue was tightened and alternative delivery systems were promoted through the use of compulsory competitive tendering (CCT) for certain services and the transfer of responsibilities to quasi-autonomous non-governmental organisations (quangos).

The financial autonomy of local authorities was substantially weakened by removing much of their revenue-raising capacity. For instance, central government removed locally-determined business charges and introduced strict borrowing limits, an annual standard spending assessment (SSA) and 'capping'. Central government was thus able to exert financial discipline on local government by deciding on the level of grant that authorities should receive and placing an upper limit on the level of local tax that could be collected. In the mid-1980s, 60 per cent of local expenditure was covered by locally-determined taxes; a decade later that figure had declined to under 20 per cent (Pratchett and Wilson, 1996, p. 7). The Commission for Local Democracy argued that such financial control is 'wholly incompatible with democratic accountability. It is as offensive to local government as capping by Brussels would be to a national government' (Commission for Local Democracy, 1995, p. 42).

Economic efficiency and extending market discipline and competition in service delivery lay at the heart of the New Right vision, with local authorities conceived as 'enablers' rather than 'providers'. This is emphasised in the 1991 White Paper *Competing for Quality*:

> The Government's model for local government in the 1990s and into the 21st century is that of the *enabling authority*. Here the task of local authorities lies in identifying requirements, setting priorities, determining standards of service and finding the best way to meet these standards and ensuring that they are met. This implies a move away from the traditional model of local authorities providing virtually all services directly and a greater separation of the functions of service delivery from strategic responsibilities.
>
> (quoted in Pratchett and Wilson, 1996, p. 3, emphasis added)

Local government's primary purpose was thus taken to be 'specifying service requirements in relation to a discrete range of services which cannot be directly provided by the market, and then "enabling" these services to be provided through increased use of external agencies (including private contractors)' (Leach and Davis, 1996, p. 3). More than any other reform, it was the introduction of CCT that forced local authorities towards this enabling role. CCT required a split between the roles of purchaser and provider, with the primary role of local authorities being the former, 'contracting-out' service provision to the most economically efficient provider. Initially CCT was focused on front-line services such as refuse collection and disposal, leisure management, building cleaning and school catering, although it was later extended into 'white collar' areas. Although in many cases the contracts were won by arm's-length council direct-service organisations, critics have argued that the fragmentation of responsibilities has led to a loss of the public-service ethos and lessened the influence of elected councillors on service provision. More importantly perhaps, CCT has been charged with creating low-cost services at the expense of quality, good working conditions and sound environmental practice (Patterson and Theobald, 1996, pp. 9–18; Whitehead, 1996, pp. 20–1). Economic efficiency takes priority over environmental considerations.

Waste management offers a good example of the impact of CCT. The Environmental Protection Act (1990) forced local authorities to separate its waste regulation, collection and disposal functions. CCT has affected the last two roles.[5] The Waste Collection Authority (WCA) is required to open collection to tender and by the mid-1990s around 25 per cent of collections were run by private companies. However, at the same time the WCA is also required to produce a recycling plan including targets for recycling household waste. But it was soon discovered that progress on recycling is hampered by problems in incorporating such environmental criteria within contract specifications. Waste Disposal Authorities (WDAs) are responsible for the management of collected waste and often the day-to-day running of disposal facilities such as incinerators and landfills. Again, with the expansion of CCT policy into white-collar areas, many local authorities created arm's-length Local Authority Waste Disposal Companies (LAWDCs). This relatively complex framework for waste management, with the primary aim of maximising economic efficiency, is frequently criticised for undermining the relatively expensive environmental options of recycling and the promotion of waste minimisation. While there may have been some positive aspects of the changes, in that the separation of collection, disposal and regulation functions has had the effect of reducing the potential for corruption, the incentive structure undermined the emergence of environmental good practice.[6]

Reform did not only occur at service provision level however. The local political system was further fragmented as certain strategic local government responsibilities were transferred to newly-created quangos; for example, urban development corporations, training and enterprise councils, housing action trusts, grant-maintained schools and health trusts. In the mid-1990s it was estimated that 'there are now some 5750 agencies (90 per cent operate at the local level) which take about a third of public expenditure and have some 50,000 appointed people sitting on them' (John, 1997, p. 267). These organisations, whose boards are typically directly appointed by ministers, are rightly criticised for a lack of democratic accountability and legitimacy (Stewart, 1996a).

Conservative reforms led to a severe fragmentation of responsibilities, a lessening of local authorities' ability to coordinate action, a reduction in the available areas of discretion and continuing vulnerability to central government legislation and policy changes. However, local authorities still retained many significant functions and powers (Leach and Davis, 1996, p. 4) and a number of local authorities took an activist stance towards the fragmented local political environment. Alternative conceptions of 'enabling' emerged, with the local authority attempting to coordinate policy and service delivery across their localities through the development of local partnerships and networks which engaged communities directly. This vision of *community governance* was central to the modernisation agenda of the Labour administration.

Labour's reforms of local government have created a new political environment at local level, although they have not returned the original extensive powers and responsibilities to local government as many of its supporters hoped (Rao, 2000; Hill, 1999). In the Local Government Act (1999) the CCT regime was abolished and replaced by Best Value. This moved beyond simple economic efficiency, but the new Best Value regime nonetheless now covers all functions of local government. Best Value requires performance reviews (typically incorporating national performance indicators) to ensure efficient and effective service provision. The incentive structure is clear: there is increased autonomy for authorities achieving excellent service performance (Beacon Councils) and intervention (including private-sector management) for those who fail to achieve targets. Requirements for audit and inspection are increased, but at least now environmental criteria can form part of service specifications and performance targets.

Beyond service delivery, Labour's modernisation agenda also focused heavily on political structures, the aim being to make decision-making processes more accountable and transparent, increase citizen participation and develop the capacity of local government to play a leadership role in community governance. As the government stated in its White Paper, *Modernising Local Government: Democracy and Community Leadership*:

> The prize is an ever closer match between the needs and aspirations of communities and the services secured for them by their local authority, better quality services, greater democratic legitimacy for local government and a new brand of involved and responsible citizenship: in short reinvigorated local democracy. Increasingly, the degree to which an authority is engaged with its stakeholders may become a touchstone for general effectiveness.
>
> (DETR, 1998c, p. 23)

The Local Government Act (2000) introduced a more streamlined system of decision making. The traditional committee system, where responsibility lay with the whole council (but power was wielded by party groups behind closed doors), was replaced with an executive who would be clearly responsible and accountable for decisions. Although Blair promoted the idea of directly-elected mayors, councils were given a choice and most opted for a cabinet with a leader elected by the council (thus replicating the structure of the House of Commons and retaining executive power *within* the council itself). The Act also included a statutory power for local authorities 'to promote the economic, social and environmental well-being of their area'. As we shall discuss in more detail towards the end of this chapter, this power explicitly mentions sustainable development and requires local authorities to prepare a community plan in consultation with stakeholders. Given the impact of earlier Conservative reforms, the Labour administration also promoted the establishment of Local Strategic Partnerships (LSPs) to bring the different parts of the public sector together at local level with the private, community and voluntary sectors. The intention was to overcome fragmentation through partnership working and can be seen as an attempt to realise community governance. The government also originally flirted with the idea of innovative mechanisms for increasing citizen participation, such as citizens juries, but in the end little was forthcoming, except for a duty on local authorities to consult citizens within the new community planning (not to be confused with land-use planning) and Best Value processes.

Land-use planning

The planning system is the primary instrument through which local authorities are able to balance demand for development and the protection of the environment. Where there is a two-tier local authority system, planning control and development plans are instituted through Structure Plans and Local Plans. Structure Plans are statements of general policy produced by county councils which are applied in a more detailed manner by the Local Plan produced by district councils. Unitary authorities apply the planning process through a Unitary Development Plan which combines general policies and detailed proposals for land use in a single document. Both Structure and Unitary Development Plans require approval from the Secretary of State responsible for local government affairs.

The land-use planning system dates back to the 1947 Town and Country Planning Act and has proved relatively successful in demarcating urban and rural environments, checking urban sprawl.[7] However, the system has been less successful in incorporating more contemporary environmental problems: in planning documents the environment has typically been compartmentalised and treated within a separate chapter, usually focusing on historic monuments and nature conservation. As a 1993 Town and Country Planning Association (TCPA) report states, the planning system

> has been an effective instrument for achieving the policy objectives of the 1940s, particularly the demarcation of built-up areas from the countryside and the designation and protection of national parks, landscape areas, and nature reserves. . . . But it has been far less successful in responding to new kinds of environmental concerns.
>
> (Hall *et al.*, 1993, p. 20)

So, for instance, the planning system has to a certain extent succeeded in protecting rural areas from development pressures, but has had no influence on the direction and environmental impact of commercial agricultural policy and practice.

The planning system is ill-equipped to deal effectively with 'the integrated nature of environmental processes and policies', in particular the trans-media, trans-sectional and trans-boundary nature of environmental problems (Blowers, 1993b, pp. 14–17). To avoid shifting environmental problems from one medium to another, land-use planning needs to be integrated with, for example, pollution control and waste management – both responsibilities of the Environment Agency. Second, in formulating plans, environmental policy should not be considered as a discrete issue, but ought to be addressed as a fundamental component in the planning of energy use, transportation and agriculture. Third, environmental problems do not recognise political boundaries and, as such, a Structure Plan needs to be integrated with the planning process in neighbouring localities and at other levels of planning. A strategic approach to planning requires the formal integration of local planning within regional, national and even European policy frameworks (Lusser, 1994, pp. 126ff). Existing counties and unitary authorities are not always the most appropriate political units for planning purposes.

The 1980s witnessed the 'liberalisation' of planning – a definite step away from such integration, with the presumption being in favour of development over environmental concerns. Perhaps the most vivid example of this was the rapid expansion of out-of-town retail and business developments.[8] Local authorities consistently lost appeals against these developments, with the result that the vitality of city centres has been much reduced and the number of traffic (principally private vehicle) movements increased. At the same time, local authorities often competed with each other to attract economic development, often without taking any account of the wider strategic impact of their actions. Developers took advantage of the fragmented nature of the planning system, effectively playing neighbouring authorities off against one another (Whitehead, 1996, p. 20). Particularly in urban areas, traditional planning control and local authority discretion was further undermined by the introduction of Enterprise Zones and Simplified Planning Zones and the activities of (unaccountable) quangos such as Unitary Development Corporations.

By the early 1990s it was generally recognised that the planning system needed to be revitalised as it was unable to protect localities from unsustainable incursions. The Planning Policy Guidance (PPG) provided by the DOE began to treat issues such as energy, transport and tourism in a more integrated manner and in 1992, *PPG12: Development Plans and Regional Planning Guidance* introduced the concept of sustainable development into the planning process. Similarly, the 1994 and 1995 revisions of *PPG6: Town Centres and Retail Development* promoted development in town centres in preference to out-of-town retailing, while PPG13, published in 1993, allowed local authorities, when judging the merits of development projects, to take their effect on the volume of vehicle emissions into account.[9] Sustainability began to emerge as a common theme in many PPGs, although a presumption in favour of economic development still remained. During this period the DOE published *Environmental Appraisal of Development Plans* (DOE, 1993c), which continued the trend towards a more environmentally-integrated approach to development planning and allowed a number of local authorities to produce land-use plans approaching environment and development issues in a much more comprehensive manner, thereby putting the brakes on certain grossly unsustainable developments. One of the earliest examples of such an assessment was by Lancashire County Council, which allocated a sustainability score to each policy in relation to a series of environmental indicators. As a result of the assessment, a number of the policies in the Structure Plan were altered (Pinfield, 1992; Hill and Smith, 1994).

The Labour administration has strengthened the planning system, further embedding the concept of sustainable development within PPGs. Most obviously, the revised *PPG1: General Policy and Principles* states that the planning system 'has a key role to play in contributing to the Government's strategy for sustainable development by helping to provide for necessary development in locations which do not compromise the ability of future generations to meet their needs' (DETR, 1997, para. 39). The Labour government has a far stronger commitment to the idea of regional governance and planning than its Conservative predecessor, and has strengthened this strategic level of integration.[10] Again, guidance is given that environmental considerations should be integrated across all areas covered in the planning process and with the policies and plans of other agencies, such as the Environment Agency.

Early in the first administration, the Department of the Environment, Transport and the Regions (DETR) published *Planning for Sustainable Development: Towards Better Practice* (DETR, 1998a) which provided guidance for local authorities to move beyond environmental appraisal towards a more comprehensive system of sustainability appraisal. The recent EU directive 2001/42 ('The assessment of the effects of certain plans and programmes on the environment') will require the formalisation of this sort of strategic sustainability appraisal in the near future (see Chapter 6). Evidence suggests that large numbers of authorities have engaged in environmental assessments of their plans, but also that there is much inconsistency and little transparency and consultation in the process (Russell, 1999). However, it is clear that since the early 1990s, environmental issues, and specifically sustainable development, have gradually become more central considerations in the local planning process.

Local Agenda 21 and beyond: local authorities and sustainable development

> Because so many of the problems and solutions being addressed by Agenda 21 have their roots in local activities, the participation and cooperation of local authorities will be a determining factor in fulfilling its objectives. . . . As the level of governance closest to the people, they play a vital role in educating, mobilising and responding to the public to promote sustainable development.
>
> (UNCED, 1992, Chapter 28)

Agenda 21, signed at the Rio Earth Summit (see Chapter 7), appears to have had a quite profound effect on the practices of a number of UK local authorities. The national political environment at the time was still relatively hostile for local authorities: central government had reduced their powers, responsibilities and influence and had responded to the growing sustainable development agenda by making only weak commitments and developing few new policies (see Chapter 9). However, a significant number of local authorities saw the neglect of environment policy at the national level as an opportunity for them to take a leadership role in their localities. The emerging Rio sustainable development agenda provided further legitimacy for such action. Chapter 28 of Agenda 21, 'Local Authorities' Initiatives in Support of Agenda 21', recognises local authorities as the closest level of government to the general population and, as such, their functions and ability to mobilise support are seen as essential to any move towards a sustainable future. It has been estimated that over two-thirds of Agenda 21 'cannot be delivered without the commitment and cooperation of local government' (LGMB, 1992, p. 1). Similarly, the European Commission calculated that some 40 per cent of the EC Fifth Environmental Action Programme, *Towards Sustainability* (see Chapter 8), was the implementation responsibility of local government (LGMB, 1993a, p. 28).

The emergence of the environmental agenda

UK local authority activity in the areas of environment and sustainable development did not simply emerge as a response to Rio – action can be traced back to the late 1980s. Prior to Agenda 21 and the EU's Fifth Environmental Action Programme, a number of enlightened authorities in the UK had already begun to question their response to environmental issues. These authorities began to recognise the need to move beyond simply fulfilling day-to-day statutory duties in such areas as planning, transport and waste disposal, and towards the development of a more coordinated, corporate approach to environmental problems. For these authorities, international agreements and programmes provide a legitimate basis for their more challenging policies, and for others they have acted as an inspiration to move from token responses to a more holistic appreciation of the sustainable-development agenda. Initially environmental action often begins with a focus on the authority's own structure, policies and practices before moving out into the wider community activity.

The publication of Friends of the Earth's *Environmental Charter for Local Government* in 1988 is often regarded as a seminal initiative in making the transition to a more corporate approach to environmental issues. The charter – a general statement of intent – was adopted in one form or another by many local authorities and had the effect of introducing the idea that environmental issues permeate all departments, policies and service-delivery areas.

At the same time as promoting the concept of an environmental charter, FOE were working with Kirklees Metropolitan Council to produce the UK's first state of the environment (SOE) report in 1989. The collation of all available information and knowledge on local environmental conditions is essential if local authorities wish to act as stewards of the local environment. Such a report provides a clear indication of the background environmental conditions against which the local authority can measure the impact of its policies and take informed decisions on what are priority areas for action. The process of developing an SOE report is not simply a matter of collating and coordinating in-house knowledge, itself spread throughout different departments, but also requires the cooperation of other sectors in providing information; for example, the Environment Agency, privatised utilities and voluntary organisations among others. Such a process is often an early stage in the development of local partnerships and relationships of trust between actors.

Many local authorities began to recognise that if they were to take a more activist, leadership role in solving local environmental problems then they should start by getting their own house in order. A significant number have thus subjected themselves to internal environmental audits and attempted to develop awareness-training programmes, often simply focusing on such areas as energy consumption, purchasing practice and paper usage. For some this is an important first step in recognising the huge impact that councils can have on the environment.

A natural step forward from such audits, SOE reports and charters is the development of a more comprehensive environmental strategy which defines broad environmental priorities, indicates responsible actors (not always the local authority itself) and provides timetables for action. The content of these strategies varies, but typically they focus on areas such as energy, transport, waste, environmental education and awareness raising. These strategies have been complemented by environmental management systems – a number of authorities piloted the British Standard 7750 and its European counterpart, the Eco-Management and Audit Regulation.[11]

Also prior to Rio, Leicester was designated as Britain's first 'Environment City'. This was part of an initiative established by the Royal Society for Nature Conservation, Civic Trust and UK2000 which aimed to create a network of British cities as models of environmental excellence. A number of other cities competed for the designation and many of them retained the structures and mechanisms established at that time, even when they were unsuccessful. Typically, as in Leicester, a number of 'specialist working groups' were set up in areas such as energy, transport, waste and pollution, the natural and built environment. These involve individuals and representatives from the private, public and voluntary sectors who together develop an environmental strategy for the city (ICLEI, 1993, pp. 38–9). This model of stakeholder collaboration influenced the development of post-Rio initiatives in the UK.

Local authorities and the Rio process

Given that the Rio agenda had an incredibly positive effect on the work of many local authorities in the environmental field, it is perhaps surprising that only three months before UNCED there was no mention of the role of local government in any of the documents being prepared for the conference. It was not until the fourth prep-com in March/April 1992 that local government achieved any recognition. From that point onwards, when Jeb Brugman from the International Council for Local Environmental Initiatives (ICLEI) was able to introduce the text for Chapter 28 of Agenda 21, the essential role of local authorities in attaining sustainable development has been brought to the fore of the environment and development debate. As we have already noted, it is claimed that up to two-thirds of Agenda 21 cannot be delivered without the commitment of local authorities and the communities they serve.

A week before UNCED, a meeting of leaders of local authorities from around the world endorsed the *Curitiba Commitment*, a declaration calling for local authorities to develop a local action plan for sustainable development centred on principles of community education and democratic participation. In the UK, this international commitment was shadowed by the LGMB's *A Statement to UNCED* which stressed that the 'local democratic mandate enables local authorities to inform, mobilise and speak on behalf of their communities. . . . They can use these powers both to enforce and to encourage good environmental practice' (Hams, 1994, p. 31).

The important coordination, education and advocacy role that ICLEI and the Local Government Board (LGMB) played in promoting local authority action, and Local Agenda 21 (LA21) in particular, should not be understated. Both organisations aimed to build local government's institutional capacity to respond to environmental problems. At the international level, ICLEI acts as both a clearing-house for good practice by disseminating information on successful local sustainability initiatives and offering training, and building political awareness through campaigns on LA21 and particular environmental issues such as climate change and the sustainable use of water.[12] In the UK, a similar role was played by the LGMB, until its demise in the late 1990s. LGMB not only provided guidance on good practice – for instance it commissioned research on sustainability indicators (LGMB, 1995b) – but also was heavily involved in lobbying central government (LGMB, 1993b) and providing reports to the United Nations Commission on Sustainable Development (see Chapter 7) (LGMB, 1993c).

The Local Agenda 21 (LA21) process

Within Chapter 28 of Agenda 21 there was a recommendation that most local authorities should have produced an LA21 through consultation with all sectors of their communities by 1996.

> Each local authority should enter into a dialogue with its citizens, local organisations and private enterprises and adopt 'a local Agenda 21'. Through consultation and consensus-building, local authorities would learn from citizens and from local, civic, community, business and industrial organisations and acquire the information needed for formulating the best strategies.
>
> (UNCED, 1992, Chapter 28)

LA21 can be understood as 'the process of developing local policies for sustainable development and building partnerships between local authorities and other sectors to implement them' (LGMB, 1994, p. 1). Rather than being seen as a single, standard approach, the process will involve different initiatives and priorities in different localities. What is clear is that LA21 requires action within the authority itself and a new working relationship between the authority and other actors in the local community.

The key elements of Local Agenda 21: steps in the process

Action within the local authority

1 Managing and improving the local authority's own environmental performance;
2 Integrating sustainable development aims into the local authority's policies and activities;

Action in the wider community

3 Awareness raising and education;
4 Consulting and involving the general public;
5 Partnerships;
6 Measuring, monitoring and reporting on progress towards sustainability.

(LGMB, 1994, pp. 2–3)[13]

It is undeniable that LA21 requires a wholesale change in policy and practice by committed local authorities. Julian Agyeman and Bob Evans emphasise four linked themes that are essential for the achievement of the overall policy goal of sustainability at the local level: community environmental education; democratisation; balanced partnerships; integrated and holistic policy making (Agyeman and Evans, 1994, pp. 20–2). These are fundamental to any successful attempt by local authorities to develop a comprehensive and coordinated response to local environmental, social and economic issues. The success or failure of initiatives often depends upon whether these themes have been embraced and understood. To this end, committed authorities are looking to promote new working relationships with different sectors of their communities.[14] In principle LA21 is highly participatory, engaging local communities in grassroots participation in projects and decision-making processes. There is a growing recognition that the adversarial nature of many existing local political institutions, particularly in the planning process, needs to be altered if participation is to become more meaningful. As Chris Church argues, 'the needs and justifiable aspirations of local people are rarely taken into account. Traditional adversarial planning processes often offer no more than a chance to object to proposals prepared in private' (Church, 1995, p. 3). For those authorities committed to the LA21 process, a range of institutional designs and initiatives have been developed to enhance community participation, including forums, round tables, focus groups, visioning, audits and appraisals, 'planning for real' initiatives, community arts projects and information services (LGMB, 1994, p. 5; Young, 1996, pp. 17ff; DOE, 1995b).

It would appear that there are a number of stages through which a local authority passes as it develops its response to environmental problems and the principle of sustainability (Stoker and Young, 1993, pp. 89–90; Hams *et al.*, 1994, pp. 13–14). These seem to map onto the idea that there are competing approaches to, and interpretations of, sustainable development (see Chapters 2 and 6). The initial phase is *business-as-usual* where environmental policy and response to problems is fragmented. The council fulfils only its statutory duties and takes the minimal necessary notice of PPGs and pressures from the community. It pursues economic goals irrespective of the environmental impacts. In phase two, *superficial tokenism* emerges as local authorities begin to appreciate the significance of environmental issues but are only willing to tackle specific issues without taking into account the wider, overall effect of their policies. The council will normally act on high-profile issues such as cycle paths and wildlife protection, seeing these as vote winners. In the third phase, the *holistic policy approach*, councils recognise the integrated nature of the environmental impact of their policies. SOE reports, internal management systems and environmental strategies are developed to make all policies more environmentally sensitive. Sustainable development becomes a guiding principle. The final phase is the development of a *Local Agenda 21 process*. Local councils realise that they must work in partnership with and involve all sectors of the community to achieve sustainability. LA21 is then crucially tied to the reinvigoration of local democracy and to the idea of community environmental governance. Whether local authorities and local communities will be able to realise this agenda is another matter. What is clear is that some enlightened authorities are beginning to tread this path.

One of the earliest and most celebrated LA21 initiatives to date is coordinated by Lancashire County Council. In 1989, three years before the Earth Summit, the Council published a *Green Audit*, a sophisticated state-of-the-environment report. It identified areas of environmental concern and exposed where information and knowledge was limited. In the same year, the Council established the Environment Forum to be a focus for decision making in developing a plan of action to follow up the audit's findings. Four specialist groups were created by the Forum to develop proposals.[15] These were discussed, debated and challenged in a full Forum meeting and eventually converted into the *Lancashire Environmental Action Programme* (LEAP). Published in 1993, LEAP makes some 200 recommendations aimed at, among others, central government, local authorities, industry, the voluntary sector and the general public.

Aspects of Lancashire's Local Agenda 21 programme[16]

- **Green Audit**: Published in 1989, this is one of the most sophisticated state-of-the-environment reports produced, using a Geographic Information System (GIS). It identifies areas of environmental concern and exposes where information is limited.

- **Lancashire Environmental Action Programme**: LEAP was launched in 1993 and takes into account the next fifteen years. It makes 200 recommendations aimed at, among others, central government, local authorities, industry, the voluntary sector and the general public.

- **Lancashire Environment Forum**: Set up by the County Council in 1989 this is the focus of decision making for the Green Audit and LEAP. It comprises over ninety organisations from all sectors and has four specialist working groups that have developed the LEAP recommendations from an analysis of the Audit.

Central to the LA21 programme is the Lancashire Environment Forum, a 'stakeholder' design based on the principle of consensus building.[17] The Forum has a number of functions. First, it draws organisations together from a variety of perspectives and allows the development of common understandings among stakeholders. Second, those organisations are a source of important information and experience in the development of proposals. Third, the Forum is the primary decision-making mechanism for LA21. Fourth, the Forum is a key instrument for implementing proposals – proposals are more likely to be implemented given that responsible agencies have been involved in the decision-making process (they 'own' the decisions) (Doak and Martin, 2000). In principle, then, the Forum is an impressive democratic innovation and highlights the importance of institutional design in the formulation and implementation of sustainability initiatives.

In practice, the LA21 process in Lancashire has faced problems that are common to many localities. In particular it has found it difficult to draw in business and industrial support for the process: many local business leaders are sceptical of the County Council's strong environmental stance (Doak and Martin, 2000). Research carried out by Lancaster University also suggests that one of the key stakeholders – the local population – is also highly sceptical of the local authority's motives in promoting sustainability (Macnaghten *et al.*, 1995). Overcoming such perceptions is a fundamental issue for local government. Regardless of these concerns (which are common to almost all LA21 initiatives), the Lancashire programme remains one of the most innovative British responses to the challenge of LA21. Overall only a minority of councils have so far engaged with LA21 in such a coordinated fashion; for most it remains a peripheral activity.

Tensions in the Local Agenda 21 process

A number of authorities used the LA21 process as an opportunity to reorientate the way in which they operate and engage with the local community. However, for the majority of authorities the radical promise of LA21 did not have a lasting impact. In many localities the rhetoric did not match the actual outcome. There are a number of interrelated reasons that explain the limited impact of LA21 (Young, 1999; Church and Young, 2000).

First we need to consider the broad context within which local authorities operate. Earlier in this chapter we highlighted the fragmented nature of local politics and the loss of powers, responsibilities and autonomy of local government over recent decades. LA21 emerged at a time when local authorities were finding it more difficult to coordinate activities in their localities. Where LA21 requires an holistic approach to policy making and practice, CCT and other fiscal measures tended to contribute towards the fragmentation of local authority responsibilities. As Alan Patterson and Kate Theobald argued:

> CCT, linked with tight fiscal restraint on local government capital and recurrent spending, is having a considerable negative impact on the ability of local authorities to plan long term and to implement new environmental strategies such as those required by Local Agenda 21, and even on their ability to deliver more traditional environmental services to an acceptable standard . . . the means by which the principles of sustainability, subsidiarity and strategy can be implemented are being weakened or removed.
>
> (Patterson and Theobald, 1996, p. 18)

Added to this, the status of LA21 affected support for the process. LA21 is non-statutory: there is no legislation requiring its adoption and implementation. In a political environment where local authorities have a number of statutory duties (including the development planning process, air-quality management, local transport and recycling plans and economic development and local housing strategies) it is perhaps not surprising that LA21 has dropped down many local policy agendas.

Second, where the LA21 process gained a foothold, it was too often characterised and pigeonholed as just another 'environment' activity. This clearly indicates a misunderstanding of the challenging nature of the sustainable development agenda on the part of local authorities; nonetheless, it is true that for many councillors and officers it is seen as just another green initiative. In practice, many LA21s tend to concentrate on environmental projects and predominantly draw in participants with an interest in the environment. Even the two examples of good practice mentioned earlier – Leicester and Lancashire – are primarily environment-focused. This is not to suggest that the environment does not cut across social and economic policy, rather that those involved tend to have more traditional 'environmentalist' backgrounds and perspectives and this may affect the issues tackled. Thus Chris Church notes, in a review of LA21 activity:

> Crime, poverty and health are three areas where, as yet, there is little 'good practice' emerging out of Local Agenda 21. . . . If they have not emerged in discussions on Local Agenda 21 it is perhaps because people are not being given sufficient opportunity to raise their real concerns.
>
> (Church, 1995, p. 19)

For LA21 to be an effective exercise it needs to move beyond limited (but important) environmentalist concerns such as energy, transport and land-use planning, and open up the process to ensure that issues such as social justice and social exclusion are confronted and a broader number of stakeholders involved. LA21 must not simply follow traditional environmental protection lines, but needs to link environmental, social and economic agendas (O'Riordan and Voisey, 1997a, p. 20).

Finally, LA21 has suffered from a lack of political support. At a national level the sustainable development agenda has been rather confused. We have already seen that local authorities are required to produce a range of different plans and policies by central government; however, without substantial guidance and leadership from government, many local authorities were simply not willing to invest time and money on a non-statutory initiative. Under the Conservatives, no funding was allocated to the LA21 process. At the 1997 UN General Assembly Special Session (Rio+5) Blair attempted to reinvigorate the process, stating: 'I want all local authorities in the UK to adopt Local Agenda 21 strategies by the year 2000.' However, no new resources emerged; only a guidance document (DETR, 1998b). At the same time many local councils remained resistant to the forms of increased participation promoted under LA21 and balked at the potentially radical changes that LA21 might bring in its wake. LA21 was perceived as a mechanism whereby special interest groups (in this case, greens) would have undue influence on highly-protected council decision-making processes. And finally, local authorities often found it difficult to engage their local populations and organisations in the LA21 process. Business organisations in particular were often sceptical and large sections of the population were simply disillusioned with the political process and cynical of the motives of local government

(Miller *et al.*, 1996, p. 47).[18] Distrust and apathy are unlikely to be fertile ground for political institutions to engage citizens in collective action. This should be of particular concern for environmentalists. As research carried out for Lancashire County Council shows, there is a definite problem which political institutions have to overcome if they wish to promote innovative environmental practice:

> People display a pronounced degree of fatalism and even cynicism towards the country's public institutions, including national and local government. This is reflected in an apparently pervasive lack of trust in the goodwill and integrity of national government, and in doubts about the ability or willingness of local government to achieve positive improvements in the quality of people's lives (not least because local authorities' powers are seen as diminishing). . . . There is a danger that, because of people's largely negative attitudes towards (and apparent recent experience of) such official bodies, proposals by the latter for specific measures to advance sustainability will be interpreted as self-interested, and even more likely to marginalise people further (particularly those in lower income groups). . . . Overall, whilst there is substantial latent public support for the aims and aspirations of sustainability, there is also substantial and pervasive scepticism about the goodwill of government and other corporate interests towards its achievement.
>
> (Macnaghten *et al.*, 1995, pp. 3–5)

Sustainable development requires widespread changes in contemporary practices across all areas of society. Without doubt there is a substantial role to be played by local government in coordinating such action. But, it is unlikely that citizens will respond positively to proposals when there is such a profound sense of apathy, cynicism and mistrust abroad.

LA21 across Europe

Engagement with the LA21 process has varied across Europe.[19] The pioneering nation in the development of LA21 is arguably Sweden, although local authorities in both the UK and the Netherlands were also in the forefront of developments. Sweden and the Netherlands are well-known sustainable development pioneers (see Chapter 9), but the relative enthusiasm of UK local authorities is perhaps surprising. We have already argued that local councils in the UK may have viewed LA21 as an opportunity to 'reclaim' its community leadership role in the face of a central government that had weakened its powers. The relatively late engagement of local authorities from other environmentally active Scandinavian nations such as Denmark and Norway may be explained on the grounds that they were already involved in environmental projects and saw no reason to re-launch these as LA21 initiatives. Again, the fact that UK authorities had generally not developed environmental activities to the same extent meant that LA21 had an inspirational effect on many councils. The constitutional structure of nation states appears to be a key determinate in explaining why

---

continued

Scandinavian local authorities have been particularly effective in developing local environmental initiatives: the high degree of autonomy enjoyed by these authorities would seem to provide more effective conditions for the emergence of an effective LA21. The relatively successful performance of UK local government is thus an interesting anomaly (Lafferty, 1999, pp. 254–6).

Beyond LA21? The emergence of community governance

Although we have identified a number of barriers to the effective formulation and implementation of LA21, it must be reinforced that a small but significant number of local authorities in the UK have used the post-Rio period to develop impressive corporate responses. But although the majority of authorities claim to have engaged with LA21, its actual impact across the UK is probably overestimated; for most authorities the LA21 process has been unfocused and marginalised from the core functions of councils (Young, 1999; Church and Young, 2000).

At the same time as the momentum behind LA21 is weakening, the Labour administration has signalled a new approach to the question of sustainability at the local level: community planning.[20] The Local Government Act (2000) provides local authorities with a broad new power to promote the economic, social and environmental well-being of their localities:

> It will ensure that councils must, at all times, consider the long-term well-being of their area. It will put sustainable development at the heart of council decision making and will provide an overall framework within which councils must perform all their existing functions. So, in taking decisions affecting their area or its people, councils will have to weigh up the likely effects of a decision against the three objectives – economic, social and environmental – and if necessary strike a balance to ensure that the overall well-being of their area is achieved.
>
> (DETR, 1998c, para 8.10)

In order to promote such well-being, local authorities now have a statutory duty to produce a comprehensive community plan for their locality in consultation with their local population and stakeholders. Central government is also promoting the establishment of Local Strategic Partnerships (LSPs) to coordinate the implementation of community plans and other initiatives. An LSP brings together representatives of public, private, voluntary and community sectors and existing partnerships, which should include existing LA21 initiatives.

The Labour administration is attempting to create the conditions for successful community governance as a way of overcoming the fragmented nature of local politics. The power of well-being, community planning and the establishment of LSPs is seen as the necessary infrastructure for enhancing the sustainability of localities. Certainly, there are some advantages over the LA21 process, most importantly its statutory status. Local authorities are required to produce a community plan and an LSP will be a mechanism for accessing central government support and resources. Contrast this with the LA21 process, which was not mandatory, and received only rhetorical support and no new resources from central government. Again, community planning is clearly a corporate responsibility and will draw in all departments within local authorities. LA21 was often marginalised as an 'environment' initiative and was rarely embraced by the whole authority.

However, there are some concerns about subsuming LA21 under community planning. The first is that within LA21, environmental considerations were given a high priority in relation to economic and social issues (too high a priority according to many critics). The power of well-being resonates with the sustainable development discourse, requiring local authorities to balance economic, social and environmental considerations. But under present conditions, will these different aspects of well-being be considered with the same weight? In making judgements, will local authorities continue to prioritise economic considerations when there is a conflict? LA21 forced authorities to give more prominence to environmental concerns. Will the same be true for community planning? Only time will tell.

Second, LA21 was explicitly participatory in its ambition. Whether local authorities actually embraced this bottom-up approach to participation is highly questionable. However, at the heart of the LA21 ideal is a commitment to grassroots community engagement, both in decision-making processes and the development and implementation of sustainability projects. Community planning explicitly requires local authorities to consult with its population on the development of the local strategy. But the process is top-down: simple consultation with local communities on a draft version of the plan is likely to be the norm. The participatory and empowerment ethos of LA21 has all but disappeared.

It may well be that community planning will achieve more than the LA21 process. Certainly it has the resources and political will that LA21 lacked. However, implicit within the two approaches are two apparently contrasting visions of community governance. Community planning and the establishment of LSPs aims to develop the capacity of the local political system to build a common purpose and deliver improved well-being. The focus here is on civic leaders and elites from different sectors blending their resources and skills. In contrast to this pragmatic, top-down approach, the spirit of LA21 is idealist, participatory and bottom-up. Community governance here involves the active participation of citizens in the development of a sustainable society. These are not necessarily conflicting visions. Progress towards sustainable development almost certainly requires the integration of both approaches: an ongoing dialogue and engagement between civic leaders and citizens. It remains an open question as to whether the spirit of LA21 will be able to influence the trajectory of community governance and the extent to which sustainable development will be fully embraced by localities.

Conclusion

Environmental concern has the dual advantage of being able to provide some justification for the defence of some locally-produced services, whilst simultaneously allowing a demonstration of a new enabling role. It provides an opportunity to prove to a sceptical local electorate and an unsympathetic central government that they have a useful, popular role in a democratic society. Developing and promoting environmental policies is therefore a way of creating new political space for local authorities through the concept of local guardians of the environment and equally a way of defending their traditional service role.

(Ward, 1993, p. 466)

Local politics has particular resonance within green political theory and practice. The utopian vision that drives many activists is the ideal of face-to-face, small-scale political units. This vision is a long way removed from the contemporary globalised world. However, it explains why greens pay a great deal of attention to acting in their localities, often engaging directly with local authorities. And local government has been at the forefront of the emerging environment and sustainable development agendas. This is even the case in the UK, where local government powers and responsibilities have been diminished and where the local political environment is highly fragmented. Enlightened (and sometimes self-interested) local authorities have recognised that more active development of environmental policy offers them an opportunity to develop new areas of competence and engage more effectively with their local communities. The emergence of LA21 provided local government with further reasons for continuing such work.

After an initial rush of enthusiasm for LA21, only a small proportion of local authorities have seen it fundamentally alter their approach to governing. One of the problems local government has often faced is a confused and unsupportive national political framework and a lack of new resources. Central government has been keen to see local authorities take responsibility for environmental issues, but has not always provided funding or a policy climate to support such activity. Further, there still remains some doubt over whether local authorities truly have the political will and/or ability to support and nurture meaningful grassroots participation and embrace environmental and democratic innovation. LA21 remains a challenging vision for local environmental governance.

Case study: Sustainable Seattle

Seattle is a metropolitan area on the North-West coast of the United States with a population of about 1.5 million, only a third of whom live in the city itself. Common to most large American cities, Seattle has experienced a process of 'urban sprawl' or 'suburbanisation' with the population in the city itself steadily reducing and larger numbers of households becoming almost entirely dependent on their cars for mobility. This population movement has resulted in increasing economic differentials with concentrations of high levels of poverty in the inner city.

Since the late 1980s a series of initiatives focusing on the goal of making Seattle a more sustainable place to live have been developed. These initiatives, involving different sections of the community, gained widespread recognition in the United States and beyond, as many local authorities and their populations begin to develop Local Agenda 21.

Initial elements of the Sustainable Seattle project

- The Waste Reduction and Recycling Programme
- The Environmental Priorities Project
- The Comprehensive Plan
- The Sustainable Seattle Citizen's Initiative

The first of these initiatives, the Waste Reduction and Recycling Programme, emerged in 1988 initially as a citizens' campaign against the incineration policy of the City Council. The programme set a recycling target of 60 per cent. By 1994, 42 per cent of the city's solid waste was being recycled, with 90 per cent of all single-family households participating in the programme (Lawrence, 1994, p. 15).

The second initiative, the Environmental Priorities Project, began in 1990 with the objective of identifying Seattle's most serious environmental and social problems and developing an action plan to address these issues. The process is on-going with the first Environmental Action Agenda adopted by the City Council in 1992.

The Comprehensive Plan was also initiated in 1990 as an attempt to produce an integrated and anticipatory land-use and development planning process. Both this and the Priorities Project were initiated by the then Seattle Mayor, Norman Rice, who gave sustained and influential political leadership in the development of the local sustainable development agenda. One of his most interesting acts was his early appointment of Gary Lawrence as Director of the Planning Department, who readily admitted to not being a trained planner and who made the department's procedures more understandable and accessible to the Seattle public.

The fourth and most famous element, dating back to late 1990, is the citizen-driven Sustainable Seattle, 'a voluntary network and civic forum, bringing together citizens from many different sectors of the community to promote the concept and practice of sustainability. Business, environmental groups, city and county government, labor, the religious community, educators and social activists have all been represented' (Sustainable Seattle, 1993, p. 3). Its most ambitious, influential and well-documented project is the development of sustainability indicators for the Seattle area against which the effectiveness of other initiatives can be judged.[21]

What makes a good indicator?

These indicators of Sustainable Development have been selected because they meet the following criteria, which were developed by the Task Team:

Good indicators

- *are bellwether tests of sustainability* and reflect something basic and fundamental to the long-term economic, social, or environmental health of a community over generations;

continued

- *can be understood and accepted by the community* as a valid sign of sustainability or symptom of distress;
- *have interest and appeal for use by local media* in monitoring, reporting and analysing general trends toward or away from sustainable community practices;
- *are statistically measurable* in our geographic area, and preferably comparable to other cities/communities; a practical form of data collection or measurement exists or can be created.

The geographic scope of an indicator depends on the context and accessibility of the data, with some indicators referring to Seattle city limits, others to King's County (our first choice, when available), and still others placing Seattle in a statewide context.

(excerpt from Sustainable Seattle, 1993, p. 4)

In their first report, *The Sustainable Seattle 1993 Indicators of Sustainable Community*, the first twenty indicators were detailed. They covered four areas: environment; population and resource; economy; culture and society. In all four areas there are a few indicators that show some improvement or little measurable change, but overall, over half indicate moves away from sustainability.

Recent years have seen improvements in such key indicators as overall air quality, water consumption, and the diversity of the local economy. There has been little measurable change in adult literacy rates or the numbers of hours one has to work at the average wage to support a family's basic needs. But many other trends are carrying us away from sustainability and toward an uncertain – and potentially unpleasant – future.

Increasing numbers of children are being born with low birth weights, or being raised in poverty, or turning to crime. Fewer people are voting. Wild salmon are disappearing. More of us are driving more miles, consuming more energy, and producing more garbage per person every year.

Overall, the Seattle area is not moving toward the goal of long-term sustainability. Instead, it is moving in the wrong direction.

(Sustainable Seattle, 1993, p. iii)

By the time of the third report in 1998, Sustainable Seattle was reporting on forty indicators. Again the results paint a mixed picture. On the positive side, policy instruments introduced to reduce water consumption have had an impact and community volunteering among young people is high. The 'talisman' indicator of salmon runs has stabilised, but remains low. However, the report highlights the continuing problems of traffic congestion and increased movements of private vehicles.

A spirit of realism pervades the various initiatives. There is a recognition that any long-term turnaround will require major changes in citizen and organisational attitudes. The City Council has devoted resources into researching the values and attitudes of the community and, not surprisingly, has discovered that, although the public holds many political themes in common (environmental stewardship, economic security and social equity), their values often conflict. For instance, citizens value highly their freedom to drive and any reduction in that freedom is viewed as an attack on the individual's liberty. But, at the same time environmental degradation is also viewed in a similar manner: 'attacks on the environment are perceived to be the same as an attack on the person' (Lawrence, 1994, p. 12). Private cars are a major cause of pollution and so any action to alter mobility patterns needs to tread carefully between these two perceived freedoms (see the case study in Chapter 5). In the long term, the first of these freedoms will need to be rearticulated, although in such a way as not to alienate the citizens whose participation and political support are vital. It is an open question as to whether Seattle has the initiatives in place through which such a reinterpretation of values might be achievable.[22]

So why Seattle? Why should this area of America be taking such innovative steps towards a more sustainable future? Why do citizens appear to be more inclined to participate? First, there is a strong cultural connection with the local environment which can perhaps be traced to such factors as its geographical setting (the region is dominated by the sea and hills), a strong connection to native Indian traditions, and high educational standards. Second, the City Council has greater control over fiscal and planning issues by comparison with similar cities in other countries, especially in the UK. Rather than receiving most of its resources from central government, American cities raise a large proportion from local taxes. This in itself makes the Council more accountable to its local population which tends to be more interested and involved in local planning and fiscal issues. Perhaps the most important reason, however, was the political vision and leadership of Mayor Norman Rice. He had a clear understanding of the links between economic, social and environmental injustices and developed and supported initiatives which aimed to make Seattle a more equitable and livable city. Central to his vision was the idea of sustainable development and the necessary involvement, partnership and political support of all sectors of an economically- and socially-divided community. His influence, it seems fair to say, cannot be underrated.

The political, cultural and geographical features of Seattle make it a location where the concept of sustainable development resonates among significant sections of the local communities. Although in many ways the political and cultural situation is unique, the initiatives and experiences of Seattle have become the focus of attention for other areas around the world also looking to develop towards a more sustainable future.

Suggestions for further reading

There are a number of collections providing a comparative analysis of LA21 initiatives across Europe. William M. Lafferty's edited collection *Implementing LA21 in Europe* is perhaps the most comprehensive with chapters focusing on twelve nations. Versions of some of these chapters appear in *From Earth Summit to Local Agenda 21* edited by William Lafferty and Katarina Eckerberg. Lafferty's more recent edited collection *Sustainable Communities in Europe* is a follow-up analysis of implementation. *Sustainable Development in Western Europe: Coming to Terms with Agenda 21* (originally a special issue of *Environmental Politics*), edited by Tim O'Riordan and Heather Voisey, offers another interesting comparative analysis of sustainable development at the national and local level. Andrew Gouldson and Peter Roberts' edited collection *Integrating Environment and Economy: Strategies for Local and*

Regional Government provides a number of case studies of local action. Julian Agyeman and Bob Evans' edited collection *Local Environmental Policies and Strategies* examines the response of local government in different areas of policy to the emerging environmental agenda in the early 1990s. Tony Hams and colleagues consider similar ground in *Greening Your Local Authority*, but from the perspective of local government officers responsible for LA21. The journal *Local Environment* is a useful source for relevant articles by both academics and practitioners.

Useful websites

International Council for Local Environmental Initiatives: www.iclei.org
Office of the Deputy Prime Minister (responsible for local and regional policy): www.odpm.gov.uk

Notes

1   In general terms, the British 'style' of local government is also present in the Republic of Ireland, Canada, Australia and New Zealand.
2   These arguments are drawn from a number of sources, including Phillips (1996), Stoker (1996a, 1996b), Commission for Local Democracy (1995), Pratchett and Wilson (1996), Parry *et al.* (1992) and Barber (1984).
3   This is most obviously expressed by the consistently low turnouts for local elections (Pratchett and Wilson, 1996, p. 7).
4   The more proportional voting system (the additional member system) used for the GLA elections led to the election of three green representatives.
5   The Waste Regulation Authority (WRA) function has now been merged into the new Environment Agency (see Chapter 9). The WRA has the responsibility for enforcing the 'duty of care' requirements for controlled wastes and for licensing, inspecting and enforcing remedial action on landfills. Duty of care 'applies to any person who produces, imports, carries, keeps, treats or disposes of controlled waste, or, who, as a broker, has control of it' (Bell, 1997, p. 421). Such persons are responsible for the containment of the waste and for ensuring it is transferred to an authorised person.
6   For a more detailed discussion of waste management under the Conservative regime, see Cooper (1994) and Blowers (1993b).
7   It is estimated that approximately 12 per cent of England and Wales is Green Belt around urban areas.
8   For a brief discussion of the problem of land value that has led to out-of-town developments, see Hall *et al.* (1993, pp. 22–3).
9   PPGs, along with other guidance notes, for example regional and mineral planning guidance, are now provided by the Office of the Deputy Prime Minister. A listing and full text of these various guidance notes can be found at www.planning.odpm. gov.uk/policy.htm. There is some concern that the separation of environmental responsibilities (moved into the new Department of the Environment, Food and Rural Affairs, DEFRA) from the planning process will reduce the influence of sustainable development within the planning process. See Chapter 9 for a discussion of the restructuring of the environmental machinery of government within Whitehall.
10 However, there is some concern that this regional level of decision making is at present democratically unaccountable.

11   For further discussions of these initiatives, see Ward (1993), Webber (1994) and Hams *et al.* (1994). See also Chapter 5.

12   For more on ICLEI and its current activities, see www.iclei.org. See also Brugman (1997, 2001), Hams *et al.* (1994, pp. 45–6) and ICLEI (1993).

13   This LGMB document formed the basis of later guidance produced by the DETR (1998b)

14   As a rough guide, in 1996, 38.5 per cent of local authorities claimed that they strongly supported the development of Local Agenda 21 and were 'committed to change in [the] authority's operations'; 49.1 per cent gave more 'tentative support' to the process (Tuxworth, 1996, p. 281).

15   The four specialist working groups are: air, energy, transport and noise; water, waste, land and agriculture; wildlife, landscape, townscape and open space; education and public awareness.

16   For a more detailed discussion of the Lancashire initiatives, see Doak and Martin (2000), DOE (1995b).

17   In 2000, the membership of the Forum comprised 12 per cent from national government departments and agencies, 21 per cent industry and unions, 32 per cent local government, 30 per cent interest groups and 5 per cent academic establishments (Doak and Martin, 2000, p. 227).

18   Only 33 per cent of respondents agreed that 'most politicians can be trusted to do what they think is best for the country' (Miller *et al.*, 1996, p. 47).

19   The following discussion is drawn from Lafferty (1999), Lafferty and Eckerberg (1998), O'Riordan and Voisey (1997b) and Voisey *et al.* (1996).

20   Again, community planning should not be confused with land-use planning (see earlier in the chapter).

21   For more on Sustainable Seattle, including a history of the indicators project and more recent activities, see www.sustainableseattle.org.

22   It is interesting to note that the community consultation exercise threw up results that the city planners did not expect and as such is a lesson that strategies for sustainable development need to be aware of the way in which the community perceives problems. The planners in Seattle believed that one of the first problems that needed solving was peak hour congestion on major routes in Seattle: 'Yet citizen consultation revealed that people didn't necessarily want a lot spent on solving peak hour congestion because they view it as part of the working day and "the roads are supposed to jam!" For them what was imperative was finding solutions to congestion on Saturday mornings when delays cut into their own quality time' (Church, 1995, p. 50).

Concluding remarks:
the future of
environmental politics?

In the Introduction we argued that there are two fundamental and distinctive insights unique to green politics which differentiate environmental thinking from other streams of political and ethical thought. The first insight is the recognition that there are limits to growth: infinite growth in a finite system is impossible. Thus development patterns need to be sensitive to the carrying capacity of environments, whether local or global. Economic development needs to integrate environmental considerations; economies do not operate in isolation from the environment that supports them. The second insight is the recognition of the ethical standing of parts or all of the non-human world. Greens challenge the view that nature is only valuable as a resource for production and consumption processes: it has value beyond the simple instrumental use-value to humans. In combination these two insights provide a powerful position from which to critique and challenge existing political, economic and social institutions and practices that place increasing burdens on the environment.

As the book progressed we engaged in some depth with environmental philo-sophy and ethics, green political thought, the changing nature of the environmental movement and the barriers and opportunities that exist within environmental policy making. From this analysis it becomes apparent that environmental politics is a varied and contested field in both theory and practice: a wide variety of actors are involved in debating and challenging the development of green ideas and the formulation and implementation of environmental actions. No one is untouched by the emerging environmental agenda; everyone has an interest in shaping the development of environmental politics (for good or bad). Thus in theoretical debates about the nature of the green society, deep greens find themselves in contestations with free-market environmentalists; in practical debates about the future development of the emerging climate change regime, environmental NGOs clash with multinational oil companies in an attempt to shape both national and international policy.

What has also become clear as we have developed our analysis is that many of the deliberations and battles over green ideas and policy implications are now being played out under the rubric of 'sustainable development'. The concept of sustainable development has become the intellectual centre of environmental politics. Much now rests on how this essentially contested concept is interpreted theoretically and practically. A wide variety of different interpretations of sustainable development have emerged. One useful heuristic is the distinction between strong and weak interpretations, although it needs to be recognised that debates are actually much more nuanced.

Strong interpretations tend to be favoured by more radical greens who hold that a precondition for the emergence of an environmentally-sustainable society is the wide-scale restructuring of political, economic and social institutions. Effective and long-term protection of the environment requires a considerable rethink about ideas of 'progress' and 'quality of life'. Extensive and often irreversible damage to the environment has been justified on the grounds of continued economic growth. But economic prosperity is not the same as well-being; the recognition of our inter-dependence with the non-human world would require a rethink of our understanding of what it is to lead a good life. Here the fundamental insights of limits to growth and the ethical standing of non-human nature are marshalled in a wholesale critique of the institutions of contemporary industrial society. The emerging green vision is often one of small-scale, low-impact, highly-participatory, self-reliant communities. At the radical end of both green theory and practice – whether in the writings of deep ecologists, the development of green communes or the actions of Earth First! – such an analysis of the problems of existing society and the prescription of a sustainable alternative is embraced. This is one possible future for environmental politics.

However, critics contend that this vision is nothing more than green fantasy – it is utterly utopian. The ecological ideal of 'localisation' is entirely unrealistic, undesirable and, importantly, unnecessary. In the face of intensifying patterns of globalisation, there is no point 'wishing away' contemporary capitalism and the growth ethic; the future of environmental politics lies in the process of reforming (rather than restructuring) existing institutions. Although the ecological ideal may play an important role in inspiring green theorists, activists and policy makers, a realistic environmental politics needs to engage with debates over weaker interpretations of sustainable development that dominate more mainstream politics, in particular the idea of ecological modernisation. As we have noted throughout the book, advocates of ecological modernisation argue that economic growth does not need to be sacrificed in order to protect the environment. A reorientation of economic growth is itself a precondition of environmental protection; a 'win–win' situation is possible. With the extensive and consistent use of many of the policy principles, policy instruments and evaluation techniques discussed in Part II of this book, national economies can be made more environmentally efficient. The ecological ideal is redundant because capitalism can be greened. There is a technological solution to environmental problems.

Certainly it is this vision of sustainable development that is the intellectual weight behind the majority of the agreements, strategies and policies that we discussed in Part III of the book. International agreements on specific environmental problems do not directly challenge the structure of the global economy; Agenda 21, the most exhaustive international document on sustainable development, attempts to reconcile environmental protection with the current capitalist system. Production and consumption are worthy of attention, but within a framework that protects and supports multilateral economic institutions such as the WTO, World Bank and IMF and views transnational corporations as a key actor in the development of a sustainable future. Again, although the European Union has begun taking responsibility for drawing together and reinforcing international environmental regimes, its own approach to solving environmental problems is one which gives priority to continued economic growth. Similarly national sustainability strategies and Local Agenda 21s have been important in raising the status of environmental issues, but without serious attention to the role of the economy. Even the most exhaustive strategy, the Dutch *National Environmental Policy Plan*, which recognises that structural changes will be necessary in order to negotiate successfully the transition to sustainability, implicity assumes that this can be achieved through reforms of the existing political and economic systems. The future of environmental politics on this reading is a technical question of how to make capitalism more environmentally sensitive.

Should we be concerned that this is the theoretical and practical territory within which many of the debates within green politics now take place? The fact that the conception of sustainable development as ecological modernisation is taken so seriously by policy makers and that environmental pressure groups find themselves constructively engaged in policy networks highlights the significance of environmental politics. Environmental politics has come a long way over the last three decades. Implementing existing agreements and policies and attempting to realise ecological modernisation would certainly make existing societies (at least high-consumption societies) more environmentally sensitive than they currently are. Even if it is not the desired end-state for many greens, it is likely to be a worthwhile first step.

But we are not happy with this state of affairs; we are uncomfortable with this vision of environmental politics as ecological modernisation. Neither do we wish to ally ourselves wholeheartedly with the more radical ecological ideal. It is our belief that we need to go back to the fundamental insights of green politics: limits to growth and the ethical standing of non-human nature. It is our contention that, first, ecological modernisation fails to respond adequately to these insights; and second, the radical ecological ideal is not the only alternative.

The discourse of ecological modernisation and the environmental documents and policies that have emerged in recent years typically share an optimistic belief that technological solutions can be found. Ecological modernisation can 'overcome' the limits to growth by decoupling economic development from environmental impact. However, as we argued in Chapter 2, there does not seem to be evidence of consistent absolute decoupling in high-consumption societies. Ecological modernisation may be theoretically compelling, but there is a lack of evidence that it can work in practice. Again, the technical nature of the ecological modernisation discourse tends to treat the environment as a resource; admittedly one that needs to be used more efficiently, but a resource nonetheless. Resource efficiency is without doubt a fundamental element of environmental sustainability; but for greens the instrumental, use-value of non-human nature is but one aspect of value. There is a failure within ecological modernisation to appreciate the diversity of values we associate with the non-human world (see Chapter 1).

So what is left? The first thing to recognise is that ecological modernisation and the radical green utopian vision are not the only options. If we return to the themes embodied within the concept of sustainable development (see Introduction), we may be able to construct a more consistent and appealing green position. We have already argued that ecological modernisation has an inadequate account of economy–environment integration and the reasons for environmental protection. There are other factors that it also tends to neglect. The first of these is the question of justice. Where a level of decoupling of economic growth and environmental damage has taken place, it appears to be at the expense of less-industrialised nations. Environmental pollution and damage is exported and the citizens of less-industrialised nations are exposed to higher levels of environmental risk. The global reach of sustainable development is ignored; the ecological-modernisation discourse and many of the environmental agreements and strategies fail to respond adequately to the question of international justice. Second, within the theory and practice of ecological modernisation, participation is understood as engagement between government, economic and civil society elites (including the large environmental pressure groups). The role of citizens (beyond being more sensitive green consumers) is underdeveloped.

Thus an alternative vision of environmental politics emerges; one that has at its heart a commitment to both justice and participation. In Chapter 2 we termed this position *ecological democratisation*. It is our contention that only through the democratisation of our existing political, social and economic institutions (at all levels) will just and environmentally-sustainable policies emerge. The achievement of sustainable development will require creative and challenging solutions. Policies will have to be formulated which will require sacrifices on the part of many citizens in order to achieve justice for both present and future generations while respecting ecological limits and the values we associate with the environment. We do not claim that this will be an easy transition; but without extensive democratisation we do not believe that citizens will accept the necessary changes. There are an impressive array of policy principles, policy instruments and evaluation techniques that could be employed; ecological democratisation will provide a suitable context within which they might be utilised more efficiently for the common (global) good.

No doubt we will also be accused of succumbing to the utopian impulse. How do we plead? The first response is that we believe that we must work on the material and institutions we have to hand: they cannot be wished away. We need to have strategies to reform global institutions, the state, private corporations and other associations. Second, we believe that there are elements of our vision of ecological democratisation within existing agreements and strategies. So, for example, as we argued in Chapter 7, parts of Agenda 21 recognise that sustainable development requires enhanced participation and the development of the capacity of existing institutions to nurture such participation. At the international level, the United Nations Commission on Sustainable Development (CSD) can be seen as one attempt to construct a more democratic institution. Again, the Aarhus Convention visibly expresses democratic and ecological principles. At the local level, often through the Local Agenda 21 process, innovative forms of participation in environmental policy and projects have emerged. And a number of interesting projects and organisations in the social economy point to the possibility of alternative forms of organisation. However, we accept that such practices are marginal; that such ideas only tend to emerge at the edges. The question for environmental politics is whether they can be brought to the fore. Under present conditions we are not entirely optimistic.

Bibliography

Ackerman, B. and Hassler, W. T. (1981) *Clean Coal, Dirty Air: or How the Clean Air Act Became a Multibillion-Dollar Bail-out for High-Sulphur Coal Producers and What Should Be Done about it*, New Haven, Conn.: Yale University Press.

Adams, J. (1995) *Cost Benefit Analysis: Part of the Problem, Not the Solution*, Oxford: Green College Centre for Environmental Policy and Understanding.

Agyeman, J. and Evans, B. (1994) 'The New Environmental Agenda', in J. Agyeman and B. Evans (eds) *Local Environmental Policies and Strategies*, Harlow: Longman.

Alarm UK (1996) *Roadblock: How People Power is Wrecking the Roads Programme*, London: Alarm UK.

Alarm UK (no date) *A Rough Guide to the Roads Programme*, London: Alarm UK.

Andersen, M. (1996) 'The Impact of New Member States on EU Environmental Policy', *Environmental Politics* **5** (2): 339–44.

Andersen, M. and Liefferink, D. (eds) (1997) *European Environmental Policy: The Pioneers*, Manchester: Manchester University Press.

Andersen, S. and Eliassen, K. (1993) *Making Policy in Europe: The Europeification of National Policy-making*, London: Sage.

Anderson, T.L. and Leal, R.L. (1991) *Free Market Environmentalism*, San Francisco: Pacific Research Institute for Public Policy.

Anderson, T.L. and Leal, R.L. (1998) 'Visions of the Environment and Rethinking the Way we Think', in J. Dryzek and D. Schlosberg (eds) *Debating the Earth: The Environmental Politics Reader*, Oxford: Oxford University Press.

Anderson, V. (1991) *Alternative Economic Indicators*, London: Routledge.

Anon. (1995) *The Book: Directory of Active Groups in the UK*, Brighton.

Arrow, K., Costanza, R., Dasgupta, P., Folke, C., Holling, C., Jansson, B., Levin, S., Maler, K., Perrings, C. and Pimental, D. (1998) 'Economic Growth, Carrying Capacity and the Environment', in J. Dryzek and D. Schlosberg (eds) *Debating the Earth: The Environmental Politics Reader*, Oxford: Oxford University Press.

Atkins, S.T. (1990) *Unspoken Decrees: Road Appraisal, Democracy and the Environment*, London: South East Wildlife Trust.

Attfield, R. (1991) *The Ethics of Environmental Concern* (second edition), Athens, Georgia: University of Georgia Press.

Attfield, R. (1994) *Environmental Philosophy: Principles and Prospects*, Aldershot: Avebury.

Attfield, R. and Belsey, A. (eds) (1994) *Philosophy and the Natural Environment*, Cambridge: Cambridge University Press.

Bachrach, P. and Baratz, M.S. (1962) 'Two Faces of Power', *American Political Science Review* **56**: 947–52 (reprinted as Chapter 1 of *Power and Poverty*).

Bachrach, P. and Baratz, M.S. (1970) *Power and Poverty: Theory and Practice*, New York: Oxford University Press.

Bahro, R. (1986) *Building the Green Movement*, London: GMP.

Bailey, P. (1997) 'The Changing Role of Environmental Agencies', *European Environmental Law Review* **6** (5, May): 148–54.

Baker, S. (1996) 'Environmental Policy in the European Union: Institutional Dilemmas and Democratic Practice', in W.M. Lafferty and J. Meadowcroft (eds) *Democracy and the Environment*, Cheltenham: Edward Elgar.

Baker, S. (1997) 'The Evolution of European Union Environmental Policy: From Growth to Sustainable Development?', in S. Baker *et al.* (eds) *The Politics of Sustainable Development: Theory, Policy and Practice Within the European Union*, London: Routledge.

Baker, S. (2000) 'The European Union: Integration, Competition, Growth – and Sustainability', in M. Lafferty and J. Meadowcroft (eds) *Implementing Sustainable Development: Strategies and Initiatives in High Consumption Societies*, Oxford: Oxford University Press.

Baker, S., Kousis, M., Richardson, D. and Young, S. (eds) (1997) *The Politics of Sustainable Development: Theory, Policy and Practice Within the European Union*, London: Routledge.

Barber, B. (1984) *Strong Democracy: Participatory Politics for a New Age*, Berkeley: California University Press.

Barde, J. and Pearce, D. (1991) *Valuing the Environment*, London: Earthscan.

Barnes, P. and Barnes, I. (1999) *Environmental Policy in the European Union*, Cheltenham: Edward Elgar.

Barry, B. (1973) *The Liberal Theory of Justice*, Oxford: Oxford University Press.

Barry, B. (1991) *Liberty and Justice: Essays in Political Theory 2*, Oxford: Clarendon Press.

Barry, B. (1999) 'Sustainability and Intergenerational Justice', in A. Dobson (ed.) *Fairness and Futurity*, Oxford: Oxford University Press.

Barry, J. (1994) 'The Limits of the Shallow and the Deep: Green Politics, Philosophy, and Praxis', *Environmental Politics* **3** (3): 369–94.

Barry, J. (1999) *Rethinking Green Politics*, London: Sage.

Barry, J. and Frankland, E.G. (eds) (2001) *International Encyclopedia of Environmental Politics*, London: Routledge.

Bateman, I. (1991) 'A Critical Analysis of COBA and Proposals for an Extended Cost Benefit Approach to Transport Decisions', in *What Are Roads Worth?*, London: Transport 2000/New Economics Foundation.

Batley, R. (1991) 'Comparisons and Lessons', in R. Batley and G. Stoker (eds) *Local Government in Europe: Trends and Developments*, Basingstoke: Macmillan.

Baxter, B.H. (2000) 'Ecological Justice and Justice as Impartiality', *Environmental Politics* **9** (3): 43–64.

Beck, U. (1992) *Risk Society*, London: Sage.

Beckerman, W. (1990) *Pricing for Pollution* (second edition), London: Institute for Economic Affairs.

Beckerman, W. (1994) 'Sustainable Development: Is it a Useful Concept?', *Environmental Values* **3**: 191–209.

Beckerman, W. (1995a) *Small is Stupid*, London: Duckworth.

Beckerman, W. (1995b) 'How Would You Like Your "Sustainability", Sir? Weak or Strong? A Reply to my Critics', *Environmental Values* 4: 169–79.

Beckerman, W. and Pasek, J. (2001) *Justice, Posterity and the Environment*, Oxford: Oxford University Press.

Beder, S. (1996) *The Nature of Sustainable Development* (second edition), Newham, Australia: Scribe Publications.

Bell, S. (1997) *Ball and Bell on Environmental Law* (fourth edition), London: Blackstone.

Belshaw, C. (2001) *Environmental Philosophy: Reason, Nature and Human Concern*, Chesham: Acumen.

Bennie, L. (1998) 'Brent Spar, Atlantic Oil and Greenpeace', *Parliamentary Affairs* **51** (3): 397–410.

Benson, J. (2000) *Environmental Ethics*, Edinburgh: Edinburgh University Press.

Bentham, J. (1960) *An Introduction to the Principles of Morals and Legislation*, Oxford: Blackwell.

Benton, T. (1993) *Natural Relations: Ecology, Animal Rights and Social Justice*, London: Verso.

Beresford, P. (1999) 'Making Participation Possible: Movements of Disabled People and Psychiatric Survivors', in T. Jordan and A. Lent (eds) *Storming the Millennium: The New Politics of Change*, London: Lawrence & Wishart.

Beuermann, C. and Burdick, B. (1997) 'The Sustainability Transition in Germany: Some Early Stage Experiences', *Environmental Politics* **6** (1): 83–107.

Bichsel, A. (1996) 'NGOs as Agents of Public Accountability and Democratisation in Intergovernmental Forums', in W.M. Lafferty and J. Meadowcroft (eds) *Democracy and the Environment*, Cheltenham: Edward Elgar.

Bigg, T. (1994) *Report on the Second Session of the UN Commission on Sustainable Development*, London: UNED-UK.

Bigg, T. (1997) *Report on 'Earth Summit II', the UN General Assembly Special Sessions to review outcomes from the Rio Summit: A UNED-UK Report*, London: UNED-UK.

Bigg, T. and Dodds, F. (1997) 'The UN Commission on Sustainable Development', in F. Dodds (ed.) *The Way Forward: Beyond Agenda 21*, London: Earthscan.

Bigg, T. and Mucke, P. (1996) 'NGO Priorities and Concerns for the 1997 UN GA Session', in *Priorities for Earth Summit II*, London: UNED-UK.

Blowers, A. (ed.) (1993a) *Planning for a Sustainable Environment*, London: Earthscan.

Blowers, A. (1993b) 'The Time for Change', in A. Blowers (ed.) *Planning for a Sustainable Environment*, London: Earthscan.

Bomberg, E. (1996) 'Greens in the European Parliament', *Environmental Politics* **5** (2): 324–31.

Bomberg, E. (1998) *Green Parties and Politics in the European Union*, London: Routledge.

Bookchin, M. (1980) *Toward an Ecological Society*, Montreal: Black Rose Books.

Bookchin, M. (1987) 'Social Ecology versus "Deep Ecology": A Challenge for the Ecology Movement', *Green Perspectives, Newsletter of the Green Program Project*, 4/5.

Bookchin, M. (1991) *The Ecology of Freedom* (second edition), Montreal: Black Rose Books.

Boutros-Ghali, B. (1992) *An Agenda for Peace*, New York: United Nations.

Brass, E. and Koziell, S.P. (1997) *Gathering Force: DIY Culture*, London: Big Issue.

Bray, J. (1995) *Spend, Spend, Spend: How the Department of Transport Wastes Money and Mismanages the Roads Programme*, London: Transport 2000.

Braybrooke, D. and Lindblom, C. (1963) *A Strategy of Decision*, New York: The Free Press.

Brennan, A. (1988) *Thinking About Nature*, Athens, Georgia: University of Georgia Press.

Brennan, A. (1992) 'Moral Pluralism and the Environment', *Environmental Values* **1** (1): 15–33.

Bressers, H. and Plettenburg, L. (1997) 'The Netherlands', in M. Jänicke and H. Weidner (eds) *National Environmental Policies: A Comparative Study of Capacity-Building*, Berlin: Springer.

Bretherton, C. and Steven, K. (2000) 'Ambivalence and Anxiety: Women and the Techno-scientific Revolution', in A. Russell and J. Vogler (eds) *The International Politics of Biotechnology*, Manchester: Manchester University Press.

British Government Panel on Sustainable Development (1995) *First Report*, London: DOE.

British Government Panel on Sustainable Development (1996) *Second Report*, London: DOE.

Brown, C. (1997) *Understanding International Relations*, Basingstoke: Macmillan.

Brown, L., Flavin, C. and Kane, H. (1996) *Vital Signs 1996–1997*, London: Earthscan.

Brugman, J. (1997) 'Local Authorities and Local Agenda 21', in F. Dodds (ed.) *The Way Forward: Beyond Agenda 21*, London: Earthscan.

Brugman, J. (2001) 'Agenda 21 and the Role of Local Government', in F. Dodds (ed.) *Earth Summit 2002: A New Deal* (revised edition), London: Earthscan.

Bryant, B. (1996) *Twyford Down: Roads, Campaigning and Environmental Law*, London: E. & F. Spon.

Bryner, G. (2000) 'The United States: "Sorry – not our Problem"', in W. Lafferty and J. Meadowcroft (eds) *Implementing Sustainable Development: Strategies and Initiatives in High Consumption Societies*, Oxford: Oxford University Press.

Bunyard, P. and Morgan-Grenville, F. (eds) (1987) *The Green Alternative*, London: Methuen.

Cairncross, F. (1991) *Costing the Earth*, London: Business Books.

Callicott, J.B. (1990) 'The Case Against Moral Pluralism', *Environmental Ethics* **12** (3): 100–24.

Cameron, J.R. (1989) 'Do Future Generations Matter?', in N. Dower (ed.) *Ethics and Environmental Responsibility*, Aldershot: Avebury.

Carruthers, P. (1992) *The Animals Issue*, Cambridge: Cambridge University Press

Carson, R. (1962) *Silent Spring*, Boston: Houghton Mifflin.

Carter, N. (2001) *The Politics of the Environment: Ideas, Activism, Policy*, Cambridge: Cambridge University Press.

Carter, N. and Lowe, P. (1995) 'The Establishment of a Cross-Sector Environment Agency', in T. Gray (ed.) *UK Environmental Policy in the 1990s*, Basingstoke: Macmillan.

Carter, N. and Lowe, P. (1998) 'Britain: Coming to Terms with Sustainable Development?', in K. Hanf and A. Jansen (eds) *Governance and Environmental Quality*, Harlow: Addison Wesley Longman.

Cathles, G. (2000) 'Friends and Allies: The Role of Local Campaign Groups', in B. Seel, M. Paterson and B. Doherty (eds) *Direct Action in British Environmentalism*, London: Routledge.

Chandler, J. (1993) *Local Government in Liberal Democracies*, London: Routledge.

Chappell, T.D.J. (ed.) (1997) *The Philosophy of the Environment*, Edinburgh: Edinburgh University Press.

Chatterjee, P. and Finger, M. (1994) *The Earth Brokers: Power, Politics and World Development*, London: Routledge.

Christoff, P. (1996a) 'Ecological Modernisation, Ecological Modernities', *Environmental Politics*, **5** (3): 476–500.

Christoff, P. (1996b) 'Ecological Citizens and Ecologically Guided Democracy', in B. Doherty and M. de Geus (eds) *Democracy and Green Political Thought*, London: Routledge.

Church, C. (1995) *Towards Local Sustainability: A Review of Current Activity on Local Agenda 21 in the UK*, London: United Nations Association/Community Development Foundation.

Church, C. and Young, S. (2000) 'The Future of Local Agenda 21 after the Local Government Act of July 2000: A Discussion Paper', *Manchester Papers in Politics*, University of Manchester.

Clark, S.R.L. (1977) *The Moral Status of Animals*, Oxford: Oxford University Press.

Clegg, S. (1989) *Frameworks of Power*, London: Sage.

Coase, R. (1960) 'The Problem of Social Cost', *Journal of Law and Economics* **3** (1): 1–44.

Cohen, C. (1970) 'Defending Civil Disobedience', *The Monist* **54** (4): 469–87.

Cohen, J. (1989) 'Deliberation and Democratic Legitimacy', in A. Hamlin and P. Pettit (eds) *The Good Polity*, Oxford: Blackwell.

Collier, U. (1997) 'Sustainability, Subsidiarity and Deregulation: New Directions in EU Environmental Policy', *Environmental Politics* **6** (2): 1–23.

Collier, U. and Golub, J. (1997) 'Environmental Policy and Politics', in M. Rhodes, P. Heywood and V. Wright (eds) *Developments in West European Politics*, London: Macmillan.

Collingwood, R.G. (1939) *An Autobiography*, Oxford: Clarendon Press.

Collingwood, R.G. (1946) *The Idea of Nature*, Oxford: Clarendon Press.

Collins, K. and Earnshaw, D. (1993) 'The Implementation and Enforcement of European Community Environment Legislation', in D. Judge (ed.) *A Green Dimension for the European Community*, London: Frank Cass.

Commission for Integrated Transport (CFIT) (2002) *Fact Sheet No.8: A New Concept for Paying for Road Use*, London: CFIT.

Commission for Local Democracy (1995) *Taking Charge: The Rebirth of Local Democracy*, London: Municipal Journal Books.

Commission on Taxation and Citizenship (2000) *Paying for Progress*, London: Fabian Society.

Comstock, G. (2000) *Vexing Nature? On the Ethical Case Against Agricultural Biotechnology*, Boston: Kluwer.

Connelly, J. (2002) 'Who Will Save the World?', *Environmental Politics* **11** (1): 197–201.

Cooper, J. (1994) 'Waste Reduction and Disposal', in J. Agyeman and B. Evans (eds) *Local Environmental Policies and Strategies*, Harlow: Longman.

Craven, J. (1992) *Social Choice*, Cambridge: Cambridge University Press.

Crenson, M. (1971) *The Un-Politics of Air Pollution: A Study of Non-Decisionmaking in the Cities*, Baltimore: Johns Hopkins University Press.

Croall, S. and Rankin, W. (2000) *Introducing Environmental Politics*, Cambridge: Icon Books.

Dahl, R. (1957) 'The Concept of Power', *Behavioural Science* **2** (July): 201–50.

Daly, H. (1992) *Steady-State Economics* (second edition), London: Earthscan.

Daly, H. (1995) 'On Wilfred Beckerman's Critique of Sustainable Development', *Environmental Values* **4**: 49–55.

Daly, H. and Cobb, J. (1990) *For the Common Good*, London: Green Print.

de la Court, T. (1990) *Beyond Brundtland: Green Development in the 1990s*, London: Zed Books.

de la Perriere, R.A.B. and Seuret, F. (2000) *Brave New Seeds: The Threat of GM Crops to Farmers*, London: Zed Books.

Department of the Environment (DOE) (1989) *Environmental Assessment: A Guide to Procedures*, London: HMSO.

DOE (1990) *This Common Inheritance: Britain's Environmental Strategy*, London: HMSO.

DOE (1991a) *Policy Appraisal and the Environment: A Guide for Government Departments*, London: HMSO.

DOE (1991b) *This Common Inheritance: The First Year Report*, London: HMSO.

DOE (1992a) *This Common Inheritance: The Second Year Report*, London: HMSO.

DOE (1992b) *PPG12: Development Plans and Regional Planning Guidance*, London: DOE.

DOE (1993a) *Making Markets Work for the Environment*, London: HMSO.

DOE (1993b) *UK Strategy for Sustainable Development: Consultation Paper*, London: HMSO.

DOE (1993c) *Environmental Appraisal of Development Plans*, London: HMSO.

DOE (1994a) *This Common Inheritance: The Third Year Report*, London: HMSO

DOE (1994b) *Sustainable Development: The UK Strategy*, London: HMSO.

DOE (1995a) *This Common Inheritance: UK Annual Report*, London: HMSO.

DOE (1995b) *First Steps: Local Agenda 21 in Practice*, London: HMSO.

DOE (1996a) *This Common Inheritance: UK Annual Report*, London: HMSO.

DOE (1996b) *Indicators of Sustainable Development for the United Kingdom*, London: HMSO.

Department of the Environment, Food and Rural Affairs (DEFRA) (2002) *Achieving a Better Quality of Life: Review of Progress Towards Sustainable Development: Government Annual Report 2001*, London: DEFRA.

Department of the Environment, Transport and the Regions (DETR) (1997) *PPG1: General Policy and Principles*, London: DETR.

DETR (1998a) *Planning for Sustainable Development: Towards Better Practice*, London: DETR.

DETR (1998b) *Sustainable Local Communities for the 21st Century: Why and How to Prepare an Effective Local Agenda 21 Strategy*, London: DETR.

DETR (1998c) *Modernising Local Government: Democracy and Community Leadership*, London: DETR.

DETR (1998d) *Policy Appraisal and the Environment*, London: DETR.

DETR (1999) *A Better Quality of Life: A Strategy for Sustainable Development for the United Kingdom*, London: HMSO.

DETR (2000) *PPG12: Development Plans*, London: DETR.

DETR (2001) *Achieving a Better Quality of Life: Review of Progress Towards Sustainable Development: Government Annual Report 2000*, London: DETR.

Department of Transport (DOT) (1987) *Values for Journey Time Savings and Accident Prevention*, London: DOT.

DOT (1989) *Roads for Prosperity*, London: HMSO.

DOT (1991) *The Role of Investment Appraisal in Road and Rail Transport*, London: HMSO.

DOT (1992) *The Government's Expenditure Plans For Transport 1992–3 to 1994–5*, London: HMSO.

de-Shalit, A. (1995) *Why Posterity Matters: Environmental Policies and Future Generations*, London: Routledge.

Dessai, S. (2001) 'Why did the Hague Climate Conference Fail?', *Environmental Politics* **10** (3): 139–44.

Devall, B. and Sessions, G. (1985) *Deep Ecology: Living As If Nature Mattered*, Salt Lake City, Utah: Peregrine Smith.

Devlin, J. and Yap, N. (1993) 'Structural Adjustment Programmes and the UNCED Agenda: Explaining the Contradiction', *Environmental Politics* **2** (4): 65–79.

Diani, M. and Donati, P.R. (1999) 'Organisational Change in Western European Environmental Groups: A Framework of Analysis', *Environmental Politics* **8** (1): 13–32.

Dicken, L. and McCulloch, A. (1996) 'Shell, the Brent Spar and Greenpeace: A Doomed Tryst?', *Environmental Politics* **5** (1): 122–9.

Doak, J. and Martin, A. (2000) 'Consensus-building for Environmental Sustainability: The Case of Lancashire', in A. Gouldson and P. Roberts (eds) *Integrating Environment and Economy: Strategies for Local and Regional Government*, London: Routledge.

Dobson, A. (ed.) (1991) *The Green Reader*, London: André Deustch.

Dobson, A. (1993) 'Critical Theory and Green Politics', in A. Dobson and P. Lucardie (eds) *The Politics of Nature: Explorations in Green Political Theory*, London: Routledge.

Dobson, A. (1998) *Justice and the Environment: Conceptions of Environmental Sustainability and Dimensions of Social Justice*, Oxford: Oxford University Press.

Dobson, A. (ed.) (1999) *Fairness and Futurity: Essays on Environmental Sustainability and Social Justice*, Oxford: Oxford University Press.

Dobson, A. (2000) *Green Political Thought* (third edition), London: Routledge.

Dobson, A. and Lucardie, P. (eds) (1993) *The Politics of Nature: Explorations in Green Political Theory*, London: Routledge.

Dodds, F. (ed.) (1997) *The Way Forward: Beyond Agenda 21*, London: Earthscan.

Dodds, F. (ed.) (2001) *Earth Summit 2002: A New Deal* (revised edition), London: Earthscan.

Doherty, B. (1992) 'The Fundi-Realo Controversy: An Analysis of Four European Green Parties', *Environmental Politics* **1** (1): 95–120.

Doherty, B. (1997) 'Direct Action Against Road-building: Some Implications for the Concept of Protest Repertoires', in J. Stanyer and G. Stoker (eds) *Contemporary Political Studies*, Nottingham: Political Studies Association.

Doherty, B. (1999) 'Paving the Way: The Rise of Direct Action Against Road-building and the Changing Character of British Environmentalism', *Political Studies* **47** (2): 275–91.

Doherty, B. (2000) 'Manufacturing Vulnerability: Protest Camp Tactics', in B. Seel, M. Paterson and B. Doherty (eds) *Direct Action in British Environmentalism*, London: Routledge.

Doherty, B. and de Geus, M. (eds) (1996) *Democracy and Green Political Thought*, London: Routledge.

Dower, N. (ed.) (1989) *Ethics and Environmental Responsibility*, Aldershot: Avebury.

Downs, A. (1972) 'Up and Down with Ecology – the "Issue–Attention Cycle"', *The Public Interest* **28**: 38–50.

Dryzek, J. (1987) *Rational Ecology*, Oxford: Blackwell.

Dryzek, J. (1990) 'Green Reason: Communicative Ethics for the Biosphere', *Environmental Ethics* **12**: 195–210.

Dryzek, J. (1992) 'Ecology and Discursive Democracy: Beyond Liberal Capitalism and the Administrative State', *Capitalism, Nature, Socialism* **3**(2): 18–42.

Dryzek, J. (1995a) 'Political and Ecological Communication', *Environmental Politics* **4** (4): 13–30.

Dryzek, J. (1995b) 'Democracy and Environmental Policy Instruments', in R. Eckersley (ed.) *Markets, the State and the Environment*, London: Macmillan

Dryzek, J. (1997) *The Politics of the Earth: Environmental Discourses*, Oxford: Oxford University Press.

Dryzek, J. (2000) *Deliberative Democracy and Beyond*, Oxford: Oxford University Press

Dryzek, J. and Schlosberg, D. (eds) (1998) *Debating the Earth: The Environmental Politics Reader*, Oxford: Oxford University Press.

Duff, A. (ed.) (1997) *The Treaty of Amsterdam: Texts and Commentary*, London: Sweet & Maxwell.

Dunn, J. (1990) *Interpreting Political Responsibility*, Oxford: Blackwell.

Dworkin, R. (1977) *Taking Rights Seriously*, London: Duckworth.

Eckersley, R. (1992) *Environmentalism and Political Theory*, London: UCL Press.

Eckersley, R. (ed.) (1995a) *Markets, the State and the Environment*, London: Macmillan.

Eckersley, R. (1995b) 'Liberal Democracy and the Rights of Nature: The Struggle for Inclusion', *Environmental Politics* **4**(4): 169–98.

Eckersley, R. (1996) 'Greening Liberal Democracy: The Rights Discourse Revisited', in B. Doherty and M. de Geus (eds) *Democracy and Green Political Thought*, London: Routledge.

Eckersley, R. (1999) 'The Discourse Ethic and the Problem of Representing Nature', *Environmental Politics* **8**(2): 24–49.

The Ecologist (1993) *Whose Common Future?*, London: Earthscan.

Ehrlich, P. (1972) *The Population Bomb*, London: Pan/Ballantine.

Ekins, P. (ed.) (1986) *The Living Economy: A New Economics in the Making*, London: Routledge & Kegan Paul.

Ekins, P. (1995) 'Economics and Sustainability', in C. Ravaioli (ed.) *Economists and the Environment*, London: Zed Books.

Elkington, J. and Burke, T. (1987) *The Green Capitalists*, London: Gollancz.

Elkington, J. and Hailes, J. (1988) *The Green Consumer Guide*, London: Gollancz.

Elliot, L. (2001) *The Global Politics of the Environment*, Basingstoke: Macmillan.

Elliot, R. (ed.) (1995) *Environmental Ethics*, Oxford: Oxford University Press.

Environmental Data Services (ENDS) (1994) 'Advancing the Sustainable Development Agenda', *ENDS Report*, No. 228 (January): 18–21.

ENDS (1995a) 'Round Table on Sustainable Development starts work', *ENDS Report*, No. 240 (January): 6.

ENDS (1995b) 'European Environment Agency gets under way', *ENDS Report*, No. 240 (January): 20–3.

ENDS (1995c) 'Treasury put to test over sustainable development', *ENDS Report*, No. 242 (March): 29.

ENDS (1995d) 'Lords urge step-by-step move to EC environment inspectorate', *ENDS Report*, No. 242 (March): 30–1.

ENDS (1995e) 'Taking cost/benefit analysis too far', *ENDS Report*, No. 243 (April): 2.

ENDS (1996a) 'Commission outlines ideas for improving implementation', *ENDS Report*, No. 257 (June): 44–5.

ENDS (1996b) 'Disappointing response to Round Table report', *ENDS Report*, No. 258 (July): 35–6.

ENDS (1996c) 'Breaches of EC environmental rules remain commonplace', *ENDS Report*, No. 261 (October): 39–40.

ENDS (1996d) 'Commission treads softly on decentralisation of enforcement', *ENDS Report*, No. 261 (October): 40–1.

ENDS (1996e) 'Green Ministers who barely meet', *ENDS Report*, No. 263 (December): 24.

ENDS (1997a) 'Sustainable development becomes Treaty goal for EC', *ENDS Report*, No. 269 (June): 44–5.

ENDS (1997b) 'Commission proposals to ease work of European Environmental Agency', *ENDS Report*, No. 270 (July): 40–1.

369

ENDS (1999) 'Audit Committee keeps up pressure on "greening government"', *ENDS Report*, No. 294 (July): 33–4.

ENDS (2000) 'Ministers press on with greening government', *ENDS Report*, No. 310 (November): 12–13.

ENDS (2001a) '"Decoupling" ambition for EC's sixth environmental programme', *ENDS Report*, No. 313 (February): 46–7.

ENDS (2001b) 'EMAS-2 opens for business', *ENDS Report*, No. 316 (May): 6.

ENDS (2001c) 'Commission sets out priorities for sustainability strategy', *ENDS Report*, No. 316 (May): 47.

ENDS (2001d) 'Mixed feelings as Bonn climate talks succeed', *ENDS Report*, No. 318 (July): 49.

ENDS (2001e) 'Directive on environmental liability takes shape', *ENDS Report*, No. 322 (November): 42–4.

ENDS (2002a) 'Business gets extra defences in proposed EU liability rules', *ENDS Report*, No. 324 (January): 40–1.

ENDS (2002b) 'Pieces fall into place for emissions auction', *ENDS Report*, No. 324 (January): 6–7.

ENDS (2002c) 'EU study highlights barriers to green tax reform', *ENDS Report*, No. 324 (January): 8–9.

ENDS (2002d) 'Inspections slump to record low as Agency struggles with IPPC', *ENDS Report*, No. 325 (February): 6.

Environment Challenge Group (1994) *Green Gauge: Indicators for the State of the UK Environment*, London: ECG.

Environmental Audit Committee (EAC) (2001) 'Environmental Audit: First Parliament and Next Steps', Press Notice No. 5, Session 2000–01 (9 January) www.parliament.uk/commons/selcom/eapnt05.htm.

European Commission (1985) *Council Directive on the Assessment of the Effects of Certain Public and Private Projects on the Environment*, Luxembourg: Commission of the European Communities.

European Commission (1992) *Towards Sustainability: The Fifth Environmental Action Programme*, Luxembourg: CEC.

European Commission (1999) *Europe's Environment: What Directions for the Future?*, Luxembourg: CEC.

European Commission (2001) *A Sustainable Europe for a Better World: A European Union Strategy for Sustainable Development*, Luxembourg: CEC.

European Commission (2002) *Environment 2010: Our Future, Our Choice: The Sixth Environmental Action Programme*, Luxembourg: CEC.

European Environment Agency (EEA) (1995) *Europe's Environment (The Dobris Assessment)*, Luxembourg: Office for Official Publications of the European Communities.

EEA (1998) *Europe's Environment: The Second Assessment*, Luxembourg: Office for Official Publications of the European Communities.

EEA (1999) *Environment in the European Union at the Turn of the Century*, Copenhagen: EEA.

EEA (2001) *Reporting on Environmental Measures: Are We Being Effective?* (Environmental Issue Report No. 25), Copenhagen: EEA.

EEA (2002) *Environmental Signals 2002*, Copenhagen: EEA.

Falk, R. (1995) *On Humane Governance*, Cambridge: Polity Press.

Feinberg, J. (1991) 'The Rights of Animals and Unborn Generations', in J. White (ed.) *Contemporary Moral Problems*, St Pauls, MN: West Publishing Co.

Fischer, F. (2000) *Citizens, Experts and the Environment: The Politics of Local Knowledge*, Durham, NC: Duke University Press.

Fitzpatrick, T. and Caldwell, C. (2001) 'Towards a Theory of Ecosocial Welfare: Radical Reformism and Local Exchanges and Trading Systems (LETS)', *Environmental Politics* **10** (2): 43–67.

Foley, M. and Edwards, B. (1999) 'Is It Time To Disinvest in Social Capital?', *Journal of Public Policy* **19**: 669–78.

Foster, J. (ed.) (1997) *Valuing Nature: Economics, Ethics and Environment*, London: Routledge.

Foster, M.B. (1992) *Creation, Nature, and Political Order in the Philosophy of Michael Foster* (edited by C. Wybrow), Lewiston: Edwin Mellen Press.

Fox, W. (1990) *Towards a Transpersonal Ecology*, Boston: Shambhala.

Frankel, B. (1987) *The Post-Industrial Utopians*, Cambridge: Polity Press.

Frankena, W. (1979) 'Ethics and the Environment', in K.E. Goodpaster and K.M. Sayre (eds) *Ethics and Problems of the Twentieth Century*, Notre Dame and London: University of Notre Dame Press.

Freeden, M. (1995) *Green Ideology: Concepts and Structures* (OCEES Research Paper No. 4), Mansfield College, Oxford.

Friends of the Earth (1988) *Environmental Charter for Local Government*, London: FOE.

Friends of the Earth (1996) *Earthmatters: 25th Anniversary Issue*, No. 30 (Summer).

Gallie, W.B. (1964) *Philosophy and the Historical Understanding*, London: Chatto & Windus.

Garner, R. (2000) *Environmental Politics: Britain, Europe and the Global Environment* (second edition), Basingstoke: Macmillan.

Gaventa, J. (1982) *Power and Powerlessness: Quiescence and Rebellion in an Appalachian Valley*, Oxford: Clarendon Press.

George, S. (1996) *Politics and Policy in the European Union* (third edition), Oxford: Oxford University Press.

Georgescu-Roegen, N. (1971) *The Entropy Law and the Economic Process*, Cambridge, MA: Harvard University Press.

Giddens, A. (1998) *The Third Way*, Cambridge: Polity Press.

Gillies, D. (1999) *A Guide to EC Environmental Law*, London: Earthscan.

Golding, M.P. (1972) 'Obligations to Future Generations', *The Monist* **56**: 85–99.

Goldsmith, E. (ed.) (1992) *The Future of Progress: Reflections on Environment and Development*, Bristol: International Society for Ecology and Culture.

Goldsmith, E. and Mander, J. (eds) (2001) *The Case Against the Global Economy*, London: Earthscan.

Goldsmith, E., Allen, R., Allaby, M., Davoll, J. and Lawrence, S. (1972) *A Blueprint for Survival*, Harmondsworth: Penguin.

Goldsmith, M. (1996) 'Normative Theories of Local Government: A European Comparison', in D. King and G. Stoker (eds) *Rethinking Local Democracy*, Basingstoke: Macmillan.

Golub, J. (1996a) 'Sovereignty and Subsidiarity in EU Environmental Policy', *Political Studies* **44** (4): 686–703.

Golub, J. (1996b) 'British Sovereignty and EC Environmental Policy', *Environmental Politics* **5** (4): 700–28.

Goodin, R. (1992) *Green Political Theory*, Cambridge: Polity Press.

Goodin, R. (1996) 'Enfranchising the Earth, and its Alternative', *Political Studies* **44** (5): 835–49.

Goodin, R. (1998) 'Selling Environmental Indulgences', in J. Dryzek and D. Schlosberg (eds) *Debating the Earth: The Environmental Politics Reader*, Oxford: Oxford University Press, pp. 237–54.

Goodpaster, K.E. (1978) 'On Being Morally Considerable', *Journal of Philosophy* **75**: 308–25.

Gorz, A. (1980) *Ecology as Politics*, London: Pluto.

Gouldson, A. and Murphy, J. (1997) 'Ecological Modernisation and Restructuring Industrial Economies', in M. Jacobs (ed.) *Greening the Millennium*, Oxford: Blackwell.

Gouldson, A. and Murphy, J. (1998) *Regulatory Realities*, London: Earthscan.

Gouldson, A. and Roberts, P. (eds) (2000) *Integrating Environment and Economy: Strategies for Local and Regional Government*, London: Routledge.

Grant, W. (1989) *Pressure Groups, Politics and Democracy in Britain*, London: Philip Allan.

Gray, J. (1993) *Beyond the New Right: Markets, Government and the Common Good*, London: Routledge.

Gray, T.S. (ed.) (1995) *UK Environmental Policy in the 1990s*, Basingstoke: Macmillan.

Gregory, R. (1989) 'Political Rationality or "Incrementalism"?', *Policy and Politics* **17**: 139–53.

Gruen, L. and Jamieson, D. (eds) (1994) *Reflecting on Nature*, Oxford: Oxford University Press.

Gunderson, A.G. (1995) *The Environmental Promise of Democratic Deliberation*, Madison: University of Wisconsin Press.

Gyford, J. (1991) *Citizens, Consumers and Councils*, Basingstoke: Macmillan.

Haas, P. (1989) 'Do Regimes Matter: Epistemic Communities and Mediterranean Pollution Control', *International Organisation* **43**: 377–403.

Haas, P., Keohane, R. and Levy, M. (eds) (1993) *Institutions for the Earth*, Cambridge, Mass.: MIT Press.

Haigh, N. (1989) *EEC Environmental Policy and Britain* (second edition), London: Longman.

Haigh, N. and Irwin, F. (eds) (1990) *Integrated Pollution Control in Europe and North America*, Washington, D.C.: The Conservation Foundation.

Haigh, N. and Lanigan, C. (1995) 'Impact of the European Union on UK Environmental Policy Making', in T.S. Gray (ed.) *UK Environmental Policy in the 1990s*, Basingstoke: Macmillan.

Hajer, M.A. (1995) *The Politics of Environmental Discourse: Ecological Modernisation and the Policy Process*, Oxford: Oxford University Press.

Hall, D., Hebbert, M. and Lusser, H. (1993) 'The Planning Background', in A. Blowers (ed.) *Planning for a Sustainable Environment*, London: Earthscan.

Hamer, M. (1987) *Wheels Within Wheels*, London: Routledge.

Hams, T. (1994) 'Local Environmental Policies and Strategies After Rio', in J. Agyeman and B. Evans (eds) *Local Environmental Policies and Strategies*, Harlow: Longman.

Hams, T., Jacobs, M., Levett, R., Lusser, H., Morphet, J. and Taylor, D. (1994) *Greening Your Local Authority*, Harlow: Longman.

Handler, T. (1994) *Regulating the European Environment*, London: Wiley.

Hardin, G. (1977) 'Lifeboat Ethics: The Case against Helping the Poor', in W. Aiken and H. La Follette (eds) *World Hunger and Moral Obligation*, Englewood Cliffs: Prentice-Hall.

Hardin, G. (1998) [1968] 'The Tragedy of the Commons', in J. Dryzek and D. Schlosberg (eds) *Debating the Earth: The Environmental Politics Reader*, Oxford: Oxford University Press.

Harding, R. and Fisher, E. (eds) (1999) *Perspectives on the Precautionary Principle*, Sydney: Federation Press.

Harris, P.G. (2001) 'Assessing Climate Change: International Cooperation and Predictions of Environmental Change', *Politics* **21** (1): 11–22.

Hay, P.R. (1988) 'Ecological Values and Western Political Traditions: From Anarchism to Fascism', *Politics* **8**: 22–9.

Hayward, T. (1995) *Ecological Thought*, Cambridge: Polity Press.

Heap, S.H., Hollis, M., Lyons, B., Sugden, R. and Weale, A. (1992) *The Theory of Choice: A Critical Guide*, Oxford: Blackwell.

Held, D. and McGrew, A. (eds) (2000) *The Global Transformations Reader*, Cambridge: Polity Press.

Held, D., McGrew, A., Goldblatt, D. and Perraton, J. (1999) *Global Transformations*, Cambridge: Polity Press.

Helm, D. (ed.) (1991) *Economic Policy Towards the Environment*, Oxford: Blackwell.

Henry, R. (1996) 'Adapting United Nations Agencies for Agenda 21: Programme Coordination and Organisational Reform', *Environmental Politics* **5** (1): 1–24.

Hill, D. (1999) *Urban Policy and Politics in Britain*, Basingstoke: Palgrave.

Hill, D. and Smith, T. (1994) 'Environmental Management and Audit', in J. Agyeman and B. Evans (eds) *Local Environmental Policies and Strategies*, Harlow: Longman.

Hindess, B. (1996) *Discourses of Power*, Oxford: Blackwell.

Hirst, P. and Thompson, G. (1999) *Globalisation in Question* (second edition), Cambridge: Polity Press.

HM Treasury (1991) *Economic Appraisal in Central Government: A Technical Guide for Government Departments*, London: HMSO.

Hoffmann, J. (1999) 'From a Party of Young Voters to an Ageing Generation Party?', *Environmental Politics* **8** (3): 140–6.

Holm, J. and Bowker, J. (eds) (1994) *Attitudes to Nature*, London: Pinter.

Humphrys, J. (2001) *The Great Food Gamble*, London: Hodder & Stoughton.

Hurrell, A. (1993) 'The 1992 Earth Summit: Funding Mechanisms and Environmental Institutions', *Environmental Politics* **1** (4): 273–9.

Hurrell, A. and Kingsbury, B. (eds) (1992) *The International Politics of the Environment*, Oxford: Clarendon Press.

Imber, M. (1993) 'The United Nations' Role in Sustainable Development', *Environmental Politics* **2** (4): 123–36.

The Independent (2002) 'Editorial: Charge Motorists to Use Busy Roads – But Not the Mayor of London's Way', *The Independent*, 25 February.

Ingham, A. (1993) 'The Market for Sulphur Dioxide Permits in the USA and UK', *Environmental Politics* **2** (4): 98–122.

International Council for Local Environmental Initiatives (ICLEI) (1993) *Local Initiatives: ICLEI Members in Action 1991–1992*, Toronto: ICLEI.

International Institute for Sustainable Development (IISD) (1997) *Assessing Sustainable Development: Principles in Practice*, Winnipeg: IISD.

Irvine, S. and Ponton, A. (1988) *A Green Manifesto: Policies for a Green Future*, London: MacDonald Optima.

Irwin, A. (1995) *Citizen Science: A Study of People, Expertise and Sustainable Development*, London: Routledge.

Jacobs, M. (1991) *The Green Economy*, London: Pluto.

Jacobs, M. (1994) 'The Limits to Neoclassicism', in M. Redclift and T. Benton (eds) *Social Theory and the Global Environment*, London: Routledge.

Jacobs, M. (1995a) 'Sustainable Development: Assumptions, Contradictions, Progress', in J. Lovenduski and J. Stanyer (eds) *Contemporary Political Studies: Proceedings of the Annual Conference of the Political Studies Association*, London: PSA.

Jacobs, M. (1995b) 'Financial Incentives: The British Experience', in R. Eckersley (ed.) *Markets, the State and the Environment*, London: Macmillan.

Jacobs, M. (1995c) 'Sustainable Development, Capital Substitution and Economic Humility: A Response to Beckerman', *Environmental Values* **4**: 57–68.

Jacobs, M. (1999a) 'Sustainable Development as a Contested Concept', in A. Dobson (ed.) *Fairness and Futurity: Essays on Environmental Sustainability and Social Justice*, Oxford: Oxford University Press.

Jacobs, M. (1999b) *Environmental Modernisation: The New Labour Agenda*, London: Fabian Society.

Jänicke, M. and Jörgens, H. (1998) 'National Environmental Policy Planning in OECD Countries: Preliminary Lessons from Cross-National Comparisons', *Environmental Politics* **7** (2): 27–54.

Jänicke, M. and Weidner, H. (eds) (1995) *Successful Environmental Policy: A Critical Evaluation of 24 Cases*, Berlin: Sigma.

Jänicke, M. and Weidner, H. (eds) (1997) *National Environmental Policies: A Comparative Study of Capacity-Building*, Berlin: Springer.

Jeffrey, S. (2002) 'Congestion Charges', www.guardian.co.uk/livingstone.

Jiménez-Beltrán, D. (1995) 'The Process of Sustainable Development and the Role of the European Environment Agency', *European Environmental Law Review* **4** (10) (October): 265–9.

John, P. (1997) 'Local Governance', in P. Dunleavy, A. Gamble, I. Holliday and G. Peele (eds) *Developments in British Politics 5*, Basingstoke: Macmillan.

Johnson, G. and Corcelle, S. (1995) *The Environmental Policy of the European Communities* (second edition), London: Kluwer.

Jordan, A. (1993) 'Integrated Pollution Control and the Evolving Style and Structure of Environmental Regulation in the UK', *Environmental Politics* **2** (3): 405–27.

Jordan, A. (2000) 'Environmental Policy', in P. Dunleavy, A. Gamble, I. Holliday and G. Peele (eds) *Developments in British Politics 6*, Basingstoke: Macmillan.

Jordan, A. and Fairbrass, J. (2001) 'European Union Environmental Policy after the Nice Summit', *Environmental Politics* **10** (4): 109–14.

Jordan, G. (2001) *Shell, Greenpeace and the Brent Spar*, Basingstoke: Palgrave.

Jordan, G. and Maloney, W. (1997) *Protest Businesses? Mobilising Campaigning Groups*, Manchester: Manchester University Press.

Jordan, G. and Richardson, J. (1987) *British Politics and the Policy Process*, London: Allen & Unwin.

Jordan, T. and Lent, A. (eds) (1999) *Storming the Millennium: The New Politics of Change*, London: Lawrence & Wishart.

Judge, D. (ed.) (1993) *A Green Dimension for the European Community*, London: Frank Cass.

Kant, I. (1963) *Lectures on Ethics*, New York: Harper Torchbooks.

Kay, P. (1992) *Where Motor Car is Master: How the Department of Transport Became Bewitched by Roads*, London: CPRE.

Keat, R. (1997) 'Values and Preferences in Neo-Classical Environmental Economics', in J. Foster (ed.) *Valuing Nature: Economics, Ethics and Environment*, London: Routledge.

Kemp, R. (1985) 'Planning, Public Hearings, and the Politics of Discourse', in J. Forester (ed.) *Critical Theory and Public Life*, Cambridge, Mass.: MIT Press.

Khor, M. (1992) 'Development, Trade and the Environment: A Third World Perspective', in E. Goldsmith (ed.) *The Future of Progress: Reflections on Environment and Development*, Bristol: International Society for Ecology and Culture.

Khor, M. (1994) 'CSD Still Alive, But not yet Kicking into Action', *Third World Resurgence* **47** (July): 3–4.

Khor, M. (1997) 'Effects of Globalisation on Sustainable Development after UNCED', *Third World Resurgence* **81/82** (May/June): 5–11.

Kinrade, P. (1995) 'Towards Ecologically Sustainable Development: The Role and Shortcomings of Markets', in R. Eckersley (ed.) *Markets, the State and the Environment*, London: Macmillan.

Knetsch, J. (1990) 'Environmental Policy Implications of Disparities between Willingness to Pay and Compensation Demanded Measures of Values', *Journal of Environmental Economics and Management* **18**: 227–37.

Krämer, L. (1993) *European Environmental Law Casebook*, London: Sweet & Maxwell.

Krämer, L. (1995) *E.C. Treaty and Environmental Law* (second edition), London: Sweet & Maxwell.

Krämer, L. (1997) *Focus on European Environmental Law* (second edition), London: Sweet & Maxwell.

Krasner, S. (ed.) (1983) *International Regimes*, Ithaca: Cornell University Press.

Kunzlik, P. (1994) *Environmental Policy*, London: Longmans.

Kuper, R. (1997) 'Deliberating Waste: The Hertfordshire Citizens' Jury', *Local Environment* **2** (2): 139–53.

Labour Party (1994) *In Trust for Tomorrow*, London: Labour Party.

Laferrière, E. and Stoett, P. (1999) *International Relations Theory and Ecological Thought*, London: Routledge.

Lafferty, W. (ed.) (1999) *Implementing LA21 in Europe*, Oslo: ProSus.

Lafferty, W. (ed.) (2002) *Sustainable Communities in Europe*, London: Earthscan.

Lafferty, W. and Eckerberg, K. (eds) (1998) *From Earth Summit to Local Agenda 21: Working Towards Sustainable Development*, London: Earthscan.

Lafferty, W. and Meadowcroft, J. (eds) (2000) *Implementing Sustainable Development: Strategies and Initiatives in High Consumption Societies*, Oxford: Oxford University Press.

Lamb, R. (1996) *Promising the Earth*, London: Routledge.

Lang, P. (1994) *LETS Work*, Bristol: Grover Books.

Lang, T. and Hines, C. (1993) *The New Protectionism: Protecting the Future Against Free Trade*, London: Earthscan.

Laver, M. (1983) *Invitation to Politics*, Oxford: Blackwell.

Lawrence, G. (1994) 'Sustainable Seattle, USA', in Department of the Environment, *Partnerships for Change*, London: HMSO.

Layton, C. (2001) *A Climate Community: A European Initiative with the South*, London: The Federal Trust.

Leach, S. (1996a) 'The Dimensions of Analysis: Governance, Markets and Community', in S. Leach and H. Davis (eds) *Enabling or Disabling Local Government*, Buckingham: Open University.

Leach, S. (1996b) 'Conclusion: Scenarios for Change', in S. Leach and H. Davis (eds) *Enabling or Disabling Local Government*, Buckingham: Open University.

Leach, S. and Davis, H. (1996) 'Introduction', in S. Leach and H. Davis (eds) *Enabling or Disabling Local Government*, Buckingham: Open University.

Leahy, M. (1994) *Against Liberation*, London: Routledge.

Lee, K. (1994) 'Awe and Humility: Intrinsic Value in Nature', in R. Attfield and A. Belsey (eds) *Philosophy and the Natural Environment*, Cambridge: Cambridge University Press.

Lee, N. (1989) *Environmental Impact Assessment: A Training Guide*, Occasional Paper No. 18 (second edition), EIA Centre, Department of Planning and Landscape, University of Manchester.

Lee, N. and Walsh, F. (1992) 'Strategic Environmental Assessment: An Overview', *Project Appraisal* **7** (3): 126–36.

Levy, M., Keohane, R. and Haas, P. (1993) 'Improving the Effectiveness of International Environmental Institutions', in P. Haas, R. Keohane and M. Levy (eds) *Institutions for the Earth*, Cambridge, Mass.: MIT Press.

Liberatore, A. (1997) 'The Integration of Sustainable Development Objectives into EU Policy-making: Barriers and Prospects', in S. Baker, M. Kousis, D. Richardson and S. Young (eds) *The Politics of Sustainable Development: Theory, Policy and Practice Within the European Union*, London: Routledge.

Lightfoot, S. and Luckin, D. (2000) 'The 1999 German Tax Law', *Environmental Politics* **9** (2): 163–7.

Lindblom, C. (1959) 'The Science of Muddling Through', *Public Administration Review* **19**: 79–88.

Lindblom, C. (1965) *The Intelligence of Democracy*, New York: Free Press.

Lindblom, C. (1979) 'Still Muddling, Not Yet Through', *Public Administration Review* **39**: 517–26.

Local Government Management Board (LGMB) (1992) *Agenda 21: A Guide for Local Authorities in the U.K.*, Luton: LGMB.

LGMB (1993a) *Towards Sustainability: A Guide for Local Authorities*, Luton: LGMB.

LGMB (1993b) *A Framework for Local Sustainability*, Luton: LGMB.

LGMB (1993c) *The UK's Submission to the UN Commission on Sustainable Development: An Initial Submission by UK Local Government*, Luton: LGMB.

LGMB (1994) *Local Agenda 21 Principles and Processes: A Step by Step Guide*, Luton: LGMB.

LGMB (1995a) *The Sustainable Management of Solid Waste*, Luton: LGMB.

LGMB (1995b) *Sustainability Indicators Research Project: Consultants' Report of the Pilot Phase*, Luton: LGMB.

Lomborg, B. (2001) *The Skeptical Environmentalist*, Cambridge: Cambridge University Press.

London Economics (1992) *The Potential Role of Market Mechanisms in the Control of Acid Rain*, Department of the Environment, Environmental Research Series, London: HMSO.

Lovelock, J. (1979) *Gaia: A New Look at Life on Earth*, Oxford: Clarendon Press.

Low, N. and Gleeson, B. (1998) *Justice, Society and Nature: An Exploration of Political Ecology*, London: Routledge.

Lowe, P. and Goyder, J. (1983) *Environmental Groups in Politics*, London: Allen & Unwin.

Lowe, P. and Ward, S. (eds) (1998) *British Environmental Policy and Europe: Politics and Policy in Transition*, London: Routledge.

Lukes, S. (1974) *Power: A Radical View*, London: Macmillan.

Lusser, H. (1994) 'Environmental Planning', in J. Agyeman and B. Evans (eds) *Local Environmental Policies and Strategies*, Harlow: Longman.

Macnaghten, P., Grove-White, R., Jacobs, M. and Wynne, B. (1995) *Public Perception and Sustainability in Lancashire*, Preston: Lancashire County Council.

Maddison, D., Pearce, D., Johansson, O., Calthrop, E., Litman, T. and Verhoef, E. (1996) *Blueprint 5: The True Costs of Road Transport*, London: Earthscan.

Malthus, T. (1968) *An Essay on the Principles of Population*, Harmondsworth: Penguin.

Manning, F. (2000) 'Biotechnology: A Scientific Perspective', in A. Russell and J. Vogler (eds) *The International Politics of Biotechnology: Investigating Global Futures*, Manchester: Manchester University Press.

Marin, A. (1997) 'EC Environmental Policy', in S. Stavridis, E. Mossialos, R. Morgan and H. MacHin (eds) *New Challenges to the European Union: Policies and Policy-Making*, Aldershot: Dartmouth.

Markandya, A. (1991) 'Global Warming: The Economics of Tradeable Permits', in D. Pearce, E. Barbier, A. Markandya, S. Barrett, R.K. Turner and T. Swanson (eds) *Blueprint 2: Greening the World Economy*, London: Earthscan.

Marman, K. (1996) 'Road Rave', *Green Line* **137** (September): 3–5.

Marsh, D. and Rhodes, R. (1992) *Policy Networks in British Government*, Oxford: Clarendon Press.

Martell, L. (1994) *Ecology and Society*, Cambridge: Polity Press.

Mathews, F. (1991) *The Ecological Self*, London: Routledge.

Mayo, E. (1994) 'What Happened When We Measured "Real" Wealth', *New Economics* **29** (Spring): 6–7.

McCormick, J. (1991) *British Politics and the Environment*, London: Earthscan.

McCormick, J. (1993) 'Environmental Politics', in P. Dunleavy, A. Gamble and G. Peele (eds) *Developments in British Politics 4*, London: Macmillan.

McCormick, J. (2001) *Environmental Policy in the European Union*, London: Palgrave.

McKay, G. (1996) *Senseless Acts of Beauty: Cultures of Resistance Since the Sixties*, London: Verso.

McKay, G. (ed.) (1998) *Party and Protest in Nineties Britain*, London: Verso.

McLean, I. (1987) *Public Choice*, Oxford: Blackwell.

Meadows, D.H., Meadows, D.L., Randers, J. and Behrens, W.W. (1972) *The Limits to Growth*, London: Pan.

Mensah, C. (1996) 'The United Nations Commission on Sustainable Development', in J. Werksman (ed.) *Greening International Institutions*, London: Earthscan.

Meyer, A. (2000) *Contraction and Convergence – The Global Solution to Climate Change*, Dartmouth: Green Books

Midgley, M. (1983) *Why Animals Matter*, Harmondsworth: Penguin.

Midgley, M. (1994) 'The End of Anthropocentrism?', in R. Attfield and A. Belsey (eds) *Philosophy and the Natural Environment*, Cambridge: Cambridge University Press.

Mihevc, J. (1995) *The Market Tells Them So: The World Bank and Economic Fundamentalism in Africa*, London: Zed.

Mill, J.S. (1874) *Three Essays on Religion*, London: Longmans.

Mill, J.S. (1909) *Principles of Political Economy*, London: Longmans.

Miller, D. (1992) 'Deliberative Democracy and Social Choice', *Political Studies Special Issue: Prospects for Democracy* **40**: 54–67.

Miller, W., Timpson, A. and Lessnoff, M. (1996) *Political Culture in Contemporary Britain*, Oxford: Clarendon Press.

Ministry of Housing, Physical Planning and Environment (1989) *National Environmental Policy Plan: To Choose or to Lose*, The Hague: SDU.

Ministry of Housing, Physical Planning and Environment (1990) *Report Recommendations on and Responses to the NEPP*, The Hague: SDU.

Mishan, E.J. (1988) *Cost–Benefit Analysis*, London: George Allen & Unwin.

Mol, A.P.J. and Sonnenfield, D. (eds) (2000) *Ecological Modernisation Around the World: Perspectives and Critical Debates*, London: Frank Cass.

Mol, A.P.J. and Spaargaren, G. (2000) 'Ecological Modernisation Theory in Debate: A Review', *Environmental Politics* **9** (1): 17–49.

Mol, A.P.J., Lauber, V. and Liefferink, D. (eds) (2000) *The Voluntary Approach to Environmental Policy*, Oxford: Oxford University Press.

Monbiot, G. (2000) *Captive State*, London: Macmillan.

Monbiot, G. (2002) 'Business of Betrayal', *The Guardian*, 15 January, p. 15.

Moran, A. (1995) 'Tools of Environmental Policy: Market Instruments versus Command-and-control', in R. Eckersley (ed.) *Markets, the State and the Environment*, London: Macmillan.

Morriss, P. (1987) *Power: A Philosophical Analysis*, Manchester: Manchester University Press.

Mueller, D. (1989) *Public Choice II*, Cambridge: Cambridge University Press.

Müller-Rommel, F. and Poguntke, T. (eds) (2002) *Green Parties in National Governments*, London: Cass.

Naess, A. (1973) 'The Shallow and Deep Ecology Movement', *Inquiry* **16**: 95–100.

Naess, A. (1989) *Ecology, Community and Lifestyle*, Cambridge: Cambridge University Press.

Nasr, H. (1990) *Man and Nature*, London: Unwin.

New Economics Foundation (no date) *Participation Works!*, London: New Economics Foundation.

Newell, P. (1998) 'Who "CoPed" Out in Kyoto? An Assessment of the Third Conference of the Parties to the Framework Convention on Climate Change', *Environmental Politics* **7** (2): 153–9.

Newell, P. (2000) *Climate for Change: Non-state Actors and the Global Politics of the Greenhouse*, Cambridge: Cambridge University Press.

Nijkamp, P. and Perrels, A. (1994) *Sustainable Cities in Europe: A Comparative Analysis of Urban Energy-Environmental Policies*, London: Earthscan.

Norton, A. (1994) *The International Handbook of Local and Regional Government: A Comparative Analysis of Advanced Democracies*, Aldershot: Edward Elgar.

O'Brien, R., Goetz, A.M., Scholte, J.A. and Williams, M. (2000) *Contesting Global Governance: Multilateral Institutions and Global Social Movements*, Cambridge: Cambridge University Press.

Offe, C. and Preuss, U.K. (1991) 'Democratic Institutions and Moral Resources', in D. Held (ed.) *Political Theory Today*, Cambridge: Polity Press.

Office for National Statistics (1992–2001) *Social Trends*, 22–31.

Official Journal of the European Communities (OJ) (1993) C138.

Olson, M. (1971) *The Logic of Collective Action* (second edition), Cambridge, Massachusetts: Harvard University Press.

O'Neill, J. (1993) *Ecology, Policy and Politics: Human Well-Being and the Natural World*, London: Routledge.

Ophuls, W. (1973) 'Leviathan or Oblivion', in H. Daly (ed.) *Toward a Steady-State Economy*, San Francisco: W.H. Freeman.

Ophuls, W. (1977) *Ecology and the Politics of Scarcity*, San Francisco: W.H. Freeman.

Organisation for Economic Cooperation and Development (OECD) (1989) *Environmental Policy Benefits: Monetary Valuation*, Paris: OECD.

O'Riordan, T. (1981) *Environmentalism* (second edition), London: Pion.

O'Riordan, T. (1999) 'The Politics of the Precautionary Principle', in R. Harding and E. Fisher (eds) *Perspectives on the Precautionary Principle*, Sydney: Federation Press.

O'Riordan, T. and Cameron, J. (eds) (1994) *Interpreting the Precautionary Principle*, London: Earthscan.

O'Riordan, T. and Jordan, A. (1995) 'The Precautionary Principle in Contemporary Environmental Politics', *Environmental Values* **4**: 191–212.

O'Riordan, T. and Voisey, H. (1997a) 'The Political Economy of Sustainable Development', *Environmental Politics* **6** (1): 1–23.

O'Riordan, T. and Voisey, H. (eds) (1997b) *Sustainable Development in Western Europe: Coming to Terms with Agenda 21: Special Issue of Environmental Politics*, London: Frank Cass.

O'Riordan, T. and Weale, A. (1989) 'Administrative Reorganisation and Policy Change: The Case of Her Majesty's Inspectorate of Pollution', *Public Administration* **67** (Autumn).

Osborn, D. (1997) 'The Way Forward Beyond Agenda 21: Perspectives on the Future from Europe', in F. Dodds (ed.) *The Way Forward: Beyond Agenda 21*, London: Earthscan.

Ostrom, E. (1990) *Governing the Commons: The Evolution of Institutions for Collective Action*, Cambridge: Cambridge University Press.

Ostrom, E. (1997) 'Investing in Capital, Institutions, and Incentives', in Christopher Clague (ed.) *Institutions and Economic Development: Growth and Governance in Less-Developed and Post-Socialist Countries*, Baltimore, MD: Johns Hopkins University Press.

Ostrom, E. (1998) 'A Behavioural Approach to the Rational Choice Theory of Collective Action', *American Political Science Review* **92** (1): 1–22.

Ostrom, E. and Keohane, R. (1994) 'Introduction', *Journal of Theoretical Politics* **6** (4): 403–28.

Paehlke, R. and Torgerson, D. (eds) (1990) *Managing Leviathan: Environmental Politics and the Administrative State*, Peterborough, Ontario: Broadview Press.

Park, P. (2001) 'The UK Greenhouse Gas Emissions Treading Scheme: "A Brave New World" or The Result of Hurried Thinking?', *European Law and Management* **13** (6): 292–9.

Parkin, S. (1989) *Green Parties: An International Guide*, London: Heretic Books.

Parry, G., Moyser, G. and Day, N. (1992) *Political Participation and Democracy in Britain*, Cambridge: Cambridge University Press.

Parson, E. (1993) 'Protecting the Ozone Layer', in P. Haas, R. Keohane and M. Levy (eds) *Institutions for the Earth*, Cambridge, Mass.: MIT Press.

Passmore, J. (1980) *Man's Responsibility for Nature* (second edition), London: Duckworth.

Paterson, M. (1992) 'The Convention on Climate Change Agreed at the Rio Conference', *Environmental Politics* **1** (4): 267–72.

Paterson, M. (1996) *Global Warming and Global Politics*, London: Routledge.

Paterson, M. (2000) *Understanding Global Environmental Politics*, Basingstoke: Macmillan.

Patterson, A. and Theobald, K. (1996) 'Local Agenda 21, Compulsory Competitive Tendering and Local Environmental Practices', *Local Environment* **1** (1): 7–20.

Peacocke, A. and Hodgson, P. (1989) 'The Judaeo-Christian Tradition', in R. Attfield and K. Dell (eds) *Values, Conflict and the Environment*, Oxford: Ian Ramsey Centre.

Pearce, D. (1983) *Cost–Benefit Analysis* (second edition), London: Macmillan.

Pearce, D. and Barbier, E.B. (2000) *Blueprint for a Sustainable Economy*, London: Earthscan.

Pearce, D. and Turner, R.K. (1990) *Economics of Natural Resources and the Environment*, London: Harvester Wheatsheaf.

Pearce, D., Markandya, A. and Barbier, E.B. (1989) *Blueprint for a Green Economy*, London: Earthscan.

Pearce, D., Barbier, E., Markandya, A., Barrett, S., Turner, R.K. and Swanson, T. (1991) *Blueprint 2: Greening the World Economy*, London: Earthscan.

Pearce, F. (1991) *Green Warriors*, London: Bodley Head.

Pepper, D. (1991) *Communes and the Green Vision: Counterculture, Lifestyle and the New Age*, London: Green Print.

Pepper, D. (1993) *Eco-Socialism: From Deep Ecology to Social Justice*, London: Routledge.

Pepper, D. (1999) 'Ecological Modernisation or the "Ideal Model" of Sustainable Development? Questions Promoted at Europe's Periphery', *Environmental Politics* **8** (4): 1–34.

Peters, B.G. and Hogwood, B. (1985) 'In Search of an Issue–Attention Cycle', *Journal of Politics* **47**: 238–53.

Phillips, A. (1996) 'Why Does Local Democracy Matter?', in L. Pratchett and D. Wilson (eds) *Local Democracy and Local Government*, Basingstoke: Macmillan.

Pigou, A. (1932) *The Economics of Welfare* (fourth edition), London: Macmillan.

Pinfield, G. (1992) 'Strategic Environmental Assessment and Land Use Planning', *Project Appraisal* **7**: 157–63.

Plant, R. (1991) *Modern Political Thought*, Oxford: Blackwell.

Plumwood, V. (1986) 'Ecofeminism: An Overview and Discussion of Positions and Arguments', *Australasian Journal of Philosophy* **64** (Supplement): 120–38.

Poguntke, T. (1993) 'Goodbye to Movement Politics? Organisational Adaptation of the German Green Party', *Environmental Politics* **2** (3): 379–404.

Porritt, J. (1984) *Seeing Green: The Politics of Ecology Explained*, Oxford: Blackwell.

Porter, G. and Brown, J. (1996) *Global Environmental Politics* (second edition), Boulder, CO: Westview Press.

Porter, G. and Brown, J. (2000) *Global Environmental Politics* (third edition), Boulder, CO: Westview Press.

Pratchett, L. and Wilson, D. (1996) 'Local Governance under Siege', in L. Pratchett and D. Wilson (eds) *Local Democracy and Local Government*, Basingstoke: Macmillan.

Princen, T. and Finger, M. (1994) *Environmental NGOs in World Politics*, London: Routledge.

Quinton, A. (1982) *Thoughts and Thinkers*, London: Duckworth.

Raghavan, C. (1996) 'TNCs Control Two-Thirds of World Economy', *Third World Resurgence* **65/66** (Jan/Feb): 31–2.

Rao, N. (2000) *Reviving Local Democracy: New Labour, New Politics?*, Bristol: Policy Press.

Rawcliffe, P. (1998) *Environmental Pressure Groups in Transition*, Manchester: Manchester University Press.

Rawls, J. (1972) *A Theory of Justice*, Oxford: Clarendon Press.

Real World Coalition (1996) *The Politics of the Real World*, London: Earthscan.

Real World Coalition (2001) *From Here to Sustainability: Politics in the Real World*, London: Earthscan.

Regan, T. (1984) *The Case for Animal Rights*, London: Routledge.

Renn, O., Webler, T. and Wiedemann, P. (eds) (1995) *Fairness and Competence in Citizen Participation*, Dordrecht: Kluwer.

Rhodes, R.A.W. and Dunleavy, P. (eds) (1995) *Prime Minister, Cabinet and Core Executive*, London: Macmillan.

Richardson, D. and Rootes, C. (eds) (1995) *The Green Challenge: The Development of Green Parties in Europe*, London: Routledge.

Richardson, J. and Jordan, G. (1979) *Governing Under Pressure*, Oxford: Robertson.

Ritchie, D.G. (1894) *Natural Rights*, London: Allen & Unwin.

Road Alert! (1997) *Road Raging: Top Tips for Wrecking Roadbuilding*, Newbury: RA!.

Roberts, J., Cleary, J., Hamilton, K. and Hanna, J. (eds) (1992) *Travel Sickness: The Need for a Sustainable Transport Policy for Britain*, London: Lawrence & Wishart.

Robertson, J. (1989) *Future Wealth*, London: Cassell.

Robinson, M. (1992) *The Greening of British Party Politics*, Manchester: Manchester University Press.

Roddick, J. (1994) 'Second Session of the Commission on Sustainable Development', *Environmental Politics* **3** (3): 503–12.

Roddick, J. and Dodds, F. (1993) 'Agenda 21's Political Strategy', *Environmental Politics* **2** (4): 242–9.

Roemer, J.E. (1989) 'A Public Ownership Resolution of the Tragedy of the Commons', in E.F. Paul, F.D. Miller and J. Paul (eds) *Socialism*, Oxford: Blackwell.

Rolston, H. (1981) 'Values in Nature', *Environmental Ethics* **3**: 113–28.

Rolston, H. (1994) 'Environmental Ethics: Values in and Duties to the Natural World', in L. Gruen and D. Jamieson (eds) *Reflecting on Nature*, Oxford: Oxford University Press.

Rootes, C. (1995) 'Britain: Greens in a Cold Climate', in D. Richardson and C. Rootes (eds) *The Green Challenge: The Development of Green Parties in Europe*, London: Routledge.

Rootes, C. (ed.) (1999) *Environmental Movements: Local, National and Global*, London: Frank Cass.

Ross, A. (2000) 'Greening Government: Tales from the New Sustainability Watchdog', *Journal of Environmental Law* **12** (2): 175–96.

Routley, R. and Routley, V. (1995) 'Against the Inevitability of Human Chauvinism', in R. Elliot (ed.) *Environmental Ethics*, Oxford: Oxford University Press.

Rowell, A. (1996) *Green Backlash*, London: Routledge.

Royal Commission on Environmental Pollution (RCEP) (1976) *Fifth Report: Air Pollution Control – An Integrated Approach*, London: HMSO.

RCEP (1988) *Best Practicable Environmental Option*, London: HMSO.

RCEP (1995) *Transport and the Environment*, Oxford: Oxford University Press.

Rucht, D. and Roose, J. (1999) 'The German Environmental Movement at a Crossroads?', *Environmental Politics* **8** (1): 59–80.

Rüdig, W. (ed.) (1999) *Environmental Policy*, Cheltenham: Edward Elgar.

Russell, A. and Vogler, J. (eds) (2000) *The International Politics of Biotechnology: Investigating Global Futures*, Manchester: Manchester University Press.

Russell, S. (1999) 'Environmental Appraisal of Development Plans', *Town Planning Review* **70** (4): 529–46.

Ryle, M. (1988) *Ecology and Socialism*, London: Century Hutchinson.

Sachs, W. (ed.) (1993) *Global Ecology: A New Arena of Political Conflict*, London: Zed.

Sagoff, M. (1988) *The Economy of the Earth*, Cambridge: Cambridge University Press.

Sale, K. (1985) *Dwellers in the Land: The Bioregional Vision*, San Francisco: Sierra Club Books.

Salih, M. (1997) 'Global Ecologism and its Critics', in C. Thomas and P. Wilkin (eds) *Globalisation and the South*, Basingstoke: Macmillan.

Salt, J. (1998) 'Kyoto and the Insurance Industry: An Insider's Perspective', *Environmental Politics* **7** (2): 160–5.

Sandbrook, R. (1996) 'Rio Plus Five – What has Happened and What Next?', in *Priorities for Earth Summit II*, London: UNED-UK.

Sandler, T. (1997) *Global Challenges: An Approach to Environmental, Political and Economic Problems*, Cambridge: Cambridge University Press.

Sargisson, L. (2001) 'Politicising the Quotidian', *Environmental Politics* **10** (2): 68–89.

Scheffler, S. (1994) *The Rejection of Consequentialism*, Oxford: Clarendon Press.

Schlosberg, D. (1999) *Environmental Justice and the New Pluralism*, Oxford: Oxford University Press.

Schumacher, E.F. (1973) *Small is Beautiful*, London: Sphere.

Scruton, R. (2000) *Animal Rights and Wrongs* (third edition), London: Claridge Press.

Seel, B., Paterson, M. and Doherty, B. (eds) (2000) *Direct Action in British Environmentalism*, London: Routledge.

Sen, A. (1977) 'Rational Fools', *Philosophy and Public Affairs* **6**: 317–44.

Sen, A. (1987) *On Ethics and Economics*, Oxford: Blackwell.

Shaw, B. and Willis, R. (2002) 'Handshakes All Round?', *Green Futures* **32**: 24–6.

Shiva, V. (1988) *Staying Alive: Women, Ecology and Development*, London: Zed Books.

Shiva, V. (1992) 'Recovering the Real Meaning of Sustainability', in D.E. Cooper and J.A. Palmer (eds) *The Environment in Question: Ethics and Global Issues*, London: Routledge.

Shiva, V. (2000) *Stolen Harvest: The Hijacking of the Global Food Supply*, London: Zed Books.

Simon, H. (1957) *Administrative Behaviour* (second edition), New York: Free Press.

Simon, J. and Kahn, H. (1984) *The Resourceful Earth: A Response to Global 2000*, Oxford: Blackwell.

Singer, P. (1983) [1975] *Animal Liberation*, London: Thorsons.

Skea, J. and Smith, A. (1998) 'Integrated Pollution Control', in P. Lowe and S. Ward (eds) *British Environmental Policy and Europe: Politics and Policy in Transition*, London: Routledge.

Slater, D. (1994) 'How IPC is Facilitating Environmental Protection', in J.A.G. Drake (ed.) *Integrated Pollution Control*, Cambridge: Royal Society of Chemistry.

Smith, G. (2000) 'Pluralism, Democratic Deliberation and Environmental Values', in C. Pierson and S. Tormey (eds) *Politics at the Edge*, Basingstoke: Macmillan.

Smith, G. (2001) 'Taking Deliberation Seriously: Institutional Design and Green Politics', *Environmental Politics* **10** (3): 72–93.

Smith, G. and May, D. (1980) 'The Artificial Debate Between Rationalist and Incrementalist Models of Decision Making', *Policy and Politics* **8** (2): 147–61.

Smith, M.J. (ed.) (1999) *Thinking Through the Environment*, London: Routledge.

Soper, K. (1995) *What is Nature?*, Oxford: Blackwell.

Spretnak, C. and Capra, F. (1986) *Green Politics: The Global Promise*, London: Paladin.

Sprigge, T.L.S. (1997) 'Respect for the Non-Human', in T.D.J. Chappell (ed.) *The Philosophy of the Environment*, Edinburgh: Edinburgh University Press.

Standing Advisory Committee on Trunk Road Assessment (SACTRA) (1992) *Assessment of the Environmental Impact of Trunk Roads*, London: HMSO.

SACTRA (1994) *Trunk Roads and the Generation of Traffic*, London: HMSO.

Stewart, J. (1996a) 'Reforming the New Magistracy', in L. Pratchett and D. Wilson (eds) *Local Democracy and Local Government*, Basingstoke: Macmillan.

Stewart, J. (1996b) 'Innovation in Democratic Practice in Local Government', *Policy and Politics* **24** (1): 29–41.

Stewart, J., Kendall, E. and Coote, A. (1994) *Citizen Juries*, London: Institute for Public Policy Research.

Stewart, M. (1996) 'Urban Regeneration', in S. Leach and H. Davis (eds) *Enabling or Disabling Local Government*, Buckingham: Open University.

Stoker, G. (1996a) 'Introduction: Normative Theories of Local Government and Democracy', in D. King and G. Stoker (eds) *Rethinking Local Democracy*, Basingstoke: Macmillan.

Stoker, G. (1996b) 'Redefining Local Democracy', in L. Pratchett and D. Wilson (eds) *Local Democracy and Local Government*, Basingstoke: Macmillan.

Stoker, G. and Young, S. (1993) *Cities in the 1990s*, Harlow: Longman.

Stone, C. (1987) *Earth and Other Ethics: The Case for Moral Pluralism*, New York: Harper & Row.

Stone, C. (1988) 'Moral Pluralism and the Course of Environmental Ethics', *Environmental Ethics* **10**: 139–54.

Straaten, J. van der (1992) 'The Dutch National Environmental Policy Plan: To Choose or To Lose', *Environmental Politics* **1** (1): 45–71.

Straaten, J. van der (1994) 'Recent Developments in Dutch Policy', *Environmental Politics* **3** (4): 226–32.

Strange, S. (1988) *States and Markets*, London: Pinter.

Sunstein, C.R. (1991) 'Preferences and Politics', *Philosophy and Public Affairs* **20**: 3–34.

Sustainable Seattle (1993) *The Sustainable Seattle 1993 Indicators of Sustainable Community: A Report to Citizens on Long-Term Trends in Our Community*, Seattle: Sustainable Seattle.

Sverdrup, L.A. (1997) 'Norway's Institutional Response to Sustainable Development', *Environmental Politics* **6** (1): 54–82.

Therivel, R., Wilson, E., Thompson, S., Heaney, D. and Pritchard, D. (1996) *Strategic Environmental Assessment*, London: Earthscan.

Third World Network (1992) *Earth Summit Briefings*, Penang: TWN.

Thomas, C. (1992) *The Environment in International Relations*, London: Royal Institute of International Affairs.

Thomas, C. (1993) 'Beyond UNCED: An Introduction', *Environmental Politics* **2** (4): 1–27.

Thomas, C. (ed.) (1994) *Rio: Unravelling the Consequences*, Newbury: Frank Cass.

Thomas, C. (1997) 'Globalisation and the South', in C. Thomas and P. Wilkin (eds) *Globalisation and the South*, Basingstoke: Macmillan.

Thompson, J. (1990) 'A Refutation of Environmental Ethics', *Environmental Ethics* **12** (2): 147–60.

Tietenberg, T.H. (1991) 'Economic Instruments for Environmental Regulation', in D. Helm (ed.) *Economic Policy Towards the Environment*, Oxford: Blackwell.

Tindale, S. and Holtham, G. (1996) *Green Tax Reform: Pollution Payments and Labour Tax Cuts*, London: Institute for Public Policy Research.

Toner, G. and Doern, B. (1994) 'Five Political and Policy Imperatives in Green Plan Formation: The Canadian Case', *Environmental Politics* **3** (3): 395–420.

Torgerson, D. (1999a) *The Promise of Green Politics: Environmentalism and the Public Sphere*, Durham, NC: Duke University Press.

Torgerson, D. (1999b) 'Limits to the Administrative Mind', in J. Dryzek and D. Schlosberg (eds) *Debating the Earth: The Environmental Politics Reader*, Oxford: Oxford University Press.

Turner, R.K., Pearce, D. and Bateman, I. (1994) *Environmental Economics*, London: Harvester Wheatsheaf.

Tuxworth, B. (1996) 'From Environment to Sustainability: Surveys and Analysis of Local Agenda 21 Process Development in UK Local Authorities', *Local Environment* **1** (3): 277–98.

Tyme, J. (1978) *Motorways Versus Democracy*, London: Macmillan.

UK Round Table on Sustainable Development (1996) *First Annual Report*, London: DOE.

UK Round Table on Sustainable Development (1997) *Second Annual Report*, London: DOE.

United Nations Association Sustainable Development Unit (UNA SDU)/Community Development Foundation (CDF) (1995) *Towards Local Sustainability: A Review of Current Activity on Local Agenda 21 in the UK*, London: UNA.

United Nations Conference on Environment and Development (UNCED) (1992) *Agenda 21: A Programme for Action for Sustainable Development*, New York: United Nations.

United Nations Development Programme (UNDP) (2001) *Human Development Report 2001*, New York: UNDP.

United Nations Environment and Development UK Committee (UNED-UK) (1996) *UNED-UK Annual Report 1995/96*, London: UNED-UK.

van der Heijden, H. (1997) 'Political Opportunity Structure and the Institutionalisation of the Environmental Movement', *Environmental Politics* **6** (4): 25–50.

van Muijen, M. (2000) 'The Netherlands', in W. Lafferty and J. Meadowcroft (eds) *Implementing Sustainable Development: Strategies and Initiatives in High Consumption Societies*, Oxford: Oxford University Press.

Vidal, J. (1996) 'The Seeds on Stony Ground', *The Guardian*, 16 October, pp. 2–3.

Vincent, A. (1992) *Modern Political Ideologies*, Oxford: Blackwell.

Vincent, A. (1993) 'The Character of Ecology', *Environmental Politics* **2** (2): 248–76.

Vincent, A. (1998) 'Is Environmental Justice a Misnomer?', in D. Boucher and P. Kelly (eds) *Social Justice from Hume to Walzer*, London: Routledge.

Vogel, D. (1993) 'The Making of EC Environmental Policy', in S. Andersen and K. Eliassen (eds) *Making Policy in Europe: The Europeification of National Policy-making*, London: Sage.

Vogler, J. and Imber, M. (eds) (1996) *The Environment and International Relations*, London: Routledge.

Vogler, J. and McGraw, D. (2000) 'An International Environmental Regime for Biotechnology', in A. Russell and J. Vogler (eds) *The International Politics of Biotechnology: Investigating Global Futures*, Manchester: Manchester University Press.

Voisey, H. and O'Riordan, T. (1997) 'Governing Institutions for Sustainable Development: The United Kingdom's National Level Approach', *Environmental Politics* **6** (1): 24–53.

Voisey, H., Beuermann, C., Sverdrup, L.A. and O'Riordan, T. (1996) 'The Political Significance of Local Agenda 21: The Early Stages of Some European Experiences', *Local Environment* **1** (1): 33–50.

Walker, P. and Goldsmith, E. (2001) 'Local Money: A Currency for Every Community', in E. Goldsmith and J. Mander (eds) *The Case Against the Global Economy*, London: Earthscan.

Wall, D. (1994) *Weaving a Bower Against Endless Night . . . An Illustrated History of the UK Green Party*, London: Green Party.

Wall, D. (1999) *Earth First! and the Anti-Roads Movement*, London: Routledge.

Walters, J. (2002) 'Why Only Satellites Can Stop Gridlock', *The Observer*, 24 February, p. 14.

Walters, J. and Jeffries, S. (2001) 'War on the Driver', *The Observer*, 26 August, p. 13.

Ward, H. (1996) 'Green Arguments for Local Democracy', in D. King and G. Stoker (eds) *Rethinking Local Democracy*, Basingstoke: Macmillan.

Ward, H., Grundig, F. and Zorick, E. (2001) 'Marching at the Pace of the Slowest: A Model of International Climate-Change Negotiations', *Political Studies* **49** (3): 438–61.

Ward, S. (1993) 'Thinking Global, Acting Local? British Local Authorities and Their Environmental Plans', *Environmental Politics* **2** (3): 453–78.

Warren, K.J. (1987) 'Feminism and Ecology: Making Connections', *Environmental Ethics* **9** (1): 3–20.

Warren, K.J. (ed.) (1994) *Ecological Feminism*, London: Routledge.

Warren, M.A. (1991) 'The Rights of the Nonhuman World', in J. White (ed.) *Contemporary Moral Problems*, St Pauls, MN: West Publishing Co.

Wathern, P. (ed.) (1988) *Environmental Impact Assessment: Theory and Practice*, London: Unwin Hyman.

Watson, M. and Sharpe, D. (1993) 'Green Beliefs and Religion', in A. Dobson and P. Lucardie (eds) *The Politics of Nature*, London: Routledge.

Weale, A. (1992) *The New Politics of Pollution*, Manchester: Manchester University Press.

Weale, A., O'Riordan, T. and Kramme, L. (1991) *Controlling Pollution in the Round*, London: Anglo-German Foundation.

Webber, P. (1994) 'Environmental Strategies', in J. Agyeman and B. Evans (eds) *Local Environmental Policies and Strategies*, Harlow: Longman.

White, J. (ed.) (1991) *Contemporary Moral Problems*, St Pauls, MN: West Publishing Co.

White, L. (1994) 'The Historical Roots of Our Ecologic Crisis', in L. Gruen and D. Jamieson (eds) *Reflecting on Nature*, Oxford: Oxford University Press.

Whitehead, A. (1996) 'Can Local Authorities Deliver Local Agenda 21?', *Interdisciplinary Strands* **5** (2): 17–21.

Wiesenthal, H. (1998) 'The German Greens: Preparing for Another New Beginning', in J. Dryzek and D. Schlosberg (eds) *Debating the Earth: The Environmental Politics Reader*, Oxford: Oxford University Press.

Wilkin, P. (1997) 'New Myths for the South: Globalisation and the Conflict between Private Power and Freedom', in C. Thomas and P. Wilkin (eds) *Globalisation and the South*, Basingstoke: Macmillan.

Wilkinson, D. (1997) 'Towards Sustainability in the European Union?', *Environmental Politics* **6** (1): 153–73.

Williams, B. (1973) 'A Critique of Utilitarianism', in J. Smart and B. Williams, *Utilitarianism: For and Against*, Cambridge: Cambridge University Press.

Williams, B. (1985) *Ethics and the Limits of Philosophy*, London: Fontana.

Williams, B. (1995) 'Must a Concern for the Environment be Centred on Human Beings?', in *Making Sense of Humanity*, Cambridge: Cambridge University Press.

Williams, C.C. (1995) 'Local Currencies *are* Getting Through', *New Economics* **35** (Autumn): 4.

Winpenny, J.T. (1991) *Values for the Environment: A Guide to Economic Appraisal*, London: HMSO.

Winter, G. (ed.) (1996) *European Environmental Law: A Comparative Perspective*, London: Dartmouth.

Wissenburg, M. (1998) *Green Liberalism: The Free and Green Society*, London: UCL Press.

Witherspoon, S. (1996) 'Democracy, the Environment and Public Opinion in Western Europe', in W. Lafferty and J. Meadowcroft (eds) *Democracy and the Environment: Problems and Prospects*, Cheltenham: Edward Elgar.

Wolman, H. (1996) 'Theories of Local Democracy in the United States', in D. King and G. Stoker (eds) *Rethinking Local Democracy*, Basingstoke: Macmillan.

Wood, C. and Dejeddour, M. (1992) 'Strategic Environmental Assessment: EA of Policy, Plans and Programmes', *Impact Assessment Bulletin* **10** (1): 3–22.

Worcester, R. (1997) 'Public Opinion and the Environment', in M. Jacobs (ed.) *Greening the Millennium: The New Politics of the Environment*, Oxford: Blackwell.

World Commission on Environment and Development (WCED) (1987) *Our Common Future* (Brundtland Report), Oxford: Oxford University Press.

Wrong, D. (1979) *Power: Its Forms, Bases and Uses*, Oxford: Blackwell.

Wynne, B. (1996) 'May the Sheep Safely Graze? A Reflexive View of the Expert–Lay Knowledge Divide', in S. Lash, B. Szerszynski and B. Wynne (eds) *Risk, Environment and Modernity: Towards a New Ecology*, London: Sage.

Yearley, S. (1991) *The Green Case*, London: HarperCollins.

Yearley, S. (1994) 'Social Movements and Environmental Change', in M. Redclift and T. Benton (eds) *Social Theory and the Global Environment*, London: Routledge.

Young, S.C. (1992) 'The Different Dimensions of Green Politics', *Environmental Politics* **1** (1): 9–44.

Young, S.C. (1993) *The Politics of the Environment*, Manchester: Baseline Books.

Young, S.C. (1996) *Promoting Participation and Community-Based Partnerships in the Context of Local Agenda 21*, University of Manchester: Department of Politics.

Young, S.C. (1997) 'Community-based Partnerships and Sustainable Development: A Third Force in the Social Economy', in S. Baker, M. Kousis, D. Richardson and S. Young (eds) *The Politics of Sustainable Development: Theory, Policy and Practice Within the European Union*, London: Routledge.

Young, S.C. (1999) 'Slowing Down on LA21 – or Pausing before Acceleration?', in W. Lafferty (ed.) *Implementing LA21 in Europe*, Oslo: ProSus.

Young, S.C. (2000) 'The United Kingdom: From Political Containment to Integrated Thinking?', in W. Lafferty and J. Meadowcroft (eds) *Implementing Sustainable Development: Strategies and Initiatives in High Consumption Societies*, Oxford: Oxford University Press.

Index

Aarhus Convention 244–5
Agenda 21 239–40, 243–4, 246–7, 359, 361;
    Local Agenda 21 328, 339–40, 341–9, 361
Agyeman, J. 328
Alarm UK 116–17
Allman, T. 117
anarchism 60–2
Anderson, T.L. 171
Anderson, V. 206–7, 208
animals: duties towards 21–2; rights 21–2,
    56; suffering 20
anthropocentrism; 26, 28–9; strong 18, 28;
    weak 18, 28
Atkins, S.T. 114–15
Attfield, R. 18
authoritarianism 54–5

Bachrach, P. 137
Bahro, R. 90, 109
Bailey, P. 290
Baker, S. 260, 282
Baratz, M.S. 137
Barde, J-P. 190
Barry, B. 36,37, 124
Barry, J. 49, 52
Bateman, I. 190
Baxter, B. 37
Beck, U. 70
Beckerman, W. 51, 211
Bentham, J. 20, 56
Bigg, T. 246
bioregionalism 60

Blair, T. 313, 317–8, 346
Blowers, A. 338
Blueprint for Survival 51–2
Bomberg, E. 279
Bookchin, M. 60
Bretton Woods institutions 226–7
British Government Panel on Sustainable
    Development 312, 315
Brown, C. 221, 223, 225
Brown, J. 223, 228, 242
Brundtland Report (*Our Common Future*) 5,
    34, 66, 219, 237–8, 309
Bryant, B. 115
Bush, G. (Jnr) 223, 253
Bush, G. (Snr) 242, 253

Cairncross, F. 151, 168
Cameron, J.R. 36, 39
Carruthers, P. 21
Carter, N. 296–7, 306
Centre for Alternative Technology 109
Chatterjee, P. 243
Christianity 17–19
Christoff, P. 68
Church, C. 343, 346
civil disobedience *see* direct action
climate change negotiations 222–3, 249–54,
    263; clean development mechanisms
    (CDM) 251; and collective action
    problem 250–4; Intergovernmental Panel
    on Climate Change (IPCC) 231, 249, 250,
    253; joint implementation (JIM) 251;

385